THE
CANADIAN
FEDERAL
ELECTION OF
2006

THE CANADIAN FEDERAL ELECTION OF 2006

Edited by
Jon H. Pammett &
Christopher Dornan

DUNDURN PRESS
TORONTO

Copy-editor: Jennifer Gallant
Design: Jennifer Scott
Printer: Transcontinental

Library and Archives Canada Cataloguing in Publication

The Canadian federal election of 2006 / Jon H. Pammett, Christopher Dornan, editors.

Includes bibliographical references.
ISBN-10: 1-55002-650-X
ISBN-13: 978-1-55002-650-4

1. Canada. Parliament--Elections, 2006. 2. Canada--Politics and government--2006-. 3. Elections--Canada--History--21st century. I. Pammett, Jon H., 1944- II. Dornan, Chris

JL193.C358 2006   971.07'2   C2006-903854-6

1   2   3   4   5   10   09   08   07   06

  Canada

We acknowledge the support of the **Canada Council for the Arts** and the **Ontario Arts Council** for our publishing program. We also acknowledge the financial support of the **Government of Canada** through the **Book Publishing Industry Development Program** and **The Association for the Export of Canadian Books**, and the **Government of Ontario** through the **Ontario Book Publishers Tax Credit program**, and the **Ontario Media Development Corporation**.

Care has been taken to trace the ownership of copyright material used in this book. The author and the publisher welcome any information enabling them to rectify any references or credits in subsequent editions.

J. Kirk Howard, President

Printed and bound in Canada.
Printed on recycled paper.

www.dundurn.com

Dundurn Press	Gazelle Book Services Limited	Dundurn Press
3 Church Street, Suite 500	White Cross Mills	2250 Military Road
Toronto, Ontario, Canada	High Town, Lancaster, England	Tonawanda, NY
M5E 1M2	LA1 4XS	U.S.A. 14150

TABLE OF CONTENTS

PREFACE

A Canadian federal election is a complex event, and the editors count themselves extremely lucky to be able to assemble a prestigious team of authors who agree to drop all their other work and produce a chapter analyzing the election within a very short time after the results are in. Please note that the chapters in this book, including the data appendix, cite preliminary election results as issued by Elections Canada immediately following the Canadian Federal Election of 2006. Certain of these figures may be at small variance with the official corrected results released subsequently by Elections Canada, but the timing of the book's publication did not allow these data to be updated.

The editors would like to thank staff at Elections Canada, and particularly Chief Electoral Officer Jean-Pierre Kingsley, for their co-operation in 2006 and in previous election years. Thanks are also due to Diane Dodds of the Political Science Department at Carleton University, who assembled the appendix.

We would also like to thank Jennifer Gallant and the staff at Dundurn Press for their professionalism and good cheer in bringing this book to press.

The Editors
Ottawa

CHAPTER ONE

From One Minority to Another
Jon H. Pammett and Christopher Dornan

U nlike the 2004 campaign, which was precipitated by the Liberals at a time of their own choosing, the 2006 campaign was initiated when the combined opposition defeated the Liberal government on a motion of non-confidence. This action was taken despite the fact that there were few indications that the Canadian public was clamouring for an election or collectively wanted to install a new government. Published polls showed that the party standings were roughly similar to the results of the 2004 election. On November 29, the *Globe and Mail* reported a poll by the Strategic Counsel that showed the Liberals with 35 percent of decided support, the Conservatives with 29 percent, the New Democrats with 17 percent, the Bloc Québécois with 14 percent, and the Greens with 5 percent. The 2006 election was to be fought between the same parties, with the same leaders and many of the same candidates, on similar issues to those of 2004. The prevailing feeling in late November of 2005 was that the upcoming election would likely lead to a result similar to the previous one.

Nevertheless, the state of the parties was somewhat different than it had been a year and a half earlier. The Liberals had been in disarray ever since their near defeat in 2004 and the resulting minority situation in the House of Commons. Stephen Clarkson, in Chapter Two, shows that ineffective and indecisive leadership, combined with the continued pressure of external events like the inquiry into the sponsorship scandal, served to render the Liberals vulnerable to a credible alternative. And all of the opposition parties had strengthened themselves to present such an alternative.

The Conservative Party of Canada, which fought its first election in 2004, had learned from its mistakes, as Faron Ellis and Peter Woolstencroft explain in Chapter Three. The party moved its policy agenda further toward the centre of the spectrum, and its message became simplified and more attractive. Central control was tightened so that the party would speak with a coherent voice. The Conservative Party thus came more and more to resemble the old Progressive Conservative Party, rather than the more extreme Reform and Alliance parties that had contributed to its formation. The Conservatives made a deliberate attempt to associate themselves with the previous conservative parties in Canadian history, including the Progressive Conservative Party led by Brian Mulroney and John Diefenbaker, and ultimately the party originally led by John A. Macdonald. One measure of their success is the extent to which the news media tended to treat the Conservative Party as simply the current manifestation of earlier conservative parties. As Chris Waddell and Chris Dornan show in Chapter Nine, the media gave the Conservative campaign generally positive coverage in 2006.

The New Democratic Party was also in a better position to fight the election of 2006 than it had been in 2004. In this case, it was the party's performance in the minority Parliament that had improved its image. Alan Whitehorn shows in Chapter Four how the NDP, under the effective leadership of Jack Layton, had received recognition for a number of positive legislative and budgetary outcomes of the short-lived Parliament through exacting concessions from the Martin Liberals as a price for keeping them in power. The NDP had also learned from its fate in the 2004 campaign, when it suffered from strategic voting decisions made by people who wanted to ensure the Conservatives did not win and hence voted Liberal even if the NDP was their first choice. Though they could never totally prevent such strategic decisions from affecting them, their campaign in 2006 would directly address the problem.

The Bloc Québécois was probably the party that was most eager for the election to take place. Given that the continual pounding of the Gomery inquiry and report was destroying the reputation of the Liberal Party in Quebec, the Bloc felt that it would sweep the province in a new election. It would do so by profiting from what the party saw as the unpopularity of all its opponents in Quebec. The federal Liberals were discredited, and furthermore, the provincial Liberal government was extremely unpopular. The Conservatives, sporting a Western leader and a reputation for hostility to any special status for French Canada, were not considered a threat. The NDP, for which Quebec voters might have some ideological affinity, had little organization in the province and was not competitive anywhere. Éric Bélanger and Richard Nadeau describe in Chapter Five the initial high expectations nurtured by the Bloc that they would dominate the politics of the province, with the ultimate goal of sovereignty for Quebec.

The Green Party of Canada also was in a better position for the 2006 election. Although the 2004 election had seen a national vote total of just over 4 percent, this result represented a tremendous increase in support for the party. Susan Harada in Chapter Six portrays the Greens' high hopes that they could build on their 2004 result and achieve the breakthrough of electing an MP. Louis Massicotte outlines in Chapter Eight how the new electoral financing legislation had put enough money in the Green coffers to expand the party's ability to campaign in the new election.

THE ISSUE AREAS

At the outset of the campaign, the minimal Liberal advantages that had led to their minority government after the 2004 election still appeared to be in place. In the area of social policy, the Liberals had infused cash into the health care system, no matter that some of this had come as a result of a deal with the NDP to sustain the government in the spring of 2005. An additional move in the social policy area was to negotiate financial agreements with the provinces to provide additional public day care spaces. As well, the Liberal mini-budget of November 2005 increased support to post-secondary education. They felt that financial moves in those three areas would allow them to claim that they were the party that would guarantee an improved level of social services. This, together with residual public suspicion of the Conservatives as privatizers of social services and advocates of fiscal retrenchment when it came to public expenditure, could be expected to sustain support for the Martin government.

The second area of Liberal strength that appeared to be intact was values. The Liberals felt they could argue that the morally and socially conservative positions taken in the days of the Reform and Alliance parties still lingered under the Conservative banner, with the consequence that the fear-oriented advertising the Liberals had used in the past ("Choose Your Canada") could be hauled out again. Furthermore, since the previous election, the Liberal Party had put in place legislation permitting the marriage of gay and lesbian Canadians, against the continued opposition of most of the Conservatives. The Conservative opposition to gay marriage had been reinforced by resolutions of that party's Montreal policy congress of March 2005. Canadians, the Martinites felt sure, would not support in large numbers the merchants of intolerance and regressive social conservatism.

To add to the lead they felt they had on the social policy and value dimensions, the Liberals moved in November to reinforce their position in the economic policy arena. Although economic policy issues had not been prominent in 2004, the Liberals felt they could make them work in 2006. For one thing, the main economic indicators looked rosier than they had for many years — a large budget surplus of more than $11 billion, favourable progress in national debt retirement, high economic growth, low unemployment, and a tolerable inflation rate. "You never had it so good" was the implicit message of the economic statement, which went on to promise Canadian taxpayers that they would now reap the dividends from the Liberals' beneficent economic management. A cut in the income tax was promised, which would go into effect immediately and benefit taxpayers in all income groups, assuming the Liberals stayed in office. Once the campaign started, this income tax cut would provide ammunition for the message that a tangible benefit was to be gained by voting Liberal.

On the remaining three elements of electoral victory — leadership, competence and trust, and national unity — the Liberals remained hopeful as the campaign began. The fact that the first Gomery report on the sponsorship scandal had not produced new accusations against the Martin government meant that the Liberals could promise to implement the recommendations that would be contained in the second Gomery report, which now would not appear until after the election was over. On the national unity front, the Liberals knew they were vulnerable in Quebec but felt that gains by the Bloc Québécois in that province could be offset by their own successes elsewhere. The Conservatives were not seen as a threat in Quebec and were also not seen as having credibility as defenders of national unity elsewhere in the country, since they could be painted as defenders of the rights of rich Western provinces. Finally, since the cast of leaders was exactly the same as in 2004, and since they all seemed to be acting in a similar manner as before, the Liberals felt they would be able to neutralize the leadership factor. And perhaps Paul Martin would do better this time. At the very least, Stephen Harper could be portrayed as "scary" once again.

The story told in this book outlines the reasons the scenario painted above did not come to pass. Until the midpoint of this two-part election campaign, however, it seemed to be a plausible version of events. Public opinion polls remained relatively stable until Christmas, with the

Liberals maintaining a moderate lead. On December 22, 2005, the *Globe and Mail* published a Strategic Counsel poll that showed the Liberals at 34 percent, the Conservatives at 30 percent, the NDP at 16 percent, the Bloc Québécois at 15 percent, and the Greens at 5 percent, numbers very similar to those of the poll mentioned above at the start of the campaign. The first half of the election campaign seemed to have produced very little change, either because voters had already made up their minds or because they were not yet paying attention.

With the evidence we have in retrospect, it appears that the electorate was relatively evenly divided between those two positions. As pointed out in Table 4 of André Turcotte's Chapter Eleven, about half the electorate claimed to have decided either before the election was called or at that moment, while the other half decided during the campaign or in the final days before the election. These findings from POLLARA are similar to those of a poll published by SES Research on February 23, 2006, in which approximately one-third of the electorate claimed to have made up their minds either on the final weekend or at the poll when about to cast a vote. It must be said that this is not a particularly unusual result for Canadian election surveys; many voters say they leave the final decision to the end. Nevertheless, it does show that there was plenty of scope for the parties to make a significant impact with their campaign appeals.

There is considerable evidence that, in contrast to some elections, campaign developments did make a major difference to the 2006 result. Between Christmas and New Year's, despite the fact that little if any actual campaigning was taking place because of a self-imposed moratorium on electioneering, the Liberals and Conservatives more or less reversed places in party standings, and they maintained those positions, with minor ebbs and flows, up to the final result. An examination of the way the issue elements played out in the election campaign gives some reasons for this development.

In their campaign, the Conservatives directly took on the two main areas in which the Liberals had an advantage in 2004: values and social policy. In a controversial move, Stephen Harper chose to announce his party's policy against gay marriage right at the beginning of the campaign, in the context of acknowledging its existence and then assuring people that the issue would be decided by a free vote in Parliament. The clear implication of this announcement was that it was an embarrassing party policy holdover from the Reform Party days that would be disposed of at some point and then forgotten. It was to be the first of many signals from Harper that the Conservatives were to be a centrist party with a broad national and sectoral appeal. Although this announcement generated negative publicity for a few days, the attempt to put values questions to the side was ultimately successful. While the Conservatives certainly did not win national advantage on the values question, they did manage to neutralize it to the extent that later attempts by the Liberals to raise it did not succeed in the face of more important issues.

Another crucial Conservative strategy was to develop simple and specific policies in the social and economic policy areas in an effort to overcome the impact of the Liberal budget announcements. The policies were carefully designed to be appealing without being extravagant, given the problems the Liberals faced with their blitz of funding announcements. On the social policy front, there were two major promises. Instead of a grandiose pledge such as Martin's 2004 promise to "fix health care for a generation," Harper proposed a "patient wait times guarantee" for prompt treatment of a variety of health conditions. This approach was not new; the Liberals and others had promised to reduce wait times in 2004. But despite the increased funding to the health care system, it was not evident to most that waiting times for surgery or treatment were being reduced. Thus the "guarantee," although the Conservatives were not specific about the lengths of time they would guarantee for different procedures. This proposal appeared to be a reasonable approach to improving the health care system — the *public* health care system, the Conservatives made a point of stressing.

The second chink in the Liberal social policy armour came with the day care issue. A national child care program had been announced, first as a goal, then as the object of an intergovernmental agreement, for a considerable period of time. Perhaps because the progress was slow and the actual day care spaces did not seem to be materializing outside Quebec (where they were created by a provincial government program), the Conservatives felt they had an opening to advance a different kind of proposal. The Conservative plan was to give families a cheque for $1,200 a year for each child under six years old to help with day care expenses. Criticism was immediate about the inadequacy of this amount of money, but the Conservative plan had at least two advantages over the Liberals'. First, it was an immediate unilateral federal solution to what had always been portrayed as an intractable intergovernmental problem. Second, it recognized that parents with small children might need help with child care even if one of the parents was staying at home to look after the child. The Conservative hope was that the plan might appeal to more traditional families (who were more likely to be predisposed to the Conservatives in any case because of "values") and offset any support the party might lose from families in which both parents were working outside the home. Even if working families had their doubts about the Conservative plan, they could at least feel that the party was taking the issue seriously and might be worthy of support if other issues were working in their favour.

The same approach of appealing directly to voter self-interest was employed in the economic policy issue area. As we have pointed out before in this series of books, the prominence of economic policy issues during an election seems to be inversely related to the overall state of the economy; the better the economy, the less likely voters are to base their decision on economics. About all that is left of the great national elections fought over inflation, unemployment, and free trade is a concern for the level of taxation. The Liberals, as mentioned previously, hoped their proposed income tax cuts would carry the day. The Conservatives, however, chose to compete in the taxation sweepstakes by offering a cut in the Goods and Services Tax (GST). This tax, implemented by the Progressive Conservative government led by Brian Mulroney, had been the subject of intense criticism, particularly by the Liberals in 1993. At that time, Jean Chrétien promised to get rid of the GST if elected, which he was, but the tax stayed in place. With this Conservative promise to lower the GST by a point or two, the Liberals were forced to argue that their income tax reduction plan was actually better for people, even though that reasoning was debatable and in any event was not clearly explained. It did not help that under other circumstances one could well imagine the Liberals themselves promising to reduce the GST.

National unity was the issue where the Conservative gain was most unexpected. The party had not elected anybody in the province of Quebec in 2004, nor had its predecessors the Reform and Alliance parties. The Progressive Conservatives had only two Quebec members in 1998 when their leader, Jean Charest, left to become the leader of the provincial Liberals in Quebec. At the outset of the campaign, the battle in Quebec was between the Bloc Québécois and the Liberals, with the Liberals in a distinct losing position.

It was the initial surge of support for the Bloc, with commentators predicting that they would greatly increase their vote and seat totals, that gave the Conservatives a chance to make inroads on the national unity issue. Quebec federalists were able to turn to the Conservatives, once that party had established some momentum, knowing that a vote for the Conservatives might be more effective in electing a federalist MP than a vote for the discredited Liberals. The lacklustre Bloc campaign, which seemed to assume rather arrogantly that everybody in the province would flock to them ("*Ici, c'est le Bloc*"), provided further impetus for a move to the Conservatives. The failure of the Bloc to mention a prominent element of their *raison d'être*, sovereignty, in their campaign blunted some of their reputation for honesty.

Outside Quebec, the Liberals lost their cachet of being the party that could deal best with that province. It was not that the Liberals were supplanted by the Conservatives as the party that could best preserve national unity so much as it was that the national unity bonus that attended the Liberal image was lost. Judgements between the parties based on other factors were not accompanied by this reserve of Liberal support, once it became clear that Quebec was rejecting the Liberals.

These developments were accentuated by two factors: renewed public attention to the sponsorship scandal and some signals given by Harper that the Conservatives would be attentive to Quebec's interests. During the campaign, the Conservative leader spoke of the opportunities a Conservative government would give to Quebec to participate in international affairs, particularly in cultural policy. Quebec would be able to represent Canada in UNESCO, for example. Going along with these specifics was the Conservative image of being more attuned to provincial rights (long an appealing position of the Reform and Alliance parties in the West), which raised hopes in Quebec among those of a more sovereigntist point of view. The fact that Quebec voters were willing to consider the Conservatives, however, was motivated primarily by their general disgust with the Liberals over the sponsorship scandal. Day after sordid day of hearings before the Gomery Commission had taken their toll in the province. A general desire to be rid of the Liberals was in the wind, and it was not clear that the Martin Liberals were essentially different from the Chrétien Liberals, despite the fact that Martin himself was not tied to the scandal.

It seems more than coincidental, however, that the situation both inside and outside Quebec worsened for the Liberals after the announcement in the last week of December by the RCMP that they were conducting an inquiry into another potential scandal affecting the Liberals, a leak of financial information that may have preceded the mini-budget of November 15. Liberal denials that anything untoward had happened seemed reminiscent of the initial denials that the Quebec sponsorship program had brought illicit profits to friends of the party. It was at this point that the Liberals lost a good deal of the public trust that they had been grudgingly conceded with the launching of the Gomery inquiry and the promises to implement the eventual recommendations of this commission. It seemed the final straw. The Conservatives began to look more attractive to voters across the country. Public opinion polls began to show a lead for the Tories, and Harper himself began to be rated best choice for prime minister.

The New Democratic Party was, as often happens, placed in the position of having to campaign against both the Liberals and the Conservatives. Their initial assumption was that the Liberals were their main competition, particularly in Ontario and British Columbia, two areas of party strength, an impression reinforced by the attention the Liberals had paid in 2004 to trying to win over NDP supporters for strategic reasons. As the tide of the campaign turned towards the Conservatives, the NDP realized that some of their supporters might be more likely to consider a Conservative vote for strategic reasons than a Liberal one. This forced an adjustment in NDP campaign rhetoric and advertising, which had some effect on the coherence of the NDP message.

THE LEADER IMAGES

Since the main political parties were all led in 2006 by the same men who held those positions in 2004, the ability of any of the leaders to markedly improve his image appeared to be limited. In the past, leader images have almost invariably deteriorated over time rather than improved; whether through inadequate job performance or unpopular policy choices, familiarity has seemed to breed contempt of Canadian political leaders. Even leaders who were initially extremely popular, such as Pierre Trudeau or Brian Mulroney, suffered major declines in public support.

Paul Martin was no exception to this dominant trend. As André Turcotte shows in Chapter Eleven of this book, Martin's popularity declined everywhere in 2006. This decline was particularly painful for him in Quebec and the Prairie provinces, where the party lost seats. These were areas where Martin, upon assuming the Liberal leadership, had been seen as improving the Liberal Party's fortunes. Not only did this not happen, but Martin's stock plunged lower in these areas than Jean Chrétien's had ever been. Martin's mannerisms became more and more distracting, if not necessarily more and more pronounced. His stumbling speech patterns, repetition of stock phrases ("I want to make this very clear…"), and constant gesticulations did not make his public addresses convincing. They detracted from his answers in the leaders' debates by making him appear nervous and distracted. Martin's uncharismatic mannerisms seemed to thwart any genuine public affection for the man.

Stephen Harper in 2005 and 2006 was in desperate need of a softer, more acceptable image. Humourless in public, shy, and apparently uninterested in being personally appealing to the public or the media, Harper preferred to be evaluated on the basis of his messages rather than his image. In 2004, his popularity rating was somewhat lower than Martin's and also below the neutral midpoint on a popularity scale. In 2006, Harper managed to improve his popularity everywhere, most surprisingly in Quebec. In part, the extra length of the 2006 campaign, and the double set of leaders' debates, allowed his low-key style to be put on display to a greater extent than previously. Obviously, many voters were taking another look at Harper, given the deficiencies that had become apparent with his main rival. He managed to give substantive answers to questions, to speak in coherent and well-paced sentences, and to smile. His French was acceptable. He didn't seem "scary," and he even exhibited a certain degree of charm. The advantage on the leadership factor shifted in the Conservatives' direction.

THE HORSE RACE

It is common to decry the preoccupation of parties and the media in contemporary elections with the mechanics of the contest, at the expense of the issues and substantive policy differences on which elections should properly be fought. Sometimes this is manifested in a preoccupation with public opinion polls, as analyzed by Michael Marzolini in Chapter Ten. In addition, it is said that too often the parties and the media attend to matters of tactical advantage or disadvantage, to electoral one-upmanship, to the personalities and the comportment of the leaders, to blunders, to accusations and counter-accusations, to the political mosh pit of jostling contestants. All this serves only to obscure a clear understanding on the part of voters of how the various parties differ from one another in policy, priority, and approach to governance; to undermine the possibility of reasoned debate between them; and to disenchant the electorate with the entire exercise. It reduces the vote to a referendum on electoral machines and tactics rather than a contest between political philosophies.

As familiar a complaint as this is, in the election of 2006 it rather misses the point. Sometimes, attention to the horse race aspects of the campaign is more than warranted. After all, if a party cannot run a disciplined, coordinated, and well-organized election campaign it hardly bodes well for its ability to manage the infinitely more complex affairs of the federal government. In that regard, the Martin Liberals entered the campaign saddled with the unflattering image of being hapless tacticians while in government. They were seen as unfocused and directionless, personified by a leader who had been caricatured in the media as "Mr. Dithers" for his apparent inability to take swift and firm decisions. The vaunted Liberal electoral machine had been grievously damaged by long years of internecine fighting, and an entire wing of the party — those who had been supporters of the previous prime minister — had been sidelined or made unwelcome. This was a party seething with resentments it had done little to ameliorate. And the performance of the party in the 2004 election, in which a minority government was secured only in the dying days of the campaign by a near-hysterical attempt to demonize the Conservatives, did not inspire confidence in either its strategic or tactical competence.

The Harper Conservatives, by comparison, had been deeply stung by their loss in 2004. In the final weeks of that election, they had tasted the prospect of forming the government (and unwisely mused aloud about winning a majority) only to see the Liberals surge in the closing lengths, not on the strength of any proposed policy or electoral promise, but simply through scare tactics. In the aftermath of that outcome, the party under Harper's leadership set about digesting the mistakes of the 2004 campaign with a view to never repeating them and to assessing the errors and weaknesses of the Liberal government.

The mechanics of getting elected in the 2006 campaign were therefore just as important as the policies each party promised to implement should they win. The Conservatives may have had a slight advantage over the Liberals in each of the issue areas detailed above, but this would have been worth little had the Liberals managed to tactically outmanoeuvre their main opponents. In fact, what happened was the opposite: in the day-to-day jockeying for position over the course of the campaign, the Conservatives bested the Liberals at almost every turn.

Partly, of course, this was the result of the Liberals' own miscalculations. Mistakenly assuming that the campaign would not begin in earnest until after the Christmas break, the Liberals surrendered an early advantage to the Conservatives, who seized the agenda from the outset through their methodical release of policy positions. The Liberals also assumed the Conservatives' chief weapon would be to hammer the Liberals on the issue of integrity in government, using the sponsorship scandal as their cudgel. They banked on the fact that the misdeeds detailed by the Gomery Commission were not the doing of the Martin regime and that the public would eventually find such harping tiresome. They were therefore taken by surprise when the Conservatives chose to emphasize their own policy positions rather than the Liberals' record. The Liberals also appeared to believe that the Conservatives would be the authors of their own misfortune, as they had been in 2004. Loose talk by the Conservatives on a variety of issues during the 2004 campaign, from immigration to the prospect of foreign ownership of the Canadian media, had provided the Liberals with the ammunition to paint their opponents as extremists out of step with mainstream thinking, and therefore to portray themselves as the defenders of core Canadian values. The Liberal game plan in 2006 seemed to place great faith in the likelihood that the Conservatives would hobble themselves, following which the Liberals would pounce.

The Conservatives, meanwhile, had determined that their electoral prospects hinged on denying the Liberals any such opportunity. They therefore imposed a message discipline on their campaign that was unprecedented for a party that was still a relatively recent amalgam of Reform/Alliance and Progressive Conservative elements. As the campaign unfolded, the attack opportunities the Liberals assumed would emerge as a matter of course simply never presented themselves in anything approaching the frequency or seriousness the Liberals needed. Instead, it was the Liberals who found themselves rocked by gaffes and missteps, from a campaign worker comparing NDP candidate Olivia Chow, wife of party leader Jack Layton, to a chow-chow dog on his website, to Martin communications director Scott Reid's intemperate dismissal of the Conservative day care plan as giving people "$25 a week to blow on beer and popcorn."

Sometimes a gaffe is just a gaffe. Sometimes, however, it can galvanize existing suspicions or perceptions in such a telling way that it takes on a life beyond a mere unfortunate slip of the tongue. More than anything else, Reid's blunder helped to contrast the Liberal and Conservative approaches to child care in vivid terms not at all helpful to the Liberals. The Liberals, it suggested, simply did not trust parents to care responsibly for their own children. By extension, it was not the Conservatives who were contemptuous of Canadian values, it was the Liberals who were contemptuous of Canadians themselves.

Measured attention to electoral mechanics — such as that offered in the chapters of this book — is necessary, therefore, not simply because these can be crucial to election outcomes, but because in contemporary elections the distinction between substantive policy concerns and the horse race no longer holds. They are by now inextricably enmeshed. The proof of that is to be found in the 2006 Conservative strategy of releasing a policy announcement each day as a means of simultaneously presenting their positions to the voters, distinguishing themselves from the Liberals, forcing their opponents to scramble in response, seizing control of the news cycle, and keeping the media occupied. Policy, strategy, tactics, and mechanics — they are now all of a piece.

THE CONSERVATIVE MANDATE

In terms of the six important factors in winning elections that we have discussed in this chapter, the Conservative victory was fashioned by the party's having a slight advantage in all six rather than being substantially ahead in a subset as the Liberals were in 2004 and in previous elections. On the three issue areas of economic policy, social policy, and national unity, the Conservative proposals were attractive to some but weren't the overwhelming choice of voters. On the trust and competence factors, the public did not so much trust the Tories as distrust the Liberals. On the leadership factor, Harper's advantage was fashioned once again in a comparative context, against a backdrop of a Liberal leader with an unappealing personal manner.

The Conservative proposals in the three issue areas were also short term in nature and deliberately oriented to the ostensible personal benefit of voters. A few hundred dollars may stay in peoples' wallets temporarily because of a lower GST, and $1,200 dollars may go some small way to buying child care for a family with a small child. A patient wait times guarantee may persuade some people they are able to more speedily access health care. While the successful implementation of these electoral promises may bring plaudits (though the day care promise may also bring controversy), these initiatives will have to be followed quickly by more sustained action in these fields and an expansion of the legislative agenda to other areas. Political scientists who study elections are wary of the sustained electoral appeal of "pocketbook issues" such as those that dominated the Conservative campaign. Voters are more likely to make their choices on "sociotropic issues" that emphasize the overall benefit to the society, the economy, or the country. To be ultimately successful, the Conservatives will have to develop a vision that persuades Canadians that the party has these overall goals in mind.

There are several warning signs for the Conservatives in the entrails of the 2006 election results. In the first place, the Conservative vote increase (up 6.7 percent over 2004) was not matched by an increase in Canadian party identification with the Conservatives, which increased only slightly. The 36.3 percent that the Conservatives achieved in 2006 still does not match the combined Canadian Alliance and Progressive Conservative vote totals in 2000 (37.7 percent). The Conservatives were not the second choice of the majority of Canadians who did not vote for them, whereas the majority who did not vote for the Liberals identified that party as their second choice. There is still a gender gap, where women are reluctant to support the Conservatives; the bulk of the vote increase for the party came from men. There is also a large group of Canadians who feel that the Conservatives are too right wing, too com-mitted to conservative social and moral views, and who declared in sur-veys at the time of the election that they would never vote for them. The challenge for the Conservatives in dealing with all these reservations is to pursue a moderate course and try to build support.

The challenge for the Liberals is not a simple one. The party will need, in the selection of its new leader and beyond, to build support in areas of the country where they are currently weak, particularly in Quebec. They must avoid taking for granted the heartening conclusions they might draw from survey findings that people voted for the Conservatives "to give the Liberals a time out" and by extension are just waiting for the right moment to put them back in power. Policy propos-als that the Liberals make will have difficulty gaining currency in the atmosphere of the blizzard of promises put forward before and during the 2005–06 election campaign, where they promised cash infusions to provincial and municipal governments and aid to Aboriginals, hospital patients, day care searchers, students, university researchers, environ-ment groups, and many others. They must place their agenda for the future in the context of a national vision and try to contrast this with the ideas of their opponents.

The NDP made gains in the 2006 election, improving its vote by just less than 2 percent and electing ten more members. The NDP leader, Jack Layton, also improved his leader rating in 2006, lending credence to the view that the other leaders benefited from the problems faced by Martin. The bulk of the twenty-nine seats won by the NDP, however, came from

Ontario and British Columbia. The challenge facing the party is to sustain this growth without falling victim to the decisions of voters who feel the necessity of choosing strategically between the other parties. In this regard, the decision of the NDP to run the 2006 campaign asking for more NDP members to allow the party influence in a minority Parliament does not seem to have created a problem for it, despite some predictions at the time. It appears that the overall result of a change of government but a narrow plurality for the Conservative victors suited many voters. If either of the larger parties is able to persuade the public that a majority is important, however, the NDP will once again be vulnerable.

Despite initial predictions, the 2006 Canadian Federal Election was an exciting contest in which the parties were more competitive than they had been just a couple of years earlier. As Lawrence LeDuc and Jon Pammett point out in Chapter Twelve, this rise in competition is one factor that stemmed the tide of voter abstention in 2006 and contributed to a small but significant rise in turnout. In addition, the tone of the electoral discourse was, for the most part, positive and respectful, at least in comparison with the recent past. Parties put the focus on their policy proposals. The leaders' debates were conducted in a format that allowed the participants to speak to their records and ideas without constant interruption. The media reported on the substance of the issues as well as the tactics of the campaigners. Despite the relative lack of histrionics — or, indeed, in part because of the campaign's positive tone — the 2006 election was one of the most exciting in recent memory. Whatever else they may be, elections are a form of public theatre. This one was genuinely engaging. We fondly hope that this is one lesson the various players will take from the election of 2006, since the outcome — a second minority government — suggests that Canadians will return to the polls in the shorter rather than the longer term.

CHAPTER TWO

How the Big Red Machine
Became the Little Red Machine
by Stephen Clarkson

PLUS C'EST LA MÊME CHOSE, PLUS ÇA CHANGE

In late November 2005, political analysts were singing a common refrain: the election campaign triggered by the opposition parties' non-confidence vote would be a carbon copy of 2004's experience. The same four leaders — the frenetically over-achieving Paul Martin, the remote and rigid Stephen Harper, the relentlessly programmed Jack Layton, and the doggedly outraged champion of Quebec's eternal grievances, Gilles Duceppe — would run on the same issues. Their same four parties — the Liberal Party of Canada (LPC), the Conservative Party of Canada (CPC), the New Democratic Party (NDP), and the Bloc Québécois (BQ) — would employ the same strategies. As a result, the same Canadian voters would respond in the same way they had seventeen months before and duly return a Liberal minority to preside over Ottawa's affairs for more of the same lean-to-the-right government and lean-to-the-left politicking that it had practised for over a century. Indeed, if Canadians knew what you were talking about when you mentioned the "big red machine," it was because the Liberal Party was "adept at patronage, skilled at brokerage, a purveyor of pan-Canadian messages, and an apostle of globalization" — in short, skilled at adapting itself to the challenges of governing as well as at getting its members re-elected.[1]

The replication theory was solidly grounded in past lore and present data. Historically, every federal minority government but two had returned to office. Polling numbers confirmed that, were the election to be held immediately, the Liberals would resume control of the House of Commons. Indeed, they had good reason to be optimistic. With a sound economy linked to Paul Martin's strong fiscal record as finance minister and his moderate record of accomplishments as a prime minister, it was the Liberals' election to lose.

It quickly became evident that the conventional wisdom was exactly wrong. The leaders may have been the same, but one, Stephen Harper, had changed. The teams were similar, but one, the Conservatives, had learned the lessons of 2004. The issues remained the same, but the valence of one, corruption, had shifted. The press corps was also largely the same, but its mood had changed. As a result, the Liberals' campaign was almost a mirror reflection of their 2004 effort[2] — at first glance identical, but actually reversed:

- The Liberals' descent was accomplished under their own power, leaving them vulnerable to a premature election.
- Their campaign organization was a surprisingly inept version of the vaunted big red machine.
- Their platform was inaudible to a public interested in policy.
- Paul Martin, as his campaign's messenger, was unable to deliver a convincing message.
- The media turned from ally to enemy.
- The regions proved largely unfriendly, particularly Quebec.
- Only at the last minute did the 2006 campaign resemble its predecessor by giving the Liberals a reprieve from disaster, leaving it well-positioned to consider how to renew its leadership, review its policies, and set about regaining office.

CONTEXT: DESCENT UNDER THE POWER OF A HYPERACTIVE GOVERNMENT

To understand how a talented prime minister who controlled the main levers of power and used them to generate a significant record of accomplishment could have been positioned for electoral defeat requires us to review how his attractive qualities were offset by debilitating weaknesses. Paul Martin's strategic achievements — legislative, personal, diplomatic, and federal — and his tactical triumphs in Parliament failed to generate enough political capital for him to withstand his opponents' attacks by the time new writs were issued and the political playing field was levelled.

Mr. Dithers: The Psychology of a Muddling Leader

Whatever their technical sophistication may be, the eerie truth about Canadian political parties is that their fate rests in the hands of their leaders, whether for better or for worse. To understand how Paul Martin did his party both great good and great harm in the year and a half since June 2004, we need to review his personal assets and liabilities.

As the son of a social-reforming career politician, Paul Martin Jr. was fed politics at the family's kitchen table. A Young Liberal at law school with a passionate interest in public affairs, he delighted in the cut and thrust of policy debates, all the more since he could grasp all sides of an argument. Curiously, he seemed to develop no personal philosophy that would help him define his own position in these discussions or let him distinguish those issues that had high priority from those that were less pressing. What did emerge was his ambition to avenge his father, who, though a stalwart member of Mackenzie King's, Louis St. Laurent's, Lester Pearson's, and Pierre Trudeau's cabinets, had failed to become prime minister himself.

As minister of finance, Martin brought with him a horizontal management style that had served him in the private sector when CEO of Canada Steamship Lines. The advisers and civil servants with whom he surrounded himself debated fiscal issues ad nauseam and in secret as they gestated the department's annual offspring, the federal budget. Eleven such documents built him a reputation as Canada's most successful and most popular finance minister for eradicating the government's escalating deficit and reducing its dangerous debt load.

Once installed in the Prime Minister's Office (PMO), where a multitude of issues had to be handled urgently and communicated to reporters answering to hourly deadlines, Paul Martin's apparent virtues turned out to be serious vices. His compulsion to control everything caused him to centralize still more powers in an already over-centralized cabinet system. His comfort with managerial chaos led to the establishment of a horizontally structured PMO in which debates seemed never to conclude and decisions were always reversible.

Prototypical of the Martin circle's decision-making style was the lengthy process it initiated to produce the International Policy Statement that was to define Canada's global stance for the decade ahead. The document reportedly went through thirty-seven drafts as different players insisted on adding their ideas and deleting others, and the job of achieving some overarching coherence was outsourced to a Canadian foreign-policy scholar at Oxford University. In the end, a document that was billed as selecting a few objectives on which Canada's role in the world would concentrate actually proposed a bewildering cornucopia of priorities on every page.

Rather than hire a staff that could harness his attributes, offset his defects, and protect him from the press, he brought with him the loyalists whose ruthlessness, fresh from their successful ousting of Jean Chrétien, was tailor-made to perpetuate ill will within the party, exacerbate it without, and allow the Prime Minister to exhaust a himself with long days spent reading endless documents and micromanaging every issue. Despite his critique of his predecessor's democratic deficit — getting on as a cabinet minister depended not on what you knew but who you knew, he had complained — his clique isolated him from cabinet colleagues, caucus members, officials, outside experts, and the public.

Even though Paul Martin represented his country in international meetings and spoke for his government on national issues, his delayed decisions, his muddled explanations, and his nervous, stammering performance in media scrums ultimately produced a prime ministerial persona that the *Economist* magazine definitively dubbed "Mr. Dithers."[3]

Strategic Governing

When reviewed with hindsight, Paul Martin's strategic achievements in less than a year and a half were considerable but often undermined by his own actions. Some eighty-two legislative measures were enacted. Although a bill to decriminalize the possession of small amounts of marijuana was allowed to stall, Bill C-38, which legitimated marriage between same-sex partners, passed in the face of more than two dozen backbenchers' opposition and one cabinet minister's resignation. With Canada only the third country to endorse gay marriage, the Martin government was known for being socially progressive, not for being tough on crime, but it also passed various measures toughening the Criminal Code to prevent the sexual exploitation of children, combat human trafficking, and give police more power to extract DNA samples from suspects. A significant number of bills fulfilled the Liberals' commitment to ameliorate the conditions of Aboriginal nations through augmenting their economic powers, settling many land claims, and promoting their self-government. The LPC passed whistleblower legislation and gave low-income citizens a rebate to offset higher energy prices, but nothing seemed to accrue. As opposition parties criticized these accomplishments for being too much or too little, Paul Martin proved unable to explain to the public how his government's individual achievements fit into a larger picture.

Governing is about managing people as well as policy. Martin's daring and spectacular appointment of a vivacious journalist who had as a girl immigrated to Canada from Haiti as Governor General was tarnished by poorly handled speculation about Michaëlle Jean's sovereigntist sympathies. New ministers Ujjal Dosanjh (Health), David Emerson (Industry), and Ken Dryden (Social Development) gave Martin's cabinet a heft that was undermined by accusations of impropriety made against Judy Sgro (Citizenship and Immigration) and revelations of John Efford's (Newfoundland) poor attendance from ill health.

In his diplomacy, Martin completed Canada's successful support for the United Nations' initiative to buttress international law by declaring the global community's "responsibility to protect" citizens whose security is jeopardized in failed states. At UNESCO, the Canadian campaign to protect cultural diversity achieved stunning success in the face of the United States' opposition.

Ironically, Martin's ineptitude in dealing with the United States marred his fundamentally pro-American approach to North American integration. Bill C-26 established the Canada Border Services Agency to increase security and facilitate the sharing of intelligence data with the U.S. Department of Homeland Security. Bill C-25 governing the operation of remote sensing space systems allowed the United States to use Canadian data for its ballistic missile defence system (BMD), and an amendment of NORAD positioned Canada at the table for BMD's warning and risk assessment work. Reversing his intention to support BMD, Martin caved in to pressure from party activists, but rather than having the fortitude to tell President Bush of his decision at a summit both attended in Europe, he left this information to be relayed by his foreign affairs minister, Pierre Pettigrew, to Condoleezza Rice, the U.S. Secretary of State. Although his government had increasingly supported U.S. positions in the UN favouring Israel over Palestine, had reorganized the military in a Canada Command to mirror the Pentagon's Northern Command, had radically increased the defence budget, and had recommitted troops to Kandahar in Afghanistan, where they relieved American soldiers in their continuing war against the Taliban, Paul Martin managed to present himself as anti-American.

A further irony bedevilled Martin's federal-provincial diplomacy. Awash in budget surpluses, Finance Minister Ralph Goodale's 2005 budget had allocated fresh billions to health care, green measures, city infrastructure, and tax relief. Playing a year-round Santa Claus, the Prime Minister had personally and very publicly negotiated deals worth billions more with Newfoundland and Nova Scotia and effectively changed the federal-provincial equalization formula by promising not to clawback offshore petroleum revenues. For Quebec, Martin offered over $2 billion for its municipalities and day care. Ultimately responding to Premier Dalton McGuinty's loud complaint about Ontario's $23-billion fiscal imbalance, Martin signed an arrangement with Queen's Park worth some $6 billion, and he also inked handouts for large if lesser amounts with the other provinces. Yet, Martin's frenetic province-by-province deal-making yielded him little political credit.

Tactical Triumphs

Governing without majority control in the House of Commons is a precarious business. Although roundly criticized in the press for opportunism,[4] Martin did what minority prime ministers have to do when he bargained with Jack Layton for the NDP's support to withstand an impending non-confidence vote in April 2005 by committing another $4.6 billion for such social programs as affordable housing, post-secondary education, pension protection, the environment, and foreign aid. Further evidence that the Martin team had regained the Liberal Party's capacity for tactical smarts came the next month when Belinda Stronach abandoned the Harper Conservatives, crossing the floor of the House, accepting a seat in Martin's cabinet, and, on May 19, saving the Liberals from defeat.

Shrewd political judgment had not become endemic to the Martinites, as they showed the following October when they refused to make another deal with Jack Layton, who was pressing for more commitments on health care in return for helping the Liberals beat off another expected Conservative non-confidence attack. It was not for lack of money, as Finance Minister Goodale demonstrated a few weeks later with the $39 billion in spending commitments that he announced in his Economic and Fiscal Update of November 14. Clearly the men and women running the Martin shop felt they could call Stephen Harper's bluff and take to the hustings. This was not to be the only sign of the Martin group's overconfidence, but it was the crucial miscalculation that abandoned its much safer position in government and exposed it to the vicissitudes of electoral combat when the media would give as much coverage to the three opposition parties' attacks on the governing party as to its pleas for continued public support.

THE BIG RED MACHINE THAT COULDN'T

If little had changed in "the Board" — the tight-knit group that managed Paul Martin's prime ministerial office — it followed that there was little in the way of personnel change between the Liberals' 2004 and 2006 campaign organizations. Terrie O'Leary, one of Martin's top advisors while finance minister; Tim Murphy, the chief of staff in the PMO; and communications director Scott Reid travelled on the plane with the Liberal leader throughout the campaign, along with Senator Francis Fox, national party director Steve MacKinnon, and party president Mike Eizenga.[5] Besides David Herle, campaign co-chairman John Webster and national campaign director Karl Littler operated from Liberal Party headquarters in Ottawa. Scott Feschuk wrote speeches for the leader, and Cyrus Reporter, a former Alan Rock strategist, headed the Liberal war room, which was responsible for researching opposition party positions and disseminating quick ripostes to their policies and attacks. The caucus research bureau responded to requests for policy information.

Each of the three most seat-rich provinces — Quebec, Ontario, and British Columbia — had its own largely autonomous organization responding to the media, co-ordinating policy announcements, and implementing specific regional messages and advertisements. In Quebec, the controversial former separatist Jean Lapierre remained Martin's choice to direct the party's fortunes. Charles Bird, vice-president of government affairs for Bell Globemedia and a former Earnscliffe senior consultant, was the campaign director in Ontario. In British Columbia, Mark Marissen, husband of former deputy premier Christy Clark, was the party's chief organizer in charge of its "Made-in-B.C. Agenda."

More striking than this continuity in personnel was the continuity, a.k.a. immobility, in the Board's thinking and attitudes. Its practice had been consistently to hype expectations about their leader's performance, "Making History" being the prototypically inflated title they had given Martin's all-things-to-all-people acceptance speech at his leadership convention victory two years before. Having ousted Chrétien and ostracized their rivals by the time they took power in Ottawa, they had proceeded to deepen divisions and alienate other Liberals rather than heal wounds and bring together the party's different camps.

The tone was set by David Herle, who seemed temperamentally unable to tolerate disagreement. With dissent taken for disloyalty, anyone who had a different approach was dismissed as a virtual enemy. Since grudges were held, they were returned in spades. Sheila Copps, who had been effectively prevented from running in the 2004 election, openly attacked the Liberals in 2005, advising the Conservative candidate in her riding and formally supporting the NDP against her nemesis, Tony Valeri. Warren Kinsella, who had run Chrétien's war room, now sustained an open vendetta from his popular web log where he wrote inflammatory comments about the Martinites' failings. John Manley remained sidelined but discreet in his unhappiness. Jean Chrétien and his close associates, John Rae and Eddie Goldenberg, kept out of the campaign entirely. Peter Donolo, another Chrétien team alumnus, commented sagely but distantly in the media.

Although there was no pretender to the throne in the caucus and no mobilized opposition in the extra-parliamentary party, there was much grumbling about the Martinites' cronyism and much disappointment with their record. Cut out of the party's decision-making loop, the party's middle levels were bitter. Acrimony persisted, with many committed Liberals sitting on their hands. Many actually wanted what they called the Martin party to lose because it had gone astray and needed to be put out of its misery so that the real Liberal Party could rebuild itself. It was not just dissenters who were marginalized. The Young Liberals, an important internal party organization, were not actively engaged in relaying the campaign's priorities in a form appealing to youth. These neophytes' exclusion from the party apparatus sacrificed a traditional advantage the LPC enjoyed over the Conservatives, who do not have a youth wing in their structure.

In striking contrast with normal campaign practice, David Herle filled the functions of both campaign director and campaign pollster. Quite apart from the evident conflict of interest — his company stood to gain financially from his role — it left the campaign with no one able to generate an overall perspective that could transform the endless printouts of attitudinal analysis into a coherent vision. In the summer of 2005, he had briefed the national caucus in Regina at its annual retreat, indicating that the party faced a "daunting task" trying to win a fifth consecutive mandate. Suggesting his high-wire approach to campaigning, he predicted that "either we win a majority or we could lose entirely."[6]

Sensing the latter, there was a great deal of disengagement among the grassroots. Even some of Martin's people were cranky, refusing to volunteer. That the Liberals' campaign appeared to be directionless was especially true at the riding level, where candidates and staffers received few directives from the national campaign. Conference calls were cut out on the grounds that they might be tapped, and the stream of email from the party's national and regional headquarters slowed to a trickle, especially in regions like the Prairies without a strong Liberal organizational presence, either federally or provincially.

Astonishingly, it turned out that, apart from taking distinct approaches to the campaign's three phases, the Herle group did not have an overall strategy for the campaign, which, as it proceeded, seemed to have no focus, no conscious direction, no core message, and no continuing theme. The Board even dithered about its slogan, using several spasmodically throughout the campaign until it ended up with what it had used in 2004. The Liberals' reissuing of "Choose your Canada" made it easier for the Conservatives to protect themselves against the recycled "values" attack.

These problems became immediately evident in the Liberals' failure to convey a coherent policy message, but they also sapped their leader's performance and resulted in media coverage that was anything but positive. Given the length of the campaign and its clearly differentiated phases, the interplay of these three factors needs to be analyzed stage by stage.

PHASE I: THE CAMPAIGN BEFORE CHRISTMAS

Invisible Policy and Platform

The Board had opted for an unusually long — eight-week, fifty-six-day — campaign on the assumption that Stephen Harper was their biggest asset, because opinion polls showed he scored well below Paul Martin on leadership qualities. In the *Globe and Mail*, Jeffrey Simpson had recently written, "Most journalists gave up trying to see Harper months ago. He's barricaded himself behind a wall of media resentments."[7] The Liberals felt they could afford to run a low-key campaign before Christmas, because they believed the public was not paying attention. Instead, they would concentrate the "air war" on their advertising and leave their touring leader to highlight the government's notable economic achievements. Neither approach was effectively executed, since the Liberals seemed to be hesitant in each case.

Using insider sources, the media had predicted a wave of American-style negative attack ads before the election had even been called.[8] In actual fact, the Liberal agency, Red Leaf Communications, held back and started on a positive note. Releasing only five ads up to December 16, compared to the Conservatives' fourteen, the Liberals spent a mere $2 million (one-half of their rivals' expenditures) to broadcast them. Lacking visual consistency, one ad addressed the Charter of Rights and Freedoms and one the United States, while three ads, ending with the tag line "30 million reasons to vote Liberal," concentrated on the economy, an issue that less than 10 percent of the public considered the most important facing Canada.[9]

At first, it seemed that this restrained approach would work, as Stephen Harper appeared to put his foot in his mouth on Day 1 by announcing his intention to hold a free vote that could delegitimatize same-sex marriage and on Day 2 by getting into a dispute with his deputy leader, Peter McKay, about creating a new public prosecutor. But the Conservative leader appeared to hit his stride when he announced his striking proposal to cut 2 percent off the universally unpopular Goods and Services Tax (GST). The Conservatives' daily announcement of a concrete, voter-friendly, centrist policy caused the journalists on the Liberal tour to press the Prime Minister for his comments. His response to the GST cut was to claim that his 2005 budget's income tax cuts were more progressive. Reacting to Harper's initiatives pushed Paul Martin off his feel-good, economic-prosperity message, causing him to lose control of the campaign's agenda.

If Week 1 was a battle for unearned media coverage, the Conservatives had clearly won. They were mentioned first on every day of CBC-TV's *The National* except one. Qualitatively, the net balance in the tone of newspaper reporting as measured at McGill University was 16 percent positive for Harper and 5 percent negative for Martin.[10]

With its stand-aside approach failing, the Liberal campaign made a tactical shift in Week 2 in order to give some policy response to Stephen Harper, who kept making daily promises, notably a direct grant to parents of $1,200 per child under six years of age to help with day care and specific tax cuts for small business, trades people and apprentices, students, and seniors. But when Martin announced his $11-billion national child care plan on Day 8, linking it to medicare, it appeared in the press as an amorphous response to Harper's more concrete proposal to put cash in the hands of families.[11] The next day, Martin played his prime ministerial card by attending the United Nations conference on climate change that Canada was hosting in Montreal, where he criticized the United States for not supporting the Kyoto Protocol and indirectly admonished the Bush administration by adding sanctimoniously, "there is such a thing as a global conscience."[12] On Day 10, when Martin announced his first new plank, a ban on handguns, the policy was widely reported as ineffective.[13] The change in tactic did not yield better results in the press, where net negatives for Paul Martin in Week 2 increased from 5 to 18 percent.

Week 3 offered the public a strange spectacle about who could make the biggest gaffe. On Day 13, during a Sunday evening TV panel, the Liberals' communications director, Scott Reid, dismissed the Conservative day care plank (which amounted to $23 per child per week) by quipping that parents would spend the cash on "beer and popcorn." The partisan jibe was blown up in the media on Day 14 as a major mistake and was exploited by the opposition parties as living proof of Liberal arrogance. Luckily for the Liberals, the U.S. State Department had instructed its representative in Canada to respond to the Prime Minister's slur of the previous week. Accordingly, on Day 15, U.S. Ambassador David Wilkins stepped into the campaign during a high-profile Canadian Club speech in Ottawa when he intoned that "criticizing your friend and number one trading partner … was a slippery slope, and all of us should hope that this doesn't have a long-term impact on our relationship." The ambassador's intervention was manna from heaven for Paul Martin, who in a carefully orchestrated press conference at a sawmill in B.C. on Day 16 tied his "anti-Americanism lite" with the long-standing softwood lumber dispute by stating very pointedly that he "would not be dictated to" by the Americans as to which issues he could or could not discuss.[14]

Paul Martin, the Messenger without a Message

The newly redefined Stephen Harper appeared for everyone to see at the campaign's first leaders' debates, held in Vancouver in French on Day 17 and then in English on Day 18 with a format that eliminated incomprehensible yelling matches and allowed each leader equal time to express his views. Where Harper kept his cool and appeared comfortable in front of the cameras, at which he had learned to smile almost genuinely, Paul Martin looked harried as the target for attacks by the other three leaders. His hands gesticulating, his expressions earnestly righteous, his furrowed brow communicating as much anxiety as intensity, Martin appeared overheated and agitated. Beyond his nervous demeanour, his delivery was stuttering and awkward, his syntax sometimes incomprehensible. Only occasionally did he deliver a strong and pithy point.

It was the beginning of the end for the incumbent. Polling that had tracked the question "Which leader would make the best prime minister?" had seen Martin's numbers rise from 29 percent on Day 1 to 33 percent by Day 17, the time of the first French debate. From that moment, his numbers drifted down, while Harper's, which had been hovering around 21 percent, started a slow rise.[15]

The next week also marked the beginning of the end for the Liberal Party as the federalist champion in Quebec. On Monday, December 19, Stephen Harper promised Quebecers an "open federalism" in which their province would be given a stronger voice on the world stage, primarily at UNESCO, and would gain greater autonomy along with a correction of the fiscal imbalance between the federal and provincial governments. Jean Charest, Quebec's Liberal premier, and Mario Dumont, leader of Action démocratique du Québec, warmly welcomed these undertakings, which Paul Martin had refused to make. It was a policy position that would place the CPC on Quebec's map for the first time in more than a decade.

The Media: From Ally to Enemy

As the campaign wound down for the Christmas break, public opinion polling did not yet suggest that the Liberals had lost, although their lead had narrowed to 1 percent. Nevertheless, as had been predicted well before the writs were issued,[16] the crucial contextual factor in moving opinion was how the media treated the various campaigns. From the beginning, when Harper's campaign was plagued by gaffes, the media blandly reported these mistakes and then dropped them. The Conservative leader turned out to be more approachable than expected, his bus and plane accommodation was better organized, and his campaign speeches contained frequent, solid, understandable material for the press corps to report.

By contrast, almost every failing of Martin and of members of his party was given prominence by a press corps that seemed intent on not giving the Liberal team the benefit of the doubt as it had in 2004. Journalists had become fed up with being continually "spun" by Martin's handlers and resented being harangued for having written stories that the Board found displeasing. The press gallery was particularly upset at the Prime Minister's failure to keep his much-hyped promise, when campaigning for the leadership, to eliminate Parliament's democratic deficit. The "beer and popcorn" comment by Scott Reid received extensive, even exuberant, coverage by reporters who could gleefully get back at a communications director they despised for his overbearing behaviour over the previous two years. Marc Garneau's years-old disparaging comments about disabled people were brought back to the public's attention. Issues such as the already-disproven allegations against former minister of citizenship and immigration Judy Sgro resurfaced. The net negative tone of stories about Martin before Christmas was 12 percent and for the Liberal Party 15 percent, whereas the net positive tone for Harper was 8 percent and the Conservative Party's coverage was statistically neutral. As journalist Lawrence Martin wrote, "There is already a sense that the Conservatives are gaining credibility morsel by morsel, while the Liberals are losing it in the same small degree."[17]

PHASE II: THE CHRISTMAS BREAK

When the Board opted for a long campaign, it assumed little would happen before Christmas and still less during the intermission before New Year's. In fact, the Christmas break turned out to be the week that broke the Liberals' back.

First came the dramatic shooting death in broad daylight on Boxing Day of a fifteen-year-old high school student out shopping with her family on Toronto's busy Yonge Street. Although the Martin Liberals had done enough to burnish their credentials for toughness on crime that they had received rare praise from Premier Dalton McGuinty and Mayor David Miller on Day 10, such was the change in the public's mood that the tragic death played to the Conservatives' traditional strength on law-and-order issues.

Next, and far worse, came the announcement on December 29 that the Royal Canadian Mounted Police had launched a criminal investigation into whether advance notice of Ottawa's tax policy break for income trusts had been leaked to the financial markets by Finance Minister Ralph Goodale's entourage just before the campaign began. Suddenly the questions of ethics and accountability stemming from the Chrétien-era sponsorship scandal in Quebec, which had been largely downplayed during the campaign to date, burst onto the front pages.

The RCMP protested that its announcement had no political motivation and affirmed that it had no evidence of wrongdoing (although the information it had collected had presumably been deemed sufficiently incriminating to warrant the investigation), but it stretched credulity that this action had been taken in the middle of an election campaign without a clear understanding that it would deal the Liberal Party a body blow. Whether this was payback time for the RCMP's integrity having been impugned through the Gomery inquiry or for the RCMP's implication in the torture of Maher Arar in Syria could be suspected but not known.

What was known was the devastating impact of the RCMP action on public perceptions of the Liberals. They showed no capacity to reframe the disputed stock action as the market's anticipation of the finance minister's announcement following the irresistible pressure brought to bear on the government by many financial institutions. From December 22 to January 4, one leadership index saw Martin plunge from eighty-eight to sixty-eight.[18] In a matter of days — just in time for the campaign's final phase — the Conservatives had taken a lead in the polls.

PHASE III: AFTER DECEMBER

Having kept their policy and publicity powder dry before Christmas, the Martinites had assumed they would return to power on the basis of a positive platform presented by their leader through the news media and a negative ad campaign that would scare the public away from the Conservatives once again. The only problems with this plan were the planners, who had no capacity to convey their policy; their leader, who could not make his message heard for all his shouting; Quebec, which had turned its back; the creative team, which could not mount an effective attack; the press corps, which was more interested in scandal; the other regions, which could not save the party; and the Conservatives, who proved to be the real masters when it came to marketing negativity.

Invisible Policy and Platform

The Liberal Party of Canada may have been in power for more than twelve years, but it had not run out of ideas for new governing initiatives. Its problem was how to get the voters to heed them. Although the Martinites tried every marketing technique they could think of — a wholesale policy platform, retail policy announcements, even a jumbo policy fire sale — they managed to communicate confusion rather than coherence.

The jumbo policy fire sale technique had been used on the eve of the election when Finance Minister Ralph Goodale's Economic and Fiscal Update offered a massive $30 billion worth of tax cuts and $9 billion for other programs such as student aid ($2.1 billion), funds to provinces and territories for post-secondary education ($1 billion), and lesser monies for such projects as diversifying trade away from the United States ($0.5 million).[19] None of these massive giveaways appeared to work for the LPC as it campaigned before Christmas.

Nor had the Liberals' efforts at policy retailing succeeded, whether because they seemed to be responding to Conservative initiatives, because their proposals were dismissed by reporters more interested in probing for scandal, or because they mismanaged their announcements — all problems that persisted after December. For instance, on Thursday, January 5 — Week 6, Day 38 of the campaign — Paul Martin announced his multi-billion-dollar education package, with its 50/50 promise to cover half of every undergraduate's first and last years' tuition. Although the event was planned to take place at the University of Waterloo, the organizers had chosen a hockey rink rather than a classroom as their venue. At 9:00 a.m., they were still frantically looking for students to provide live bodies to frame the stage. When the Liberal leader turned up an hour late to make his pitch, he faced a barrage of questions from surly reporters about why the policy had been leaked the night before, why he had suddenly apologized for the century-old Chinese head tax, and other campaign glitches. As a result, the next day's *Globe and Mail* blared, "Harper trumpets get-tough crime plan" on its front page above the fold, while only the fine print of a small article at the bottom of the page revealed that Martin had released his education plan.[20]

Even wholesaling their policy proved problematic for the Liberals when, on January 11, they finally released their campaign platform. *Securing Canada's Success* was a comprehensive, fully costed document that highlighted the Liberals' record of achievement and presented a strong vision for the future. The platform was broken into five main sections:

- "Meeting Canada's Demographic Challenge" trumpeted the government's past fiscal success and laid out policies on health care, seniors' issues, immigration, and aboriginal affairs.
- "Succeeding in a New World of Giants" envisaged Canada's future prosperity, addressed child care and higher education, research and development, plans for the cities and the regions, and international trade and NAFTA issues.

- "The New Liberal Plan for Growth and Prosperity" was a short section that recounted what the government had done for Canadians in the preceding 2005 Economic and Fiscal Update, including the Liberals' tax relief plan for lower- and middle-class Canadians.
- "Building the Canada We Want" addressed the Charter and values issues Martin had emphasized throughout the campaign, while also describing the Liberal plans for crime control, cultural development, the environment, and foreign affairs.
- "Accountable and Efficient Government" was the final, shortest, and weakest section, which recycled Martin's often-used rebuttals to attacks on Liberal corruption — his cancellation of the sponsorship program, establishing the Gomery Commission, and creating Canada's first independent ethics commissioner and senate ethics officer — plus the repeated promise to submit the expected second Gomery report to a parliamentary committee, along with a vague assertion that a Liberal government would continue to explore "the underpinnings of democratic renewal."

Typical of previous Red Books, the platform spoke to both the left and right, balancing a commitment to social programs and Charter rights with promises of tax cuts and continued fiscal conservatism. The platform drew heavily on the accomplishments of the Liberal government under Paul Martin: policies on child care, health, and Aboriginal issues were framed in terms of delivering on agreements forged with provinces and interest groups during the preceding Parliament. There were also echoes of the Liberals' last policy convention resolutions, particularly with respect to seniors' issues. While there was little included in the platform that had not already been released during the campaign or in the 2005 Economic and Fiscal Update, the platform did provide further details on some key commitments, such as the Canada Health Care Guarantee. Other planks, such as the 50/50 Plan for education, provided more detailed accounts of the amount of money required. According to the Liberals' own costing, of the $9.6 billion in policy initiatives announced during the campaign and in the platform, only $4.1 billion represented new spending.

Apart from one commitment to draft an international treaty banning the weaponization of space, all of the platform had been announced previously or was a residue from the Liberals' time in government. In some cases, policies contained in the platform were restated for the fifth time (having been previously mentioned in the Speech from the Throne, the 2005 Budget, the Economic and Fiscal Update, and on the campaign trail). The prevailing perception that the Board had been drafting policy on the fly was reinforced by the highlighted quotations that appeared throughout the document: many were dated only days before the platform's official release. Too little and too late, it was greeted with a general lack of interest by reporters, several of whom had received leaked copies the previous night, when the entire document had been posted on the right-leaning *Western Standard* magazine's website. It was a tribute to the 2006 Red Book's monumental failure that the *Toronto Star* simultaneously endorsed Paul Martin editorially on January 12 and made no mention at all of the Liberal platform's unveiling the previous day. It was also an indicator of Paul Martin's personal failure that, in the same edition, the country's largest and most Liberal-leaning paper carried a front-page skewering of the leader that argued, "This election isn't about Stephen Harper. It's about expectations Martin couldn't meet, a pinball government that ricochets bumper-to-bumper."[21]

Paul Martin, the Messenger with Too Many Messages

While opposition parties campaign on change and renewal, incumbents have to address their record. Seeking a fifth consecutive term in office for the LPC, Paul Martin had entangled himself in a paradox, at once embracing Liberal success stories while running away from the scandals that had plagued his party. "You can't cherry-pick Charter rights" had been one of his much-overused attack lines against Harper, but he had been flagrantly cherry-picking elements of the Liberal record to suit his electoral aspirations. Having tried to distance himself from the Chrétien record during 2004, the first weeks of his 2006 campaign offered an unapologetic but selective boast about twelve years of Liberal success.

Martin's self-styled Captain Canada image as guardian of the Charter, protector of national unity, and David to the American Goliath all hearkened back to features of the Chrétien legacy he had spent years criticizing. Even more disconcerting, Martin often found himself promoting policy positions that had defined his predecessor's reign but contradicted his own earlier stances. During the first English debate, Martin heatedly attacked Harper for his position on same-sex marriage, yet his own position whilst Chrétien was pushing the same-sex marriage bill through the House of Commons had been noticeably unenthusiastic. An impassioned defence of federalism against separatism — "fighting for national unity is in my genes"[22] — rang false from the mouth of one who had questioned the necessity of Chrétien's signature Clarity Act in the aftermath of the 1995 referendum and had made former Bloc Québécois founder Jean Lapierre his Quebec lieutenant in 2003. During the second English debate, Martin praised the Liberals' long tenure for rescuing the Canadian economy, while also referring to it in the context of ethics and accountability as "a disgraceful period."[23]

Archetypical of their intellectual disarray was the Board's last-minute decision to have Martin throw a policy grenade into the middle of the last English-language debate: "The first act of a new Liberal government is going to be to strengthen the Charter, and we will do that by removing, by constitutional means, the possibility for the federal government to use the notwithstanding clause, because quite simply, I think governance says that the courts shouldn't be overturned by politicians."

Constitutional experts were dismayed at the thought that a Liberal government would provoke a long, probably doomed, struggle to amend the constitution by abolishing this key component of the compromise that had allowed Pierre Trudeau and the provincial premiers to agree in 1981 to a Charter of Rights and Freedoms while retaining the principle of parliamentary sovereignty. Liberals such as Deputy Prime Minister Anne McLellan were nonplussed, admitting that they first heard of the notwithstanding clause brainwave when their leader announced it in prime debate time on Day 42 of the campaign.[24] Confirmation that this idea had been pulled out of thin air by the Board came two days later when the party platform turned out not to contain any mention of what Martin had declared would be the "first act of a new Liberal government."

Quebec

On the same day that Paul Martin dropped his notwithstanding clause clunker, a book entitled *Les secrets d'Option Canada* revived an old accusation that the Liberal Party had provided almost $5 million to an advertising agency during the 1995 referendum campaign in apparent violation of Quebec's campaign-financing law. With Martin unable to refute accusations that had been dismissed eleven years before or to turn the tables on the Parti Québécois for having massively subsidized the "Yes" campaign, the brilliantly timed and well-orchestrated polemic dominated the francophone media for ten days, reanimating outrage around the province about the original sponsorship scandal. The previous winter, the hard evidence of the *machine rouge*'s corruption, which the Gomery inquiry's revelations had turned into a daily soap opera, had enraged Quebecers, who were insulted that the Liberals believed they could buy their votes by positioning Canadian flags around the province. Now the Option Canada affair extended Quebecers' scorn for Jean Chrétien to Paul Martin, reminded them why they hated the Liberals, and boosted the CPC's prospects in formerly Créditiste ridings that had previously been considered safe Bloc turf.

By this time, the Martinites' disaster was largely a *fait accompli* in Quebec. Trusting a Léger Marketing report that two-thirds of the Quebec electorate had put the AdScam issue behind them and were willing to consider what the LPC had to offer for the future,[25] and true to their propensity for raising expectations, members of the Board had indicated that they expected to pick up seats from the BQ. Although less than 3 percent of the Quebec electorate deemed national unity an important issue, they had chosen to launch Phase I of their campaign by having Paul Martin suggest that, with Gilles Duceppe and new Parti Québécois Leader André Boisclair in cahoots, "this really is a referendum election."[26] When it turned out that Duceppe was gaining enough ground that he might win the symbolically powerful 50 percent plus 1 of the votes, the Liberal leader backed away from this futile scaremongering.

Then Martin challenged Duceppe during the first English TV debate to a one-on-one debate "on every street corner, in every city, and in every town and village in Quebec,"[27] but when the Bloquiste leader accepted the offer, the Liberal leader backed off again. Public cynicism about the *Rouges* all but obscured the personal tragedy of Paul Martin, who had spent his adult life becoming bilingual, living and working in Montreal, and relaxing and breeding sheep in the Eastern Townships. No doubt he meant it when he rose during the same debate to a memorable tirade against Duceppe: "This is my country, and my children were born and raised in Quebec. And you're not going to go to them and say that you're going to take my country, or divide Quebec family against Quebec family."[28]

His emotions played well in the rest of Canada but fell on deaf ears in Quebec, largely because the francophone reporters had also turned against the Liberals. They knew that Martin's clique was anglophone and disconnected from the province. They resented that during campaign scrums Paul Martin took fewer questions in French than did Stephen Harper. They had noticed that the Liberal blog was initially written in English only.

Week 2's polls had revealed that the major issues in Quebec were health care, the provincial debt, employment insurance, and the environment.[29] Yet the Quebec Liberals had nothing to say on any of these issues, at least nothing significant enough to warrant newspaper coverage, and Martin made no specific promises to the people of Quebec in the entire pre-Christmas campaign, despite spending its first few days in the province. With their leader being indecisive and uninspiring, with their candidates having nothing to communicate in the way of program, with Jean Lapierre remaining a liability by associating a Duceppe comment with Nazism, the Liberals' Quebec campaign was foundering.

By the end of the campaign, the province's two-party race had become a three-party competition in which the *Rouges* were running third. New Brunswick Premier Bernard Lord personally canvassed the province to support the Conservatives' Quebec campaign, but the Liberals had no such luck in winning high-profile assistance at the provincial level. In the beginning, Premier Jean Charest's involvement in the campaign was limited to urging voters to support anyone other than the BQ candidates. Whereas endorsement from Charest might have been a mixed blessing for the Martinites given his unpopularity, it boosted the Conservatives' fortunes when he enthusiastically cheered Harper's decentralizing support for Quebec's aspirations and covertly directed his organizers to work for CPC candidates.

Realizing in the last two weeks that even his formerly safe seats were now in jeopardy, Martin came back to Quebec in the hope of holding on to the traditionally Liberal ridings surrounding Montreal. Outside the major urban centres, however, the party candidates were left to fend for themselves. Even in Brome-Missiquoi, where Martin's farm is located, *Rouge* chances were slim. Polls even suggested that the Liberals were in a dogfight to retain any seats outside of the anglophone Montreal ridings. Some of the Liberal team's most acclaimed members found themselves in trouble — Liza Frulla, Pierre Pettigrew, Marc Garneau, and even Jean Lapierre — and pollsters started to predict that the Conservatives would win a half-dozen seats in rural Quebec.[30]

No Comfort in the Regions

Unlike the 1997 election campaign, which was fought with a nationally directed but regionally specific strategy,[31] the Liberals' 2006 campaign repeated 2004's pan-Canadian approach in which most of the Liberals' policy announcements were national in scope and few significant regional policies were introduced, even in Quebec. Martin was selective

in making announcements relating to specific provinces or regions, preferring to announce policies that applied to multiple regions and so
maximize their impact.

Atlantic Canada

Paul Martin spent only four days in this region, since the Liberals were
confident they could retain most of their seats there. He paid a rare visit
to Prince Edward Island to make his first policy statement of the campaign, an announcement that the Liberals would spend another $11 bil-
lion on a national child care program and make it a permanent program
similar to medicare.[32] On Day 22, Fisheries Minister Geoff Regan provided more regionally targeted fare by announcing the Liberals' plan
not to tax fishing businesses handed down to family members and to
increase the amount beyond which survivors would have to pay tax if
sold to a non–family member to $750,000.[33] This policy would also
apply to farmers passing their property down to family members and
hence was designed to appeal throughout the country.

Securing Canada's Success did make regionally specific commitments
to innovation and economic development in agriculture, fisheries, and
natural resources in Atlantic Canada.[34] On the issue of offshore fishing by
foreign entities, the Red Book promised that, if elected, "a Liberal government will take whatever action is needed, including direct enforcement to
protect the straddling stocks on the Grand Banks."[35] On Day 46, Scott
Simms, the incumbent in Bonavista–Gander–Grand Falls–Windsor,
announced the relocation of seventy-five federal jobs to Newfoundland
and Labrador, and said the Liberals would reopen the Gander weather
centre, an issue involving four or five jobs on which they had been silent
earlier in the campaign.[36]

With all Atlantic provincial governments under Conservative control,
Harper received early endorsements from premiers Pat Binns (Prince
Edward Island), John Hamm (Nova Scotia), and Bernard Lord (New
Brunswick), proving that Martin had received little return for the billions
of dollars of largesse he had showered on the East earlier that year.
Perhaps in acknowledgment of this Liberal munificence, Premier Danny
Williams of Newfoundland had initially said he would not endorse any
party,[37] but, upon receiving Martin's reply to his pre-campaign letter ask-
ing the three party leaders to respond to Newfoundland issues, Williams
called the Liberals' response "disappointing" and endorsed Harper.[38]

Throughout the campaign, premiers Binns and Lord took shots at the Liberal Party. In P.E.I., Premier Binns was reportedly "irate" when Martin snubbed his request for a meeting.[39] Premier Lord came out early against the LPC, saying, "I do not accept the proposition of the Liberals that only they can keep this country together when you realize that they're like pyromaniacs with the matches and gasoline in their hands."[40] Lord also accused Ottawa of sending conflicting signals about the cleanup of the Saint John Harbour[41] and stalling on providing the federal government's share of compensation to victims of the previous spring's flooding of the Saint John River.[42]

Ontario

Martin spent the largest portion of his time in Ontario, where the Liberals had won many of their seventy-five seats by less than 5 percent in 2004. He picked the province to announce major parts of the Liberals' policy, including the handgun ban, the party's proposed improvements to the health care system, and the plan for education funding. Few policy announcements were made specifically for Ontario. In North Buxton on Day 18, Martin unveiled his party's agricultural policy, which proposed a national fuels standard requiring biofuel to be mixed with gasoline and diesel, and promised more money for the development of export markets for agri-food products.[43] The Liberals' environmental commitment of $1 billion to clean up several major Canadian waterways applied not just to Ontario's Great Lakes but also to the St. Lawrence Seaway and Lake Winnipeg.[44]

Paul Martin received endorsements by three key political figures in Ontario. The biggest surprise came first. On Day 4, at the Canadian Auto Workers annual meeting, union leader Buzz Hargrove hugged Martin, who was wearing a union jacket, and gave him a clear endorsement, saying, "We want a clear minority government led by Paul Martin, with as many New Democrats holding the balance of power as possible."[45] Hargrove told his membership to vote strategically, for example, by supporting Olivia Chow against Tony Ianno in Trinity-Spadina.

On Day 10, in an area of Toronto known for gang violence, Martin was endorsed by Premier Dalton McGuinty and Toronto Mayor Miller after announcing that, if re-elected, the Liberals would implement a ban on handguns. McGuinty had not appeared publicly with Martin in the 2004 election campaign because of his highly unpopular health care tax. In the 2006 campaign, his silence was supportive: he kept quiet about Ontario's putative fiscal imbalance with Ottawa. Unlike his Atlantic counterparts, Premier McGuinty was acknowledging a political debt — appreciation for the Liberals' significant move to correct big Canadian cities' own fiscal imbalance. As with Quebec, the Liberal campaign in Ontario had its own war room to service candidates' policy needs, provide organizational support — particularly for first-time candidates — and relate to the media. With a Liberal government in power in Queen's Park, the federal campaign also benefited from sharing volunteers and staffers.

The Prairies

Martin made only seven campaign stops in the Prairies. Even if the LPC had come second throughout the Prairies, it was a very distant second, as their one-ninth share of the region's fifty-six seats had indicated in 2004. This time, the party made no specific Prairie appeal. Indeed, in response to a question on Western alienation in the second TV debate, Martin said that "never again would issues in Western Canada be treated as regional issues only, they would be national issues" and noted that several key cabinet members are from the West.[46] In Saskatchewan, Martin was careful not to suggest that the federal government would conclude an energy accord with Saskatchewan similar to the Atlantic Accord of the previous February, in which the federal government agreed, because of Newfoundland's deeply rooted deprivation, not to claw back equalization payments despite escalating provincial resource revenues.[47]

The most significant regional policy document released by the Liberals in the West was the "Made-in-Alberta Agenda," introduced by Anne McLellan in Calgary on Day 21, which celebrated a number of previous Liberal commitments, including the GST rebate for cities, money for renewable energy development, and the Pacific Gateway strategy. The agenda reaffirmed the Liberals' pledge for new funding to support access to post-secondary education, to help farmers access new markets, and to explore Senate reform.[48] Martin's six-thousand-word response to the letter written by Alberta Premier Ralph Klein on behalf of other premiers and territorial leaders[49] explained general Liberal policies but was not explicitly directed at the West.

British Columbia

Like its Alberta counterpart, the "Made-in-B.C. Agenda" produced by the party's B.C. wing recalled the government's commitments made to the province in the last Parliament. It made specific commitments to resolving the softwood lumber issue, ensuring funds for the 2010 Olympic Games, and protecting Canada's fisheries.[50] Leaked to the *Vancouver Sun* the day before its official release by high-profile candidates Ujjal Dosanjh and David Emerson, the provincial platform was criticized as being little more than a wish list written by B.C. candidates.[51] The Red Book highlighted the party's $1.5-billion commitment to help Canada's forestry industry and outlined the government's initiatives to boost competitiveness and sustainability in this sector, including the promotion of wood products in growing markets (read China) and more loan insurance for businesses suffering from the softwood lumber dispute.[52]

For several days, confusion reigned within the party over its stance on the Chinese head tax issue. David Emerson reversed his earlier opinion on the controversial topic and said the government should issue a formal apology, while Raymond Chan said the government would do no such thing. Taking a position in between, Ujjal Dosanjh advocated more consultation and perhaps an apology.[53] Former Chrétien environment minister David Anderson upbraided the Liberals, who had downplayed the contamination that offshore oil and gas drilling could cause, for being "two-faced" on drilling for petroleum along the B.C. coast.[54]

The North

Aside from reiterating the commitments to Aboriginals made by the Martin government in the November 2005 agreement concluded by the federal and territorial governments and Aboriginal leaders in Kelowna, B.C., the LPC's Red Book contained pledges to buy ten to twenty unmanned aerial vehicles to enhance surveillance capabilities in the Arctic and to create a new search-and-rescue unit based in Yellowknife.[55] Although protecting First Nations' financial interests in such major resource developments as the MacKenzie Valley gas pipeline was also promised in the document, the Liberals did not discuss resource-revenue sharing, the one issue that Northwest Territories Premier Joe Handley wanted the leaders of the three main federal parties to address before he offered his support.

Early in the campaign, a report by the Canadian Arctic Resources Committee stated the petroleum and mining companies were "plundering the North for hyper-profits" and that the North had been deprived of approximately $500 million in resource revenue since 1996.[56] Premier Handley, who had demanded the Northwest Territories get 40 percent of resource revenues, the same share as the provinces,[57] had rejected signing a devolution agreement without a resource-revenue deal, lest the territory be "taking on program responsibilities without the money."[58] When Martin did not respond to a letter from the premier asking the leaders for their positions on resource-revenue sharing, Handley, who had endorsed the Liberals in 2004, withheld his support.

Campaigning was most difficult for Northern candidates because of the cold, the long hours of darkness, the difficulty of raising money, and the cost of flying by chartered plane to reach remote communities.[59] Unable to campaign in the traditional knocking-on-doors style used throughout most of Canada, candidates in this region relied on radio and the Internet to get their messages out to voters.

THE E-CAMPAIGN

From being little more than online brochures a few years before, in 2006 LPC campaign websites could bolster efforts to reach and engage voters, to test market campaign messages, and even to map supporters according to psycho- and geo-demographic segmentation. Some candidates featured their website addresses on campaign lawn signs, underscoring the central role these sites can have in raising money, organizing the grassroots, targeting core communities, boosting supporters, and communicating core messages. These websites also offer a means to enable party grassroots to "self-serve" — that is, they allow party activists to organize, mobilize, share practices, download key campaign tools, and coordinate outreach. How successfully these e-tools were used at the riding level is not yet known. For the national campaign, they seemed once again to have been of tertiary importance.

On November 29, the LPC website appeared with a much simpler user interface, allowing visitors to access profiles of each Liberal Party candidate and incumbent. On December 2, a new prompt screen was added that asked for the user's email address, postal code, and name so the party could learn more about the people accessing the website. On the same day a new link, "Tell a Friend," turned out to be hosted by a private company, Sequentia Communications, whose mission statement read, "We help you bring in new customers, forge relationships with them, and keep them loyal for life!"

For all its high-tech wizardry, the Liberal web capacity seems to have been of minor utility. Although it allowed the user to sign up for e-news announcements, members of this list serve received about one message per week from such LPC figures as party president Mike Eizenga, soliciting donations and reminding recipients of the cut-off date for tax credits. A total of only seven messages were sent out to members of this mass Liberal Party list serve — the same number of messages that the Green Party of Canada sent out. The website's "Events" section helped to track the Prime Minister's movements throughout the election campaign and also featured television, radio, and online ads. However, these multimedia links were not working when they were released on November 30, 2005. A link to Prime Minister Paul Martin's address to the Liberal Caucus following the non-confidence vote was also not working from November 29 to December 2. Since features on the CPC and NDP sites also were not functioning at times, this suggests that the LPC's website troubles were more characteristic of the technology and its need for substantial webmaster resources during a campaign than an indicator of LPC incompetence. The Liberals may have been unable to exploit the new technology to their advantage, but they were able to be its victim. It was in the mainstream media that the e-campaign seems to have been effective — in accelerating the Liberals downfall.

THE NEGATIVE MEDIA AND THE NEGATIVE ADS

The asymmetry between the media's positive treatment of the Conservatives and negative response to the Liberals continued during the campaign's final phase. When Martin made an announcement on Day 39 about new programs for the elderly and the disabled, including benefits for caregivers, at a campaign stop in Whitby, Ontario, the reporters' questions were all about the income trust scandal and Options Canada; none dealt with the policy message. As reporter Andrew Coyne put it, "The story of this election versus 2004 is not so much that the Tories made fewer mistakes, as that the media were less interested in reporting them. Tory blunders that would have excited a feeding frenzy in the previous election barely rated a mention this time around — while everything the Liberals did or said was filtered through a lens of scepticism, if not derision."[60]

Derision morphed to disgust when the Liberals' long-ballyhooed negative ad campaign was finally unveiled. Or, rather, unmasked, because "the media coverage focused on the negative blitz rather than on the substance of their message."[61] On January 11, the *Globe and Mail* ran on its front page screen shots from ten of the ads, underlining the overwhelming negativity of the Liberal campaign and so confirming Harper's own pre-emptively negative message that the Liberals would be nasty.

Bensimon-Byrne, the Liberals' ad firm, had actually created a series of positive ads designed to highlight recent policy announcements but shelved them in favour of the predicted attack ads, because "we felt we had a lot of reasons for Canadians to be concerned about the things that Stephen Harper had stood up for throughout his political career."[62] But voters and the media alike were already familiar with this old Liberal perspective on the Tories, and the ads were harshly criticized.

Quantity was one problem, but content was another. Snide allegations like "Who financed Stephen Harper's rise to the top? We know he's popular with right wingers in the U.S." fit well with public perceptions of the Liberal Party as arrogant. One of the phrases repeated in the ads — "We're not making this up" — became a national joke. Parodies of the ads circulated the Internet, and headlines in newspapers ridiculed the language. The *Toronto Sun* ran a story with a caption "This election — We did not make this up."[63] The ads were even mentioned on American comedy shows. Jon Stewart from *The Daily Show* created an anti-Canada ad mocking the Liberals for not being able to create a real attack ad. All of this meant that it was difficult to take the Liberal attack ads seriously.

One unused ad, which was inadvertently posted on the LPC website, suggested in threatening-sounding language that Stephen Harper would put soldiers in all Canadian cities, as if he would impose some kind of martial law.[64] The non-ad became a national news story, even eclipsing the French leaders' debate.[65] A comedy of confusion around the military ad helped the media define the Liberal campaign as confused, unorganized, and inept. First, Liberal Party spokesman Ken Polk stated that, although the ad was inadvertently posted, "the ad has not been aired. It may still." A few hours later, he emailed journalists again, stating that "the ad will not air in its present form, and was never intended to."[66] Paul Martin also seemed confused about the ad, at first stating that he had approved it,[67] then claiming he had approved the script but not the final ad.[68] Since it had upset many veterans and military families, Martin lamely tied to explain it was intended to show differences in military policy between the Liberals and the Conservatives.

The confusion was increased by the fact that a version of the same ad continued to run in Quebec.

The Conservatives took advantage of their rivals' disarray by releasing an attack ad about Liberal negative ads that featured quotes from Liberals who had criticized the ad and showed a clip of Martin stating, "I approved the ad, there is no doubt about that." They also responded to the Liberal attacks the day after they were released, effectively dealing with the onslaught. The ad "Can We Believe Him?" attacked Martin's credibility. Harper had spiked Martin's guns so that, in the end, a series of ads that might have been successful were severely discredited and became a national joke.

In apparent recognition that their campaign was falling apart, the Liberals released a final apologetic ad in the last few days of the campaign. "Values, Hopes and Dreams" featured a pleading Martin telling undecided voters, "Our government hasn't been perfect, but we have tried our best to govern according to Canada's values and act upon our great national objectives, our hopes and our dreams." By comparison, Harper was calm and confident in his final advertisements, which showcased him as a leader and as a family man.

Even the Liberals' war room seemed to have imploded. One reporter marvelled that, though she had registered with the Liberal campaign as she had with the others, she never once received a news release or itinerary. Nor were her calls returned. By comparison, the Conservatives always returned her calls and bombarded her with from ten to fifteen emails every day that pointed out contradictions between what the Liberals were saying and what they had said or done in the past — the kind of critical information that was easy to slip into a story as a deadline approached.[69] Early in the campaign, the press carried a photograph of Paul Martin driving a horse-drawn wagon whose rear tire was flat. Now it appeared that at least one of the big red e-machine's wheels was punctured.

REPRIEVE FROM DISASTER

The Liberal Party's fall from grace in 2006 spoke to the unerring propensity of its leader and his clique for strategic miscalculation and tactical ineptitude, which had already brought them from political hegemony in November 2003, when they had wrested control of the party from Jean Chrétien, to near defeat in June 2004 following a prematurely triggered and poorly managed election campaign. The night of Canada's thirty-ninth federal election brought the party two compensating surprises: the moderate dimensions of its by then expected rout, and its leader's rare display of decisive good judgment.

Defeat without Rout

The Liberals won thirty-two seats fewer than they had in 2004. Although this meant defeat, it also meant that they took up their new job as Official Opposition with a robust caucus of 102 members. For a party that had been dismissed as confined to its Ontario base, it turned out to have fared better outside Central Canada. In the Atlantic provinces, the Liberals retained twenty of the region's thirty-two ridings. They kept all four seats in Prince Edward Island and retained their six of eleven seats in Nova Scotia. In Newfoundland, the party lost retiring regional minister John Efford's seat, falling to four of seven, and fell from seven to six of New Brunswick's ten. None of their four cabinet ministers was defeated.[70]

Of the Prairies' fifty-six seats, the Liberals' minuscule share of six fell to five. In Manitoba, Treasury Board President Reg Alcock's loss in Winnipeg South by 110 votes was offset by a political neophyte's win in Churchill. In Saskatchewan, the Liberals picked up one seat, while Finance Minister Ralph Goodale kept his by a healthy 22 percent margin — notwithstanding the RCMP investigation into alleged leaks before his income trust announcement. In Alberta, the Liberals hit rock bottom, losing not just Edmonton–Mill Woods–Beaumont, which David Kilgour had won in 2004, but also Edmonton Centre, which Deputy Prime Minister "Landslide Annie" McLellan had held by narrow margins since 1993. In British Columbia, the Liberals actually picked up one of the province's thirty-six seats. Even though retiring David Anderson's seat in Victoria was lost, two others were won, so that B.C. voters sent nine rather than eight MPs to the Liberal benches in Ottawa, including all four cabinet ministers.[71] In the North, where Liberals won all three seats in 2004 by slim margins, the party held Yukon and Nunavut while cabinet minister Ethel Blondin-Andrew (Northern Development) was defeated in her Northwest Territory riding of Western Arctic.

Ontario was the province where the Liberals lost most, twenty-one seats. They fell from seventy-five to fifty-four of the province's 106 seats and lost four cabinet ministers. However, the Liberal Party remained dominant in Toronto, losing two more to the NDP but still retaining nineteen of the twenty-two seats. The next best region for the LPC was the suburban "905" semicircle around Toronto, where the party lost six seats, falling to eighteen of the area's thirty-two. In Northern Ontario, the Liberals dropped three, falling to seven of thirteen. Worst was Eastern Ontario, where the Liberals lost five, holding only three of seventeen ridings. Nevertheless, the party still held the most seats in the province — fifty-four compared to the CPC's forty and the NDP's twelve. It fell 5 percent in the popular vote but still received 40 percent, compared to the Conservative Party's 35 percent and the NDP's 19 percent.

Although the Liberals lost only eight seats in Quebec, retaining thirteen of seventy-five, the disaster in terms of votes was far greater — a fall from 34 to 20 percent. The Conservatives did better in the popular vote, winning 24 percent as they jumped from zero to ten seats. Only in Alberta was the LPC share of the popular vote lower. Considering how misguided had been their repeat-2004 strategy, how inept their use of policy, how inconsistent their advertising message, how ineffective their e-campaign, how inarticulate their leader, how plagued by allegations of scandal, returning to Ottawa with more than one hundred MPs in their caucus was something of a miracle for the Liberals.

Prospects

Although his two years in office as prime minister had been marked by indecisive and poor political judgment, Paul Martin delivered a surprise announcement after the results were in on election night. Appearing relaxed, even relieved, as he stood before the national media to concede his party's defeat, he thanked his family and his supporters, congratulated his victorious opponent — and announced he would step down as leader of his party. In one short sentence he put the Liberal Party on a fast track to reconstruction. Martin's decision not to cling to party office short-circuited what could have been a long and protracted rearguard action by his entourage to delay its inevitable ousting. Resigning his position and appointing Bill Graham interim leader of the party and leader of the Opposition cleared the way for the Liberal Party to devote itself to choosing a leader and redefining its policies.

After two decades of internal strife between Jean Chrétien and John Turner, then Paul Martin and Jean Chrétien, the Liberal Party had become hostage to its feuding backrooms. The challenge was considerable but it was clear. Could a negative culture of vendetta be replaced by a positive capacity to generate a policy program reflecting the grassroots' commitments and putting the Liberal Party back in the political centre, able to appeal once more to its urban, progressive, multicultural, low-income voting base?

Whereas the Liberals had enjoyed a thirty-six-seat advantage over the Official Opposition in the thirty-eighth Parliament, the Conservative Party of Canada came to power with only a twenty-one-seat lead. Despite the strong possibility that the Conservatives would be defeated before too long, the most experienced potential candidates declined to run for the Liberal Party leadership despite a virtually sure ticket to 24 Sussex Drive. Liberal optimists maintained that this sudden vacuum at the top offered the party a chance to find undiscovered leadership talent in its ranks.[72]

Less sanguine observers wondered whether a traditionally leader-driven party would be able to reverse its downward trend without a strong captain able to smooth over the rifts in the ranks, attract strong candidates, reanimate the party's rank and file, redesign its policies, and appeal once again to progressives and professionals, urban sophisticates and the less advantaged, the multicultural and the francophone. Whether the now shrunken red machine could regain its historical place in the Canadian sun would depend more than anything else on whether the new minority prime minister would follow in the dithering steps of his hapless predecessor.

NOTES

This chapter is based on research carried out by Lisa Brylowski, Alison Corbett, Kevin Corcoran, Kathryn Kotris, Stephen Mancer, Omar Soliman, Evan Sotiropoulos, Christine Van Geyn, and Jennifer Vibert. It also profited from the counsel of Stephen Deckbert, Peter Donolo, Warren Kinsella, and Michael Valpy.

1   Stephen Clarkson, *The Big Red Machine: How the Liberal Party Dominates Canadian Politics* (Vancouver: University of British Columbia Press, 2005), 284.

2   Stephen Clarkson, "Disaster and Recovery: Paul Martin as Political Lazarus," in *The Canadian General Election of 2004*, ed. Jon H. Pammett and Christopher Dornan (Toronto: Dundurn Press, 2004), 28–65.

3   "'Mr. Dithers' and his distracting 'fiscal cafeteria,'" *The Economist*, February 19, 2005, 35–6.

4   Bill Curry, Brian Laghi, and Gloria Galloway, "Martin buys NDP support," *Globe and Mail*, April 27, 2005, A1.

5   "Veteran campaigners back Liberal re-election bid," *Ottawa Citizen*, December 8, 2005, A6.

6   Jane Taber, "Liberal majority in sight, chief strategist tell MPs," *Globe and Mail*, August 25, 2005, A1.

7 Jeffrey Simpson, "The media are just the messenger, Mr. Harper," *Globe and Mail*, October 12, 2005, A23.

8 Jane Taber, "PM plans negative election campaign: onslaught of Liberal ads to follow Christmas hiatus," *Globe and Mail*, November 24, 2005, A1.

9 Strategic Counsel Poll, "Federal Election — Vote Intention, Likely Election Winner: A Report to The Globe and Mail and CTV," January 6, 2006.

10 Observatory of Media and Public Policy, McGill University, "2006 Federal Newspaper analysis," *Weekly Report*, http://www.ompp.mcgill.ca.

11 Les Whittington, "Martin pledges to expand daycare plan," *Toronto Star*, December 7, 2005, A6.

12 Paul Martin speaking at the UN Conference on Climate Change in Montreal, Quebec, December 7, 2005. The Canadian prime minister's criticism received favourable coverage in the *New York Times* and arguably pushed the United States to make a concession in Montreal — agreeing to take part in multilateral deliberations about global warming — that it had denied Tony Blair at the G-8 summit in Glen Eagles the previous summer.

12 Anne Dawson and Allan Woods, "Critics assail gun plan: Liberal proposal 'won't change a lot': expert," *National Post*, December 9, 2005, A1. However, Martin's "tough on crime" subtext was popular in the major urban centres of Toronto, Vancouver, and Montreal, where it received over 70 percent approval. Strategic Counsel Poll, "Federal Election — Vote Intention, Ownership of Handguns: A Report to The Globe and Mail and CTV," December 12, 2005.

14 Andrew Mills and Les Whittington, "'I'm going to call it like I see it', P.M. insists," *Toronto Star*, December 15, 2005, A7.

15 Peter Goddard, "How Harper beat Nixon," *Toronto Star*, January 29, 2006, C6.

16 Stephen Clarkson, "Are we playing with the media or are the media playing with us? *Globe and Mail*, October 14, 2005.

17 Lawrence Martin, "No more Mr. Ice Guy: Harper's makeover turns Tory tide," *Globe and Mail*, December 22, 2005, A21.

18 CPAC-SES Polling, http://www.sesresearch.com.

19 Steven Chase and Brian Laghi, "Martin's Christmas bonus," *Globe and Mail*, November 15, 2005, A1.

20 Campbell Clark, "Setbacks aside, Martin 'happy' with campaign," *Globe and Mail*, January 6, 2006, A1.

21 James Travers, "Liberal party's scattered campaign a reflection of Martin's leadership," *Toronto Star*, January 12, 2006, A1.

22 CBC-TV, *The National*, December 20, 2005.

23 CBC-TV, *Leaders Debate 2006*, January 9, 2006.

24 Doug Beazley, "Liberal party hangs McLellan out to dry," *Edmonton Sun*, January 14, 2006, http://www.edmontonsun.com.

25 Quebecers also believed the Liberal Party the most capable of upholding national unity. Carolyn Ryan, "Playing the Quebec game," CBC: Canada Votes, December 22, 2005, http://www.cbc.ca/canadavotes/leadersparties/quebec_game.html.

26 Paul Martin speaking to reporters in Toronto, December 2, 2005.

27 CBC-TV, *Leaders Debate 2005*, December 16, 2005.

28 John Ibbitson, "New synergy aims to limit Liberal vote," *Globe and Mail*, December 17, 2005, A5.

29 Quoted in: "Enjeux électoraux: Les Québécois et les Canadiens préoccupés par la santé," Canadian Press, December 7, 2005.

30 Conversation with Peter Donolo.

31 R. Kenneth Carty, William Cross, and Lisa Young, *Rebuilding Party Politics* (Vancouver: UBC Press, 2000), 187–90.

32 Keith Leslie, "Paul Martin jumps into policy parade with other $11 billion for childcare," *CP Atlantic Regional News*, December 6, 2005.

33 "Liberals promise fishermen tax break," CBC News Online, December 21, 2005.

34 Liberal Party of Canada, *Securing Canada's Success*, January 11, 2006, 42–3.

35 Ibid, 39.

36 "Liberals find money for Gander jobs," CBC News Online, January 13, 2006.

37 "Williams to stay on election sidelines," CBC News Online, November 29, 2005.

38 "PM's response falls flat, Williams says," CBC News Online, January 17, 2006.

39 Wayne Thibodeau, "Binns irate Martin snubbed his request for equalization meeting," *The Guardian* (Charlottetown), December 12, 2005.

40 Allan Woods, "Lord says Martin playing with fire," *Leader-Post* (Regina), December 7, 2005.

41 "NB says Ottawa sending conflicting signals about harbour cleanup," Canadian Press, December 9, 2005.

42 Chris Morris, "NB sceptical of Ottawa's offer to cost share compensation for river flood," CP Atlantic Regional News, December 16, 2005.

43 "Liberals would mix ethanol with gasoline," CBC News Online, December 20, 2005.

44 Ibid, 66–7.

45 Campbell Clark, "Liberals touted by CAW leader," *Globe and Mail*, December 3, 2005, A1, A6.

46 CBC-TV, *Leaders Debate 2005*, December 16, 2005.

47 James Wood, "Equalization a key economic issue," *Leader-Post* (Regina), December 12, 2005.

48 Tony Seskus, "Deputy PM McLellan touts Liberals' plan for Alberta," *Calgary Herald*, December 20, 2005.

49 Rob Ferguson, "Provinces in mix, PM says," *Toronto Star*, December 23, 2005, A6.

50 Team B.C., "Made-in-B.C. Agenda," January 6, 2006.

51 Michael Smyth, "Liberals' 'Made in B.C.' agenda a waste of paper," *Province* (Vancouver), January 8, 2006.

52 *Securing Canada's Success*, 40.

53 Petti Fong, "Emerson backs head-tax compensation," *Globe and Mail*, January 4, 2006, S3.

54 "Former environment ministers issue green challenge," CBC News Online, January 13, 2006.

55 *Securing Canada's Success*, 42.

56 Nathan VanderKlippe, "NWT missing out on $500M in royalties," *Leader-Post* (Regina), December 17, 2005.

57 Ibid.

58 "Liberal's fall could jeopardize devolution deal, says MP," CBC News Online, January 5, 2006.

59 "Election rules keep Nunavut candidates grounded," CBC News Online, December 20, 2005.

60 Andrew Coyne, "This election campaign was predicted to be a repeat of the one held in June, 2004. What happened?" *National Post*, January 14, 2006, A10.

61 Keith McArthur, "New Tory ad attacks Martin's credibility: Liberals call spots false and misleading," *Globe and Mail*, January 12, 2006, A7.

62 Jack Bensimon, president of Bensimon Byrne, quoted in Keith McArthur, "A Tale of two election advertising campaigns: Strategic use of attack ads shaped

outcome of slugfest between Liberals, Conservatives," *Globe and Mail*, January 28, 2006.

63 Linda Williamson, "218 Reasons NOT to vote for the Liberals," *Toronto Sun*, January 22, 2006, A1.

64 Mike Duffy interviews John Duffy, "Countdown with Mike Duffy," *CTV News*, January 10, 2006.

65 James McCarten, "Duffy vs. Duffy: Liberal ad sparks on-camera clash between journalist, Grit strategist," *Globe and Mail*, January 11, 2006, A8.

66 John Ibbitson, "Here's the Story Behind the Story," *Globe and Mail*, January 11, 2006, A7.

67 Lorrie Goldstein, "Stand back, he's about to blow," *Ottawa Sun*, January 22, 2006.

68 Michelle Macafee, "Martin approved script, but ditched finished ad," *Brandon Sun*, January 13, 2006.

69 Beth Duff-Brown (Canadian correspondent for the Associated Press), interview with the author, February 1, 2006.

70 Cabinet ministers from Atlantic Canada re-elected: Andy Scott (Indian Affairs) of Fredericton, N.B.; Joe McGuire (Atlantic Canada Opportunities) of Egmont, P.E.I.; Scott Brison (Public Works) of Kings-Hants, N.B.; and Geoff Regan (Fisheries and Oceans) of Halifax West, N.S.

71 Cabinet ministers from British Columbia re-elected: Raymond Chan (Multiculturalism) of Richmond; Ujjal Dosnajh (Health) of Vancouver South; Stephen Owen (Western Economic Diversification) of Vancouver Quadra; and David Emerson (Industry) of Vancouver Kingsway. Subsequently, Emerson defected to the Conservatives to become Minister of International Trade, Minister for the Pacific Gateway and the Vancouver-Whistler Olympics and returned the B.C. Liberals to their 2004 level of eight seats.

72 Peter Donolo, "How the race is run will matter," *Globe and Mail*, February 23, 2006, A19.

CHAPTER THREE

A Change of Government, Not a Change of Country:
The Conservatives and the 2006 Election
by Faron Ellis and Peter Woolstencroft

When Stephen Harper succeeded Stockwell Day as leader of the Canadian Alliance in 2002, few would have predicted that in less than four years he would lead a united Conservative Party to victory and become Canada's twenty-second prime minister.[2] Indeed, despite the electorate's apparent interest in change, only eighteen months before his victory the Conservatives' hopes for forming a government had gone unfulfilled when a dramatic final weekend shift in Ontario voters' preferences led to a minority win for the Liberals. The most widely accepted — and certainly most compelling — reason for the Liberals' sharp recovery in the final stages of the 2004 campaign was their ability to portray Harper and the Conservatives in negative terms and the Conservatives' inability to counter the charges effectively. Equally important was the Conservatives' inability to project a competent, ready-to-govern image throughout that campaign. When Liberal television attack commercials labelled Harper and his party as too scary, too right-wing, too extreme, and certainly too unknown to be entrusted with power, several Conservative candidates' off-message musings on hot-button issues and the leader's announcement that he was already planning the transition to power seemingly validated the accusations and solidified voters' concerns.[3]

Beyond the specific campaign dynamics, however, the 2004 election demonstrated one fundamental deficiency with the new party: it had not yet developed an identity and could therefore not plant a positive image for itself in voters' minds. How, then, would the Conservative Party address its identity crisis in attempting to broaden its support?[4] How would it position itself on social issues like abortion, same-sex marriage, and euthanasia? Could it successfully navigate the troubled waters of French-English relations? What role would it prescribe for the courts, especially in relation to the Charter of Rights and Freedoms? What was its vision of federalism, the role of government, and the welfare state? In the fashion of a missionary movement, would it revert to the populist, moralistic, and right-wing rhetoric of the Reform Party, one of its founders?[5] Or would it develop more moderate and balanced positions in the manner of a broker-oriented, centre-seeking party, akin to the Progressive Conservative Party, the other part of its heritage?[6] Or would it seek to find some compromise between the two poles and risk leaving itself still undefined and open to charges of harbouring hidden agendas?

Conservatives would begin the work of answering these questions immediately following their 2004 election loss. They held the party's first convention in Montreal to determine the policies upon which its identity would be crafted. They then set out to build an organization capable of clearly communicating the party's vision, of rehabilitating its leader's image, and of wresting power from the Liberals. But the long ten months between the March 2005 convention and the January 2006 election were fraught with setbacks. The Conservatives tried but failed to defeat the government in May when former Conservative Party leadership candidate Belinda Stronach and former Reform MP Chuck Cadman helped sustain the Liberals. Harper's media coverage was generally unenthusiastic, often negative, and by summer's end the Conservatives continued to be mired in second place in national opinion polls and seemed destined to fulfill predictions that they were incapable of dethroning the Liberals. The Conservative consolidation project seemed to be stalled, so much so that when the government was defeated in late November of 2005, the popular opinion was that the election would not produce materially different results from those of 2004.

However, the 2006 contest provided evidence that election campaigns matter. An innovative and strategically sound campaign by the Conservatives, a disastrous Liberal campaign (see Chapter Two), and a series of exogenous dynamics — a Boxing Day shooting death in a downtown Toronto shopping area and the late-December announcement by the RCMP that they were investigating leaks about the Liberals' income trusts policy, among others — combined to produce an outcome few would have predicted with much confidence only a few months earlier. Not only did the Conservatives form a minority government, but they did so by bringing many PC voters back into the coalition and at the same time building substantial support in Quebec. Although the party fell short of making significant inroads with recent immigrant voters, leaving it shut out of Montreal, Toronto, and Vancouver, given the state of electoral competition at the campaign's start, the Conservatives' 2006 results were quite extraordinary.

THE 2004 POST-MORTEM

The Conservatives began planning for the 2006 election by engaging in a series of critical evaluations of the 2004 effort. Harper, campaign manager Tom Flanagan, executive director Ian Brodie, and director of field organizations Doug Findlay spontaneously and independently set about to evaluate their operations and make recommendations for improvement. Flanagan assumed a coordinating role in an overall review that went on for months, but Harper held many meetings independently of Flanagan, while Brodie attended to post-election party organizational matters. Given the personal and professional characteristics of each of the principals involved, the various processes often involved frank, no-holds-barred critiques that have taken on a mythical status in much of the early post-election analysis, leading to a misrepresentation of the process as being much more coordinated than it actually was. What can be said is that the learning exercise produced an approach to the 2006 campaign that was very different than that taken less than two years earlier.

Initially, the Conservatives' ability to counter Liberal negativity with a simple, comprehensive vision would be central to inoculating the party against opposition tactics that strategists accurately assumed would be used again. The Conservatives' 2004 campaign, only two-thirds scripted at the outset, suffered because it lacked an overall narrative that would have defined the party's image and simplified its message for voters. The policy platform was too detailed, at times far too abstract, and not connected well to the advertising and communications strategies. In its sophistication, it also did not connect well with voters. The 2006 campaign needed better scripting and communication of a comprehensive narrative delivered to voters by way of more and varied television advertising.

Logistics, including media management, needed to be improved. In attempting to define the embryonic party's image during the 2004 contest, strategists decided to release entire platform planks early in the campaign, including detailed subsets of policies associated with the main plank. This resulted in one-day media hits that were often overshadowed by other events, campaign related or otherwise, and a frustrated national media looking for fresh material on non-release days. The 2004 platform's Saturday release stood out as an example of how to ensure minimal print and television exposure. For a time, however, the policy-up-front strategy appeared to be paying dividends. But when the full force of Liberal attack ads came in the later part of the campaign, the Conservatives were left spinning their wheels, with all of their major announcements having been made. As a result, they were forced into damage control for much of the last ten days of a short, five-week campaign.

The 2004 leader's tour was also less than optimally effective in communicating the platform. Although for the most part the tour ran according to plan, Harper and his immediate staff had taken on too many responsibilities for themselves and there was little use made of secondary tours featuring prominent MPs. Events were typically scheduled later in the day or evening, with travel scheduled in the morning, creating deadline problems for reporters and surrendering upwards of half of the twenty-four-hour news cycle to their opponents. At times, such as when Harper was preparing for the debates, the party organized no photo ops and the leader received no media exposure. Other strategic decisions such as the final weekend return to the western base provided dramatic and powerful visuals, but these images seemingly contradicted the most important goal of reaching out to the voters of Central Canada. An under-resourced war room and poor communication between it and the tour also contributed to the late-campaign drift. Research and media communications needed systematic improvements for the 2006 effort, including the establishment of an organization that provided journalists with Conservative attack material, reality checks, and backgrounders.

Logistic and strategic problems were compounded by a breakdown of discipline on the part of several Conservative candidates, the party's war room, and the leader himself. Harper's speculation about a Conservative majority and comments about a transition team — designed to demonstrate competency and alleviate concerns about how ready the party was to govern — distracted from the party's message and were easily counter-spun by opponents as reflective of an inexperienced and arrogant leader who was in too big a hurry to implement his hidden agenda. When a number of candidates' socially conservative comments, past and present, were ferreted out and seemingly substantiated by an excessively inflammatory war room news release accusing Paul Martin of supporting child pornography, opponents pronounced that the hidden social conservative agenda had been exposed. When Harper had trouble dealing with the aftermath of these developments, Conservative momentum stalled, and then reversed, as the chastened leader's tour seemingly limped home to Alberta on the final weekend.

In spite of the mistakes, for a party that was only six months old, the Conservatives ran a remarkably successful 2004 campaign. Where problems occurred, they tended to be compounded by, or in some cases caused by, the new party's lack of a firm identity. The merger of the missionary-like, Western-based Canadian Alliance with the brokerage-oriented, Atlantic-based Progressive Conservative Party was not yet institutionalized, and the new Conservatives faced a conundrum: Could they successfully complete the union and compete with the Liberals in Canada's two most populous provinces? A widely held interpretation of Canadian centre-right politics was that a structural constraint existed between the PC and Alliance ideological and organizational cultures. Their differences were neither idiosyncratic nor accidental but deep-seated enough to be a significant barrier in the consolidation project. The 2004 election results confirmed the premise that "uniting the right" was a more troubled concept than many of its proponents had imagined or let on.[7] So despite the relative success that had been achieved by conservative leaders, the time had come for members of the new party to weigh in on policy matters and help answer some of the identity questions.

THE MONTREAL CONVENTION, MARCH 2005

By the time more than twenty-four hundred Conservative delegates gathered in Montreal for their first policy convention as a united party, much of the sting of not forming a government in 2004 had worn off. Delegates tended to think about how far they had come in just over one year rather than be disappointed about not achieving power in their first united effort. They also recognized how significant their deliberations would be in forming a new identity for the party, as much for what they would take off the party's agenda as for what they would include in its policy declaration manual.

The choice of Montreal as the convention site was considered by many to be odd, if not quixotic. The party had no MPs from Quebec,[8] and with polls suggesting the Bloc Québécois was benefiting enormously from the sponsorship scandal revelations, the Conservatives seemed to lack growth prospects. Moreover, the party's membership in Quebec was minuscule, almost assuring that Québécois participation would be minimal. Indeed, there was considerable danger that even a debate on the social conservative agenda, no matter what its outcome, would only solidify the party's image as anathema to Quebec's notoriously secular, socially liberal voters. Although many party strategists preferred Ottawa or Toronto, because

Harper was so committed to building the party in Quebec he determined that the convention would be held in that province.

To the surprise of many — media commentators and opponents alike — the convention was generally free of the fear and loathing that had characterized the relations between the Alliance and PC parties and had been apparent in some electoral district associations after the merger. In a sense, the convention's proceedings presaged the election campaign of 2006; its overall tenor was of control, discipline, and focus, and its overarching theme was a party united, moving ever closer to the centre, and readying for government. Despite some spirited debates, there was little evidence of the "Tory syndrome" on display in Montreal.[9]

The convention's opening video and Stephen Harper's speech contained a surprising and ironic invocation: the Conservative Party was described as a family with deep roots throughout Canada's history, extending from John A. Macdonald to Brian Mulroney, the last Progressive Conservative prime minister, and Preston Manning, founder of Reform, the party that destroyed the PC base in Western Canada. The effect of the judiciously considered combination was palpable: Unity was essential. A significant number of prominent former Progressive Conservatives in attendance reinforced the success the party was achieving in becoming something more than an Alliance takeover of the old PC party. Former Clark and Mulroney cabinet members such as John Crosbie, Walter McLean, Tom Siddon, and Michael Wilson[10] were visible throughout the event. Also prominent was long-time PC strategist and 1998 PC leadership candidate Hugh Segal, who would soon be appointed by Martin to the Senate, sit in the Conservative caucus, and advise Harper's 2006 campaign team.[11]

Harper's speech was also instructive. He acknowledged social conservatives by promising to bring forward legislation that, "while providing the same rights, benefits and obligations to all couples, will maintain the traditional definition of marriage as the union of one man and one woman." In the next sentence, however, he acknowledged the progressive agenda by declaring that he would "not bring forth legislation on the issue of abortion." He went further by promising both factions that "as your leader, if you disagree with me on these matters, I will not call you stupid or label you a threat to Canadian values. As leader, I care less about your views on these matters than whether you are prepared to respect the views of those who disagree with you."[12] Although the speech was moderate in tone and addressed the unity issue by offering something for both factions,[13] its strong pronouncements about what Harper would do as Conservative prime minister, delivered before delegates had even debated policy, was antithetical to Harper's Reform roots. While former PC delegates took little notice, former Reformers mused openly about how Manning would have been pilloried for such pronouncements before Reform delegates had made their deliberations.

An earlier indication of the direction Harper would lead the new party was the founding principles adopted at the time of the merger, especially when compared to those of its foundational entities, the PC, CA, and Reform parties. The 2003 agreement between then Alliance leader Harper and PC leader Peter MacKay identified nineteen founding principles.[14] These were phrased exactly as they had been in the "Aims" and "Principles" sections of the last constitution of the federal PC Party.[15] When combined with the adoption of the PC method of leadership selection and convention delegate entitlements, as well as the Conservative brand name, the leaders' agreement demonstrated that, at least in these important respects, the merger was dominated by PC norms and values. Gone were most of the Reform-Alliance populist and Western declarations in support of a "Triple E Senate," referenda, citizens' initiatives, recall, opposition to "unaccountable judges and human rights bureaucrats," and support for the "legitimate use of the Section 33 notwithstanding provision." Also jettisoned was the Reform-Alliance rhetoric in support of "fundamental justice," "a balanced federation of equal provinces and citizens," and an unqualified commitment to a "broadly based free enterprise economy."[16] In summary, taking Reform's stated principles as a baseline, over time there has been a clear moderation in principles, attempted first by the Canadian Alliance and significantly furthered by the new Conservatives, with the latter reflecting much more the PC rather than the Reform-Alliance side of its past.

The extent to which the new Conservative Party is based on its progressive conservatism is also seen in three other aspects of the merger. First, the party name fits closely the PC brand, which was often abbreviated by dropping the "Progressive."[17] Second, the Conservatives adopted the PC system whereby the individual electoral district rather than the individual party member is used for electing the leader and determining the number of delegates electoral districts are allowed to send to conventions. The system is based on the equality of electoral districts, so the district with ten thousand members counts no more than one with one hundred members. A strict "one member, one vote" system would have rendered Eastern Canada politically unimportant and resulted, presumably, in a differently constituted 2005 policy convention.[18] Third, in policy terms, the party adopted various resolutions that spoke to its desire to move toward the political centre. Although there were some motions that had Reform-Alliance overtones, the resulting "Policy Declaration" effectively eliminated most of the social conservative and populist hot button issues that allowed their opponents to label the Conservatives as extreme and accuse them of harbouring hidden agendas.

Although the convention supported including property rights in the Charter, ending minimum sentences and statutory release for serious offenders, and upholding the traditional definition of marriage by a vote of 74 percent in favour, they quashed several other socially conservative proposals. By a vote of 54.9 percent to 44.1 percent, delegates supported Harper's position not to re-engage the abortion debate.[19] They also overwhelmingly defeated a motion that would have committed the party to striking a Royal Commission to investigate euthanasia, assisted suicide, and palliative care. They backed Harper's Quebec outreach agenda by overwhelmingly supporting official bilingualism, dedicated the party to restoring the constitutional balance of power through limiting the federal spending powers, and adopted a resolution to address the fiscal imbalance, a motion that had been killed at the previous day's workshops but was resurrected by the party brass and placed before the plenary session. They also agreed with their leader on the use of free votes in Parliament but systematically defeated all other populism proposals, including a citizens' assembly on electoral reform, recall, referenda, and citizen-sponsored initiatives.

Exorcising the populist ghosts and taming the social conservative agenda demonstrated that even most former Reformers now conceded that the damaging electoral consequences of these policies had stalled the drive to build a national coalition of voters.[20] Former Progressive Conservatives concurred with that wisdom and those interviewed for this chapter indicated their beliefs that former leaders of the PC Party — from MacKay to Diefenbaker — would have had little or no problem with what transpired at the Conservative policy convention in Montreal.

AN ELECTION AVOIDED AND AN ELECTION ACHIEVED

The eight months between the Montreal convention and the Martin government's defeat was like a roller coaster ride for the Conservatives. An immediate post-convention bump in the polls indicated that Conservative prospects were improving. Testimony to the ongoing

Gomery Commission into the sponsorship affair was constantly bad for the Liberals, especially in Quebec, where people followed the proceedings intently. Liberal vulnerability emboldened Harper to seek the defeat of the government on a non-confidence motion in the spring of 2005, but his plans were scuppered. The critical event was the defection to the Liberals (and appointment to cabinet) of former Conservative leadership candidate Belinda Stronach. With the help of Chuck Cadman, a former Canadian Alliance MP elected as an independent in 2004, two other independents, and the NDP, the Liberals survived. Conservatives took some solace in the belief that the Liberals were clearly desperate to hang onto power because of what was forthcoming in the Gomery hearings, for which they would eventually be punished. However, they were soon tarnished themselves by the rather bizarre accusations from one of their MPs, Germant Grewal, that he had been approached by both Martin's Chief of Staff Tim Murphy and Health Minister Ujjal Dosanjh to cross the floor to the Liberals. Taped recordings of the discussions that allegedly supported the accusations were of dubious authenticity, and when this affair was combined with the government's survival, the Conservatives seemed to have lost the momentum they had gained in Montreal.

Nevertheless, once the parliamentary session ended, Harper embarked on a highly publicized "Summer BBQ Tour," with the requisite appearances at fairs, rodeos, and stampedes. The tour was designed to reconnect the leader with the grassroots and demonstrate that, despite the frustration of failing to bring down the government, the leader was still engaged, working hard, and motivated to win the next election. By the party's standard, the summer tour was a great success in buoying the spirits of and re-energizing both the leader and the troops. Behind the scenes Harper continued to make critical decisions, including the restructuring of his office, a process that lasted until September. The national media, however, was underwhelmed with both initiatives.

By the time Harper met his caucus in mid-summer, media reports pointed to concerns about the ineffectiveness of the summer outreach program. Public opinion polls had reversed, with most measuring Conservatives support at around 25 percent and the Liberals in the high 30s. An SES poll from mid-August indicated that Jack Layton, the leader of the NDP, was more favourably viewed than was Harper, and both were far behind Paul Martin. Moreover, the sponsorship scandal was losing its saliency and being eclipsed by traditional issues of health care and social policies. But Harper plodded on. In late August the Conservatives began to run four television commercials that featured Harper and one or more of his MPs discussing — in a rather stilted and self-conscious manner — health care, lowering taxes, choice in child care, and assisting immigrants to enter the workforce. Media evaluation of the party's commercials was generally negative, and the extensive restructuring of Harper's office led to counterproductive press reports about unrest at the Conservative caucus meeting in Halifax just after Labour Day.

In the fall of 2005, a number of nominated candidates stepped aside because of the uncertainty about when the election would happen and the unlikelihood of success given the party's weak poll numbers. In Quebec, former candidates and party organizers criticized Harper for the party's falling support levels and for various organizational difficulties. Tensions between MacKay and Harper were widely reported, and long-time conservative activist Carol Jamieson publicly called for Harper's resignation. The leadership issue was so prominent that the two co-chairs of the election campaign — Michael Fortier, a prominent Quebec Conservative, and John Reynolds, a long-term B.C. MP and former interim opposition leader — issued a statement claiming that the party and its leader were on the right path. They insisted that their internal polling showed the party was doing better than media-reported polls would suggest and claimed that a growing proportion of voters were considering the Conservatives. But with the Conservatives strategically deciding to keep their platform "powder dry" until the election was called, members and supporters had little to substantiate the campaign chairs' claims.[21]

The underlying tensions were reignited when speculation began about whether MacKay would leave the federal party to pursue the premiership of Nova Scotia after John Hamm announced his intention to retire as provincial Conservative Party leader. Although MacKay would decline the opportunity, questions about whether the deputy leader would stick with the federal unity project were often compounded by speculation about whether Harper even wanted him to stay. All in all, it seemed that the project was failing. Illustrative of the widespread criticism were two articles in *Policy Options* that dismissed Harper's chances. Graham Fox, former chief of staff for Joe Clark, criticized Harper for not broadening the party's base and for making the sponsorship scandal the pivotal argument for seeking to defeat the Liberals. Robin Sears labelled Harper as a politician more interested in the purity of ideas than in building coalitions.[22]

Throughout the fall parliamentary session, Harper, his caucus, and the party continued their election preparations but continued to keep policy closeted until after Justice Gomery released his report on the sponsorship scandal. As the session became more and more acrimonious, Gomery's conclusions about a "culture of entitlement" left the NDP with little option but to withdraw its support of the government. As the Liberals embarked on a pre-election spending spree, the Prime Minister refused to support an NDP motion that would have seen the election campaign begin in January 2006. Although the Conservatives were trailing in the polls, they believed that the government was vulnerable on the trust issue, and, moreover, that their strategic planning was proceeding very well; most electoral districts had nominated candidates and were ready to roll. With many Conservative strategists fearing that the Prime Minister's promised February election start date would give the Liberals time to recover from the Gomery Commission's fallout, a confidence vote was called, the government fell, and what was expected to be one of the most bitterly negative campaigns in Canadian history began.

CAMPAIGN ORGANIZATION AND STRATEGY

The Montreal convention and policy manual put the party on a reasonably secure footing as it drafted its 2006 campaign platform. Delegates had moderated the party's position on a number of social conservative issues, although its position on the same-sex marriage issue remained a question. They had thoroughly inoculated the party against charges of harbouring hidden agendas disguised as populism and developed a centrist, conservative policy manual as the foundation for establishing an identity for the merged party. One indication of the success of the consolidation project was found in the federal electoral histories of 2006 Conservative candidates.

The most striking feature of Table 1 is that about 70 percent of the candidates had no previous candidacies or party-office incumbency with either of the founding streams.[23] The second is the differences east and west of the Manitoba-Ontario border. To the west, most incumbents came from the Reform/Alliance pillar. In Atlantic Canada seven of ten candidates with electoral histories had PC backgrounds (again mostly incumbents). In Ontario, which had given the Conservatives twenty-four seats in 2004, two-thirds of candidates with federal electoral histories had PC backgrounds, suggesting that PC stalwarts were comfortable with the direction taken by the Conservatives.[24]

It remained to develop and execute a strategic plan that could improve on the 2004 gains without making similar mistakes. The Conservatives'

Table 1

Federal party backgrounds of Conservative candidates, 2006 election

Province/ Region	PC	Reform/ CA	Both	None	Number of Districts
Atlantic	7	3	0	22	32
Quebec	4	6	1	64	75
Ontario	24	10	3	69	106
Manitoba	0	1	2	11	14
Saskatchewan	0	6	0	8	14
Alberta	0	19	1	8	28
British Columbia	0	11	2	23	36
North	0	0	0	3	3
Total	35	56	9	208	308

Source: CBC candidate biographies; www.cbc.ca/canadavotes/riding
Centre for Election Studies, University of Waterloo.

Note: Candidates were categorized on the basis of having run for the indicated parties or holding national party office. "Both" means having PC and Reform/CA electoral histories.

planning presupposed that enough Canadian voters would support a change in government if presented with a competent, moderate, and national alternative to the Liberals. Accordingly, rather than underemphasize the pre-Christmas campaign, they sought to build credibility by emphasizing the party's well-considered and attractive policies as the foundation for its new image.

Against much advice, Harper decided that there would be no negative advertising in the first part of the campaign or overplaying of the sponsorship scandal, leaving that ground to the NDP and Bloc. Rather, he would trot out a policy a day in an attempt to reclaim ownership of issues typically considered to be areas of Conservative strength — Canada–U.S.A. relations, managing the economy, and tax cuts — but where party pollster Dimitri Pantazopoulos was still measuring Liberal strength. Once credibility was established on traditional ground, they would continue with the relentless policy rollout to establish credibility on more centrist issues such as health and child care.

There would be little Christmas break; the thinking was to use informal campaign events and policy announcements to keep fresh images of the leader and party in the media during what was widely assumed to be downtime. The final, post–New Year's phase of the campaign would open by simplifying the message and reducing it to five key priorities that would emphasize the ballot question Conservatives were trying to establish: a change in government is a relatively low-risk proposition with the now more moderate and competent Conservatives representing the only option for voters wanting change.

The strategy was predicated on Harper's ability to articulate a policy vision for the country while revealing himself as a rather ordinary, middle-class family man. The policy focus also assumed that voters would be paying attention to the pre-Christmas phase of the campaign and that by the time the Liberals were fully engaged, the Conservatives would have sufficiently defined themselves positively to withstand Liberal negativity in the campaign's second half.

Communications, internal and external, would be key. The 2004 campaign taught the Conservatives that they needed more coordinated and extensive internal communications in order to ensure that everyone, including the leader, stayed on-message. To that end, the Conservatives established a communications plan that involved upwards of five daily conference calls between the campaign team's key members. Each day opened with a morning communications call that included various senior members of the war room, the leader's tour, and media advisors. Each morning senior staff would also be involved in a daily strategy call with the leader. Several other scheduled calls involving the leader and upwards of twenty staff followed throughout the day. University of Western Ontario political scientist Ian Brodie, who had been promoted in the fall of 2005 from executive director of the party to Harper's chief of staff, provided the vital communications link between the tour and the war room. University of Calgary political scientist and long-time Harper confidant Tom Flanagan was the war room's communications linchpin.

Campaign manager Doug Findlay, new director of communications William Stairs, press secretary Carolyn Stewart-Olsen, strategist Bruce Carson, and French media liaison Dimitri Soudas travelled with the leader on tour. Conservative senator and new Harper confidant Marjorie LeBretton, executive assistant Ray Novak, and often Harper's wife, Laureen Teskey, joined them on a tour that was supported by a chartered Air Canada plane and three Greyhound buses that were used almost exclusively in Ontario and Quebec.[25] The tour schedule focused on

Central Canada. Only three trips were made to the West prior to the tour's final return to Calgary on election eve, and one of those was associated with the first set of leaders' debates in Vancouver, while another was for Christmas.[26] The Conservatives also made much more extensive use of a secondary tour in the 2006 campaign; MPs such as Jim Prentice, Peter MacKay, Monte Solberg, Rona Ambrose, Jason Kenny, and campaign co-chair John Reynolds, among others, filled the media void when the main tour was distracted with other matters such as debate preparation.[27]

Political marketer Patrick Muttart was hired in the summer of 2005 and became the central scripter of the overall campaign message and master of strategic communications. He was responsible for giving the campaign a narrative that pulled together the often disjointed aspects of abstract policy, advertising, and messaging by providing a new style that reflected the party's more moderate identity. Once the campaign began, Muttart moved to advertising full-time, provided a link between the virtual agency the Conservatives had established and the rest of the organization, while managing the team that determined which type of photo ops and settings would be used to provide visual backup to the top-line message of the day. As the creative mind of the campaign, Muttart took a "political marketing" approach to how the Conservatives presented themselves to the electorate. In its most sophisticated expression, the political marketing approach analyzes voters in terms of their values and policy positions. Critical components include segmenting the electoral marketplace, strategic positioning, intensive research of voters through surveys and focus groups, use of television to frame issues, and micro-messaging to target voter groups.[28]

British political scientist Jennifer Lees-Marshment uses a threefold typology for understanding the interactions between politicians and electorate within the context of election campaigns.[29] One type of party — the market-oriented — prepares itself to win an election by conducting research "to identify and understand public priorities, concerns, and demands before then designing a product that reflects them."[30] The essential strategic task is to identify "the key groups within the electorate whose support is required to secure election."[31] Alex Marland, in his examination of the 2000 Canadian case, argued that the Liberals took a market-oriented approach while the other major parties essentially were sales-oriented, with the exception of the Bloc Québécois, which took a product-oriented approach.[32]

In 2006 the Conservatives successfully adopted a market-oriented approach by avoiding generalities and offering specific policies that appealed not to general demographic groupings but to voters with specific concerns and policy preferences within the party's commitment to smaller government, controlling spending, and putting more money in people's pockets. The influence of Muttart's political marketing approach was reflected in numerous Conservative policies, including those most central to the campaign such as the GST cut, monthly child care cheques, sports tax credit, and workers' tools credit. Each has the virtue of being hands-on, personally identifiable, and good for consumers rather than for corporations, public policy specialists, or newspaper editorialists.

Each morning of the campaign began with a new policy announcement or, later in the campaign, a central message about one of the main themes. Communications proceeded on two tracks. The first involved a relatively small scripting team headed by Ken Boessenkool, on leave from his position as general manager of Hill and Knowlton's Calgary office, and included Mark Cameron and Guy Girono, all of whom worked with Harper on crafting the top-line message for the day that would be announced in the leader's speech and supported by news release and backgrounders. Flanagan provided editorial support and worked with translators to ensure the French versions were accurate. The second track involved a larger communications strategy group of more than twenty people that was responsible for all the other material being churned out by a very active war room.[33] Calgary Southeast MP Jason Kenny specialized in putting out attacks on the Liberals, while party research director Keith Beardsley managed the research staff. Yarislov Baron provided strategic advice and managed the war room assignments and activities. Flanagan was officially responsible for signing off on all of the material produced by this group, but most decisions were agreed upon by at least three, if not by all four, of the principals.

The war room also provided much more candidate support than it had in 2004, including extra support for targeted ridings. It also ensured that the party's spin team was well stocked with talking points and plenty of research prior to engaging spokespeople from the other parties on television and radio programs. Sandra Buckler[34] managed the spin team of a half-dozen media panellists, including Goldy Hyder, Tim Powers, and others, who battled their opponents on CBC Newsworld, CTV Newsnet, and various regional television and radio programs on an almost daily basis. LeBretton and Stairs provided spin on the leader's tour.

All told, the Conservatives built a rather sophisticated organization to win favour with the English media.[35] They had learned from 2004 and arranged their scheduling on the premise that helping journalists do their jobs is more likely to lead to fair coverage than a campaign that made it difficult for reporters to file their stories and meet deadlines. The Conservative team provided the media with the top-line message first thing in the morning, supported it throughout the day with a blizzard of substantiating information, and scheduled tour travel for evenings after reporters had met their deadlines. The strategy was highly effective in forcing the other parties, particularly the Liberals, to play defence as the media began most days by asking them to respond to the Conservatives' message. It also endeared the Conservative campaign to most journalists, who tended to soften their often harsh coverage of Harper. Furthermore, the more the campaign kept the focus on Harper, and as long as he stayed on-message, there was much less likelihood of reporters seeking out comments from some of the party's more outspoken candidates, although most candidates recognized and had been coached on the consequences of getting off-message.[36]

ADVERTISING

Conservative strategists recognized that in 2004 they had not fought a competitive advertising "air war." They did not pre-purchase enough television advertising time, especially towards the end of the campaign, and were not nearly creative enough in their advertising strategies. As a corrective for the 2006 contest, television ads would constitute the bulk of Conservative advertising efforts. Some radio spots would be purchased, but the party would buy no national print advertising. Another change was that advertising would not be done out of the war room but rather would be produced by a virtual agency in Toronto.

After providing the campaign with an overall narrative and working closely with the scripting group, once the campaign began, Muttart was assigned personal responsibility for advertising and acted as the link between the advertising agency and the war room. Rather than use an existing, independent advertising firm as the party had done in 2004, Wurstlin adman Perry Miele was recruited in the summer of 2004 to build the Conservatives a virtual advertising agency similar to that used by the Liberals. He put together a couple of creative teams, a media buyer, and production people in Toronto for English ads, plus another agency in Montreal to handle French production.

Over two dozen ads were produced that eventually aired. There were nine versions of the original homespun, positive ads featuring a rather stiff

Harper in a set of staged interviews. Pundits criticized the ads as being too folksy, if not amateurish, but they were nevertheless charming in their lack of glitz and were intentionally designed to distinguish the Conservative campaign from the glitzy, entitlement image with which they were intent on tarring the Liberals. A half-dozen negative ads were produced, including a pre-emptive attack ad warning voters that the Liberals would use negative advertising, as well as attack ads that appeared at various stages in the campaign as dynamics dictated. For example, over the Christmas break the party produced attack ads in response to the RCMP announcement of its probe into the income trust affair. Later in the campaign, more attack ads were designed to counter, or take advantage of, the Liberals' counterproductive attacks on the Conservatives over their urban military plans. Some Quebec-specific ads were produced early in the campaign, with each spot ending in a disclaimer that the advertisement was paid for with clean money. Some of the English ads were also translated into French.

FINANCING THE CAMPAIGN

Party and election campaign financing reform benefited the Conservatives tremendously. The party was heir to the direct marketing techniques introduced by the Clark Progressive Conservatives in the seventies and the highly successful Reform-Alliance procedures for collecting large numbers of small donations from members and supporters. These factors, combined with the elimination of corporate donations, restrictions on individual contributions, and the taxpayer-funded allowances based on votes received in the previous election, vaulted the Conservatives past the Liberals as Canada's most financially successful federal party. First under the guidance of Brodie, and more recently his replacement as executive director, Mike Donison, the party outpaced other parties in fundraising.

By way of example, in 2003, the last year before financing reforms took effect, the Liberals raised $24 million, with $10 million collected from the corporate sector. That same year, the Canadian Alliance and the Progressive Conservatives raised a combined $12.6 million, with approximately $2.4 million coming from business. In 2004, the Conservatives raised almost $11 million in contributions and received almost $8 million more in public allowances for a total of almost $19 million, surpassing the Liberal totals (over $5 million in contributions and $9 million in public allowances for a total of $14.4 million) by more than $4.5 million.

In 2005 the Conservatives continued to outperform their competitors by securing a combined total of $25.5 million, compared to almost $18 million raised by the Liberals (almost evenly split between contributions and public allowances). For the Conservatives, funding a campaign would not be a problem. In fact, sticking to the approximately $18.3-million limit and deciding how to stretch it over the course of an eight-week campaign would become a more immediate campaign concern.

Table 2

Conservative Party of Canada financing, 2004–05

	Value of Contributions	Number of Contributors	Dollar Value per Contributor
2004 Contributions	$10.95 million	68,382	$160
2004 Allowances	$7.91 million		
2004 Totals	$18.86 million		
2005 Contributions			
Q1	$2.65 million	28,624	
Q2	$4.98 million	46,119	
Q3	$3.25 million	32,714	
Q4	$7.32 million	59,519	
Total Contributions	$18.19 million	166,976	$107
2005 Allowances	$7.33 million		
2005 Totals	$25.52 million		

Source: Elections Canada.

THE *STAND UP FOR CANADA* PLATFORM

The Conservatives' complete platform, released in its entirety late in the campaign, consisted of sixty policies grouped into six main planks. In some respects, it mirrored the party's policy declaration: support for a free vote on the same-sex marriage issue, inclusion of property rights in the Charter, and no mention of abortion legislation. In other areas, platform policies were significantly tweaked from those that emanated from

Montreal, where the party had voted to provide Canadians with "immediate and long-term broad based tax relief, starting with reducing personal income tax."[37] Yet the GST reduction (from 7 percent to 6 and then to 5 percent) had become the centrepiece of Conservative tax policies and, as Harper would admit in the final weeks of the campaign, would require the reversal of the Liberals' promised income tax reductions. The explanation for such an apparently blatant disregard of membership direction lies in how the Conservative leadership viewed the distinction between the platform and the policy declaration and reveals how far they had moved from the old Reform model of grassroots supremacy.

The policy declaration was viewed as long-term guidance, similar to the party's principles but more detailed. The platform was viewed as a strategic document designed to win an election and to define the government's mandate. Although the grassroots of the party and many caucus members played key roles in the declaration's development, the platform was the purview of the leader, his advisors, and senior caucus critics. From this perspective, the GST decision is rational. It incorporated the overall policy of lowering taxes, provided the party with a strategic response to the Liberals, who had co-opted the personal income tax reduction position, and fit nicely with the Conservative campaign's aims of simplifying the message by appealing to Canadians' psychological aversion to the very visible tax. The Conservatives' child care platform policies, among others, were designed with similar strategic goals in mind.

The *Stand Up for Canada* platform declared that an accountable government could get things done — for all of us — and placed its "Stand Up for Accountability" plank at the forefront. The thirteen sub-policies included furthering the reform of federal party financing, toughening the Lobbyist Registration Act, cleaning up government procurement procedures, providing whistleblower protection, strengthening the authority of the accountability watchdogs, and creating a new directory of public prosecutions.

The eleven policies comprising the "Stand Up for Opportunity" plank contained the Conservatives' economic plans such as reducing taxes, limiting the growth of government spending, focusing federal education policy on research and the trades, and supporting traditional industries, including agriculture, forestry, mining, and fisheries.

Eleven policies indicated how Conservatives would "Stand Up for Security," including getting tough on crime and strengthening border security, providing effective gun control, implementing a national drug strategy, and appointing a national victims' ombudsman. Conservatives had eight "Stand Up for Families" policies, including the party's health care waiting lists proposals, the $1,200 child care allowance, support for seniors and students, and the free parliamentary vote on the definition of marriage. "Stand Up for Our Communities" was built on eight policies, including improving Canada's military capabilities, housing policies, public transit and other environmental policies, Aboriginal policies, charities, the arts, sports, and culture.

The platform was rounded out with nine policies declaring how the Conservatives would "Stand Up for Canada" by strengthening national unity through open federalism, curing the fiscal imbalance, protecting and promoting both official languages, enshrining property rights in the constitution, defending Canada internationally, and creating jobs through international trade.

Two weeks prior to the formal release of the entire platform, Harper had already narrowed his focus to five priorities: passing the Federal Accountability Act, providing tax relief for businesses and individuals by cutting the GST, cracking down on violent crime, providing a subsidy for child care, and reforming health care. When the Conservatives won the election, Harper declared these the top priorities of his mandate.

CAMPAIGN DYNAMICS

Harper opened the campaign with an upbeat address to his caucus. Declaring that "opposition is not enough," he warned that the campaign would not be easy, as the Liberals would again use negative tactics to maintain power. He set the early theme by framing the Conservatives' ballot question: "This is not just the end of a tired, directionless, scandal-plagued government. It is the start of a bright new future of this great country."

Harper began the first full day of campaigning with a cleverly devised and strategically risky manoeuvre. He intentionally lingered at his first news conference until a reporter asked about his party's position on same-sex marriage. Harper surprised most observers by declaring that a Conservative government would hold a free vote by asking the House if it wanted to table legislation to change the definition of marriage. The motion's defeat would end the matter; if, however, it passed, he would initiate legislation to redefine marriage based on its traditional definition. He qualified the proposal by ensuring that existing same-sex marriages would continue to maintain their full legal standing. The gambit surprised many, not because it was inconsistent with party policy, Harper's speech to the March convention, the subsequent resolution debate, or the near unanimity within his caucus. It was not. But many observers believed it was a mistake to focus on the issue on the campaign's first day. It seemingly played to the Liberals' strategy of casting the Conservatives as social conservatives opposed to Charter rights.

As the campaign played out, however, the manoeuvre appeared to be strategically astute. By not shirking from the party's position, Harper substantiated his rhetoric of trust and honouring commitments. Furthermore, had he not addressed the issue early, Harper would have exposed himself to charges of hiding a social conservative agenda. Most observers surmised that a minority Parliament would likely witness the opposition parties defeating the motion, and so, having effectively neutralized the issue, the Conservatives could campaign on more salient and vote-winning policies.

Having been the party's greatest advocate for expending scarce resources in what many party members thought to be an electoral wasteland, Harper quickly headed to Quebec to begin the long process of building visibility, if not credibility, amongst that province's voters. His initial campaign foray into the province, however, did not go smoothly. After his proposal to create a special independent federal prosecutor was criticized as an intrusion into provincial jurisdiction (blasphemy for any federal politician seeking votes in Quebec), and Deputy Leader MacKay appeared to contradict Harper on the issue, it appeared as though the party was picking up where its 2004 contest left off: disorganized, with ad hoc policy announcements and miscommunications. Matters were not helped when the leader got surly with the media for pointing out that he didn't bother to introduce the eight Quebec Conservative candidates he was attempting to showcase.

The rough start was turned around quickly. Harper announced the GST reduction centrepiece of his economic plank, followed the next day with his health care policies, and then with a tough stand on crime. By week's end the media had positively re-evaluated the wisdom of the same-sex strategy and caught the rhythm of the Conservative campaign at the same time they were becoming more critical of the lethargic Liberal effort. Despite critical reviews of the first round of Conservative television ads, most analysts declared the Conservatives to have controlled the early campaign agenda.

Harper continued rolling out policy announcements on an almost daily basis through the campaign's pre-Christmas phase. The strategy largely achieved the multiple goals of defining the Conservative agenda positively, softening the leader's image with the electorate, targeting middle-income suburban voters, and improving relations with the media. Selected tax cuts for middle-income voters were added to the party's child care policies to demonstrate that the new Conservatives were not averse to governmental support for important initiatives. But the collection of policies had a common thread that distinguished Conservative principles from those of its competitors. While supporting a positive role for government, Conservatives would emphasize individual choice; avoid creating large, centralized, state monopolies as the solution to social problems; and put money into people's hands.

The Conservatives deftly used their child care policies to highlight these differences. When Martin advisor Scott Reid handed the Conservatives a gift by declaring the Liberal approach was superior because it would prevent Canadian parents from blowing child care money on "popcorn and beer," Edmonton Conservative MP Rona Ambrose declared Reid's remarks "offensive" and said that the comments served to highlight that "the Liberals don't trust people with their own money. They don't trust Canadians to make the best decision for their children." Despite Reid's quick apology, the damage to the Liberals' credibility was done.

Making his first tour of the Maritimes, Harper received endorsements from a number of provincial Progressive Conservatives, including New Brunswick Premier Bernard Lord. For his part, Harper brought some tough talk to Newfoundland and Labrador, stating that he planned to use the military to unilaterally police the Atlantic fishing industry, even in international waters beyond Canada's two-hundred-mile custodial limits. In subsequent days he unveiled more military polices, including $2 billion for Arctic sovereignty and the creation of new territorial battalions stationed in major urban centers, a proposal that the Liberals attempted to exploit later in the campaign, much to their detriment.

When the Prime Minister and Frank McKenna, Canada's ambassador to the United States, got into a dust-up with David Wilkins, U.S. ambassador to Canada, over Martin's comments concerning the American administration's decision not to sign the Kyoto climate change protocol, Harper quickly moved to partially inoculate himself from Liberal charges that he would kowtow to the Americans by not crafting an independent foreign policy. He appeared statesmanlike by criticizing both Wilkins, for inappropriately intervening in the election campaign, and Martin, for acting like a tough-talking schoolyard coward who revelled in name-calling from a safe distance but "couldn't throw a punch to save his life."

After this brief sojourn into the international arena, the party leaders headed to Vancouver for the first round of leaders' debates. Martin telegraphed his debate strategy by attempting to prime the rights issue. He resurrected a tactic from the 2004 campaign, accusing Harper of concealing his planned use of the notwithstanding clause to override same-sex marriage rights. For his part, Harper took advantage of the debate's locale to remind voters that his accountability planks still included a number of items designed to appeal to alienated westerners: particularly the election of senators, fixed election dates, and the prohibition of parachuting "star" candidates into ridings over the objections of local party members.

Harper emerged from the first round of debates relatively unscathed as all the opposition leaders turned their guns on Martin. NDP Leader Jack Layton, while frequently stating that he disagreed with Harper on policy, focused his most critical attacks on the Liberals. Bloc Québécois Leader Gilles Duceppe, subscribing to the conventional wisdom that the Conservatives presented little threat in Quebec, followed suit. More importantly for his fortunes, Harper succeeded in reinforcing the Conservatives' "need for change" ballot question by presenting his party as a low-risk option for those who no longer wished to support the Liberals. His calm, somewhat reserved, and certainly not angry manner effectively showcased a softer side of Canadian conservatism. Martin stuck to the Liberal strategy of attempting to define Harper as an excessively right-wing conservative who harboured a secret agenda designed to trample on Canadians' Charter rights, at one point insisting that "if you can't defend the Charter of Rights, then you've got to ask why you want to be the prime minister." Harper routinely dismissed the criticisms by suggesting that the Prime Minister's rhetoric revealed an arrogance implying that Martin believed only those who share his values are fit to govern.

In a debate format that stifled any meaningful exchanges between the leaders, Harper was judged to have performed at least as well as Martin and was declared by the media to be one of the winners. Despite being considered the least likely to have won the previous day's French-language debate, that encounter allowed Harper to plant the seeds of Conservative resurgence in Quebec.[38] Arguing that the Conservatives were the only party capable of replacing corrupt and arrogant Liberals, Harper set the stage for an immediate post-debate trip to Quebec that would fundamentally change the campaign dynamics in Quebec and the nation.

During the debates and throughout the later days of the campaign's pre-Christmas phase, Harper began to link the Conservatives' main ballot question of change to the national unity issue. Declaring that "the only way Quebec is ever going to separate from Canada is if we create a federal government that is so tarnished in their eyes, so corrupt, so disrespectful of their jurisdictions that we drive them that way," Harper arrived in Quebec to deliver one speech that would lend the Conservatives enough credibility to trigger their unanticipated surge in the province. Harper promised Quebec a stronger voice at home and in the international arena along with better funding arrangements. He reiterated Conservative plans to respect provincial autonomy while allowing Quebec to play a role in international institutions, such as UNESCO. He did not say whether Quebec should have powers that other provinces would not share and explicitly stopped short of committing to any full-scale constitutional changes. "But when you get into some areas," he declared, "particular areas that touch upon culture and language, obviously it's not a surprise that the government of Quebec would seek arrangements that may be of little interest to other provinces." He continued to frame the Conservatives as an option, not only for federalists who were tired of the Liberals, but also for nationalists who desired more than the protest option provided by the Bloc. He declared that "making a real change means having an honest government that can help Quebec be more than just a powerless spectator in the House of Commons, or totally absent from the cabinet table."[39]

The speech had two important effects on campaign dynamics. First, the Quebec media immediately began to re-evaluate the Conservative leader, as evidenced by the front-page coverage of his speech in almost every daily newspaper in the province. Quebec voters also began to take a serious look at the Conservatives, led by their Liberal premier, Jean Charest. Second, Martin's response reinforced a central theme the Conservatives had been attempting to establish over the course of the pre-Christmas phase. Martin responded that "you don't strengthen Canada by weakening the federal government," thereby echoing Chrétien's, if not Trudeau's, strong central government approach to Quebec. It did little to endear the Liberals to soft nationalists and other important swing voters. Furthermore, Martin's continued over-the-top rhetoric about Canada "speaking with one voice internationally" appeared inconsistent with his recent asymmetrical experiments, thereby further eroding his credibility on the issue.

Harper's next stop, Ontario, found him continuing to push the national unity issue. He initiated a bitter spat with Martin when he accused the Liberals of secretly desiring a Parti Québécois victory in the next Quebec provincial election so as to provide the Liberals with a crisis that they believed only they could resolve. Martin was incredulous and demanded an apology. Harper flatly refused and calmly explained that his accusation arose only because Martin had been talking about a referendum and having a PQ government in Quebec. He concluded that since the Prime Minister "has pledged that he will stop talking that way ... then frankly our problem is solved." More than his position on the issues, it was Harper's changed demeanor that was drawing him his most notable early accolades.

Just before the Christmas break, the Conservatives' relatively stagnant national polling numbers started to trend upward and it appeared that the Liberals' had stalled. The Conservatives were gaining in Ontario, had rebounded in the West, and their once moribund Quebec campaign was starting to show signs of life.[40] More importantly, the strategy of showcasing Harper appeared to be bearing fruit. His performance indicators began to catch up with Martin's while the media provided increasingly positive coverage. Momentum was bolstered when the RCMP announced a criminal investigation into possible advance notice of the Finance Department's decision on the taxation of income trusts. Confident that the NDP would take the lead in further eroding the Liberals' credibility on the accountability issue, Harper chose to continue articulating his own platform and generally refrained from commenting on the RCMP investigation beyond saying that the Liberals had a lot to explain. When full campaigning resumed after New Year's, the Conservatives found themselves tied with the Liberals for first place in national polls and beginning a steady climb towards competitiveness in Quebec.[41]

For Harper, there was little Christmas break, as his strategists kept him in the media throughout the season. First, Harper's young family provided ample photo opportunities, including greeting him with hugs at the Calgary airport. These were followed by media coverage of the bespectacled father shopping at an outlet toy store for last-minute Christmas gifts. After spending Christmas Day with family, Harper participated in a menorah lighting ceremony at the home of Calgary Rabbi Menachem Matus, with media in attendance. He then embarked on a three-day tour of British Columbia, where he announced the party's public transportation and environment policies, as well as more military policies, including his planned use of the military for urban disasters. The media were provided with more Christmas-break photo ops when Harper cast a mail-in ballot before returning to Ottawa to resume full campaigning.

The campaign's final phase saw Harper simplify his focus to the five Conservative priorities, while the increasingly frantic Liberals attempted to characterize Harper as dangerously right-wing and ideologically similar to former Ontario premier Mike Harris. Heading into the second round of leaders' debates, the Conservatives were forced to account for their spending plans in the face of Liberal claims that they would lead to multi-billion-dollar deficits over the next five years.[42] Admitting that his government would have to cancel the Liberals' 1 percent income tax reduction, Harper left his finance critic, Monte Solberg, to chastise the Liberals for their "ridiculous" accounting and blatant attempt to repeat their successful scare tactics of the 2004 campaign.[43]

In the second round of debates, Harper stuck to his game plan of talking policy from beginning to end. When Martin invoked a ten-year-old speech that Harper had given to a right-wing U.S. think tank as evidence that he was an extremist,[44] Harper accused Martin of attacking his patriotism.[45] He also countered with accusations that someone who had registered his company's ships offshore to avoid paying Canadian taxes should not be counted an authority on patriotism. By staying calm throughout the debate, smiling regularly, and using self-deprecating humour about his lack of passion, Harper skillfully juxtaposed his leadership style against Martin's increasing hyperbole.

He challenged Martin's commitment to crime prevention, an issue of Conservative strength, by exposing contradictions between the Prime Minister and his defence minister over mandatory sentences. He aggressively attacked the government's ethics and continued to link the accountability issue with national unity as he trolled for more Quebec votes. But Harper's best performance may have come courtesy of Martin's surprise announcement that his first priority would be to initiate full constitutional negotiations aimed at stripping the federal government of its authority to use the notwithstanding clause. Harper, likely as surprised as anyone, sprang to the defence of the notwithstanding clause. By arguing that it provides a balance between parliamentary sovereignty and judicial authority, Harper ended up supporting the current construction of the constitution and the Charter of Rights and Freedoms, an irony not lost on most observers, including high-profile Liberal cabinet ministers who plainly were unaware of the new policy.[46]

The second French-language debate also provided a new dynamic. For the first time in memory, a non-Quebecer became the focus of the proceedings. Bloc Québécois Leader Gilles Duceppe abandoned his focus on the Liberal sponsorship scandal in favour of attempting to link the

Conservatives to allegations that Option Canada had violated the 1995 Quebec referendum rules. He also introduced a slogan that the Bloc would use to try to stop the late-campaign Conservative surge in Quebec.[47] Declaring that "parties run out of Toronto and Calgary cannot respond to Quebec's aspirations," Duceppe publicly recognized that Harper had made the Conservatives serious contenders in many Quebec ridings.[48] Harper responded with a staunch defence of federalism by stating that it is the prime minister's duty to promote federalism in Quebec and that he would not shirk from that responsibility. He ended the debate with an appeal that the Conservatives would use to close their campaign efforts in Quebec. Attempting to marginalize the Bloc as a perpetually ineffective opposition party, he told the "people of Quebec" that the Conservatives were the alternative they sought to a corrupt Liberal Party and Bloc MPs who do little more than criticize from the sidelines. In essence, and backed by national opinion polls suggesting the Conservatives had opened up as much as a ten-point lead over the Liberals,[49] he suggested the Conservatives were going to form the next government and that Quebecers would be well advised to have MPs inside his caucus and cabinet.

Independent of their debate strategy, the Liberals were preparing to ratchet up the negativity in the campaign air war. They produced twelve television ads designed to rekindle some of the discomfort voters had with Harper in 2004. The "Choose Your Canada" ads showed a blurry black-and-white image of Harper with military music playing in the background as a female voice read ominous text about his alleged opinions and plans. The ads accused Harper of, among other things, harbouring extreme, pro-American, right-wing attitudes, of planning to run Canada as Mike Harris ran Ontario, of supporting the Iraq war, of being anti-Kyoto, and of having insulted Atlantic Canada. The most bizarre of the ads — pulled from the to-be-aired list but inadvertently posted on the Liberal website — appeared to accuse Harper of planning to invoke some kind of military dictatorship based on his plans to post one hundred regular force officers and four hundred reservists in major Canadian cities for disaster relief purposes. The text of the ad read as follows: "Stephen Harper actually announced he wants to increase military presence in our cities. *Canadian cities. Soldiers with guns. In our cities. In Canada.* We did not make this up."

Negative fallout from the "pulled" ad was swift, brutal, and damaging for the Liberal campaign. The ad's content became instant fodder for radio talk show hosts, their guests and callers, television panellists, newspaper columnists, and satirical bloggers. The situation worsened when the

Prime Minister admitted that he had approved the creation of the ad. Liberal candidates and cabinet ministers chimed in to condemn the tactics. The "pulled" ad undercut the credibility of the remaining ads, and the Liberal campaign more generally, again allowing Harper to take a dignified and calm approach by expressing disappointment rather than outrage and accusing the Liberals of insulting Canadian soldiers, not him. The Conservative war room immediately went on the offensive by contrasting the ads to Martin's statements about the need to "have a more intelligent debate" and to stop "drive-by smears." They prepared counterattack ads that linked Martin's admission of having approved the ads to one of his own candidate's comments about "some idiot" having released them. Harper decided the direct link was too negative and ordered the ads recast. They eventually aired with the various Liberal members' quotations, but without the "idiot" insult linked directly to the Prime Minister.[50]

With just over one week remaining in the campaign and the Conservatives peaking in the polls,[51] Harper unveiled the entire Conservative platform document. Few surprises remained, as most of the $60.7 billion in policies had been previously announced. Had the vote been held at this point in the campaign, senior Conservative strategists believe they would have elected a much larger minority, if not won a slight majority. However, the vote was then still ten days away and the Conservatives, without an aggressive end-game strategy, again began to drift. With their fiscal plans now under attack from all sides, they continued to campaign hard in Central Canada and the Maritimes. But without the discipline of an issue-a-day script, Harper stumbled in attempting to ease concerns about the possibility of a Conservative majority. He stated that he wasn't sure there was such a thing as a true Conservative majority given that he would face limits on his ability to operate that a Liberal government would not face. "The reality is that we will have, for some time to come, a Liberal Senate, a Liberal civil service ... and courts that have been appointed by the Liberals. These are obviously checks on the power of a Conservative government. That's why I say ... there is certainly no absolute power for a Conservative government and no real, true majority."

Opponents pounced on the statement as tantamount to an admission of harbouring a hard right-wing agenda that would result in an assault on the courts, the bureaucracy, and the Charter. When asked to state if he would never restrict abortion rights, Harper responded that "never is a long time," providing Martin with the ammunition he believed he needed for a last-week turnaround. After altering their plans to include more time campaigning hard in urban southern Ontario, organizing four events in the province on the last Friday before the vote and returning to the West Coast for only the final day of campaigning, the Conservatives were under increasing pressure to allow media interviews with some of their more socially conservative candidates. Conservative strategists refused, deciding it was better to take a hit for appearing to be muzzling candidates than risk a last-minute incendiary headline that could undercut what had been a notably disciplined effort to that point. The strategy succeeded in as much as the Conservative campaign coasted through the final week, garnering editorial endorsements from across the country and an unexpected announcement from Action démocratique du Québec Leader Mario Dumont that he would be voting Conservative.

CONCLUSION

As vote counting began on election night, many Conservatives could be forgiven for sensing a certain déjà vu when early returns hinted at another final weekend shift. In the end, however, voters rewarded the Conservatives with a minority victory of 124 seats based on 36.3 percent of the national vote. Importantly, the Conservatives elected members in every province except Prince Edward Island, including ten members from Quebec, and would be able to claim a national, albeit limited, victory.

The Conservatives improved on their 2004 results by 6.7 percent nationally and achieved gains in every province and territory. The party made substantial seat gains in Ontario (sixteen) and Quebec (ten) but lost seats in the West, particularly in B.C. (five), despite slight gains in popular support. The Conservatives could justifiably claim that the old Reform mantra of "the West wants in" had been finally realized, with more than half of all its members being elected from the region (52.4 percent, sixty-five seats). They could also make a better claim to national voter support than any other conservative party since the Mulroney PCs. In electing almost one-third of its caucus from Ontario, winning ten contests in Quebec, and securing nine of Atlantic Canada's thirty-two seats, Harper had MPs from each region for his cabinet.

As prime minister, Harper continued his quest to build a truly national government by distributing cabinet positions more equitably across the country than voters had returned Conservative members. Westerners, at over one-third of the total (37 percent), were prominent but smaller as a percentage of cabinet than their caucus proportion.

Ontario was rewarded with nine cabinet positions (one-third of the total), including many senior economic portfolios. Quebec's five cabinet positions represented nearly one in five of the total (18.5 percent), while one minister came from each of the three Atlantic provinces that elected Conservatives.[52]

Having been shut out in Canada's three largest cities, Harper made two controversial cabinet appointments to provide better representation for those regions. He appointed his Quebec campaign co-chair, Montrealer Michael Fortier, to the Senate and as minister of public works, a decision that seemingly contradicted the party's already diminished commitment to Senate reform. More controversially, he convinced Vancouverite and former Liberal industry minister David Emerson to cross the floor and take up cabinet duties as minister of international trade. Emerson joined two other cabinet ministers that were at one time elected provincially as Liberals. Harper also appointed nine ministers with PC pedigrees, including the three with Ontario provincial experience, a former federal PC leader, and another federal PC leadership candidate. In comparison only seven members of the new cabinet had been previously elected as Reform or Alliance members, including Harper.

There is little doubt that the Conservatives made considerable movement to the centre of Canada's political spectrum since the merger of the PC and CA parties.[53] They quelled many voters' anxieties by dropping the most problematic Reform-Alliance policies that had enabled their opponents to label them as extreme or harbouring hidden agendas. Their *Stand Up for Canada* platform was inclusive and absent of attacks on any "enemies" or perceived problem segments of society such as unions, public sector employees, special interests, Québécois, immigrants, francophones, Central Canada, or even government itself.

The campaign — predicated on the belief that there was great interest in change but only if it was moderate, balanced, and circumspect — reflected the further maturing of the Conservatives after the 2004 election. From Harper, to his organization, down to the candidates in the most marginal of districts, control, discipline, and moderation were the mantra. The campaign proceeded as scripted, advantage was taken of opportunities, big mistakes were avoided, and minor missteps were few. The carefully directed policy planks gave the Conservatives the wherewithal to expand their coalition incrementally without upsetting their base.

The historically minded know that Conservative governments have been infrequent and generally brief in tenure. Harper's next electoral challenge will be to expand his party's support base beyond what was constructed in 2006, at a time when the Liberals, Canada's natural governing party, were in bad odour. For Canadian voters, party strategists, and political scientists, the 2006 election presented an unusually interesting question. Was the victory an aberration or the beginning of a critical period of electoral realignment? Realignment of the party system will be an enormous challenge. But many have erred by dismissing Harper's chances at each stage of his remarkable rise to power, and few would now disagree that he has the grit, purposefulness, and willingness to do what is necessary to achieve clearly established goals.[54]

Table 3
2006 Conservative caucus and cabinet

	Total Seats	Seats won	Change from 2004	% of vote	Change from 2004	% of Seats won in province	Seats as % of caucus	Cabinet seats	Seats as % total cabinet
BC	36	17	-5	37.3	+1.1	47.2	13.7	4	14.8
AB	28	28	+2	65.0	+ 3.4	100.0	22.6	4	14.8
SK	14	12	-1	48.9	+ 1.0	85.7	9.7	1	3.7
MB	14	8	-1	42.8	+ 3.7	57.1	6.5	1	3.7
ON	106	40	+16	35.1	+ 3.6	37.7	32.2	9	33.3
QC	75	10	+10	24.6	+ 15.8	13.3	8.1	5	18.5
NB	10	3	+1	35.8	+ 4.7	30.0	2.4	1	3.7
PEI	4	0	0	33.4	+ 2.7	0.0	0.0	0	0.0
NS	11	3	0	29.7	+ 1.7	27.3	2.4	1	3.7
NL	7	3	+1	42.7	+ 10.4	42.9	2.4	1	3.7
YT	1	0	0	23.7	+ 2.8	0.0	0.0	0	0.0
NWT	1	0	0	19.8	+ 2.6	0.0	0.0	0	0.0
NU	1	0	0	29.6	+ 15.5	0.0	0.0	0	0.0
Total	308	124	+25	36.3	+ 6.7	40.3	100.0	27	100.0

Source: Elections Canada.

NOTES

This essay reflects in part interviews with a number of people associated with the Conservative Party's campaign. We have committed to not identify our interviewees. We sincerely thank all of those who consented to interviews for their time, insights, and help in making this a more accurate and complete analysis of the campaign.

1   Stephen Harper, victory address, January 23, 2006, Calgary, Alberta.
2   See the discussion in André Blais, *Anatomy of a Liberal Victory: Making Sense of the Vote in the 2000 Canadian General Election* (Peterborough, ON: Broadview Press, 2002).

3   See Faron Ellis and Peter Woolstencroft, "New Conservatives, Old Realities: The 2004 Election Campaign," in *The Canadian General Election of 2004*, ed. Jon H. Pammett and Christopher Dornan (Toronto: The Dundurn Group, 2004), 66–105.

4   For a debate about the long-term prospects for Canadian conservatives and the Conservative Party see Nelson Wiseman, "Going Nowhere: Conservatism and the Conservative Party," 57–69, and Faron Ellis, "Twenty-First Century Conservatives Can Succeed," 70–82, in *Crosscurrents: Contemporary Political Issues*, 5th edition, ed. Mark Charlton and Paul Barker (Toronto: Nelson, 2006).

5   Faron Ellis, *The Limits of Participation: Members and Leaders in Canada's Reform Party* (Calgary: University of Calgary Press, 2005).

6   For an interpretation of the "brokerage-missionary" debate and the Conservative Party, see Graham Fox, "The Conservatives and a Minority House: A Tale of Two Harpers," *Policy Options*, October 2005.

7   The Conservatives' 29.6 percent of the 2004 vote compared poorly to the combined PC and CA total of over 38 percent in 2000.

8   All but a handful of Conservative Quebec candidates had done badly in 2004, with the party wining about one-third fewer votes than the combined PC-CA total in 2000.

9   George Perlin, *The Tory Syndrome* (Montreal: McGill-Queen's University Press, 1980).

10 Wilson, one of Mulroney's leading cabinet ministers, was appointed Canada's ambassador to the United States by Harper, one of the new government's first acts.

11 Segal also penned a weekly column for the *National Post* throughout the campaign as part of a three-party punditry panel.

12 Address by Stephen Harper to the Conservative Party of Canada Convention, Montreal, Quebec, Friday, March 18, 2005.

13 The speech helped Harper receive an 84 percent endorsement of his leadership.

14 Of the twenty-three principles adopted by the Conservative convention, nineteen were from the Agreement-in-Principle that led to the merger. Three new principles affirmed that "English and French have equality of status" in Parliament and the Government of Canada; that "Canadians should have reasonable access to quality health care regardless of their ability to pay"; and that the "greatest potential for achieving social and economic objectives is under a global trading regime that is free and fair." See, Agreement-in-Principle on the establishment of the Conservative Party of Canada, Ottawa: October 15, 2003, 1–2.

15 Progressive Conservative Party of Canada, Constitution, as amended, Edmonton, Alberta, August 24, 2002, 1–3.

16 As contained in parties' constitutions; Reform Party of Canada, "Statements of Principle," as amended, 1998; Canadian Alliance, "Statement of Principles," 2000; Progressive Conservative Party, "Aims and Principles," 2002; Conservative Party, Constitution, as amended on March 19, 2005, and consolidated by the executive director under the review of the National Council.

17 The media also continues to refer to the Conservatives as "Tories" although little traditional Toryism remains, at least in its anti-American and nationalistic interventionism forms.

18 This issue provided the only significant dust-up at the 2005 Conservative convention when Harper confidant and Conservative MP Scott Reid led a move to reduce the equality provisions for constituency associations with fewer than one hundred members. Peter MacKay declared it a betrayal of the PC wing of the new party and a "deal breaker" for maintaining the merger. The motion was defeated, leaving the PC procedures in place. Also see Lloyd Mackey, *The Pilgrimage of Stephen Harper* (Toronto: ECW Press, 2005), 121.

19   These support levels are very similar to those measured by Ellis and Archer at the 1992 Reform Assembly (61.5 percent of Reform delegates indicated a pro-choice position with 7.5 percent uncertain and 30.9 percent opposed) and by Ellis at the 2002 Alliance convention (56.2 percent indicated a pro-choice position with 9 percent uncertain and 34.8 percent opposed). See Faron Ellis and Keith Archer, "Ideology and Opinion within the Reform Party," in *Party Politics in Canada*, 8th edition, ed. Hugh Thorburn and Alan Whitehorn (Scarborough: Prentice Hall, 2001), 122–34; and Faron Ellis "Summary of Results from 2002 Alliance Convention Delegate Study," *Citizen Society Research Lab*, Lethbridge College.

20   See Ellis, "Conservatives Can Succeed."

21   One important internal debate concerned the timing of the platform's release. Some wanted an early release, allowing Harper to define himself and the party. The contrary argument was that the Liberals, as they had in the past, would "steal" Conservatives policies if they tipped their hand too early. For the most part, Harper accepted the latter argument and few commitments were made through the summer and into the autumn.

22   Fox, "The Conservatives and a Minority House." Robin Sears, "Fundamentalism on the Right: the road to another defeat," *Policy Options*, October 2005.

23   In Manitoba, half of the candidates had been elected previously as provincial PC MLAs, by far the highest ratio across the country. In Quebec, almost all candidates were new to politics in that they had no provincial or municipal experience.

24   In Ontario, Jim Flaherty, Tony Clement, and John Baird, three prominent members of the Harris government, much touted for being right-wing, ran for the Conservatives. Each was elected and appointed to cabinet.

25   The 2004 campaign taught the Conservatives that there was little utility in booking a second fleet of three buses for Western Canada. Not only would the tour spend much less time in the Western provinces than in 2004, but the vast distances between the West's urban centers, the only districts that needed tour campaign support, made bus travel impractical.

26   The tour also made three swings through the Maritimes as well as one quick late-campaign trip to Prince Edward Island.

27   Michael Coates managed the debate preparation team as he had done in 2004.

28   See Fritz Plasser, *Global Political Marketing: A Worldwide Analysis of Campaign Professionals and Their Practices* (Westport, CT: Praeger Press, 2002), 3.

29   See Jennifer Lees-Marshment, *Political Marketing and British Political Parties* (Manchester: Manchester University Press, 2001).

30   Darren G. Lilleker and Jennifer Lees-Marshment, "Introduction," in *Political Marketing: A Comparative Perspective*, ed. Darren G. Lilleker and Jennifer Lees-Marshment (Manchester: Manchester University Press, 2005). The product-oriented party focuses on its ideology and correlated policies. The sales-oriented party is distinguished by its use of communication media — especially television — to sway voters. Research is limited to finding out what voters are thinking in order to develop messages and advertising. The sales-oriented party "does not change its behaviour to suit what people want, but tries to make people want what it offers," Lilleker and Lees-Marshment, 9.

31   Ibid., 11.

32   Alex Marland, "Canadian political parties: market-oriented and ideological slag-brains," in Lilleker and Lees-Marshment, *Political Marketing*, 59–78.

33   The communications strategy group produced a vast quantity of research that was

used to support the many "reality checks," "prebuttals," attacks, counterattacks, and talking points for media spokespersons and candidates.

34   Buckler would replace William Stairs as Harpers communications chief shortly after the election.

35   The Conservatives' French-language media team of approximately ten people worked in Montreal and supported candidates in that province. Initiatives such as building sympathetic relations with Mario Dumont's Action démocratique au Québec and Liberal Quebec premier and former PC MP and federal leader Jean Charest were executed primarily by Harper.

36   What could not be controlled was external Internet communications, particularly web logs (blogs) by various campaign workers and other supporters. Although the party hosted two official blogs they were little more than casual versions of the official party rhetoric. Despite Jason Kenny misinterpreting a blog by Martin's speech writer Scott Feschuk early in the campaign and holding a news conference to chastise Feschuk (for which Kenny apologized), and one Edmonton campaign manager who was forced to resign after blogging about joining an Alberta separatist movement should the Liberals win the election, blogging was not as explosive a problem for the Conservatives as it was for the Liberals. In fact, bloggers benefited the Conservatives tremendously by regularly making available material that highlighted problems in the Liberal campaign. Bloggers also provided the most savage parodies of the Liberal "soldiers in the streets" and "radical U.S. links" ads, many of which broke through from the blogosphere into the mainstream media.

37   Policy Declaration, Conservative Party of Canada, March 19, 2005.

38   Ipsos-Reid reported that Martin (32 percent) and Harper (30 percent) led as winners of the English debate. In French, Harper was least likely to be viewed as having won (6 percent) compared to Layton's 14 percent, Martin's 17 percent, and Duceppe's 52 percent.

39   Address by Stephen Harper to the Quebec City Chamber of Commerce, Quebec City, December 19, 2005. The speech was accompanied by a four-point mini-platform for Quebec entitled "For Real Change: The Conservative Party of Canada's Commitment to Quebecers."

40   CPAC-SES Nightly Tracking, see http://www.sesresearch.com.

41   Strategic Counsel. See "A Report to The Globe and Mail and CTV: Federal Election — Vote Intention," January 22, 2006, http://thestrategiccounsel.com.

42   The Liberals claimed that the Conservatives' campaign promises would lead to a $12.4-billion deficit over five years and could balloon to as high as $23.4 billion to $52.4 billion.

43   The Conservatives counterattacked by releasing a letter dated December 22 from Paul Darby, deputy chief economist of the Conference Board of Canada, in which he stated that the platform "is affordable" from now to 2011, and would allow for $3 billion a year in debt repayment.

44   Harper gave the speech to the U.S. think tank Council for National Policy in June of 1997, shortly after retiring as MP for Calgary West and beginning his career with the National Citizens Coalition.

45   Quotations from the speech would be used by the Liberals throughout the campaign as well as by various interest groups opposed to the Conservatives such as the His Own Words Coalition, which includes as members the Council of Canadians, the Carpenters Union Central Ontario Regional Chapter, Egale Canada, First Peoples for Progressive Government, and Friends of Nature. The group ran two-page newspaper ads with text from the speech on the final weekend of campaigning.

46 Deputy Prime Minister Anne McLellan, in acknowledging that there had been "glitches in Liberal campaign," admitted that she did not discuss Martin's notwithstanding clause announcement with him prior to the debates.

47 The Strategic Counsel was measuring Conservative support in Quebec (22 percent) moving ahead of the Liberals' (19 percent) for the first time during their January 7 to 9 polling period. See http://thestrategiccounsel.com.

48 The Bloc ran ads on final weekend of campaign that targeted Harper's Alberta roots, stating, "We will not let Calgary decide for Quebec." Duceppe defended the ads as merely symbolizing the fact Conservatives "are defending interests that are not ours" and that "Quebec will never accept having Calgary or Toronto dictate our priorities to us." In response Harper praised Bill 101 as having a positive effect and restated his long-time deference to provincial autonomy on language.

49 The Strategic Counsel was measuring national Conservative support at 38 percent compared to the Liberals' 28 percent during their January 7 to 9 polling period. See http://thestrategiccounsel.com.

50 The attack ad issue dominated the news for almost a week and tended to overshadow other developments such as the Liberal and Conservative leaders each having to eschew one of their candidates. Harper moved quickly to distance himself from Derek Zeisman, a B.C. candidate facing smuggling charges. Given it was too late to formally withdraw his Conservative credentials, Harper assured voters that if Zeisman were to win he would not be welcome in the Conservative caucus unless acquitted of the charges.

51 The Strategic Counsel measured the absolute Conservative peak at 42 percent during their January 14 to 16 polling period. CPAC-SES measured a similar peak in Conservative support at 40 percent on January 12. See http://thestrategiccounsel.com and http://www.sesrearch.com.

52 The cabinet also included six women, 22.2 percent of the total, four members who were under forty yeas of age (14.8 percent of the total cabinet), and two visible minority members (Bev Oda and Michael Chong).

53 For a contrary view, see, Steve Patten, "New Right Politics," in *Canadian Politics: Democracy and Dissent*, ed. Joan Grace and Byron Sheldrick (Toronto: Pearson Prentice-Hall, 2006).

54 For a sympathetic presentation, see William Johnson, *Stephen Harper and the Future of Canada* (Toronto: McClelland and Stewart, 2005).

CHAPTER FOUR

The NDP and the Enigma of Strategic Voting
by Alan Whitehorn

In the fourteen elections from the New Democratic Party's founding in 1961 to 2004, the NDP has averaged 15.3 percent of the national vote and almost twenty-three seats. The nineties was a difficult decade for the NDP. In January 2003, Jack Layton, a former university professor, long-time Toronto city councillor, and former president of the Federation of Canadian Municipalities, became the NDP's federal leader. Under his leadership, NDP support rose in public opinion polls, as did membership and income — crucial developments for a fourth-place party. The NDP made significant gains in the next election, rising from 8.5 percent of the vote in 2000 to 15.7 percent in 2004. Because of the bias of our electoral system, the number of NDP seats increased by just six, from thirteen to nineteen.[1] Particularly in a minority Parliament, even a caucus of nineteen could have an impact. During the dramatic 2004–05 minority Parliament, Layton's national profile grew still further, and increasingly he became a key asset for the party.

To a significant degree, the federal NDP's prospects are greatly affected by the strength and popularity of its provincial sections. The B.C. NDP had done exceedingly well in the provincial election in spring 2005, and expectations were high that the party might make gains in the upcoming federal election. In Saskatchewan, historically the CCF-NDP heartland, the provincial NDP government of Lorne Calvert continued to struggle in popularity, but there was hope that the federal NDP might regain some seats after having been shut out in 2004. In Manitoba, Gary Doer's NDP government remained popular and gave hope that Manitoba could continue to be fertile ground for the federal party. In Ontario, while the provincial NDP had struggled, it was felt that the mayoralty victory in Toronto by David Miller gave reason for optimism in Jack Layton's home province. With no provincial NDP in Quebec, this province would again be a challenge for the federal party, even though it was Layton's place of birth. In Nova Scotia, the provincial NDP was the official opposition and highly competitive in a tight three-party system.

The NDP was formed in 1961 as a partnership between the Co-operative Commonwealth Federation (CCF) and the Canadian Labour Congress (CLC). The linkage between the trade union movement and the NDP has been pivotal in terms of organization, finances, and ideology. However, the 2004 reform of party financing regulations dramatically reduced corporate and trade union donations to all political parties. The 2006 election would be the second test of the new financing system and the labour movement's adjustment to the regulations. In addition, the 2006 campaign would be a test once more of the compatibility of the strategies and tactics of left-leaning interest groups and the social democratic NDP.

Of particular note in the pre-election period was the heightened profile and greater political instability of the minority Parliament. For a fourth-place party, the situation in the House of Commons was both an opportunity for more visibility and an electoral challenge. Layton and the NDP acquired a higher profile and generally received positive assessments. The NDP received praise for trying to make the minority Parliament work. The spring 2005 budget amendment, later referred to by Layton as the "NDP budget," promised more government spending for infrastructure and social programs. The NDP also pointed to examples of its positive parliamentary role in Canada's resisting involvement in the U.S. missile defence system and in prodding the Martin Liberals to pass the same-sex marriage legislation. On a more acrimonious note, many of the last days of the minority Parliament dwelled on the Liberal sponsorship scandal and the findings from the Gomery inquiry.

A key catalyst for the election call was the Supreme Court's ruling on the Chaoulli case, which stated that it was unconstitutional to ban the use of private medical care in light of lengthy waiting lists in the public health care system. The Court's ruling seemed to open the door for greater privatization of health care, an issue of great concern to social democrats. For NDP strategists and activists, this was a core issue on which to confront the Liberals, both in Parliament and, if necessary, in a general election. When Paul Martin and Health Minister Ujjal Dosanjh (a former B.C. NDP premier) did not respond sufficiently to NDP demands for a guarantee to protect public medicare, the election clock countdown commenced.

Both the media and the public were critical of the NDP's willingness to defeat the government and trigger an election. Even the CLC, the party's key ally, which had not wanted a spring 2005 election,[2] was surprised by the timing of the winter 2005–06 campaign. Perhaps not surprisingly, in late November the NDP's polling numbers started to dip from a high of around 20 percent recorded earlier. Still, party strategists were optimistic that at last they might have a wedge issue between the NDP's commitment to public health care and the Liberal Party's seeming inaction on such a key social issue.

NDP INTERNAL POLLING

In the 2006 campaign, the NDP's polling was directed by the Winnipeg-based Viewpoints Research, owned and led by Ginny Devine and Leslie Turnbull. The company had extensive involvement in past NDP campaigns, including the 1997 and 2000 federal contests and a number of provincial elections, and had worked a number of times previously with the Now Communications team. Viewpoints commenced in April 2005 with focus group testing in the key cities of Toronto and Halifax. In late August 2005, the party pollster completed an important pre-election baseline survey of eight hundred persons, conducted in forty ridings. During the campaign itself, shorter surveys posed questions regarding party standings, the leaders, the mood for political change, the most effective messages and phrasing, and the impact of emerging issues in the campaign. Additional focus groups tested the viability of party ads.

In the August baseline survey of the sampled ridings, the "NDP universe" (i.e., those who would consider voting NDP) was found to be in the 40 percent range. This was second place to the number in the Liberal universe.[3] The leader continued to grow in name recognition, particularly after the NDP's pivotal role in the minority Parliament of 2004–05 and the 2005 budget amendments. About 54 percent of those polled gave Layton a positive assessment and 24 percent selected him as the person who would be the best prime minister. Clearly, Layton was increasingly perceived to be a major asset for the party, a reason his name would be used more in election materials.

Given the limited amount ($660,000) budgeted for NDP polling, the party had to be selective and hence decided to survey only forty ridings. These included almost all of the incumbent ridings, along with a number seen as most promising, based primarily on the 2004 NDP vote. To strengthen analysis, ridings were selected in small regional clusters, usually three to seven ridings. There were eight regions, four in the West and four in the East: B.C. Lower Mainland, Vancouver Island/B.C. Interior, Saskatchewan, Manitoba, Northern Ontario, Southern Ontario, Toronto, and Atlantic. The surveys were based on a five-day rolling sample (usually Sunday to Thursday) of about 240 persons per day for a total of about 1,200 over the week. The sample size and number of ridings polled remained fairly consistent over the campaign and included the last weekend, unlike in 2004. Over the campaign period, more than a dozen riding polls were commissioned for the leader and some sitting MPs whose ridings did not fit into regional clusters.

The primary voter target was soft Liberals. Given the 2004 federal election experience, party election planners were acutely aware that strategic vote-switching to the Liberals might occur if it looked as if the Conservative Party could win. Health care was seen as the top issue, and while the public had a positive perception of the NDP, they also perceived the party as inclined towards greater government spending, reflecting the old "tax and spend" stereotype. Three key themes favouring the NDP emerged in the polling data: cutting health care waiting lists, providing more affordable seniors' care, and improving education — messages that would become key planks in the party's 2006 campaign. During the actual campaign period, the party's internal polling of selected ridings found that NDP support ranged from 28 percent to 35 percent, with local NDP candidate support slightly higher. Public preference for Layton as the best person for prime minister hovered in the low 20 percent range.

NDP STRATEGY AND THE ENIGMA OF STRATEGIC VOTING

Coming out of a minority Parliament, the challenges for any smaller party playing the precarious role of "balancer" are, first, to retain the party's independent ideological identity, and, second, not to suffer an electoral decline in votes and seats, as had happened to the NDP in 1974, in the public's desire for a majority government.[4] Without a doubt, the roots of the NDP's 2006 campaign strategy are to be found in the last few days of the 2004 campaign, when the Liberals unleashed a last-minute barrage of ads to persuade NDP-leaning voters to cast their ballot for the centrist Liberals in order to stop a possible right-wing Conservative victory. On election day in 2004, a considerable number of left-leaning voters begrudgingly opted for the Liberal Party, and a number of seats the NDP had projected to win fell into the opposition camp.

NDP planners had to find a way to counteract Liberal Party appeals to NDP voters to engage in strategic voting. One possible solution was to inoculate NDP supporters by making the Liberal Party seem so unappealing to social democrats that the gulf between the Liberal Party and the NDP would widen. To accomplish this, NDP ads targeted the Liberals and were more negative. The other side of the strategy was to lessen the fear of the Conservative Party and its Alberta-based leader. In order to achieve this, the NDP had to resist the inevitable temptation to portray the Conservatives as extremely right-wing and their leader as a scary man with a hidden agenda. Instead, the Conservative Party would be characterized as simply being wrong on policies and not congruent with most Canadians' values.

The key elements of the NDP's 2006 campaign strategy can be summarized as follows:

- support the Liberal minority government for as long as it continued to make concessions in exchange for the NDP's support;
- take advantage of the Liberal Party's lack of election readiness and be prepared, if necessary, to defeat the Liberal government before it made a spate of pre-election announcements;
- go negative on the Liberal Party early and hard;
- avoid demonizing the Conservative Party and its leader;
- run on the NDP legislative record in the minority Parliament (e.g., social programs for working people rather than tax breaks for corporations);
- make the case that if only nineteen NDP MPs could produce such positive legislative results, then even more could be accomplished with a larger NDP caucus;
- tap Jack Layton's growing profile, positive persona, and credibility;[5]
- maintain national media visibility but also run a focused and disciplined campaign targeting a realistic number of ridings (a tactic summarized in the phrase "big air, tight ground campaign");
- try to ignore the Green Party; and
- be flexible enough to respond quickly to breaking developments.

In summary, the leader was seen as the party's best asset, the "NDP budget" was its proven record, and the party was on the side of people, not corporations.

Over the past few years, the issue of health care continued to generate headlines and be ranked by Canadians as the most important issue. The NDP has had a long and heroic history in the pioneering of medicare. It is one of the reasons that Tommy Douglas, a former leader of the federal NDP and Saskatchewan premier, was voted the greatest Canadian by CBC viewers in 2004. For the NDP, the growing drift to the privatization of medicare under the watch of Paul Martin was potentially a useful wedge issue between the centrist Liberal Party and the social democratic NDP. If an election were to be triggered upon a principle, the sustained commitment to public medical care was an ideologically sound one for the NDP. Amongst the key targeted socio-demographic groups were women, young voters, and unionists in NDP incumbent and priority ridings.

Would the NDP achieve its goal of making it more difficult for the Liberals in the last days of the campaign to convince NDP voters to "come over"? The strategy was not without its critics, even within NDP circles. While New Democrats such as Ed Broadbent have aptly described the two old-line capitalist parties as the "Bobbsey Twins of Bay Street," most social democrats are also aware that it has been the Liberals, working in conjunction with social democrats, that have at times helped to build the welfare state in Canada. Would NDP voters embrace a strategy of directing more criticism towards the centrist Liberal Party than towards the right-wing Conservative Party?

Given that a tight ground campaign was a key component of the strategy, a smaller number of ridings were targeted than in the previous election. The NDP targeted about forty ridings that either had an NDP incumbent or were most promising, selected primarily based on 2004 voting results. Of the total targeted ridings, the largest number were located in Ontario, followed by British Columbia, Manitoba, Saskatchewan, Nova Scotia, New Brunswick, and the Territories. The largest growth in seats (over three-quarters) was projected to occur in Ontario and British Columbia. The number of the targeted ridings in the West was roughly equal to those in the East.

Analysis of the 2004 election results indicated that of the most promising additional twenty ridings, eleven would have NDP candidates competing primarily with Liberal incumbents, while nine would be competing primarily with Conservatives. Most of the projected potential victories over the Conservatives were to be in the West (notably B.C.), while most of the hoped-for victories over the Liberals were anticipated in the East (notably Ontario). Strong efforts were made to ensure that the leader would be re-elected in his home riding of Toronto-Danforth and that his spouse, Olivia Chow, running in Trinity-Spadina, would join him this time in Parliament.

CANDIDATES

The NDP nominated candidates in all 308 ridings. With the growth in party membership in Quebec, there were fewer nominal campaigns in Quebec than in the recent past. Amongst the more notable candidates were former Canadian governor general and Manitoba premier Ed Schreyer, former B.C. cabinet minister Penny Priddy, former MP and B.C. cabinet minister Ian Waddell, former Ontario MPP Marilyn Churley, and former MPs Dawn Black and Lorne Nystrom. In candidate selection, the NDP has been a strong advocate of affirmative action. It had the highest number and percentage of women nominated of any major party, although it did not meet the party's stated goal of 50 percent. Amongst the nominated candidates, 108 were women (35 percent, a slightly higher percentage than in 2004), 36 were youth, 21 were visible minorities (including the high-profile Olivia Chow), 13 were lesbian, gay, or trans-gendered individuals, 5 were Aboriginals, and 3 were individuals with dis-abilities, for a total of 156 (51 percent) affirmative action candidates. A significant number of the candidates had a union background.

ELECTION ORGANIZATION AND COMMITTEE STRUCTURE

Between NDP conventions, the Federal Executive and Federal Council are the principal decision-making bodies of the party, but in the run-up to and during an election several specialized committees are creat-ed. The Election Planning Committee (EPC) was created just over a year before the election, with its first teleconference meeting occurring in December 2004 and in-person meeting in January 2005. Including key party staff, its membership was about forty, with representatives from every province and territory. It was composed of leader Jack Layton, the party's federal officers, and a number of co-opts, including co-chairs Brian Topp and Sue Milling (also the campaign director and deputy director respectively); parliamentary caucus representatives Judy Wasylycia-Leis, Peter Julian, and Jean Crowder; the CLC's NPAC representative, Danny Mallett; director of communications Brad Lavigne; and platform and communications chair David Woodbury. Staff members who were involved included Russ Neely, acting director of organization; Bob Gallagher, chief of staff; Jamey Heath, director of caucus communications and research; and Anne McGrath, director of operations at caucus services.

Early on, the EPC divided into four working teams: tour and events, communications and platform, fundraising and finance, and organization and candidate search. The EPC designed the strategic election plan, operating closely with its four working teams during the campaign, with the sixteen-person EPC Working Group. The full EPC usually met once a month, and more often as the election neared, usually by teleconference call to save time and money and to allow greater representation from across the country. Given the size of the full committee, the four smaller working teams (composed of top planners, key federal staff from Ottawa, and, later, contracted polling and media consultants) met more frequently before the writs were issued. During the election the EPC Working Group met daily to decide on details of managing the ups and downs of the campaign. During the election, the full EPC convened by teleconference call at three key times — just prior to the election, in mid-December to approve the platform draft, and in January to review the election-in-progress — ostensibly to oversee the campaign. In practice, the EPC Working Group, along with the war room, meeting each morning, collectively guided the campaign direction.

The communications and platform committee, drawing upon past party conventions' resolutions and reports, drafted an integrated policy platform intended to maximize the party's electoral appeal. An outline was presented to an expanded Federal Council at the October Breakthrough Conference. A draft of the forty-six-page document entitled "Getting Results for People," penned under the direction of Hugh Mackenzie, was circulated to the EPC and caucus on the eve of the election call.

During the campaign, a series of groups supervised and, where necessary, modified the election strategy. At the pinnacle of the decision-making hierarchy were the campaign director and deputy director, who led the inner circle of campaign strategists. The communications and research group (war room) and the EPC Working Group met in person (or in the case of a few by teleconference) at the beginning of each day at 6:30 and 7:30 respectively. The fifteen-person war room, chaired by Raymond Guardia, included staff assigned to quick response, media monitor, press, and research. The Working Group included the federal secretary, campaign director, and assistant campaign director (also serving as the EPC co-chairs), assistant federal secretary, various section directors (communication, organization, the leader's tour, research, administration, and fundraising), a representative from the labour movement, and the party's pollster and media consultant.

The Working Group analyzed both strategy and tactics, while drawing upon reports from daily tracking of polling, the war room's account of communications/research, and updates on the leader's tour, organization, and finance. Amongst the topics raised were focus group testing of campaign slogans and phrasing, the final changes of the ads, when and how to replace the first round of ads with subsequent ones, and preparations for and reaction to the leaders' debates and the party's platform release.

Co-ordination and feedback between the national headquarters and the leader's tour on the plane was achieved through key discussions each day between Brian Topp and Sue Milling, the campaign directors, and David Mackenzie, the lead political staff on the plane. More specific details were coordinated by Laura Nichols, the tour director in the federal office, and Diane O'Reggio, later Sandra Clifford, wagon-masters on the plane. In terms of background, what is striking is the number of key players who came from Quebec and the union movement.

ELECTION FINANCES

In January 2004, the most sweeping election financing legislation changes since the mid-seventies came into effect. Union donations were severely restricted at the local level and banned at the national level. Perhaps potentially even more crucial, the trade union movement is no longer permitted to guarantee the party's bank loans for election campaigns.

The NDP's pre-election campaign was seen as a key building block to the campaign that was expected to take place in the spring of 2005, when the government was expected to fall. But when the government was not defeated, the pre-election campaign period was extended and expenditures intended for a spring election campaign (e.g., a deposit for reserving a plane, polling, and staff training) were now rolled into the larger-than-usual pre-election budget of $1.8 million.[6] By October 2005, the projected cost of the upcoming NDP campaign was $13.4 million, but by the eve of the writs being issued, projected spending had risen to almost $14.48 million.[7] The longer campaign period of fifty-five days (instead of the normal thirty-six) and the winter season (involving costly plane de-icing) meant that costs were likely to be greater than in recent past elections.

Increasingly, the largest expense for a political party during modern election campaigns is for mass advertising. For the 2006 campaign, the

NDP planned to increase spending on advertising. The media budget was set at $4.76 million, of which $4.5 million was for media buy and $150,000 for creative work and production. Echoing past practices, the largest amount of NDP advertising was allocated to the powerful medium of television. The leader's tour, the second largest portion of the campaign budget, was projected to cost $4.08 million, including $2.5 million for plane transportation. In the past, one of the largest categories of election expenses listed involved union labour releases (under the heading goods and services), but since 2004 this was no longer permitted. Such personnel must now either be paid by the party or take vacation time or personal leave from their unions. The NDP now has to pay for the hiring of more staff. Accordingly, the budget for organization rose to $2.81 million, with the greatest amount for salaries, at $1.85 million. Telephone call centres were projected to cost $500,000. In addition, $275,000 was earmarked for information technology and $50,000 for the website. Costs for communications and the platform were set at $730,000 (of which $250,000 was for leaflets, posters, and buttons), followed by $660,000 for public opinion research (about half for tracking polls, one-third for riding polls, and one-sixth for focus groups), $300,000 for direct mail (plus another $200,000 for donor "special requests"), and a modest contingency fund.

Prior to the 2004 election, donations of money and goods and services from the trade union movement accounted for a considerable proportion of the NDP's projected revenues. With state reimbursement proportional to vote totals (in effect, financial PR), each and every vote currently brings in $1.82 per year. Accordingly, the state has now become the key source of income for Canadian parties, including Canada's social democratic party. In terms of general annual revenues, government financing provided about $1.9 million and was based on the party's total of 15.7 percent of the vote in the 2004 general election.[8]

Turning to election income, the total was projected to be $9.89 million. The specific election reimbursements from the state were projected as follows by the NDP: the central rebate, covering 50 percent of permissible expenses, had been projected at $6.34 million and to account for about two-thirds of the NDP's election revenues; the local riding rebate from the state, operational if 10 percent of the vote is received, was estimated to provide an additional $2 million.[9] Under the new election financing legislation, apart from the state, individual donors were the other key source of funding. Revenue was projected as follows: $700,000 from direct mail requests for individual donations, $500,000 from the leader's tour, $200,000 from "direct ask" (telephone requests from larger donors), and $150,000 from the website/miscellaneous accounting.

Initially, the NDP sought an $11.5-million loan from the Citizens' Bank, an Internet/phone virtual e-bank set up by the B.C.-based VanCity Credit Union. Later, the party sought an additional $2-million loan. It also had a $1.5-million line of credit. As collateral, the NDP employed three major assets — the building in which its headquarters were located and central and riding rebates to be provided by the state.

NDP CAMPAIGN PLATFORM AND MAIN MESSAGE

The campaign platform document was a forty-six-page booklet entitled "Getting Results for People." It was drafted under the general supervision of the party's election platform committee, co-chaired by David Woodbury and Peggy Nash (later Jean Crowder) with key staffers. A draft of the document, penned under the direction of Hugh Mackenzie, was circulated to the EPC and caucus on the eve of the election call. Aspects of the platform's themes had been mentioned previously in the leader's speeches. However, given some problems and controversy with aspects of the platform in 2004, there was some reluctance to issue it early on. In addition, the holiday break and dramatic shootings in Toronto contributed to the decision to delay its release. The booklet was printed in English and French in sufficient quantities for NDP candidates, riding campaign managers, and the media. The document was also posted on the party's website, where it could be downloaded in its entirety or in sections.

The catalyst that triggered the election, the Liberals' failure to address the NDP's demand for a promise to halt the spread of the privatization of public health care, was front and centre in the platform. Drawing upon the legacy of Tommy Douglas, the NDP made a solemn commitment to expand medicare to include a national prescription drug plan and foster more long-term and home care for seniors. A commitment to a national child care program and more education and training rounded out some of the major expenditure items. A less frequently cited promise was for a balanced budget and no new taxes. This part of the platform was designed to give credibility to the party on financial matters and inoculate it against a "tax and spend" stereotype. In response to the revelations from the Gomery inquiry, the NDP platform called for an end to the Liberals' scandals and corruption, for cleaning up government and addressing the democratic deficit. The latter was to be achieved by electoral reform through establishing fixed election dates, introducing elements of proportional representation, imposing greater limits on spending in party leadership contests, and ensuring more MP accountability (the Broadbent Ethics Plan). In the end, the platform reminded Canadians of what the NDP had been able to accomplish in the minority Parliament with its budget amendments on infrastructure spending instead of tax cuts for corporations. The platform suggested that the NDP was a "better choice," a party whose priority was to "put working families first."

The final version of the platform was officially unveiled quite late in the campaign, which suggests that the ideological age of party manifestoes and platforms is in decline.[10] In today's television era, the leaders' personas and the parties' television advertising seem to attract more media attention. Still, the NDP's platform was one of the most popular hits on the party's website, so perhaps Canadians were more interested than some expected.

The platform document offered detailed presentations of the NDP's stance on issues, along with sharp criticism of the Liberal Party's inaction, broken promises, and corruption. Clearly, in the platform, as in other facets of the campaign, the Liberals were the prime target of the NDP's criticism and its quest for more votes. The Conservative Party received little attention, while the Bloc Québécois and the Green Party were not mentioned at all. Given the controversy over Layton's comments on the Clarity Act and Quebec during the 2004 election campaign, the section on Quebec was brief and innocuous. By contrast, the section on urban violence, crimes, and handguns was clear and forceful. Crime on the streets was an issue that Jack Layton, former Toronto politician, wanted addressed. Another striking aspect of the document was its strong dose of nationalism regarding Canadian sovereignty, foreign ownership, and resistance to undesirable entanglements with the United States on trade and military matters. The platform's condemnation of the Liberal government's discriminatory immigration head tax and call for an apology to the Chinese Canadian community for an earlier draconian head tax is a reminder of the NDP's long history of commitment to civil liberties and an effort to reach out to Asian Canadians.

Several pamphlets were released over the course of the campaign and could be downloaded from the "Activist" portion of the party's website. While most were designed centrally, there was an attempt to accommodate regional variations and to be sensitive to local riding conditions.[11]

In the spring of 2005, when an election seemed imminent, a series of pamphlets were prepared along the theme of "Getting Results for People." The main pamphlet highlighted the achievements of the "NDP budget," and about a million copies were distributed between June and early fall.[12] Once the writs were issued, there was a need to have something for activists who were canvassing door-to-door to hand out, and so a postcard was produced (with regional variations), introducing the theme of "Getting Results for People."

In the first part of the campaign a combined candidate and issues pamphlet was circulated. "Canadians Vote NDP to Get Results" reminded voters of the NDP record, outlined NDP proposals, and suggested that the Liberals "don't deserve your vote this time." Harper and the Conservatives were said to be wrong on the issues. On the other side of the pamphlet, the riding candidate was introduced and local concerns raised. This pamphlet was the most widely distributed. Some candidates from the larger campaigns also did their own local leaflets.

In the second half of the campaign, provincial variations of an end-game pamphlet were issued, suggesting "Vote for change that puts working families first." The pamphlets outlined the main planks of the NDP program — health care, pension protection, affordable education, long-term care for seniors — and also criticized both the Conservatives, for their corporate tax breaks and cuts to services, and the Liberals, for their corruption and broken promises. The document suggested that the NDP was a better choice. In British Columbia, the pamphlet came in versions that targeted the Liberal Party or the Conservative Party or both.

In the last week of the campaign, a number of "smart cards" were issued to selected ridings, intended to aggressively target voters who had lawn signs supporting other parties. These leaflets were an example of narrowcasting and an effort to win potential strategic voters over to the NDP by suggesting that a voter's first choice of party could not win in that particular riding. Thus, one red flyer warned a would-be Liberal voter of the need to vote NDP to stop the Conservatives. Similarly, two different green brochures cautioned that a Green vote would not stop either a Liberal victory or a Conservative victory and suggested instead voting NDP. A blue card counselled that the Conservatives could not win in the riding and that the way to defeat the Liberals was to vote NDP. Relatedly, there were also targeted e-cards available online that allowed web surfers to read and forward a comparable strategic vote message. During the election, the NDP also produced a number of issue leaflets on the topics of post-secondary education, public transit, working families, and labour.

While the CLC was initially on a different timeline than the NDP and was more intent on continuing to lobby in the minority Parliament, the union organization did launch in mid-December a major issues-oriented political education and mobilization campaign that was directed at its members and families. The CLC issued more than a million copies of its major pamphlet entitled "Making a better choice. Putting working families first." The six planks in this document were health care, pensions, gender economic equality, workers' rights, education and training, and decent jobs and benefits. What is perhaps noteworthy was the shift in the phrasing in the NDP pamphlets and ads from "getting results for people" to "putting working families first." Clearly, towards the end of the election campaign, there was a partial convergence in the language employed by the NDP and the CLC campaigns.

ADVERTISING

The NDP's advertising was designed by Ron Johnson and Paul Degenstein of the Vancouver-based Now Communications team, veterans of numerous NDP campaigns, working with Brad Lavigne, director of communications, and drawing upon polling information from Viewpoints Research. Advertising was the most expensive part of the NDP's 2006 election campaign. The advertising budget was quite ambitious, growing from an initial estimate of $4.7 million to a final projection of $5.0 million. In recent decades, federal NDP campaigns have spent the largest portion of the advertising budget on TV ads, and this pattern continued in 2006. Over 90 percent of the ad budget was spent on TV, with time purchased on several networks and specialty channels. Radio was used primarily in the last week or so to reinforce the message.

Since the party has never elected an MP from Quebec in a general election, the NDP placed a primary emphasis on English ads. There were a total of eight English-language ads that aired on TV in various combinations of playing time during the election period.[13] However, there were at least four French-language TV ads. The campaign also saw some NDP ads in Chinese (in both Cantonese and Mandarin), Punjabi, and Korean, and radio advertising in several languages.

Given the minority Parliament and the possibility of an early election call, no pre-election ad campaign was designed. A variety of ads emerged over the different phases of the eight-week campaign. There were no NDP TV ads in the first two weeks of the campaign. The first ad, entitled "Gift," running from mid to late December, opened the attack on the Liberals. This negative ad spoke of the Liberals "giving their well-connected friends ... a $10 billion corporate tax giveaway. What [do] Canadians get in return? Nothing. No guarantee of a single new job, a single dollar invested, a single person trained." The imagery of this ad was timely and entertaining, as it went from a lovely Christmas-wrapped gift to a stark lump of coal and ended with a winter boot, a visual suggestion that in return Canadians should "give the Liberals the boot." The second ad, entitled "Getting Results," running in the first week and a half of January, was, by contrast, a positive ad outlining the major themes of the NDP campaign: stopping health care privatization, improving funding for long-term seniors' care, addressing drug costs, increasing funding for education, and cleaning up politics. The next negative ad, entitled "Bag," airing in early to mid-January, accused the Liberals of being "pretty smug; they think they've got your vote in the bag. They think we'll ignore their corruption ... their huge wasteful corporate tax giveaways, and their endless broken promises.... Let's send the Liberals a message." The ad showed money, "corruption", and "corporate tax giveaways" spilling from a bag labelled "Liberal." In the final scene, the winter boot, reappearing from the first ad, kicked the bag and its contents into oblivion. The ad entitled "Both," running in mid-January, was equally negative about the Liberals and the Conservatives and spoke of "Liberal corruption and scandal and ... Conservatives ignoring issues and playing political games." "Invitation," running in the last full week of the campaign, pointed out the dilemma of many Canadian voters: "If you voted Liberal in the past, but can't vote Liberal this time ... and you want to stop the Conservative agenda, there's a third option — a better choice. ... Vote for the people on your side. Jack Layton and the NDP. Working families first." The ad "Former Liberals," also running in the final full week, showed a variety of disillusioned ex-Liberal voters explaining why this time they were voting for the NDP. In the final few days of the campaign, the ad "Who?" aired. It posed the question, "Who can you trust to put working families first? After twelve years of corruption and endless broken promises, it's not the Liberals. And with their plans to expand private health care and tax breaks for banks and oil companies, it's not the Conservatives." The NDP's closing ad, "Wheels," which ran only a few days, continued the criticism of both Liberals and Conservatives. It counselled voters that "with the wheels falling off the Liberal campaign ... and the Conservatives driving recklessly toward

U.S. style health care and social values, it's time to put on the brakes." The ad showed a winter boot hitting a brake pedal, conveying the message to stop going in the wrong political direction.

The four French-language ads were variations of "Gift," "Getting Results" (one version for Quebec targeting the Liberals and the BQ, the other for New Brunswick targeting the Liberals and the Conservatives), and "Invitation." Ads in other languages (e.g., "Getting Results for Chinese Canadians" and "Strengthening Our Communities") were specifically designed for distinct ethnic communities, usually in key urban ridings.

Increasingly, there are efforts to link TV and the Internet. The TV ads showed the party's website address and all of the ads were also placed on the party's website. The magnitude of the NDP's television buy was to ensure that the party was in the game right up to the end. Accordingly, the heaviest play of NDP ads occurred after the holiday break. Given Layton's increased profile and positive assessment, the NDP leader was very much a key component of the ads.

The NDP planners' fear of strategic voting, which hurt the party in 2000 and 2004, resulted in the party's platform, TV ads, and pamphlets initially being geared to criticizing the Liberal Party and not the Conservatives. For some social democratic activists, this anti-Liberal focus was problematic, and a number of prominent party members said so. Still, as the campaign progressed and the Conservative Party rose in the polls, the target of the NDP's attacks broadened. Of the eight TV ads, most in the first half of the campaign were anti-Liberal, whereas most in the second half were both anti-Liberal and anti-Conservative. Did the shift come soon enough? "Bag" began to air as Liberal support fell and seemed slightly out of phase in the campaign. As the campaign progressed, the language of the ads shifted from a more generic "getting results for people" to a more labour-oriented "putting working families first." The role of the CLC's lobbying and parallel campaign was a key influence in the shift. There is no doubt that negative advertising is often considered more effective by many communications strategists, and the NDP's electoral gains provide yet another example. Given the regional variations of which party was the NDP's main rival, different ads were given more air time in the various regions. "Both," which attacked both the Liberals and the Conservatives, ran more in British Columbia, while "Bag," which attacked only the Liberals, ran more in Ontario. The electoral gains in both targeted regions suggest this flexibility in advertising was a sound decision.

INTERNET AND EMAIL

Just as the mass medium of television transformed the dynamics of election campaigns in the sixties, so too the Internet and email have altered how campaigns communicate.[14] In the 2006 election, the NDP allocated $50,000 for web expenditures and employed at least three staff. The NDP website was an integral part of the campaign. In the pre-election period the structure of the website reflected an emphasis on the leader and caucus and their parliamentary activity, party history, and various issues campaigns (e.g., the seniors' charter). People could join the party through the website. Fundraising from the website (projected at $150,000 versus actual $287,951) was another important and tangible endeavour.

At the start of the 2006 campaign a new, more election-oriented, site was unveiled. The structure involved several major headings each with sub-categories. The "Issues" section grew in importance, as did the "Rapid Response" category, which was critical in rebutting the political opponents' main messaging. The number of speeches and press releases available grew as the pace of the campaign accelerated. Once the platform was released, it was available for download as a whole or in sections. In the "Multimedia" section, visitors could view the full array of television ads in all languages available. The two most popular items from the website proved to be the riding/candidate locator and the NDP platform. A few days before the Vancouver leaders' debates, the NDP issued an electronic "give 'em the boot" bingo card that poked fun at Martin's over-used words and phrases and proved to be a popular download for the public and journalists alike. On the last few days of the campaign, e-cards urging strategic voting for the NDP could be read and forwarded electronically. Overall, the website was multi-purpose and touched on all aspects of the campaign.

In addition to the public access part of the NDP's website, there was also a more restricted path for party members. They could sign up for e-NDP news, while riding campaign managers and federal staff received an internal daily e-memo. NDP riding officials could receive materials (to help them stay on-message) and download items (e.g., templates for pamphlets, issue sheets, completed advocacy group issue questionnaires, and sample telephone scripts) through the "Activists" portal. As long as it had sufficient computing capacity, the riding, even a non-priority one, could get more materials sooner than in earlier decades. This suggests that the new technology can have a democratizing effect.

In the 2006 campaign, the party reported that the NDP website generated about 715,223 visits and received 45 million hits (about 50 percent higher than in 2004) from the time it was launched.[15] Overall, there was a continuing increase in the number of visits per day from the week before the campaign (3,521), through a modest mid-peak around the Vancouver leaders' debates in mid-December (10,535), to the final week of the campaign (29,215). A similar pattern emerged for number of hits. The last week broke all records, with over 1.8 million hits per day. Clearly, the new technology is of growing importance as an unfiltered communications tool enabling the party to reach the electorate directly.

THE NDP CAMPAIGN AND THE LEADER'S TOUR

The minority Liberal government fell on Monday, November 28, 2005. The 2005–06 campaign, which straddled the Christmas and New Year's holidays, would be a lengthy one at fifty-five days and, given the winter weather, would also be a more complex one logistically. The leader's tour,[16] with a projected expenditure of $4.1 million, the second biggest item in the election budget, was a major vehicle for communicating the party's national election message and was designed to highlight key issues and themes, with suitable photo ops to generate publicity for the party. The "big air" campaign also was designed to ensure that the NDP, as a fourth-place party, maintained visibility in the news. The leader also travelled to priority regions and ridings to boost the local candidates and riding organizations.

A key goal was to run a more disciplined tour in which statements by the leader, key spokespersons, and candidates stayed on-message. In 2004, Layton had deviated from the script in two controversial policy areas, homelessness and the Clarity Act, and a number of his caucus MPs had publicly disagreed with him on Quebec. In 2006, Layton spent the most time in Ontario, where the largest number of seats are located and the greatest electoral gains were expected. It is also the region where much of the English media are centred and where the leader and his wife were running as candidates. Second was British Columbia, where significant gains were projected. Next was Saskatchewan, where the NDP hoped to see some MPs elected this time. Quebec, with one-quarter of Canada's population, was the next most visited province and was pivotal if the NDP hoped to rise dramatically in national polls, even though seats were not realistically expected.

In all, more than eighty thousand kilometres were travelled and sixty cities visited.[17] The NDP tour typically went to two or three places each day, and the national media needed to be able to file their stories in time. The reality of a winter campaign meant more inside locations, greater effort to attract crowds, and an increased risk of flight delays or cancellations caused by weather. The tour never went fully dormant, even during the holidays, since the insatiable media wanted to know what Layton was doing even on non-campaign days.

Following the defeat of the government, the first week of the campaign, November 28 to December 3, saw the launch of the leader's tour. In Toronto, flanked by two high-profile candidates, Layton's wife, Olivia Chow, and Marilyn Churley, Layton opened by stating that the Liberals' record did not warrant voters' support. Instead of Liberal "broken promises," the NDP, he suggested, was "getting results for people." Two days later Stephen Harper grabbed headlines with his bold proposal to cut the GST from 7 percent to 5 percent. The NDP responded that this was an unwise tax cut. Travelling west to Saskatchewan, Layton spoke about the growing threat to public medicare. Holding up two contrasting cards in his hand, Layton counselled that all we should need is our health card, not a credit card. However, the news that dominated the headlines that day was from Ontario, where long-time New Democrat and Canadian Auto Workers union president Buzz Hargrove had weighed in on the need for strategic voting and endorsed Paul Martin's Liberals as the party most able to stop the Conservatives. The enduring image of the day was Martin wearing a CAW union jacket and embracing Hargrove. The veteran NDP personality had veered wildly off-message and undercut the thrust of the NDP's campaign of attacking the Liberals. It was too soon to discern the full impact of Hargrove's controversial deed, but at the end of the first week, NDP support ranged from 14 to 18 percent in the major public opinion polls and was under 30 percent in the party's internal polling of key ridings.

Week 2, December 4 to December 10, commenced with the Conservative leader making headlines with his proposal to give families $1,200 a year per child under six for child care expenses. Layton responded that the Conservative proposal was woefully inadequate in helping families pay for quality child care. Later that week Layton indicated that public funds should not subsidize private medical clinics. Buzz Hargrove continued to campaign with Paul Martin in Windsor on the eve of Layton's snowstorm-delayed arrival in the city. It was not a great week for the NDP campaign. The tour next focused on the western provinces and participating in the two leaders' debates in Vancouver. There, the NDP unveiled a proposed national child care act that would guarantee two hundred thousand places in a public system. A memorable moment for the NDP occurred when Layton and Shirley Douglas, the daughter of medicare founder Tommy Douglas, spoke together in Regina in defence of public health care. It would be one of several times they would appear together.

The leaders' debates are useful for giving the NDP greater parity in media coverage and also provide an opportunity to convey the party's message directly to the electorate. Given that there were four debates in 2006, Layton was coached on debate technique even before the campaign commenced. Whereas in 2004 more than a dozen people advised Layton, this time only three per language (Ron Johnson, David Mackenzie, and Anne McGrath for English; Ron Johnson, Eric Hebert, and Lynda Brault for French) were involved. Since the Liberal Party was the main target of the campaign, Layton needed to challenge Martin most during the debate. In addition, since Layton now had a higher profile and could point to the NDP's parliamentary accomplishments (e.g., the so-called NDP budget), he didn't have to intervene as urgently as he did during the 2004 debates. The more restrained debate format seemed to suit Layton.

Although Layton grew up in Quebec, was reasonably fluent in French, and spoke French extensively in Parliament, he still found debating in his second language to be a challenge. The French debate was far less important for Layton than the English debate. In the French debate, Layton went after Martin for his twelve years of delay on day care and suggested that it took a minority Parliament before any progress was made. He condemned Martin for allowing the growing privatization of health care. Layton also pointedly asked why the BQ had not supported the NDP's amendment to the budget with its social spending. Overall, Layton seemed more engaged in the French debate than he had been in 2004.

In the English debate, Layton continued his extended criticism of Martin and the Liberals and noted the "enormous failure" of 5 million people not having access to family doctors. Layton pointed to Martin's broken promises and suggested that the Liberal Party was no longer the party that was most supportive of immigrants. He pointed out that the NDP had the largest number of female candidates of any party. Finally, responding to Layton's persistent portrayal of the Liberals as preoccupied with corporate tax cuts, Martin suggested that most of the Liberal government's tax cuts were targeted at individuals. Martin's response indicated that the NDP campaign was having an effect on Liberal electoral prospects. The NDP had successfully avoided being marginalized in the debate and the campaign. The NDP played the Canadian nationalist card when Layton reminded viewers how NAFTA hindered Canadian sovereignty on energy, water, and social services issues. From the NDP's perspective, however, perhaps the most dramatic statement came in Conservative Stephen Harper's closing comments, when he suggested that his party's actions were on behalf of "ordinary working people and families." The phrase was an echo of many past NDP leaders and suggested that the Conservatives were trolling for traditional NDP voters.

The post-debate period was a bit more relaxed. The assessments of Layton's debate performances were generally positive. (See Chapter Eleven.) High-profile NDP candidate Ed Schreyer attempted to clarify and defuse the controversy around his past comments about same-sex marriage, while Olivia Chow spoke out forcefully against the Liberal government's unwillingness to apologize for the historic head tax policy and to pay only some Chinese Canadian groups a financial restitution. Layton visited his home city of Toronto to speak about transit, then travelled west to Winnipeg to speak about Aboriginals. He took an epic flight to Yellowknife in the Northwest Territories, where he celebrated the winter solstice by travelling by dogsled. It was an adventuresome entry into the Christmas holiday period. The NDP gained slightly in the public polls.

The holiday interlude, December 25 to December 31, should have been a quiet period. Instead, it was jolted by two dramatic events — perhaps key defining points in the campaign. First, on December 26, a teenage girl was killed and six others were wounded in a blaze of gunfire in a downtown Toronto shopping district. Such acts of violence (i.e., unconventional participation) can galvanize a society and lead to greater interest in civic activities such as voting (i.e. conventional participation). Second, at a December 28 press conference, NDP MP Judy Wasylycia-Leis announced that the RCMP had commenced a formal investigation into a possible leak during the Liberal government's policy change on income trusts. Layton called on Finance Minister Ralph Goodale to temporarily step down from his cabinet post. The campaign turned decidedly nastier when a comment on Industry Minister David Emerson's blog site referred to Layton as having a "boiled dog's head smile" — a denigrating comment with racist implications.

The holidays divided the eight-week campaign into two unequal portions. The longer period before New Year's was initially deemed to be the less important, and so more media buy, the platform launch, and the final debates were jammed into a hectic three-week period. The campaign relaunch in Week 6, January 1 to January 7, took place in Ottawa, with Layton flanked by Ed Broadbent and Ottawa Centre candidate Paul Dewar. The first major poll, suggesting the Conservatives had displaced the Liberals in the lead, began to dominate the news headlines. Interestingly, Harper had even begun to tap an old NDP campaign issue of questioning Martin's Canadian nationalism given the foreign flagging of Martin's company ships. Harper hinted that he could work with the NDP on accountability and ethics issues. On Friday, in the Vancouver area, Layton outlined the justice portion of the NDP platform: mandatory sentencing, denying bail, and bumping up older juveniles into adult court if a gun was used in a crime. For the NDP, it was a tough crime package that had increasing appeal in major metropolitan areas.

At the large labour-sponsored rally in Vancouver, Layton spoke of "putting working families first," a key phrase that would come into greater usage during the campaign's final weeks. Also reflecting the changing campaign dynamics, Layton now directed more of his criticisms at both the Liberals and Conservatives. Polling results indicated that the NDP climbed a bit higher, in the low 30 percent range in the NDP's sample of priority ridings and just under 17 percent in national public polls.

The next week of the campaign, January 8 to January 14, would prove to be event-filled, with the crucial leaders' debates in Montreal and the NDP's platform launch. On the eve of the debates, Layton spoke of a third choice for Canadians "beyond corruption and Conservatives." With Harper continuing to gain in the polls, the NDP would direct some of its criticism towards the Conservative Party, but the Liberal Party would continue to be its primary target. In the English debate, Layton called for electoral reform. He pointed to urban violence as evidence of the need to be "tough on crime and the causes of crime." He warned against deeper integration with the United States. In classic left populist imagery, Layton also pointed out that both Martin and Harper favoured tax breaks for corporations. Layton suggested that the Liberal government's misdeeds (as noted by the Gomery inquiry) had increased the support for the BQ and the PQ. Layton criticized the Conservatives, suggesting that the smaller NDP caucus had produced more results in Parliament than the much larger Conservative caucus.

In the French debate the next night, Layton pursued the democratic deficit theme, suggesting that proportional representation would help make citizens' votes count, and questioned both Harper's and Martin's openness regarding donations to their leadership campaigns. Perhaps feeling the continuing NDP barrage from the campaign, Martin shot back that there was a donors list and that Layton should not tell lies. On the question of urban violence, Layton noted that the young woman killed on Boxing Day was from his riding. He continued his criticism of Martin by suggesting that Martin talks a lot but offers little action. Layton closed with the reminder that to have the kind of Canada you want, you need to vote for the kind of Canada you want. While Harper was perceived to have outperformed Martin, talk of the debates was displaced by heated comments about the Liberals' ad about armed troops in Canadian cities.

The next day, the NDP platform was launched in Hamilton, a city where NDP hopes were high. Unlike in the last campaign, no controversy followed the platform's unveiling, but neither did it generate banner headlines. Later in the week, it was revealed that Layton had undergone treatment for a hernia in the nineties at the Shouldice Clinic, a private facility. Since the campaign had focused so much on stopping the privatization of medicare, this was not a desirable lead story for the NDP. However, old news about the minor treatment did not draw prolonged attention. More troubling perhaps was the "Think Twice Coalition," involving high-profile activists, including Buzz Hargrove, Maude Barlow, and others from a variety of social movements, who warned of the dangers of a Conservative victory and counselled strategic voting. Meanwhile, on Vancouver Island, Layton continued to campaign with Shirley Douglas on medicare. He flew back east for a large labour-sponsored rally in Toronto, where he suggested the Liberals "need a time out." One of the more colourful buttons in evidence at the labour rally said "Buzz off. I'm voting NDP."

With the death of a Canadian diplomat and three wounded Canadian soldiers casting a sombre mood over the final week of the campaign, January 15 to January 21, Layton called for a parliamentary debate on Canada's changing military role in Afghanistan. Poor visibility grounded part of the leader's tour in Northern Ontario, where the NDP expected a number of victories. On Monday, Layton delivered a major speech to the Toronto Board of Trade in which he encouraged past Liberal voters "for this election, this time — lend us your vote." The NDP was, in effect, endeavouring to turn strategic voting on its head and induce unhappy Liberal supporters to vote NDP in 2006. The increasing attractiveness of the NDP leader could be tracked in his steady climb in the SES-CPAC polling numbers.[18]

The week witnessed the greatest volume and variety of NDP ads. The impact of the NDP campaign caused the other parties to target the NDP. The Conservatives launched one negative ad, labelled

"Moustache," which imposed an oversized image of Layton's moustache and mouth onto the faces of Canadians and suggested the NDP would legalize drugs, be indifferent to tax cuts, tax family estates, and speak only for special interest groups. Liberal Leader Paul Martin faulted Layton for "taking a pass" on challenging the Conservatives and called for "progressive voters" to rally behind the Liberals. Layton's planned trip to New Brunswick and Quebec City was cancelled because of poor weather, the second such cancellation in the week. The much respected veteran NDP MP Ed Broadbent, who was retiring, gave a farewell speech in which he warned that the Liberal Party had become "unethical, undemocratic and unprincipled" and that its campaign was "incoherent" and "deeply offensive." Layton, echoing the point, suggested that "people have learned the lesson from the last campaign"; hence, once bitten, twice shy when it came to the Liberals. In his view, Martin was not a Liberal in the tradition of Pearson or Trudeau.

Public opinion polls during this week showed the NDP averaging its best in the campaign at almost 18 percent, while internal polling had the party holding in its targeted ridings at the mid-30 percent level.

In NDP eyes, the closing weekend of the campaign, January 22 to January 23, was a particularly crucial time period, since in 2004 the Liberals had successfully out-campaigned the NDP in the last few days. This time, the final weekend dynamics would be vastly different. The groundwork had been set to drive a much greater wedge between NDP voters and the Liberal Party, making NDP voters less susceptible to voting Liberal. In the last week of the campaign, the NDP, through its website, circulated email greeting cards appealing to voters on topics ranging from progressive values, the environment, affordable education, Conservatives, and the Greens. Meanwhile, in the final hours of campaign 2006, the NDP employed automated phone messages in key ridings targeting potential NDP voters. Trekking one last time to the West and back, Layton returned to Toronto to visit six ridings, including his own and that of his wife. In addition to having endurance, a leader on a long campaign must, like a marathoner, stay focused on the intended course. In 2004, Layton was a freshman leader, but he had learned important lessons about the risks of going off-message. As a sophomore leader in 2006, Layton was far more disciplined, perhaps even too scripted at times. But the result was a well-run and relatively error-free campaign.

ELECTION RESULTS AND ANALYSIS

With just over 2.5 million votes (17.5 percent of those cast), the NDP saw gains in both votes (an increase of almost half a million) and seats (the caucus grew by ten members). Campaign 2006 produced a vote several points above the NDP's average (15.3 percent) over the 1961–2004 period. Overall, the NDP's vote in 2006 went up in eight provinces, all but P.E.I. and Newfoundland. The largest gains in percent of the vote were in Quebec and British Columbia. As was the case in 2004, no province gave the NDP a vote higher than 30 percent,[19] although it exceeded 20 percent in five provinces, led by Nova Scotia, followed by B.C., Manitoba, Saskatchewan, and New Brunswick. In Ontario, a crucial province in terms of seats and where the leader resided, the NDP received 19 percent of the vote. The NDP vote percentage was less than 10 percent in only two provinces, P.E.I. and Quebec. It is evident that there is still need for substantial growth in support in the heartland provinces of Ontario and Quebec, where most of the seats are located, if the party is to achieve a dramatic breakthrough. The fact that state funding to parties is based on the number of votes received makes it even more important to increase the vote in these key provinces.

The percentage of votes received in each riding gives a good preliminary indication of the number of ridings in which a party is competitive in either three-way or two-way races.[20] Very few ridings (only six) gave the NDP an absolute majority of votes, an electoral reality in a multi-party system. In fourteen ridings the NDP received almost half of the votes cast (40 to 49 percent), while thirty-two ridings were in the 30 to 39 percent range and forty-five in the 20 to 29 percent range. Together, these ninety-seven ridings where the NDP acquired greater than 20 percent of the vote offer the greatest likelihood for future electoral gains. The 120 ridings in the 10 to 19 percent range reflect much more difficult prospects. While things improved in 2006, there were still 91 ridings where the NDP vote was less than 10 percent, the threshold for riding reimbursement by Elections Canada. The largest percentage gains occurred in Quebec, from a low base of 5 percent to almost 8 percent in 2006. If proportional representation had been in place, the increase in the NDP vote in Quebec would have translated into seats for the federal social democratic party.

Using party placement rankings, the data on first- (29) and second-place (53) finishes suggest that 82 ridings can be considered locations in which the NDP stands a good chance of future success. This is an increase from 70 in 2004 and only 39 in 2000, but is still far short of the degree of competition needed for the NDP to form the government or even the official opposition. In ridings where the NDP placed third (158), the party could have a reasonable chance of success if both a strong campaign and local candidate emerge.

With an increase in the NDP's vote, the party did manage to win more seats but still less than its percentage of the votes. The NDP's ratio of percent seats to percent votes was 9.4 to 17.5, for an index of 0.54 (where 1.0 would be perfect equality of percent votes and percent seats). As Alan Cairns, Fair Vote Canada, and the Law Reform Commission have documented,[21] the NDP, like its predecessor the CCF, has consistently suffered from under-representation and regional distortion in seat distribution under our current electoral system. Prominent NDP politicians have been advocates of some form of PR. The NDP perhaps should have pushed harder on this issue in the 2004–05 minority Parliament.[22]

All incumbent MPs who chose to run under the NDP banner were re-elected. The new caucus of twenty-nine MPs was the largest since 1988. Almost all of the new seats came from the two key targeted provinces: Ontario and British Columbia. A regional breakdown of candidates elected reveals twelve from Ontario (the second highest ever from the province), ten from B.C., three from Manitoba, two from Nova Scotia, one from New Brunswick, and one newly elected from the Western Arctic. For the second time in a row, a rare event occurred in that no NDP MPs were elected in Saskatchewan, despite the NDP vote in that province being over 24 percent and higher than the Liberals', who elected two Saskatchewan MPs. Overall, fourteen NDP MPs are from the West and fifteen from the East (including Ontario). The twelve women in caucus representing the NDP is by far the best percent (41 percent) in a Parliament[23] that saw the number of women elected decline overall.

The NDP campaign had primarily targeted the Liberal Party, but the NDP's major party rival often differed in the East (Liberals) and the West (Conservatives). In terms of party competition, of the eleven new seats gained, five came from the Liberals in Ontario, while in B.C. three came from the Conservatives, one from an independent conservative, and one from a Liberal. The one in Western Arctic came from the Liberal Party. The only NDP seat not retained was Churchill, where the incumbent Bev Desjarlais lost the NDP nomination, subsequently ran as an independent, and along with the new NDP candidate was defeated by a Liberal. Thirty-six of the NDP's fifty-three second-place finishes came in the West, where the Conservatives are strongest. In analyzing the ridings in which the NDP came closest, what is striking is how few seats were potentially in play. Only in three ridings did the NDP come within one thousand votes of winning. These findings offer a cautionary message for NDP strategists planning the next campaign.

CONCLUSION

A number of positive elements for the NDP came out of Jack Layton's second campaign as federal leader: increases in the party's visibility, popular vote, caucus size, and the number of women in caucus. The unique working relationship between Jack Layton and Olivia Chow, as husband and wife and now fellow MPs, has fostered positive publicity. The leader's stature continues to rise. Layton seems to possess not only inexhaustible energy but also, quite importantly, an ability to grow as a leader. Like Ed Broadbent, Jack Layton is increasingly seen as a trustworthy political leader — a valuable trait in a cynical era.

For the NDP, the primary challenge of the 2006 campaign was to avoid the adverse effects of strategic voting. The plan was to criticize the Liberals from the outset and to continue the barrage to make it more difficult for the Liberals in the last days of the campaign to convince NDP voters to "come over." However, the NDP strategy was not without its critics, even within NDP circles. CAW union president Buzz Hargrove was perhaps the most vocal doubter, even campaigning with Paul Martin in support of strategic voting to defeat the Conservatives. Hargrove, Maude Barlow, and Jim Laxer openly questioned the NDP strategy. A number of left-oriented social activists campaigned for strategic voting. While the NDP vote and seat count improved, those of the Liberals fell, and the NDP has the potential to play a key role once more in another minority Parliament. An inevitable debate within social democratic circles arose after the election about the wisdom of the NDP campaign. This was not so much in terms of the magnitude of votes and seats gained, but the indirect result — a Conservative victory.

Canada is a continental polity, and much of Canadians' identity is made up of regional or provincial loyalties. Under Layton, the NDP has made steady gains in both votes and seats in Ontario and British Columbia, with the bulk of the current NDP MPs coming from these two crucial provinces. While the NDP has made some vote gains in Quebec under Layton, the party's support level in that province remains below 10 percent. Layton's proficiency in French and his profile in Quebec continue to grow, but in 2006 Quebecers saw the Conservative Party, not the NDP, as the alternative choice to the Liberals and BQ.

While the NDP recognized that strategically it could target the Liberals, in reality it cannot run a national campaign focused exclusively on only one political opponent, particularly given the different parties' seat distributions. In much of the West, the NDP's main challenge was to defeat a Conservative rival, while in the East, it was the Liberals. The Green Party's increasing votes, money, and publicity perhaps affects the NDP the most. It seems the NDP may have to battle both foes and former friends in the election ahead. In many ways, the next campaign has already begun. The debate over which ideological path to take — left, centre, or right — and the issue of strategic voting will continue.

NOTES

I am grateful to the many who kindly consented to post-election interviews and in particular members of the NDP's Election Planning Committee and its campaign team who allowed me to observe their deliberations. I also wish to thank NDP's federal secretary Eric Hebert, campaign director Brian Topp, deputy director Sue Milling (also the EPC co-chairs), senior administrative assistant Carmel Belanger, party translator Dominique Vaillancourt, and many others without whose generous assistance this chapter would not have been possible.

1   Alan Whitehorn, "Jack Layton and the NDP: Gains But no Breakthrough," in *The Canadian General Election of 2004*, ed. Jon H. Pammett and Christopher Dornan (Toronto: Dundurn Press, 2004).

2   NDP MP Libby Davies, chief of staff Bob Gallagher, and later former NDP leaders and MPs Ed Broadbent and Alexa McDonough had helped broker the NDP's amendments to the Liberal government's budget and thereby saved the minority government from defeat in the spring of 2005.

3   The crossover point for the NDP to move into first place in the forty ridings would be around E27 to E25 for the "NDP universe" and E19 for NDP voters.

4   Interestingly, in the six minority Parliaments that the NDP has been involved from 1962 to 2005, the NDP vote has gone up in half of the cases and the MPs total increased in two-thirds of the cases.

5   As to the best person to be prime minister, public polling for the entire country generally put Layton at a range from low to mid-teens (e.g. SES-CPAC campaign polls).

6   Interview with Jess Turk Browne, assistant federal secretary.

7   At the time of the writing of this chapter, final accounting for the 2006 NDP campaign was not complete and so numbers are only preliminary estimates.

8   The NDP's increase in vote to 17.5 percent means that annual state revenues to the party would henceforth be about $4.7 million (approximately 2,590,000 votes x $1.82).

9   In the 2006 election, the NDP would get over 10 percent of the vote in 204 ridings.

10   See Chapter 3 on party manifestoes in Alan Whitehorn, *Canadian Socialism: Essays on The CCF-NDP* (Toronto: Oxford University Press, 1992).

11   Part of that sensitivity was issuing pamphlets in other languages, most notably Cantonese, Mandarin, and Punjabi.

12 I am grateful for interviews with Nammi Poorooshasb of the NDP communications team and Maya Russell of Now Communications.

13 Two ads appeared only on the Internet or free-time election broadcasts. I am indebted to Ron Johnson of Now Communications for his detailed explanation of the advertising campaign.

14 A landmark account of different eras of party systems and the influence of communications technology can be found in Ken Carty, "Three Canadian Party Systems: An Interpretation of The Development of National Parties," in *Party Politics in Canada*, 8th edition, ed. Hugh Thorburn and Alan Whitehorn (Toronto: Pearson Education, 2001).

15 Data derived from correspondence with webmasters Aylwin Lo and Jeff Debutte.

16 There was also a secondary tour of party notables to help in key ridings (e.g., Ed Broadbent, Bill Blaikie, Howard Hampton, Carole James, Judy Wasylycia-Leis, Pat Martin, and Shirley Douglas).

17 Interview with Ira Dubinsky, assistant tour director.

18 SES-CPAC reported that Harper scored 75, Martin 64, and Layton 58. This was the closest the three leaders had been in the composite leadership index, which measured trust, competence, and vision.

19 Canada's three largest cities, which shut out the Conservative party in seats, elected four New Democrat MPs, and voter support ranged from a high of 30 percent in Vancouver to 21 percent in Toronto and only 10 percent in Montreal.

20 I am grateful for the data provided by Russ Neely, the NDP's acting director of organization, and his colleagues Brad Field, Tara Peel, and Heather Fraser.

21 For a review of the literature see Henry Milner, "The Case for Proportional Representation in Canada," in *Party Politics in Canada*. The ratio of seats to votes was about one seat per 89,000 votes for the NDP; about one seat per 43,000 votes for both the Conservatives and Liberals; and one seat per only 30,000 for the BQ. Clearly, Canada's federalist NDP suffers, while the separatist BQ benefits, from our antiquated electoral system. Indeed, in terms of total votes won, the NDP, not the BQ, should be in third place.

22 One of the NDP's achievements under David Lewis in the 1972–74 minority Parliament was election party financing reform.

23 For a historic overview of NDP women in Parliament, see Alan Whitehorn, "Social Democracy and the New Democratic Party," in *Canadian Parties in Transition*, 3rd edition, ed. Alan Gagnon and Brian Tanguay (Peterborough: Broadview Press, forthcoming 2007).

CHAPTER FIVE

The Bloc Québécois:
A Sour-Tasting Victory
by Éric Bélanger and Richard Nadeau

At the outset of the 2005–06 federal election campaign, it was widely expected that the outcome of the election in Quebec would be more or less identical to that of 2004.

The Bloc Québécois' renewed dominance over the party system in Quebec appeared unchallengeable. To the eyes of Quebecers, the evidence of massive corruption under the Liberal government, uncovered by the Gomery Commission during its spring 2005 hearings, seemed to have put the last nail into Paul Martin's political coffin. Stephen Harper's Conservatives had no real party organization in Quebec and still appeared to be at odds with the Quebec population's views and aspirations. As for the other parties, they continued to show up poorly in every pre-election poll, unable to break through what had been essentially a two-party system in Quebec since 1993.

With the Liberal Party's image completely shattered, and with the lack of a viable alternative, the road appeared to be cleared for the Bloc to sweep the province. Hence party leader Gilles Duceppe's optimism when he declared early on in the campaign that it was possible for the Bloc to improve significantly over its already impressive 2004 score. The objective was to cross the symbolic threshold of "50 percent plus one" votes for the first time in the history of Quebec's sovereigntist movement. This would provide tremendous momentum for holding a third referendum on Quebec sovereignty in the next few years.

On January 23, as election night drew to a close, the Bloc Québécois remained the dominant party in the province, winning fifty-one seats out of seventy-five. But Duceppe saw voter support for his party drop from 49 to 42 percent; and while the Bloc won six new seats, it lost nine others. Eight of those seats went to the Conservative Party, which, to the surprise of many, had performed relatively well in the second half of the campaign in Quebec, as in the rest of the country.

All this resulted in a sour-tasting victory for the Bloc. In retrospect, it can be argued that the party made two strategic miscalculations in this campaign. The first mistake was to publicly raise the bar in terms of the expected outcome. The Bloc was standing so high in the polls at the start of the campaign that it is difficult to believe the party could have been able to maintain such a lead, even without the rise of the Conservatives in the province. The second error was to adopt a narrow campaign strategy that consisted of simply attacking the Liberal Party, in an attempt to knock it out for good. By focusing all of their energy on discrediting the Liberals instead of on highlighting the Canadian federal system's shortcomings, Duceppe and the Bloc left the door entirely open to the Conservatives to come up with credible proposals to better accommodate Quebec within Canada.

The next five sections provide a more comprehensive account of the 2005–06 election campaign in Quebec. We first lay out the political context in Quebec as it was during the months leading to the election. We then present an overview of the Bloc Québécois' campaign platform and publicity, before providing a summary of the campaign dynamics in Quebec. We conclude by offering some interpretations for the election outcome in Quebec and by assessing its short- and long-term consequences for the Bloc Québécois.

THE PRE-CAMPAIGN IN QUEBEC

After a period of relative decline, the Bloc Québécois came back in force in the House of Commons following the June 2004 federal election. The party received 48.8 percent of the popular vote in the province of Quebec and saw fifty-four of its candidates elected or re-elected, out of a total of seventy-five seats. With such an impressive outcome, Gilles Duceppe was able to match Lucien Bouchard's 1993 feat, when the Bloc broke through the Canadian federal party system for the first time[1] (see Table 1).

In large part, the Bloc's renewed success was attributable to an upsurge in support for the sovereignty of Quebec following disclosure, in February 2004, of what appeared to be massive corruption related to the federal sponsorship program.[2] This program was set up by the Chrétien Liberal government in the aftermath of the 1995 referendum on Quebec sovereignty that had almost been won by the "Yes" side. It aimed at improving the presence of Canadian federalism within the province of Quebec through advertising and sponsoring social, cultural, and sports

Table 1
Federal election results in Quebec since 1993

	1993	1997	2000	2004	2006
Bloc Québécois	49.3%	37.9%	39.9%	48.8%	42.1%
	(54)	(44)	(38)	(54)	(51)
Liberal Party	33.0%	36.7%	44.2%	33.9%	20.7%
	(19)	(26)	(36)	(21)	(13)
Conservative Party	n/a	n/a	n/a	8.8%	24.6%
					(10)
Progressive Conservative Party	13.5%	22.2%	5.6%	n/a	n/a
	(1)	(5)	(1)		
Reform Party/ Canadian Alliance	n/a	0.3%	6.2%	n/a	n/a
New Democratic Party	1.5%	2.0%	1.8%	4.6%	7.5%
Green Party	0.1%	0.1%	0.6%	3.2%	4.0%

Source: Elections Canada.
Note: The table indicates the percentage point share of the Quebec vote, with the number of seats in parentheses below.

events. Important irregularities in the awarding of contracts under this program were disclosed by Auditor General Sheila Fraser in her February 2004 report. Almost immediately, polls showed a significant rise in support for sovereignty, which reached 50 percent and remained at that level during the months leading up to the June 28 election (see Figure 1). This upsurge was accompanied by rising support for the Bloc Québécois and by the decline of the federal Liberal Party's popularity in Quebec.

The sponsorship scandal continued to fuel the Bloc's popularity over the next seventeen months. Further revelations were made during the Gomery Commission hearings in spring 2005 that confirmed the existence of an informal bribery system whereby some Quebec advertising firms had been giving money obtained from the sponsorship program back to the Liberal Party through unofficial channels, notably during the 1997 and 2000 election campaigns.[3] These revelations continued to undermine the

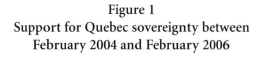

Figure 1
Support for Quebec sovereignty between
February 2004 and February 2006

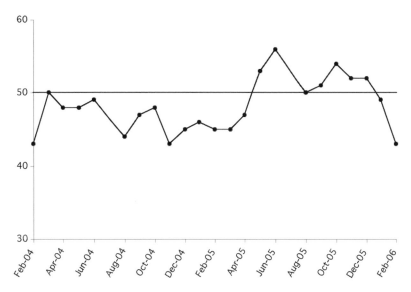

image of the federal Liberals, and of Canadian federalism more generally, in the eyes of Quebecers. Together with the other opposition parties, the Bloc kept asking the government to explain itself in the House and repeatedly said that the Liberals had lost the "moral authority" to govern. Vote intentions for the Bloc Québécois hovered around 50 percent in May 2005.[4] Perhaps more importantly, support for Quebec sovereignty rose to 53 and 56 percent, as Figure 1 illustrates, the highest level recorded in ten years by CROP. On May 19, the Bloc and the other two opposition parties made a failed attempt to defeat the minority Liberal government; but they would get a second chance at the end of November, after the release of the Gomery Commission's phase one report.

When looking at the Quebec provincial scene, the political circumstances also appeared to be very favourable to the Bloc and to the sovereigntist movement on the eve of the new federal election. Since 2004, satisfaction with Jean Charest's provincial Liberal government remained extremely low, with less than one-third of Quebecers approving of the government (according to CROP monthly polls). It appeared as though the Liberal brand in Quebec was at a low in popularity, at both the federal and provincial levels, with no viable federalist party alternative to turn to at either level. Following the unexpected resignation of their leader, Bernard Landry, in June 2005, Parti Québécois members elected thirty-nine-year-old André Boisclair as new PQ leader in the fall, just two weeks before the federal election was called. Boisclair easily won the leadership race, in good measure because he was seen as the candidate best able to renew the party, mobilize a new generation of voters in favour of Quebec sovereignty, and beat Charest in the next provincial election.[5]

All these favourable circumstances strongly suggested new momentum for the sovereigntist movement as the Bloc Québécois entered the 2005–06 electoral campaign. Late November pre-election polls indicated that support for the Bloc was skyrocketing to 60 percent, forecasting a huge sweep in the province.[6] While careful not to appear overly enthusiastic, Gilles Duceppe and his troops clearly had relatively high expectations at the start of the campaign. Some pundits even speculated on whether this was announcing a return of the "three-period" sovereigntist strategy of 1993–95 that would lead to Quebec sovereignty.[7] At the very least, the Bloc Québécois' goals were stated clearly by Duceppe early on in the campaign: to cross the symbolic 50 percent plus one threshold of voter support[8] and to push the Liberal Party off Quebec's electoral map,[9] especially by breaking through Liberal ridings populated with high proportions of cultural minorities.[10]

THE BLOC PLATFORM AND PUBLICITY

Gilles Duceppe unveiled his party's platform on November 30. The 202-page document, divided into five chapters, detailed the Bloc's position on a host of issues.[11] The first chapter was mainly concerned with the sponsorship scandal and the revelations of corruption under the Liberal government. The party proposed a series of measures to reinforce transparency and the respect of ethical standards in Ottawa. The chapter also addressed the problem of fiscal imbalance in the Canadian federation, arguing that Quebec was not receiving its share of the federal budget surpluses accumulated over the past few years. The other four chapters presented various proposals having to do with restructuring the unemployment insurance system, placing more federal investment in post-secondary education and social housing, ensuring the enforcement of the Kyoto protocol to protect the environment, expanding sustainable development policies, providing financial aid to Quebec regions affected by the softwood lumber dispute with the U.S., imposing some limits on globalization forces in order to protect cultural diversity, as well as giving more decisional powers to Quebec within international organizations on questions involving the province's jurisdiction.

Obviously, the Bloc's platform also argued that these policy areas would be better under an independent Quebec. But if one puts the sovereignty issue aside, the specific policy proposals found in the Bloc's platform suggest that the party is locating itself ideologically to the centre-left, somewhere between the New Democratic Party and the Liberals. The Bloc presents itself as the defender of Quebec's interests in Ottawa, but the party clearly defines those interests as being left-leaning. Duceppe pictures the Quebec population as holding distinct progressive values that set it apart from the rest of the country. Accordingly, it is not surprising that the Bloc Québécois shares policy positions with the NDP on several social issues. On some other questions, it is also close to the Liberal Party. One example would be the majority of Bloc MPs who voted in favour of the recognition of same-sex marriage (Bill C-38) in the free House vote of June 2005.

That being said, a close examination of the Bloc Québécois' 2005–06 campaign platform indicates that it was not much different from the party's 2004 program. Most of the policy proposals put forth in 2004 were carried through, virtually unchanged. The only substantial modification was the addition of a comprehensive account of the Gomery Commission's conclusions about the sponsorship scandal, with more direct attacks made at Paul Martin in an attempt to overcome the fact that Justice Gomery had exonerated him in his phase one report released in November. Slight updates to the platform were made in order to take into account current events, such as the hike in oil prices, the softwood lumber dispute, the legalization of assisted suicide, issues involving victims of Hepatitis C, and the Liberal government's purported inaction in reducing greenhouse gases. The Bloc also proposed a sustainable development plan for the St. Lawrence River and pushed for better federal support to francophone communities outside Quebec. Aside from these few elements, however, the Bloc basically recycled its platform from the previous election.

The Bloc Québécois' total campaign budget was $4.6 million, plus $500,000 non-refundable by the Chief Electoral Officer.[12] About $2.4 million from the budget went to publicity spending. The party's campaign slogan was "*Heureusement, ici, c'est le Bloc*" ("Thankfully, here, it's the Bloc"). While certainly lacking the cleverness of the 2004 slogan ("*Un parti propre au Québec*"), it still had the merit of conveying the party's main messages that, unlike other Canadians, Quebecers had an alternative to corrupt parties, and that the people of Quebec are different. In addition, the Bloc had several radio and television ads running throughout most of the campaign, but especially during the last two weeks, to get out the vote. The radio ads were quite negative in tone, clearly linking Paul Martin to Jean Chrétien and AdScam.[13] In comparison, the television ads were more restrained, simply showing citizens of various cultural makeups standing in front of a ballot box, saying "*heureusement*" and encouraging people to vote "*pour en donner plus pour la famille,*" "*pour faire le Québec,*" or "*pour se souvenir du scandale des commandites.*" It is important to note that no explicit mention of Quebec sovereignty was made in the ads in congruence with the party's overall campaign, which avoided the topic as much as possible.

Another $50,000 was alloted to campaigning in targeted constituencies. These ridings were those that had been won by the Liberals in 2004 by only a narrow margin. Many of these were Montreal districts with a high concentration of cultural minority groups, such as Ahuntsic, Outremont, and Papineau. It is worth noting that the Bloc printed a special pamphlet summarizing the party's positions on immigration and cultural integration issues and distributed it in most of these ridings. The pamphlet also made a point to clearly present the Bloc's definition of Quebec citizenship as being inclusive: "We believe that all the citizens living in Québec are Québécois without exception. The Bloc Québécois considers therefore that it is its political responsibility to defend and promote the specific interests of Québec's various ethnic and cultural groups."[14] In addition, the Bloc presented nine candidates from cultural minority groups, seven of these in ridings on the Montreal island.[15]

THE ELECTION CAMPAIGN IN QUEBEC

Figure 2 illustrates the trends in Quebec vote intentions during the 2005–06 federal election campaign. As in the rest of the country, we can clearly distinguish between two distinct phases, or dynamics, in the Quebec campaign: pre-holidays and post-holidays. The first half of the campaign, before the holiday break, is characterized by high stability in aggregate voter support. The Bloc Québécois clearly dominated, maintaining itself above the 50 percent threshold of vote intentions. The Liberals polled between 20 and 35 percent, while the Conservatives and the NDP persistently received between 5 and 10 percent of voting intentions.

Important shifts in voter support can be observed in the second half of the campaign, right after the new year. Vote intentions for the Bloc fell below 50 percent for good during the second week of January, while the Liberal Party saw its support crumble to 15–20 percent. As for the Conservative Party, it doubled its share of Quebec voting intentions during the first ten days of January, then saw its support rise over 20 percent (and sometimes get close to 30 percent) for the rest of the campaign. Support for the NDP and the Green Party remained stable, at a low level, throughout the campaign in Quebec.

Figure 2
Vote intentions in Quebec during the 2005–06 campaign

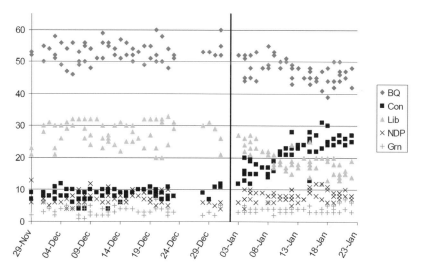

Source: 114 polls from SES Research (46), Strategic Counsel (36), Ipsos-Reid (10), Ekos (7), Decima (6), Léger Marketing (5), CROP (3), and POLLARA (1); sample sizes vary from poll to poll.

The first four weeks of the campaign went relatively smoothly for Gilles Duceppe and his troops. The campaign was concentrated to some extent in Montreal ridings. But the sovereigntist leader also travelled across the province, visiting districts in the regions of Gaspé, Beauce, Outaouais, and the Eastern Townships, without ever taking a day off.[16] He even travelled far north to the small Algonquian town of Kitcisakik, near Val d'Or, in order to denounce the Liberals' lack of structural and financial support for the Aboriginal populations of Quebec.[17] The Bloc's two main campaign themes before Christmas were AdSscam and the fiscal imbalance. The party argued that the Liberals displayed arrogance by refusing to recognize their responsibility for creating those two problems while they were in power. As Duceppe kept saying, the Liberal Party had lost the moral authority to govern, and Quebecers needed to sanction the government by supporting the Bloc.

The Liberals counterattacked by trying to prime the national unity issue. Paul Martin tried to put the Bloc Québécois on the defensive by arguing that the upcoming election was, in fact, a referendum election on the future of Quebec.[18] He stated that re-electing the Liberals was the safest way to ensure that there would be a strong opposition to Quebec separation forces in a new referendum on sovereignty. Duceppe dodged the attack by replying that the issue of separation could be decided only by Quebec's National Assembly, and that a federal election outcome had nothing to do with it.[19] The strategy of both parties was to mobilize the support of federalist voters who felt angry at the sponsorship scandal. The Liberals tried to argue that, in spite of AdScam, they remained the party best able to fight Quebec separatism, while the Bloc tried to convince federalist voters that a vote for the Bloc did not equate to a vote for Quebec independence.

Stephen Harper and Jack Layton both argued that Martin was taking for granted the defeat of Jean Charest in the next Quebec provincial election, and that the Liberals' record at defending Canadian federalism in Quebec was negative in light of their near loss of the 1995 referendum and the recent rise in sovereignty support following the sponsorship debacle.[20] Despite these criticisms, Paul Martin continued to pound the national unity issue during the first leaders' debates held in Vancouver in mid-December. He said he would continue to fight separatism and would not let Gilles Duceppe take his country away.[21] Because of the strict new debate rules, Duceppe was not allowed to reply to Martin's emotional statements, and he expressed his frustration to the media by advocating a return to the old debate formula.[22] However, if we are to believe the December poll results (Figure 2), it appears that these first leaders' debates had no real impact on Quebec public opinion.

On December 19, Stephen Harper visited Quebec City and made an important speech in which he pledged to fix the fiscal imbalance in collaboration with all provinces and said he would allow Quebec more presence on the international scene and more active participation in the negotiation of international treaties on matters dealing with provincial jurisdictions.[23] Quebec Premier Jean Charest went on the record and responded positively to Harper's openness, as did Mario Dumont, leader of the provincial opposition party, Action démocratique du Québec (ADQ).[24] Paul Martin accused the Tories of playing the sovereigntists' game by promising more decentralization. As for Duceppe, his reaction to Harper's statements was timid and cautious.[25] In private, Bloc strategists expressed concerns about the unexpected Conservative pledges, considering Harper's strategy a potential threat to the Bloc's hegemony in Quebec.[26] It was feared that the Tories would steal the angry federalist vote away from the Bloc in some districts, especially in the regions of Quebec City and Beauce.

Those concerns appeared warranted as the Conservatives started to experience a slow surge in Quebec vote intentions during the first week of January (see Figure 2). Stephen Harper continued to tour the province of Quebec, repeating his two key promises to fix the fiscal imbalance and to promote a federalism that would be more respectful of provincial jurisdictions. Perhaps more importantly, he argued that only he, not the Bloc, could actually do something to address those concerns in Ottawa. The Conservative rhetoric struck a chord with the Quebec electorate. It displayed what appeared to be a genuine openness to the needs and wants of Quebec. And it clearly contrasted, on the one hand, with the Liberals' decidedly centralist view of the federation, and on the other hand, with the Bloc's relative powerlessness to change Canadian federalism in a way that would better accommodate Quebec because of its perpetual opposition status.

It might also be argued that Harper's intentions to clean up the ethical mess in Ottawa, mentioning René Lévesque's policies as an example to follow, also resonated positively with Quebec voters, especially as the Goodale affair in late December revealed the possibility of corruption in Paul Martin's own cabinet.[27] In addition, on January 9, well-known Quebec journalist Normand Lester published a controversial book about Option Canada that detailed how this organization, created by the Canadian Unity Council and funded by Heritage Canada, purportedly spent as much as $3.5 million in illegal contributions during the 1995 referendum campaign.[28] Duceppe and the Bloc quoted the book as further evidence of anti-Quebec corruption within the federal government, and of a Liberal culture of secrecy, illegality, and immorality in Ottawa. They also argued that the Option Canada affair was a "federal scandal" in the sense that some high-profile Conservatives were supposedly involved in the organization's operations at the time. During the second leaders' debates, Duceppe named Pierre Claude Nolin, Peter

White, Yves Fortier, Jean Bazin, and Michael Meehan as examples of Tories involved with Option Canada back in 1995, even though these people were never mentioned in Lester's book.[29]

This signalled an important late-campaign shift in the Bloc's strategy. Gilles Duceppe's target was now the Conservative Party. In an attempt to halt the Tories' rise in popularity in Quebec, the Bloc tried to link the Conservatives to the Option Canada scandal and to federal corruption more generally. What is more, Duceppe and the Bloc argued repeatedly that Stephen Harper's values were at odds with those of Quebecers.[30] The Canada Harper had in mind had little to do with the progressive society that the Quebec people had worked so hard to build since the sixties. Finally, in an attempt to weaken the credibility of Harper's promises, Duceppe (and PQ Leader André Boisclair) questioned the Conservatives' will to fix the fiscal imbalance, highlighting the fact that Harper had no financial provisions about it in his platform and was refusing to evaluate how much fixing this problem would cost.[31]

Harper's attacks regarding the Bloc Québécois' powerlessness in the House of Commons continued to hurt[32] and forced Duceppe to justify his party's usefulness. The sovereigntist leader pointed out that it was the Bloc that had proposed the anti–biker gang and assisted suicide bills over the past few years. Duceppe also argued that the Bloc was the only party to defend "unconditionally" the interests of Quebec in Ottawa, implying that the election of Quebec cabinet members was no guarantee that those interests would be defended because of the inevitable compromises required in any federal cabinet.[33] And to discourage Quebec voters from trusting the Conservatives' plans for decentralization, he qualified those promises as a "*gros risque*," in a reference to Brian Mulroney's "*beau risque*" efforts that failed to reintegrate Quebec within the Canadian constitution during the eighties (Boisclair called the promises "siren songs").[34]

The new Bloc strategy appeared to be unsuccessful at stopping the rise of the Conservatives. On January 18, *La Presse*'s cover story reported the results of the most recent CROP poll, which put the Bloc at 39 percent.[35] Two days later, Léger Marketing put the party at 42 percent. Pundits were now predicting a handful of seats in Quebec for the Conservatives. Panic set in within the Bloc troops. Duceppe started to accuse Stephen Harper of wanting to strike down Bill 101 and to weaken minority rights in Canada.[36] He associated the Tories with the U.S. and George W. Bush in terms of social values and political orientations, taking the Iraq and Kyoto issues as evidence. He finally presented the Bloc as Quebec's best safeguard against a Conservative government in

Ottawa. The weekend before election day, the Bloc Québécois ran a full-page ad in two Eastern Quebec newspapers, *Le Soleil* and *Le Journal de Québec*, that said "We will not let Calgary decide for Quebec."

On election night, the Bloc Québécois won six new seats but lost nine others, for a total of fifty-one seats. Table 2 summarizes those gains and losses for the Bloc. The gains were all made at the expense of the Liberal Party. Four prominent cabinet ministers were defeated: Liza Frulla in Jeanne–Le Ber, Pierre Pettigrew in Papineau, Jacques Saada in Brossard–La Prairie, and Denis Paradis in Brome-Missisquoi. Gilles Duceppe's party actually made gains in the six ridings where the gap between the Liberals and the Bloc was the closest in the 2004 election (less than 5 percentage points). As for the seats lost by the Bloc, eight went to the Conservative Party (mostly in the Quebec City area) and one was won by independent candidate André Arthur (Portneuf–Jacques-Cartier). The Conservatives won two more seats in Quebec (Beauce and Pontiac), while the Liberals hung on to thirteen seats (down from twenty-one in 2004). Voter support for the Bloc Québécois stood at 42.1 percent, a significant drop from its 2004 result and far from the objective of 50 percent plus one. The Tories received 24.6 percent of the Quebec vote share, and the Liberals 20.7 percent. Voter turnout in Quebec was 63 percent, slightly up from 59 percent in 2004.

Table 2
Bloc Québécois seat gains and losses in the 2006 election

Gains (6)		*Losses* (9)	
District	**Change in % BQ vote**	**District**	**Change in % BQ vote**
Ahuntsic	-2.4	Beauport-Limoilou	-11.8
Brome-Missisquoi	-1.4	Charlesbourg–Haute-Saint-Charles	-13.3
Brossard–La Prairie	-3.8	Jonquière-Alma	-15.6
Gatineau	-1.1	Lévis-Bellechasse	-15.3
Jeanne–Le Ber	-0.7	Lotbinière–Chutes-de-la-Chaudière	-16.4
Papineau	+0.7	Louis-Hébert	-9.0
		Louis-Saint-Laurent	-14.2
		Mégantic-L'Érable	-12.1
		Portneuf–Jacques-Cartier	-17.0

Source: Elections Canada.

From the point of view of the public interest, it can be argued that the 2005–06 election campaign in Quebec could have dealt more with policy issues. Basically, the parties' campaigns in Quebec almost solely addressed corruption, scandals, and values, leaving Quebec voters relatively uninformed about substantive issues and actual policy proposals. The Bloc Québécois campaign primarily aimed at discrediting the federal parties by depicting the Liberals and the Conservatives as both being corrupt. Editorialist André Pratte underscored this pernicious aspect of the Bloc campaign: Duceppe first begged voters to throw the Liberals out, only to argue that a Tory government would be a disaster for Quebec. Then why did the Bloc force an election call if a government change was not going to serve the interests of Quebec?[37] In addition, the Bloc leader misquoted Stephen Harper on the Bill 101 issue during the last week of the campaign. Duceppe wanted to show that, if elected, Harper would stand against Quebec's language policy. In the complete quote from Harper, the latter said that while he did not agree with some dispositions of Bill 101, he nonetheless supported the right of the Quebec provincial government to legislate on linguistic matters.[38] Liberal Leader Paul Martin also tried to raise the stakes twice during the campaign by stating that a third referendum on Quebec sovereignty was inevitable and that Stephen Harper would curb abortion rights if elected. Such rhetorical drifts on the part of political parties and leaders should be avoided in future election campaigns.[39]

BENEATH THE SURFACE:
INTERPRETING THE BLOC VICTORY

The surprising 2006 election outcome in Quebec raises a number of questions: Does the Bloc's relative counter-performance indicate a durable defection of Quebecers toward the Conservative Party? Did the Bloc make significant gains among cultural minorities in the Montreal area? It must first be observed that support for the Bloc Québécois turns on a combination of short- and long-term factors. The intensity of nationalist sentiments, the popularity of the leaders, the issues of the day, and the dynamics of the campaign all come into play to determine the outcome of federal elections in Quebec. In this respect, the Bloc Québécois benefited from a less favourable campaign environment in 2006 compared to that of the previous election. Support for sovereignty was still high, but on the decline. Gilles Duceppe was still popular, but not as dominant as he had been in the past few years. And the disenchanted federalist voters were offered a credible alternative to the discredited Liberal Party.

Every election is unique, but common patterns are discernible. The data presented earlier in Table 1 suggest a typology for the five elections fought so far by the Bloc Québécois. The impressive victories of 1993 and 2004 stand out. The Bloc almost reached the symbolic 50 percent target of voter support on both occasions. Lucien Bouchard in 1993 and Gilles Duceppe in 2004 outperformed their opponents. Major events such as the failure of the Meech Lake Accord in the early nineties and the recent sponsorship scandal boosted support for sovereignty around the time of both elections. In addition, unpopular federalist governments on the provincial scene contributed to reduce an already low level of attractiveness for federalist parties among French-speaking Quebecers.

The 2006 election for the Bloc Québécois presents more similarities with the less successful campaigns run by this party in 1997 and 2000. Support for the Bloc dropped to around 40 percent (38 percent in 1997 and 39 percent in 2000). The upward spiral of support for sovereignty reversed its course. A federalist leader, Stephen Harper, mounted a competitive campaign in Quebec as Charest (1997) and Chrétien (2000) did before. Stephen Harper's plea for a *"fédéralisme d'ouverture"* struck the same chord among soft nationalists hit by Jean Charest in 1997 when he supported the constitutional recognition of Quebec as a distinct society.

The ability of a leader to project an acceptable image to his most moderate opponents will often win over new supporters. This pattern favoured the Bloc in 1993 and 2004. Large federalist defections to the Bloc Québécois occurred during these elections due to the popularity of Lucien Bouchard and Gilles Duceppe among francophone federalists. Jean Charest's attractiveness to sovereigntists played a very similar role in the 1997 election. An examination of the losses suffered by the Bloc in 2006 suggests that Stephen Harper appeared sufficiently attractive to induce a certain proportion of Bloc voters to defect to the Conservative Party.[40] The data in Table 2 show that the Conservatives' gains in Quebec were mostly made at the expense of the Bloc Québécois. Eight of the ten Conservative victories in the province occurred in ridings previously held by the Bloc, and the losses of Gilles Duceppe's party in these ridings averaged nearly fourteen percentage points in aggregate vote share.

A careful look at these data suggests that Stephen Harper's breakthrough in Quebec is due to two factors. First, a certain number of Bloc voters were attracted by Harper's position toward Quebec. Second, a certain proportion of federalists voted strategically for the federalist party best placed to beat the Bloc. These patterns are not peculiar to the current election. Jean Charest was an attractive option for moderate sovereigntists in 1997, and strategic voting among federalists, usually beneficial to the Liberals, favoured the Conservatives this time.[41]

The regional patterns of loyalty and defection between and among federalists and sovereigntists explain to a large extent the seat turnovers during the last federal election. Past voting patterns in the Quebec City area are revealing. Support for the Liberals in this region is usually weak, the intensity of nationalist sentiments is not particularly strong, and the attractiveness of winning parties and conservative options manifested itself repeatedly in the past. In the 1995 referendum on sovereignty, the "Yes" vote appeared surprisingly low in the Quebec City area. In the 1994 and 1998 provincial elections, the region backed the winning Parti Québécois before turning to Charest's Liberals in 2003. At that same provincial election, the Parti Québécois suffered important losses in this region to the right-wing ADQ led by Mario Dumont, who publicly supported Harper's Conservatives during the 2005–06 federal campaign.[42] As political analyst Pierre Drouilly once pointed out, it is a region that has always appeared to be fertile ground for conservative movements like the Union Nationale and the Social Credit during the fifties and sixties, and the ADQ more recently.[43] That region's *vieux fond bleu*," the defections of moderate sovereigntists, and the strategic vote of Liberal federalists all combined to produce eight of the ten Conservative victories (and eight of the nine Bloc losses) in the greater Quebec City area in the last federal election.[44]

These types of patterns also explain why the Bloc made gains in the last campaign. Table 2 shows that four of the six new Bloc victories happened in ridings of the Montreal area where the Liberals had won by slim majorities in 2004. These four ridings, which include important cultural communities, were previously considered as inhospitable lands for the Bloc Québécois. The victories of Gilles Duceppe's troops in these ridings, and most notably the defeat of high-profile cabinet ministers in two of them (Pierre Pettigrew and Liza Frulla), gave way to the speculation that the Bloc had finally made significant inroads among these long-time unfavourable groups.[45]

However, the data displayed in Table 2 do not support this interpretation. First, the Bloc did not make gains but rather lost support in five of these six ridings. While it is undeniable that, because of the rise in voter turnout, the Bloc received a *raw number* of votes in these ridings higher than in 2004, the federalist parties (taken together) nonetheless managed to mobilize an even higher number of votes this time, when we look at the *actual share* of the aggregate vote the parties received. Second, of the nine minority candidates presented by the Bloc, only Vivian Barbot in Papineau had relative success (40.7 percent, up nearly one percentage point); even Maka Kotto and Meili Faille were re-elected with a slightly smaller share of the vote than in 2004. Finally, the patterns observed in the six new ridings won by the Bloc in 2006 is the same whether or not they include ethnic minorities. All of them share a tradition of support for the Liberal Party, which has made the task of casting a strategic vote for federalists harder. As a result, the federalist vote in these ridings split between the Liberals and the Conservatives, paving the way for Bloc victories.

CONCLUSION

Three lessons can be drawn from the 2006 federal election in Quebec. First, campaigns matter. At the outset of the campaign, pundits predicted the election of a minority Liberal government and a massive sweep of the province of Quebec by the Bloc Québécois. Second, electoral choices depend to a large extent on the options put to voters. What drove the last election was not a radical change in Quebec voters' needs and demands but a significant redesigning of the political supply offered to them. Third, the last election produced more losers than winners in Quebec.

The outcome is a historical disaster for the Liberal Party. One can hardly imagine that this same party got 68 percent of the vote and seventy-four seats out of seventy-five in Quebec only a quarter of a century ago. The road to political recovery for the Liberals in Quebec will be long and perilous, and the task ahead is daunting: the rehabilitation of the party's image and credibility in the eyes of Quebecers in the aftermath of the sponsorship scandal will likely prove to be a formidable challenge for Paul Martin's successor.

The Bloc Québécois won a sour-tasting victory on January 23. The party's hope of gaining the support of more than 50 percent of the electorate appeared reasonable when the election was called. Many believed at the time that Quebecers would send up to sixty Bloc members to the next Parliament. Strategists within the sovereigntist camp speculated that the outcome of the federal election would give a solid boost to their option. A strong showing by the Bloc was considered a decisive first step in a three-period strategy (the other two being the election of the Parti Québécois in the next provincial election and the holding of a winning referendum shortly afterwards) leading to the sovereignty of Quebec.

The contrast between this optimistic picture and the political climate after the federal election is striking. The Bloc, instead of gaining ground, missed its symbolic target by a large margin. The popularity of its leader has suffered as a result. Duceppe's position as Bloc leader remains secure because of the lack of a viable successor and because the Conservative minority government's mandate will likely be short, but his image has clearly lost some of its lustre. Support for sovereignty, far from being pushed up by the performance of the Bloc, went down by several digits after the election (see Figure 1). Moreover, the defeat of the federal Liberals deprives the sovereigntists of what has been their most effective political weapon over the last few years — the sponsorship scandal. Not surprisingly, the optimism among the sovereigntist camp has waned. The 2006 election result is now perceived at best as a serious warning and at worst as a political shock that will close the window of opportunity opened up two years ago by the sponsorship scandal.

If the election in Quebec produced a catastrophic defeat for the Liberals and a quasi-defeat for the Bloc and the sovereigntist camp, one would conclude that there is at least one clear winner — the Conservative Party. We would agree with this view, but with a note of caution. Contrary to all expectations, the Conservatives received almost 25 percent of the vote in Quebec and managed to win ten seats. Thanks to Quebec voters, Stephen Harper can now claim to lead a real national party. And thanks again to Quebec voters, Harper can now present his party as the best alternative to oppose the Bloc Québécois and preserve Canadian unity. But this Tory victory may have put the federalist option at risk in Quebec. The political institution that has represented the federalist option for decades, the Liberal Party, is now discredited and its political rehabilitation may take years. This makes the political burden on the shoulders of Stephen Harper heavier. If he succeeds in offering Quebec the new brand of federalism he advocated during the campaign, the Conservatives may well gain even more ground in Quebec in the next election, primarily to the detriment of the Bloc Québécois. But if Harper fails, this may create an open field for the Bloc since Quebecers would certainly hesitate to return to the Liberal fold in the short run.

In the wake of the election outcome, Gilles Duceppe declared that the Bloc would not immediately attempt to defeat the newly elected

Conservative government and would give Harper a chance to prove himself. The sovereigntist leader also said his party might occasionally collaborate with the new government as long as such collaboration would benefit the interests of Quebec. But if Prime Minister Harper happens to disappoint Quebecers, then the Bloc will not hesitate to bring the government down.[46] For the Bloc, defeating Harper's government too soon would be a risky strategy: it could lead to a Conservative sweep in Quebec (in a repeat of the 1958 and 1984 elections), which would mean an important setback for the Bloc. It is better for the party to wait and hope for Harper to disappoint Quebecers.

To sum up, the 2006 federal election in Quebec produced a massive defeat for the Liberals, a quasi-defeat for the Bloc Québécois and the sovereigntist movement, a personal victory for Stephen Harper, and a risky situation for the federalist option. Soft nationalist French-speaking Quebecers appear to have put themselves in "wait and see" mode. So have Gilles Duceppe and the Bloc Québécois. If Harper delivers his promised "*fédéralisme d'ouverture*," the federalist option will carry the day and the Bloc will have a hard time running its next campaign. But if Harper fails to deliver, the Bloc will have a much easier time at the next election, facing two discredited federalist parties.

NOTES

We thank Stéphanie Dufresne for her helpful assistance in preparing this chapter.

1   For a recent account of the 1993 Bloc Québécois success, see Éric Bélanger, "The Rise of Third Parties in the 1993 Canadian Federal Election: Pinard Revisited," *Canadian Journal of Political Science* 37 (2004): 581–94.

2   See Alain-G. Gagnon and Jacques Hérivault, "The Bloc Québécois: The Dynamics of a Distinct Electorate," in *The Canadian General Election of 2004*, ed. Jon H. Pammett and Christopher Dornan (Toronto: Dundurn Press, 2004), 139–69. For studies about the relationship between cynicism with politics and support for the Bloc (and other third parties) during the nineties, see Éric Bélanger, "Antipartyism and Third-Party Vote Choice: A Comparison of Canada, Britain, and Australia," *Comparative Political Studies* 37 (2004): 1054–78, and Éric Bélanger and Richard Nadeau, "Political Trust and the Vote in Multiparty Elections: The Canadian Case," *European Journal of Political Research* 44 (2005): 121–46.

3   For more details, see Commission of Inquiry into the Sponsorship Program and Advertising Activities, *Who Is Responsible? Fact Finding Report* (Ottawa: Public Works and Government Services Canada, 2005).

4   Nine surveys fielded in May by five polling firms gave the Bloc between 48 and 56 percent of vote intentions (Ipsos-Reid, SES Research, Strategic Counsel, Decima, Léger Marketing).

5   During the summer, Gilles Duceppe briefly considered the possibility of entering the PQ leadership race, but decided not to because he knew a federal election was coming in a few months and he did not want to have his party spend time and energy in selecting a quick replacement for him as Bloc leader.

6   POLLARA (November 28, 2005); Ipsos-Reid (November 26) and Environics (November 28) put them at 59 percent.

7   Denis Lessard, "Le retour des 'trois périodes' de Jacques Parizeau?" *La Presse*, November 29, 2005, A10; André Pratte, "L'élection référendaire," *La Presse*, December 20, 2005, A26.

8   Said Duceppe to journalists: "Obtenir le 50% plus un, dans tout défi, c'est obtenir la majorité absolue. C'est bien sûr qu'à ce moment-là, on dit 'il y a une majorité absolue de gens qui nous appuie'. C'est drôlement important. Et pour le mouvement souverainiste, ça serait la première fois. Je ne suis pas pour cacher que, bien sûr, on serait très fiers de franchir la barre du 50% plus un." Quoted by Nathaëlle Morissette, "Gilles Duceppe souhaite une majorité absolue," *La Presse*, December 10, 2005, A9.

9   Said Duceppe in a rally of Bloc supporters: "Les libéraux, on les fait disparaître. Faites-vous un cadeau!" and "Pas question d'abandonner une seule circonscription aux mains du Parti libéral du Canada. On va faire la lutte partout, on ne reculera nulle part." Quoted by Nathaëlle Morissette, "Le Bloc veut 'faire disparaître' les libéraux de la carte du Québec," *La Presse*, December 5, 2005, A1.

10 This particular aspect of the Bloc's strategy was discussed in the foreign press. See Clifford Krauss, "Separatists in Quebec Seek Immigrant Votes," *The New York Times*, December 12, 2005, A6; Carole Duffrechou, "Les partis canadiens courtisent le 'vote ethnique'," *Libération*, January 21, 2006.

11 Bloc Québécois, *Heureusement, ici, c'est le Bloc*, 2005, 202.

12 Information about the Bloc's campaign budget come from Nathaëlle Morissette, "Le Bloc veut 'faire disparaître' les libéraux de la carte du Québec," *La Presse*, December 5, 2005, A7.

13 They were reminiscent of the strategy used in the newspaper ads that the Bloc published a few weeks before the campaign began. Those four ads showed a golf ball, a Christmas ball, a tie, and a photocopier machine, each object with the words "sponsorship scandal" and the Liberal logo printed on it, and a cap line saying "I remember, Mr. Martin and Chrétien…" in reference to some of the outrageous spending revelations made at the Gomery hearings.

14 Bloc Québécois, *An Inclusive Society in Our Own Image*, 2005, 2.

15 The nine candidates were Vivian Barbot (Papineau), Justine Charlemagne (Saint-Léonard–Saint-Michel), May Chiu (LaSalle-Émard), Meili Faille (Vaudreuil-Soulanges), William Fayad (Saint-Laurent–Cartierville), Maka Kotto (Saint-Lambert), Gérard Labelle (Honoré-Mercier), Maria Mourani (Ahuntsic), and Apraham Niziblian (Bourassa). Faille and Kotto were seeking re-election.

16 Nathaëlle Morissette, "Duceppe roule à fond la caisse," *La Presse*, December 24, 2005, A2.

17 Nathaëlle Morissette, "La misère des autochtones de Kitcisakik émeut Duceppe," *La Presse*, December 11, 2005, A1.

18 Gilles Toupin, "'Au Québec, ces élections seront référendaires'," *La Presse*, December 3, 2005, A5.

19 Marie-Claude Malboeuf, "Duceppe se défend d'être en campagne référendaire," *La Presse*, December 4, 2005, A3.

20 Joël-Denis Bellavance, "Harper accuse Martin de torpiller Charest," *La Presse*, December 4, 2005, A1; Joël-Denis Bellavance, "Stephen Harper accuse

Paul Martin de poignarder Jean Charest dans le dos," *La Presse*, December 11, 2005, A5.

21 Gilles Toupin and Joël-Denis Bellavance, "Harper isolé," *La Presse*, December 17, 2005, A1.

22 Philippe Mercure and Marie-Claude Malboeuf, "Duceppe veut revenir à l'ancienne formule," *La Presse*, December 18, 2005, A1; Vincent Marissal, "'Plates', les débats?" *La Presse*, December 19, 2005, A9.

23 Joël-Denis Bellavance, "Harper s'engage à régler la question," *La Presse*, December 19, 2005, A1; Tristan Péloquin, "Stephen Harper donnerait plus de place aux provinces," *La Presse*, December 20, 2005, A9; Robert Dutrisac, "Harper courtise le Québec," *Le Devoir*, December 20, 2005, A1.

24 Tommy Chouinard, "Charest séduit par les engagements de Harper," *La Presse*, December 20, 2005, A1; Tristan Péloquin, "Les libéraux rêvent d'un gouvernement péquiste, croit Harper," *La Presse*, December 21, 2005, A15.

25 Vincent Marissal, "Le pari québécois de M. Harper," *La Presse*, December 21, 2005, A13.

26 Hélène Buzzetti, Robert Dutrisac, and Alec Castonguay, "Onde de choc au Bloc," *Le Devoir*, December 22, 2005, A1.

27 Gilles Toupin, "Stephen Harper énonce ses cinq priorités," *La Presse*, January 3, 2006, A5.

28 Normand Lester and Robin Philpot, *Les secrets d'Option Canada* (Montréal: Éditions Les Intouchables, 2006). See also Clairandrée Cauchy, "Aide occulte pour le NON," *Le Devoir*, January 10, 2006, A1.

29 Michel David, "Le péril bleu," *Le Devoir*, January 11, 2006, A1.

30 Tristan Péloquin, "Duceppe prêt à travailler avec Harper," *La Presse*, January 6, 2006, A6; Lysiane Gagnon, "Un gouvernement sans le Québec?" *La Presse*, January 7, 2006, A23.

31 Tristan Péloquin, "Harper doit chiffrer le déséquilibre fiscal, dit Duceppe," *La Presse*, January 14, 2006, A9.

32 Said Harper in a rally of Conservative supporters in Buckingham: "Le Bloc existe depuis 16 ans à Ottawa et il n'a rien pu accomplir. Même s'il existe encore pendant 116 ans, il ne pourra faire avancer aucun dossier." Quoted by Gilles Toupin, "'La place du Québec n'est pas dans les estrades', lance Harper," *La Presse*, January 16, 2006, A7.

33 Tristan Péloquin, "'Le Bloc est utile', martèle Duceppe," *La Presse*, January 17, 2006, A7.

34 Tristan Péloquin, "Le Bloc a l'appui des fonctionnaires fédéraux," *La Presse*, January 18, 2006, A9; François Gougeon, "Boisclair en renfort à Sherbrooke," *La Presse*, January 18, 2006, A9.

35 Denis Lessard, "Le Bloc Québécois en perte de vitesse," *La Presse*, January 18, 2006, A1.

36 Tristan Péloquin, "Duceppe exige des explications," *La Presse*, January 20, 2006, A6.

37 André Pratte, "C'est ça, la démocratie," *La Presse*, January 19, 2006, A22.

38 Tristan Péloquin, "Duceppe exige des explications," *La Presse*, January 20, 2006, A6.

39 André Pratte, "Campagne de peur 101," *La Presse*, January 21, 2006, A29.

40 In their preliminary analysis of the Canadian Election Study data, Fournier and his colleagues observe that, while Quebec federalists concerned with corruption supported the Bloc in a proportion of 28 percent in the 2004 election, only 5 percent of them did so in 2006. See Patrick Fournier, André Blais, Elisabeth Gidengil, Joanna Everitt, and Neil Nevitte, "Que s'est-il passé?" *La Presse*, February 8, 2006, A23.

41   See Neil Nevitte, André Blais, Elisabeth Gidengil, and Richard Nadeau, "Why Did the Bloc Québécois Lose Ground?" in *Unsteady State: The 1997 Canadian Federal Election* (Don Mills: Oxford University Press, 2000), 117–26.

42   Denis Lessard and Tristan Péloquin, "Dumont veut freiner le Bloc," *La Presse*, January 13, 2006, A9.

43   Pierre Drouilly, "Le 'Québec tranquille', celui qui vote ADQ," in *L'Annuaire du Québec 2004*, ed. Michel Venne (Montréal: Fides, 2003), 615–8.

44   See also Réjean Pelletier, "L'énigme de Québec décortiquée," *Le Devoir*, January 28, 2006, B5. Pelletier also emphasizes that Quebec City people felt that their region had been abandoned by both levels of government in recent years and were thus highly dissatisfied with the Bloc's and the provincial Liberals' respective parliamentary work.

45   See, for example, Vivian Barbot, "Les résultats du Bloc Québécois aux élections fédérales: au-delà des chiffres, il y a des gagnants," *Le Devoir*, February 4, 2006, A9.

46   Said Duceppe during his victory speech on election night: "Si M. Harper veut régler le déséquilibre fiscal et faire vraiment une place au Québec sur la scène internationale, il trouvera le Bloc Québécois à ses côtés. [...] Par contre, si le gouvernement conservateur ne remplit pas pleinement ses engagements envers le Québec, il trouvera que le Bloc forme une opposition musclée. Le Parti conservateur a ce soir le fardeau de la preuve." Quoted by Nicolas Bérubé, "'Le Québec et le Canada ne vont pas dans la même direction,'" *La Presse*, January 24, 2006, A6.

CHAPTER SIX

Great Expectations:
The Green Party of Canada's 2006 Campaign
by Susan Harada

What Green Party strategists dubbed the sprint to the finish line —
the third phase of their campaign strategy — began on a quiet morning two days into the new year. While many Canadians were still slip-
ping back into post-holiday routines, the Green Party was already in
high gear with a simultaneous two-city launch of its 2006 election platform. At the InterContinental Hotel in Montreal, the party's Quebec
spokesperson, Claude Genest, was joined by fellow Green candidates to
unveil the platform before a small group of journalists. In Ottawa's
Lord Elgin Hotel, party leader Jim Harris and a handful of local Green
candidates took the spotlight. With cameras rolling in both cities, the
double launch began at precisely 10:30 a.m. "Happy new year," Harris
said. "Happy *green* new year."

In many respects, Harris and the party had much to feel happy
about at that moment. With the release of their 35-page, 216-point policy document entitled *We Can*, the Greens claimed the distinction of
being the second of the larger political parties to unveil a complete platform package.[1] The Ottawa launch was going live on a number of television networks, and journalists from some major media outlets were
present. In fact, the party's media team had already pulled off a coup —
in that morning's *Globe and Mail* was a 740-word pre-launch news story
that highlighted portions of the platform, as "obtained" by the paper.[2] It
was a striking difference from the attention garnered by the Greens during the campaign of 2004, when the release of the party's platform drew
barely a ripple of response in the mainstream media.

If the outward success of the platform launch was a marker of how
far the party, which not long before was routinely dismissed as "fringe,"
had come, other details served as a reminder of how far it still had to go.
In politics, the ability to fill the room, especially for something as crucial as a televised platform launch, counts for a lot. As Harris observed

during a strategy session, "it all comes back to room size," in terms of planning campaign events.[3] And though they were enthusiastic, the Green Party candidates, their families, and the party workers present that morning barely chased away the echoes in a meeting room that could comfortably hold one hundred. The otherwise empty expanse of carpet was broken only by a small media area set up in front of a podium and a Green Party backdrop.

More telling than the optics of the event, however, was the content of the formal question-and-answer session following Harris's twenty-five-minute platform presentation. Of the thirteen questions posed by journalists, only three could be considered platform-related. The rest mainly dealt with the state of the party's electoral fortunes to date. Harris was asked about the Greens' seeming lack of momentum just past the halfway point of the 2006 campaign. He was questioned about where they could find new support, and about whether the election would be a "make or break" event that would spell the end for the party if it didn't make significant gains. They were blunt questions of the sort routinely asked of any leader of any party of significance. And they underscored the great expectations that many had of the Green Party for the 2006 election. There were external assumptions about, and internal pressures for, concrete signs that the party was continuing the upward curve it had embarked upon one and a half years earlier during the 2004 campaign. That campaign was the watershed when the Greens broke out of the pack of other small political parties in a number of significant ways: it fashioned itself into a national party, geographically speaking, by running candidates in each of the 308 ridings across the country; it parlayed its failure to be included in the nationally televised federal leaders' debates into a successful public relations campaign; it captured attention when it polled as high as 7 percent in some national surveys of decided voters; and it capitalized on that attention by convincing some 582,000 Canadians to cast a ballot for Green candidates, well up from the approximately 104,000 who voted Green in 2000.

Thus, the Greens went into the election of 2006 burdened with proving that its 2004 results were not a political fluke, that Canadians had not simply parked their votes with a "novelty" party until they felt ready to gravitate back to their true political home bases. Notwithstanding Harris's exhortation that the party was on track in 2006 to elect Green MPs, realistic expectations were not necessarily that it would win seats — the Greens lack a geographically concentrated base of support, and so the first-past-the-post electoral system is a major obstacle to their dream of installing

Greens in the House of Commons. His other claim, however, that the party would win 1 million votes, did not seem, to members, to be quite so out of reach. The thinking was that if they could shoot up from a mere 0.8 percent of the vote in 2000 to 4.3 percent in 2004, it was not wildly unreasonable to believe that they could hit the 7 percent mark (approximately 1 million votes) in 2006. After all, campaign finance reform gave the party more money in its coffers, and hence more staff at its disposal, than ever before. The mainstream media were taking the Greens more seriously, based on the 2004 breakthrough. And though support seemed to undulate as the campaign unfolded, national polling data suggested that on average, the party had approximately 6 percent of decided voters onside. There was also a large pool of Canadians — those who hadn't bothered to cast a ballot in the previous election — from which the Greens hoped they could draw new support by offering themselves up as a credible and fresh alternative.

But as the numbers began pouring in from ridings across the country three weeks after the party's optimistic start to the new year, it became clear that the Green momentum of 2004 had slowed. Final results showed that the party pulled off something remarkable — it held on to its vote. Nevertheless, in light of the great expectations many had going into the campaign, that achievement was nearly overshadowed by what it didn't do. It didn't repeat the great leap forward of 2004; it didn't reach its stated goal of 1 million votes. At 4.5 percent, or approximately 666,000 votes, the Greens did manage to increase their share, but the increase was tiny — 0.2 percent, or approximately 84,000 votes. In a sense, the Greens were a victim of their own 2004 success; anything short of a repeat performance could be perceived as failure. Certainly, post-election headlines were a reflection of that: "Greens fail despite electoral changes," according to the *National Post*. "Glass half-full for Green Party," from the *Leader-Post* (Regina). In the *Edmonton Journal*, "Breakthrough eludes party, even in Canada's greenest province."[4]

Other Green election night triumphs also seemed counterbalanced by setbacks. For example, the number of Green candidates who won at least 10 percent of the vote rose from three in 2004 to eight in 2006,[5] but in two ridings where hopes had been particularly high — Saanich–Gulf Islands and Victoria — candidates Andrew Lewis and Ariel Lade actually lost support.[6] The party made inroads in Alberta, and candidate Sean Maw in Wild Rose became the first federal Green candidate to pull off a second-place finish,[7] but next door in B.C., a province considered one of the party's strongholds, the Greens' vote share dropped. Green Party Leader Jim Harris opted not to run against NDP Leader Jack Layton in Toronto-

Danforth again, and did marginally better in Beaches–East York, but he still finished well behind the top three candidates.[8]

All told, beyond the major feat of holding their vote, the Greens' results seemed to be a series of small steps forward and small steps back. It leaves the story of the Green Party's 2006 election bid to be read as one of both accomplishment and disappointment. That can mainly be attributed to the way the larger drama played out: the political climate that shifted the electoral priorities of Canadian voters and hence the fortunes of the major parties was a force beyond the Greens' control. But it can also be said that facets of the Green Party's 2006 fate were of its own making, its storyline shaped by internecine struggles common to any party trying to carve out a meaningful and principled space for itself within the electoral system. As is the case for small, activist parties accustomed to operating on the outer edges, the Greens have never really been forced to confront and resolve their internal divisions about what that space should look like in practice. Until now. If the taste of success in 2004 deposited the party at a significant crossroads in its efforts to determine a sustainable Green political path, the results of 2006 underscored the necessity of finally choosing a direction.

THE GREEN PLATFORM

For years the Green Party has been dogged by the label "single-issue," its members often dismissed as being idealistic left-wing activists who lacked solid solutions for change. For Green parties the world over, the challenge lies in translating ideals into a practical political program, one that could balance long-term ecological goals with short-term, more politically pragmatic, objectives. The German Greens are a good case in point. Over the years, they have broadened their platform to reflect the shifting priorities of the electorate, taking on such issues as job creation and a shorter work week. They developed a "social environmental" focus in an effort to move beyond a purely "natural environmental" one.[9] In Canada, the Greens also evolved out of ecological activism to develop a broad "social environmental" focus. Under former leader Joan Russow, for example, the Greens linked the environment to a wide range of issues, including human rights, poverty, health care, international law, and globalization, and hammered out specific solutions in those policy areas.[10] But it was not until the Greens parlayed their 308 candidates into headlines did the party's platform succeed in getting more mainstream attention.

In 2004, the Green Party of Canada took a page from the U.K. Green party's strategy book and positioned itself as being neither left nor right. The U.K. Greens resisted conventional political labelling largely to maintain a "distinctive Green image."[11] In Canada it can be said that the Greens tried to resist labelling in order to *create* a distinctive Green image, one with potential for more broad-based appeal. It put forward a fiscally conservative program, while reinforcing its traditionally progressive positions on social policy issues, from support of same-sex marriage to restarting the national housing program. The platform contained a mix of largely general solutions in numerous social policy areas, alongside more contentious environmentally focused proposals that involved tax-shifting — funding income tax cuts with revenue generated from "pollution taxes" — and voluntary compliance from industry through tax breaks for companies meeting certified environmental performance standards (ISO 9000 and ISO 14000).[12]

The overall effort was seen by many critics (both internal and external) as being a shift to the right, coupled with a weak environmental agenda. Russow viewed it as a betrayal of Green principles.[13] And two major Canadian environmental organizations rated the NDP higher than the Greens on the environmental front. The Sierra Club of Canada, for example, found the platform lacked depth: "The Green Party has a strong environmental commitment, but, whether through lack of experience in government or through a shortage of policy experts, the Green Platform is not as specific and does not make as many detailed commitments on as many topics as either the New Democrats or the Bloc Québécois."[14]

The Greens did not want to make that particular misstep again. In drafting the 2006 platform, staff consulted widely, seeking advice from organizations such as the Sierra Club, the Pembina Institute, and the David Suzuki Foundation, as well as a number of social justice and health care groups. The environment was placed prominently front and centre in the platform document, instead of being scattered throughout, as it had been in 2004. Taking external and internal criticisms into account, the party yanked the contentious tax breaks for ISO-certified companies. It kept the tax shift, but tempered it with a pledge to review it every three years in order to "readjust fiscal imbalances."

Being seen as a party capable of handling fiscal issues was important to the Greens; in fact, they brought in a financial expert in the fall of 2005 to help them build their document. It resulted in a platform that the party says made approximately $96 billion in promises, offset by about $79 billion in savings from such things as emission permits, select tax increases, and the cancellation of the Liberals' November 2005 mini-budget. In other words, it was looking at $17.6 billion in new spending over five years, compared to the $57.4 billion it had promised in 2004.[15] The Greens reaffirmed their support of meeting and exceeding the Kyoto targets and also offered up two broad initiatives — a promise to enshrine the right of Canadians to a healthy environment in the Charter of Rights, and a pledge to measure the country's success rate in more than purely economic terms through the introduction of a "Canadian Index of Well-being," which would also gauge such things as quality of life, health, and education. They promised to fix the fiscal imbalance between the federal and provincial levels of government, as well as tackle cash flow inequities to municipalities. They pledged to use the notwithstanding clause, along with federal spending and the Canada Health Act, to prevent two-tier health care, although the platform document did not offer up concrete solutions to fix the current troubles plaguing the health care system in Canada.[16]

The Greens' outreach and consultations were successful in that the resulting platform earned them top marks from the Sierra Club in 2006, six points more than the NDP scored. "The Green Party has substantially improved its platform since 2004. The policy proposals are, for the most part, well conceived and grounded in much of the existing policy debate," the organization observed. "The only negative comment is that the platform intrudes into provincial jurisdiction on issues of forest policy (such as banning clear-cutting), reflecting the fact that the policy capacity of the Party is still evolving."[17] It was an endorsement that gave credibility to the Greens. And it certainly softened the blunt criticism of the *Ottawa Citizen*'s editorial board. The board met with Harris a week after he launched the platform. Its assessment? The platform had some "interesting" planks, some "misguided" ones, and some "enormous gaps" in policy. The board members' take on the ability of Harris and the Greens to translate vision into practical political reality? "Getting a straight answer from Mr. Harris is like trying to put your thumb on mercury," they wrote. "It would be nice to have a few Green voices in Parliament to represent the views of those in political wilderness. But they are nowhere near reaching the maturity required to govern."[18]

Reaction to the Greens' 2006 platform was, in a sense, an echo of the party's electoral performance. In many respects, it took strides forward in terms of its policy proposals. It also took a few steps back.

THE CAMPAIGN STRATEGY AND TOOLS

At a time when the idea of electoral reform is gaining currency, and when the inclusion of *all* voices in political discourse is increasingly seen as crucial in the exercise of democracy, the role the mainstream media play during election campaigns has come under growing scrutiny. It's a development the Green Party successfully tapped into in 2004 and again in 2006 by strategically transforming the volume of coverage it gets, and its exclusion from the televised federal leaders' debates, into a symbol of democracy denied. "Mr. Harris wonders what it's going to take before the mainstream media start to give his party respect. It's a fair question," wrote *Globe and Mail* columnist John Ibbitson. "Perhaps it's time that the gatekeepers in the media started giving the fifth party the respect that it has already demonstrated it deserves."[19]

That sort of respect was not forthcoming from the consortium of major broadcasters that controlled the 2005–06 televised leaders' debates. Once again, Harris and the Green Party were left out. It should be noted that arranging leaders' debates is a tricky exercise of diplomacy at the best of times; negotiations over the rules can be excruciating. Add to that the consortium's desire to shape a program both entertaining *and* informative, while balancing individual party demands designed to maximize advantages for themselves and minimize any for the rest. Was the consortium about to be swayed by arguments that democracy would be better served if a party running 308 candidates — the party of choice for 582,247 Canadians in 2004 — were allowed to put its policies and platform forward before a national audience? It was not. "The format is set for the debates," the consortium's spokesperson said. "These things happen on a very short time frame."[20]

So, as they did in 2004, the Greens put their case to the public and found a sympathetic audience. Approximately fifty thousand people signed the party's online petition, asking that the Greens be included.[21] There were numerous editorials and letters to the editor calling for Harris's inclusion. Harris penned an opinion piece for the *National Post*, challenging the consortium's assertion that tradition dictated that a party must have parliamentary representation in order to be part of the debate.[22] The Greens formally complained to the CRTC and also called for the debates to be taken out of the hands of the consortium and administered instead by an organization such as Elections Canada. It changed nothing in terms of getting Harris up to the podium for the four nights of debate. But it successfully lined up many members of the public and the media behind the

Greens once more. And that, in the end, counts for something; sympathetic headlines during a campaign are almost the equivalent of free political ad space.

So there was a benefit to the debate about the debates. Nevertheless, its exclusion was a blunt reminder to the party that it still existed in a political grey zone — not one of the political "others" anymore, but not really a major player. The issue of money reinforced that point. The Greens had more of it than they'd ever had. Changes in election financing rules gave them $1.75 annually for each vote they won in 2004 — slightly more than $1 million in public funding, payable in quarterly chunks. It sounds like a lot until the math is done. Subtract the approximately $500,000 the party had to repay its creditors from the 2004 campaign.[23] Subtract the hundreds of thousands of dollars it took to set up basic infrastructure to enable the Greens to become more organized. In years past, the volunteer-based party largely shut down in between elections, but there was recognition that it couldn't afford to do that anymore if it wanted to grow. So, money was earmarked for a number of party-building items: salaries for twenty staff members, up from one full-time staff person three years ago; the party leader's $50,000 annual salary (as of July 2005, the party finally began paying its leader); operational costs for necessary items previously beyond the reach of the cash-strapped party, such as additional computer equipment; the 2004 national convention; and revenue-sharing with the party's provincial divisions and electoral district associations.

In the end, as one party member observed, there was little left in the war chest. The Greens had to borrow again to mount their 2005–06 effort. They secured $692,000 in loans,[24] and campaign fundraising brought in about $270,000 more. The election budget was set at approximately $700,000 — about $200,000 more than was spent in 2004, but it still had to be spread pretty thinly over the course of the longer campaign.

The campaign goals were relatively straightforward: use the Internet more effectively, both internally and externally; attract 308 high-quality candidates; support local campaigns through Green Party regional centres; run a more high profile national leader's tour; and maximize media coverage. Overall, the Greens aimed to run a more professional campaign. And that meant reinventing the political wheel in many cases, as they adopted basic electoral techniques that more established parties have used for years: professional media training for the leader and key spokespeople, for example, and tracking support in order to get out the vote. National campaign manager George Read took a page from former

U.S. presidential candidate Howard Dean's grassroots campaign book, and for the first time, the party began to track support across the country with the help of a new Internet-based management tool. Read also pushed to use the party website as more than just a passive electronic bulletin board. Total hits to the site and pages visited were analyzed regularly, with an eye to increasing interactivity through strategic placement of the spots where people could volunteer, get a sign, make a donation, or sign the online debate petition.

The Greens focused more attention on the selection of their candidates. In 2004, they were determined to establish a beachhead by running a full slate. But the pressure to find 308 people willing and able to run as Green candidates was immense; the hurdles potential candidates had to clear in order to get party endorsement were not set particularly high. Recruiting was made easier by the 2004 success, however, and so the simple one-page candidate application form was significantly toughened for 2006, now asking for detailed personal histories including bankruptcies and legal proceedings. Applicants had to write a short essay explaining why they wanted to run for the Greens; they also had to sign a waiver allowing the party to do background checks and access information filed with Elections Canada. In ridings with registered electoral district associations — approximately 130 in total when the campaign began — candidates were selected locally. All others were selected by the party's national organizing office. The national office also retained control in the selection process across the country through its power to accept or reject candidate applications. The dragnet didn't catch the candidate who planned an out-of-country vacation for the duration of the campaign, or the one who was replaced "because he failed to meet internal deadlines for filing paperwork" shortly after it was discovered he was facing an impaired driving charge.[25] But, according to the party, setting the bar higher did help identify serious, quality candidates and resulted in the recruitment of a larger number of people who had a track record in their communities and who actually lived in the riding in which they were running.[26]

The Greens also shifted their approach to their candidates *during* the campaign. If a professional electoral effort is a goal for a party based on grassroots democratic principles and doing politics differently, the balance between the extremes of total top-down control on the one hand and just cutting loose 308 candidates to do their own thing on the other must be approached with caution. It is an issue of centralization versus decentralization, and the Greens were forced to grapple with it on a number of fronts during the campaign. For example, how could they ensure candidates stayed on-message without impinging on their freedom to speak their minds?[27] The party recognized that candidates would be scrutinized more closely by voters and journalists alike, so the national team tried to run a more cohesive messaging campaign for the 2006 election. It set up a document download site for candidates and updated it daily with numerous offerings — among them, recordings of Harris, so candidates could find out what he was saying on any given subject, and speaking points on contentious subjects such as same-sex marriage. Were the speaking points mandatory? Read says his marching orders to candidates consisted of just four words: vision, hope, compassion, and honesty. "Anybody who starts their speeches or their discussions from 'vision, hope, compassion, honesty' and speaks their own truth and adheres to their values is going to be fine," he says. "And that's what makes us different from the other political parties."[28]

Centralized control, however, is more than just a question of riding herd on candidates' words — it's also a question of where the power to build and shape the party is vested. One of the Greens' most significant debates over centralization saw national party priorities versus local campaign priorities go head to head over the issue of money. The party squabbled for months over how to divide up the spoils of the 2004 election — the $1.75 earned for each Green vote. Some pushed to divide the money between the 308 candidates and ridings. Some thought the division should be regional. Still others wanted the funds to stay in the hands of the central party. It took more than a year to settle the question. Finally, after a mail-in ballot in September 2005, members agreed to a revenue-sharing formula that divided up the money three ways — between the central party, each registered electoral district association, and the provincial divisions. It was a uniquely Green solution. It was building the party from the bottom up. Everybody got something. But to some, that didn't make for smart tactical politics. Opponents of the revenue-sharing argued that at a time when the party was trying to build its national presence, a well-funded central infrastructure that could support a strong national leader's tour and an effective central communications team, as well as provide well-researched campaign materials, was essential. "Some people portray it as being anti-grassroots, and I say 'no, I *am* grassroots,'" says David Chernushenko. As both the Ottawa Centre candidate and one of the party's deputy leaders, he says he looked at the issue from both points of view and concluded that "the best thing we can do for any of our candidates, even our strong ones, is to have a strong central campaign. ... I still think that's the best way to grow the party."[29]

There was disagreement, too, over the party's regional campaign strategy that spread money and energy evenly over four urban hubs, rather than concentrating resources in the few ridings where the Greens might actually make a significant gain.[30] Money was divided instead between new offices in Vancouver, Calgary, Toronto, and Montreal to aid every regional candidate. According to Read, it was done "to increase our support overall in [those] areas, as opposed to saying 'listen, this riding is going to be the breakthrough riding.'" Media team manager Dermod Travis, who quit shortly after the 2006 election, had this to say about the party's thinking: "If you want to win a seat, then you're going to have to change your strategy. There's going to have to be very clear focusing and targeting in on ridings that can be won and they need to be worked … the day after the election. The Green Party will not win a seat by dividing its resources."[31] His recourse was to shape the leader's national tour strategically. So while Harris touched down in every province as well as Nunavut over the course of the campaign, he spent the most time in Ontario, Alberta, British Columbia, and Quebec — places where Travis figured there might be some extra return on the investment of the leader's time.

In addition to the regional strategy, however, the party did devote a little more than half of its $700,000 campaign budget to Travis's media team. Approximately $150,000 of that paid for the leader's tour — travel, accommodation, and the salaries of the two full-time staff who accompanied Harris on his six dozen campaign stops. There was money for brochures, signs, and some print advertising, but not enough for television or radio ads. Most of the rest of the budget went to media staff salaries, the goal being to carve out a profile and maximize coverage. The media team sent out nearly twice as many news releases and advances in 2006 as it did in 2004. Harris held thirty news conferences, compared to the five held in 2004. He was the first party leader to visit every province and the North. And while national media coverage wasn't plentiful, the party received more attention from regional and local media outlets than it used to, as Harris moved across the country trying to stir up support for his party and its platform.

THE LEADER'S NATIONAL TOUR

The Green Party began its 2005–06 campaign without its leader. Jim Harris was busy with his other job. In addition to heading the Green

Party, he is also a professional speaker and management consultant. His website touts him as one of "North America's foremost authors and thinkers on leadership and change."[32] And so it happened that on the November day that the Liberal government fell, Harris was in Germany on a previously booked speaking engagement, talking to representatives of a German company about "change." Back in Canada, Chernushenko was tapped to launch the Greens' election effort with an evening news conference on Parliament Hill. In Montreal, the media team was already in high gear, fielding a record number of first-day media calls: sixty, compared to the two received when the writ was dropped in 2004. In Ottawa, the membership team was working overtime to finalize a full roster of 308 candidates. In Calgary, Read set in motion the party's plan for the next fifty-five days. The Greens seemed to be in a good position going into the campaign — according to national polls, they had the popular support of 4 to 6 percent of decided voters. And by Day 2, Harris was back in the country to launch his national leader's tour from Toronto, before heading off for St. John's to throw down the gauntlet on the issue of commercial seal hunting.

The hunt has long been a point of contention within the Greens. Former leader Joan Russow refused to allow a candidate who supported the hunt to run under the party banner in the St. John's West federal by-election in May 2000.[33] But in 2002, the party voted to endorse sealing provided the entire animal was used (Russow had left the previous year). According to Harris, that motion was pushed through by a minority, against the wishes of the majority who couldn't attend the national policy convention. He, in turn, vowed to reverse the policy — and that successfully happened two years later at the 2004 convention. At the same time, Harris was determined to ensure that small groups couldn't hijack party policy anymore. He was instrumental in pushing through a motion that all policy passed at a convention must also be approved through a subsequent mail-in ballot open to all voting members. The anti-sealing resolution supported by Harris wasn't put to that test — but all future policy resolutions would be subject to the new rule.[34]

Framed in that context, Harris's announcement in St. John's that the Green Party would oppose commercial sealing — not through an outright ban but by cutting off federal subsidies to the hunt and diverting the money into developing sustainable jobs — was a loaded one, regionally. The party's Newfoundland and Labrador organizer quit. "What originally attracted my attention to the Green Party of Canada was its constitutional commitment to the concept of 'decentralization'; the idea that people living in a community could and should be the best determinants of their 'social reality,'" wrote Lori-Ann Martino in a news release. "In practice, however, the current leadership of the Green Party fails to live up to this stated commitment."[35]

Harris moved on to Charlottetown, where he signed a pledge to "campaign with the utmost respect and dignity for Canadian voters and the points of view of all political parties";[36] to Montreal, where he weighed in on the debate over the Conservatives' promised GST cuts, saying Greens would reduce the tax on healthy and environmentally friendly products, increase it on harmful products, and eliminate it altogether on items such as books, children's clothing, and school supplies. As he made his way from province to province, Harris tailored his messages to his audiences. He launched three of the party's mini-platforms from carefully chosen locations. In Iqaluit, where the impact of climate change is a pressing concern, he announced the Green Party's Kyoto Plan. From Windsor, Ontario, where air pollution is a major issue, he released the national cancer strategy — a five-year plan to reduce environmental and health hazards that contribute to the disease. And in Calgary, a city built on oil, the party's national energy platform was unveiled. It called for an investment in renewable energy for resale, to be balanced by measures such as lower taxes on green investment. It also called for an end to federal subsidies for fossil fuel sectors.

The energy platform garnered headlines, but not the kind the Greens were looking for. "Petroleum producers shrug off Greens' energy program," wrote the *Edmonton Journal*. And in the *Calgary Herald*, "Greens release energy policy: Petroleum producers say plan out of date." The reports quoted the Canadian Association of Petroleum Producers as asserting that the industry is not subsidized, and in fact is taxed at a higher rate than are other corporations.[37] Fossil fuel sector taxes and subsidies are not quite that black and white, as it turns out,[38] but by that point, the Greens were preoccupied with something else — the very public airing of their ongoing internal squabbles. Their squabbles ranged from the seemingly trivial to the more substantial, but they all spoke to a troubling party fissure created by members unable to agree on how, or even whether, to reconcile Green grassroots political beliefs with mainstream pragmatic political tactics.

THE CONFLICT WITHIN

On December 13, 2005, the party was featured on the CBC's television news program *The National* in an in-depth profile by journalist Leslie MacKinnon. "There's something ... about the Green Party that quite frankly we in the media would cover almost obsessively if it happened in any mainstream party," she reported. "The Green Party has been deeply divided."[39] MacKinnon's interviews with some "dissidents" catalogued their deep unhappiness with Harris and with the top-down way in which they felt the grassroots Greens were being managed. The profile provided a glimpse into internal divisions within a party that had, up to that point, largely managed to maintain a public image of being an idealistic group, committed to doing politics differently.

Six days later there were more national headlines, this time in the *Globe and Mail.* Canadian Press journalist Dennis Bueckert reported that Elections Canada was looking into alleged federal election law violations by Harris after receiving a complaint from the party's former assistant national organizer. The story was picked up by media outlets across the country.[40] What followed was a tangle of claims and counter-claims with respect to the credibility of the source of the allegations; the Green Party announced it would pursue legal action against the former members quoted in the report unless they retracted their statements; and there were heated internal debates when some members saw the legal threats as a betrayal — a grassroots democratic party's attempts to silence criticism through libel chill. In the end, this much seemed clear: according to the party, the only violations were "regulatory in nature" — some $600 worth of phone calls, office rent, and office supplies related to Harris's 2004 leadership campaign that he had neglected to report.[41] According to the party, Elections Canada had dismissed the remaining eleven out of fourteen allegations,[42] and the Green Party's threatened lawsuits against its former members were not pursued.

What's also clear is that the mainstream media attention had lifted the lid of the Green Party's Pandora's box. The messy internal struggles that had been fought out in the past few years largely through email and online sites subsequently escaped into the larger public domain. It was the sort of affair that has plagued many a political party, and it might have been largely ignored a few years ago when few had interest in what the Greens were up to. But coming as it did during the campaign, and at a point when the party was promoting itself as a serious and growing political alternative, it made Canadians pause and take a second look at the Greens and the man who was leading them.

Jim Harris began his political life as a member of the Conservative Party but gravitated to the Greens in the mid-eighties. He ran under the party banner in a number of municipal, provincial, and federal elections, first made a bid for the national leadership against Russow in 1997, and finally won the post in 2003. Under his leadership the Green Party experienced great change, both externally and internally. The party secured funding through private loans for the 2004 election, made electoral inroads, and presented a more professional political face to the Canadian public. Internally, however, there was turmoil, as members grappled with the challenge of redefining priorities in the face of some political success and the prospect of attaining more. A number of the party's executive — some, members with long Green histories, others, more freshly minted Greens — resigned or were forced out both before and after the 2004 election. New people arrived on the scene, not all of them carrying solid Green credentials in their back pockets.[43] Harris and some of those around him became the lightning rod for all manner of charges with respect to the shape and direction of the party's process and policy. It was perhaps inevitable that the conflict would take on a personal tone at times. Among other things, Harris's leadership style and his impact on morale was bitterly criticized.[44]

One of the party's significant internal eruptions happened in early 2005 and centred on the use of the party's Living Platform, an online interactive communications tool. It was set up as a resource to help shape platform direction and also became a forum for party members and the public to discuss policy. As tensions grew in the months following the 2004 election, frank comments about internal party matters were posted. Senior staff shut down the site temporarily, removed some material, and disallowed anonymous postings, and these actions deepened the rift. On one side were those convinced it was a case of a handful of people stifling Green grassroots democracy and open debate. On the other were those who maintained it was an attempt to protect the party's reputation and avoid getting into legal trouble. It can be difficult to push past the inevitable personality clashes that exist in any political party to get to the core of the matter. Nevertheless, the conflict over the Living Platform is illustrative of the polarization that intensified under Harris's tenure.

So, too, are resignations of members such as Kate Holloway. In early 2005 Holloway was suspended from her position as fundraising chair, and she subsequently resigned from both the party's federal council and her nomination as Toronto Centre candidate.[45] Harris attributes events connected to Holloway's suspension to an "individual personality conflict."[46] She believes that what happened to her happened within the larger context of an unwelcome change ushered in under the Harris leadership. "There was a perception before that if you did things democratically nothing would happen. That ... getting Greens organized was like herding cats," Holloway says. In her view, it was an erroneous perception that became a smokescreen for attempts to overly centralize party control, putting "expedience before democracy within the party in order to achieve the successes of the 2004 breakthrough."[47]

Membership Chair Steve Kisby saw it as yet another "flare-up" of the type that he says has plagued the party every few years, not just under Harris — flare-ups sparked by party "underperformance" that often only concluded when one side or the other eventually lost a particular round and quit. "[Harris] wanted a national executive that was also very aggressive in organizing and aggressive at putting the green message out.... He was definitely of the philosophy that leadership also meant leadership in organizing as well," says Kisby. "The party has always had this debate as to how active the central office should be at organizing. Some people have always felt that decentralization means not being so active. So there was some tension there. [But] someone like that was a breath of fresh air to the people who wanted to see the party do better and get more organized, and if that meant being a little more centralized then so be it."[48]

Personality politics? Expedient democracy? Whichever way it's perceived, there is an underlying theme, and it runs through much of the party's internal debate, whether it be over how to divide the million-dollar-plus public funding cheque, which policy paths to follow, whether there should be restrictions on online communications sites, or what sort of reaction to critical comments reported in the mainstream media is in the party's best interests. It's all linked to party identity, and it all ties into organization — it's a conflict that comes into clearer focus when viewed through the lens of the patterns that have marked the growth of the Green Party in Canada, as well as of Green parties in Europe.

THE ROOTS OF GREEN CONFLICT

Twenty-two years ago, the Green Party of Canada made its entrance onto the federal political stage by running sixty candidates scattered across six provinces in the 1984 federal election.[49] The newly minted party was led by Trevor Hancock, a prime force behind the forging of a national green ecological political entity based on the principles of environmental sustainability, peace, social justice, and participatory democracy. That last principle included electoral reform and the way politics was approached, as well as the way the party was structured. The national party was built as a bottom-up, grassroots organization with a decentralized structure, similar to other Green parties that emerged on the international scene in the eighties. The organizational structure reflected the rejection of traditional political party methods. Green parties throughout Europe, for example, "were distinguished from other established party families by their ecologically oriented disposition, an anti-professional, participatory and decentralized attitude toward party organization, and a close link to the new social movements of the 1960s and 1970s."[50]

From the beginning, the tensions inherent in maintaining a political party with a decentralized structure, while at the same time struggling to find a way to operate meaningfully and efficiently within a traditional political system, divided the Green Party of Canada. Not long after the 1984 election, a frustrated Hancock and party executive quit en masse. "We wanted a party where you could actually make decisions and not endlessly debate them," he says. "For example, one of the things that we went round and round and round about was operating on consensus. Which is fine in small groups but you start to try to do that at a national or provincial level and that becomes impossible, partly because you don't have all the party members in the room. And then it got into, 'if it's not consensus, what is it?'"[51]

The divisions in the young Canadian party were similar to those in the German Green party, factions labelled by political analysts as the fundamentalists ("fundis") and the realists ("realos"). In broad strokes, realists set their sights on attaining and maintaining political power in order to further Green goals and aren't adverse to employing pragmatic means to do so; fundamentalists believe that to organize the party with electoral gain as a priority would compromise the principles upon which the party was built.[52] As a realo, Hancock's view was as follows:

> To a certain extent if you think that Green values need to be expressed in the political process you have to play that game. We didn't make up the rules but the rules are there. So, for example, you have to be a party, you have to register, you have to have a certain number of candidates … because if you don't you don't even get to play

the game. Now the fundis would say "we don't want to play the game," but then if you don't want to play the game then you're not a party. You're not playing politics. You're doing something else, you're a movement.

With the departure of Hancock and the executive, the party fundis held sway. Steve Kisby, currently the Green Party's membership chair, was with the party in those early days. He says Hancock and the executive "wanted a much more traditional party.... However our rank and file membership wanted something much more decentralized. They didn't even want a leader, which was a big debate in the early eighties because electoral law requires you have a leader." Whether they wanted a leader or not, the Greens went through several over the next decade. As Kisby recalls, one leader was chosen during that time specifically to be a "background" leader, while the party's regional spokespeople took on leadership roles in terms of putting the party's platform forward publicly. That, too, somewhat followed the pattern set at that time by a number of international Green parties. As political analyst Jon Burchell noted, "Although the parties have had to face the practicalities of needing both a public front for the media and a reference point for contact and dissemination of information, they shunned the notion of a single party leader, opting instead for elected party spokespersons."[53]

But by the end of the decade, the Green Party of Canada phased out its spokesperson system and gave the national leader the job of national spokesperson. It was a pragmatic move, largely motivated by the need to accommodate media demands. According to Kisby, a major reason for the shift to allow the leader to speak for the party was based on the fact that the Greens wanted to fight for inclusion in televised leaders' debates; it found that broadcasters would not even *begin* to consider giving them a place at the podium if "spokespeople" were put forward in place of a leader. It was still a uniquely Green job description, however, in that being leader did not confer extra power in areas such as setting policy or party direction. The leader was still leader largely in name only.[54]

By the time Wendy Priesnitz was recruited in mid-1996 to be the party's fifth leader in twelve years, the Greens had managed to maintain a growing presence in every federal election since its first in 1984, running sixty-eight candidates in 1988 and seventy-nine in 1993.[55] But growth was incremental and the party was still labouring under the burden that all small parties in Canada carry. It was tagged with the label "fringe," relegated to the outer edges of the political scene, and largely ignored by the mainstream media. There were fundraising problems and few active members — and the internal debate over how to strike a comfortable balance between centralization and decentralization was still unresolved. Even as a proponent of the grassroots organizational model, Priesnitz says she ran into internal roadblocks in her desire to help move the Greens forward, something she attributes partially to the senior party membership still not really wanting a leader. Leadership, she says, was equated to power, and she felt there was a fear of power, or perhaps "a misunderstanding of what power can do. You know, power to work with people and power to create change rather than power *over* other people. So there certainly were some issues around that."[56]

Priesnitz saw policy development as one area that needed to be strengthened if the party hoped to move forward. At the time, she says, "there was no policy, there was no talking about policy, except that every candidate kind of just … made it up as they went along and said the party stood for the things they wanted it to stand for, which got them through most situations in the early days." So she worked with the governing council to develop a coherent policy development structure through the creation of a policy committee and shadow cabinet. Some could interpret the structure as a move toward central control; she saw it as a way to involve more people in the policy process. By all accounts, hers was a tension-filled tenure. She resigned just months after taking the position. Her sudden resignation was characterized this way, in an Alberta Green Party newsletter:

> Wendy's resignation indicates that she was disenchanted because she was unable to make the changes within the party that she wanted.… My personal feelings are that Wendy tried to move too far, too fast. In doing so, she encountered some resistance from long-time members of the party. This probably would have eventually dissipated, if she had given personality conflicts time to iron themselves out.[57]

Joan Russow's tenure as Green Party leader between April 1997 and February 2001 was no less troubled. Russow was a policy-focused academic active on the international front and acutely conscious of the Canadian party's role within the larger global Green movement. She stepped down (and eventually joined the NDP) citing disillusionment with the Green movement as a whole; specifically, the German Greens' policy shift with respect to NATO's involvement in Kosovo came as a major blow.[58] But she also faced policy-centred conflict closer to home. According to Russow, there was often trouble when she took action based on her belief that being leader meant ensuring that policy formally endorsed by the party should be implemented. "Some people felt that I was too dictatorial in a way. But it was the policy that I was always talking about. The policy was guiding me," she says. "You can have all the principles you want. But you've got to make sure you know how to operationalize. And you have policy that will bring about the realization of these principles."[59]

The pattern of internal conflict intensified with the election of Harris as leader. And while some party members may view the troubles of the last few years as simply a rite of passage — a stretch of rough water to be expected by any growing party that finds itself under greater scrutiny by the mainstream media — that provides only a partial explanation. It has been argued that the sorts of issues "new politics" Green parties face, how they deal with them, and how they set up structures to meet both internal and external challenges say much about the "new politics" they're actually practising. As one political analyst put it:

> Understanding how a party organizes itself allows us a glimpse into a party's true nature. It permits us to look beyond the persona deliberately cultivated and projected to the voters at election time. It also enables us to look beyond the activists' exalted claims of ideological commitment and purity to see how deep those claims run when faced with the ideology-sullying problems of political survival. The organization of the party is where the rhetoric meets the reality. It is the nexus between beliefs and action.[60]

It can't be said that "rhetoric" meeting "reality" has made for a harmonious storyline for a good many Green parties. Driving the discord have been the fundamentalist and the realist party factions previously mentioned. Over the years, the U.K. Green party, for example, has gone through crippling renewal debates set off by marginal electoral success and devastating failure, and fuelled by internal factions battling over how best to shape the party's path forward. Similarly, the German Greens have weathered both electoral success and setbacks, each step forward and back marked by considerable internal conflict and outright clashes. In their case, however, the success made possible by the German electoral system imposed a resolution of sorts. When real political power through coalition governance came within the Greens' grasp, thanks to Germany's form of proportional representation, the realos were pushed to the fore in the nineties, and many hard-core fundis ended up leaving the party.[61]

For Canada's Greens, operating under the first-past-the-post system, the stakes have never been quite so high. Yet the divisions have been just as real. The party's always-simmering internal conflict was reignited under Harris, first by the push to achieve electoral success in 2004, and then by the desire to match that success and better it in 2006. While party members may not fit quite as neatly into the realist and fundamentalist factions identified in European Green parties, the divisions between those pushing for change and those questioning the nature of the change have been deep and oftentimes bitter. Those divisions took on new life in the run-up to the campaign of 2006 and intensified during those long weeks, diverting energies from what might have been a singular and focused drive to consolidate the party and reinforce its values while building solidly upon the results of 2004.

CONCLUSION

The close of the election of 2006 left members of the Green Party with many things to ponder. They will definitely be pondering the party leadership — party rules dictate that a contest be held every two years, so the position comes open again in August 2006. Immediately following the election, Harris expressed an interest in fighting for the leadership.[62] So did party member Claude Genest.[63] He was drafted by a number of members, and clearly staked out his ground. "I am committed to opening our internal processes to all and doing away with the bunker mentality that so many have taken exception to," he wrote in announcing his bid. "I see the leader's role primarily as that of spokesperson with the administrative and executive powers being returned to the membership and its elected representatives." In his view, the Greens were floundering because they had strayed too far from their party ideal of grassroots democracy in the Harris years.[64]

The second to announce — the party's high-profile deputy leader, David Chernushenko — clearly staked out his ground as well. Though he says he's well aware of the importance of staying true to the party's grassroots origins, Chernushenko has his sights set on further "professionalizing" the Greens' core team. He says he's not content to see the party stay on the sidelines while others steal its ideas, even if it takes another election or two before Green MPs are elected. "We're a political party and we have to remember that and that's something I'll be stating very clearly. We're not a giant NGO … our job ultimately is to get people elected."[65]

The landscape of the Greens' leadership race took on interesting contours in April 2006. Harris announced he would not seek the job again afterall. The internal strife and criticism of his leadership style were not factors, he said. Rather, "it's the intensity of the experience, it's the amount of travel, it's the being away from my wife. It's many things." Harris said he planned to stay on with the Greens in a different capacity — as a member of the campaign committee, chief strategist, media spokesperson, or fundraiser.[66]

Weeks after Harris made his exit, Elizabeth May made her entrance. The long-time environmental activist and former head of the Sierra Club scored national headlines for the Greens when she announced her leadership bid. Backed by a number of political and environmental notables, May also secured Genest's support. He dropped his candidacy and stood by her side when she held her first news conference on Parliament Hill as a Green Party leadership contender. It's a definite shift for someone accustomed to working the process from the outside in, but according to May, now is the time to take a strong stand in the political arena, given the present lack of political will and commitment to environmental and peace issues. "Where's that voice in an election campaign? It's not going to come from NGOs because they're silenced,"[67] she says. "It's not going to come from any of the other political parties. It better come from the Green Party." May says she doesn't believe the party should operate with a hierarchical top-down structure but at the same time strongly feels a Green Party leader must do much more to actively exert influence over coverage of issues than has been the case. "What you really want to do is be a force for change," she says. "But if you're very, very careful and you're just as tepid as any other party leader in terms of being afraid to put a foot wrong for fear of offending someone, you can't do the things that a Green Party leader *could* do in an election campaign."[68]

At the time this chapter was written, then, the two candidates officially in the race for the party leadership were May and Chernushenko. Who the members decide to go with will speak volumes about how the Greens choose to shape their path ahead. And connected to the leadership are myriad other issues the party must resolve; all of those things relate to something observed by the party's campaign manager after election day, when it was clear the Greens had moved forward very little. According to George Read, the Green Party's culture has been changing, and some of its pieces are not working. And because he believes that the values underpinning the culture are solid, for him it is a question of how those values get translated by a culture that is in flux into a workable "action and command structure." In other words, he wondered, for a party that values doing politics differently, "what is the Green Party way that is successful? We don't know."[69]

It's a fundamental question that the party needs to find an answer for, and soon. All parties reach a point in their development where hard choices must be made, and the Greens are at that point, poised as they are on the edge of the possibility that they can become a bigger player. They are being considered more seriously by a good many voters, and they're being scrutinized more closely by journalists. To not face their choices squarely now would be to risk fading back into the tier of secondary Canadian political parties whence they came. The question then becomes how much does that matter, other than to those who toil endlessly for the party, who believe deeply in it, who vote for it? There are many environmentally focused organizations — some, arguably, with a higher profile than the Green Party — to champion the cause between election campaigns. Other political parties, notably the New Democrats as well as the Liberals, have shaped their own environmental policies. Certainly under the current electoral system, and especially in times of close races, Canadians are often motivated to vote strategically — a practice major parties encourage — and that doesn't translate into Green votes. But there is an argument to be made that the presence of the Green Party helped force environmental issues onto the Canadian political agenda in the first place — that the major parties wouldn't have advanced the environmental cause if the Greens hadn't been around to add some political pressure. Indeed, for some party members, it's satisfaction enough that other parties have adopted their ideas in the past, and it will be purpose enough if they continue to do so in future. But for others, the sole reason for being a political party is to get elected in order to push Green policies directly. So the party must determine something crucial: what are the great expectations that it has for itself? It can do so only by coming to a decision as to how much it is willing to compromise in either direction, how much it can *afford* to compromise in either direction. If it cannot, it will never find a meaningful answer to the question "what is the Green Party way?"

NOTES

I would like to extend my sincere thanks to all of the Green Party members and staff, past and present, as well as those outside of the party, who took the time to provide me with factual information, along with their thoughts about the party's growth and future development.

1   The Bloc Québécois released its platform on November 30, 2005. Both the Liberal Party of Canada and the New Democratic Party unveiled their platforms on January 11, 2006. The Conservative Party released its platform on January 13, 2006.

2   G. Galloway, "Greens look beyond environment; Policy platform includes proposals on foreign affairs and health care," *Globe and Mail*, January 2, 2006, A4

3   Harris made his comments during a Green Party strategy session in Montreal on January 1, 2006.

4   K. Patrick, "Greens fail despite electoral changes," *National Post*, January 25, 2006, A7; C. Weeks, "Glass half-full for Green Party," *Leader-Post* (Regina), January 24, 2006, D4; H. Brooymans, "Breakthrough eludes party even in Canada's greenest province," *Edmonton Journal*, January 25, 2006, A4.

5   Candidates in Bruce-Grey–Owen Sound, Calgary Centre-North, Calgary Centre, British Columbia Southern Interior, Wild Rose, Ottawa Centre, Calgary West, and Dufferin-Caledon won more than 10 percent of the vote, making them eligible for a partial reimbursement of some of their campaign costs. Going into the election, the party hoped at least twenty candidates would claim that distinction.

6   Andrew Lewis's vote share dropped from 16.7 percent in 2004 to 9.9 percent in 2006; Ariel Lade's vote share went from 11.69 to 8.1 percent.

7   Sean Maw finished with 10.8 percent of the vote. Although he was well behind Conservative incumbent Myron Thompson (72.2 percent), he had the distinction of beating both the Liberal (9.7 percent) and NDP (7.3 percent) candidates.

8   In 2004, Jim Harris won 5.37 percent in his home riding of Toronto-Danforth. In 2006, to avoid running against Layton again, he parachuted "800 metres to the east" into Beaches–East York. He won 6.1 percent of the vote, behind the Liberal incumbent (40.4 percent) and the NDP (35 percent) and Conservative (18 percent) candidates.

9   For more on the evolution of Green policy, see, for example, E. Bomberg, "The Europeanisation of Green Parties: Exploring the EU's Impact," *West European Politics* 25 (3): 29–50 (2002); and Jon Burchell, *The Evolution of Green Politics: Development & Change within European Green Parties* (London: Earthscan Publications Limited, 2002).

10   See Joan Russow, "The Politics of Exclusion: The Campaign of the Green Party," in *The Canadian General Election of 2000*, ed. Jon H. Pammett and Christopher Dornan (Toronto: Dundurn Press, 2001), 149–63.

11   For more on the U.K. Greens, see, for example, J. Burchell, *The Evolution of Green Politics: Development & Change within European Green Parties* (London: Earthscan Publications Limited, 2002).

12   For more on ISO standards, see, for example, Pollution Probe, "Environmental Non-governmental Organization (ENGO) Participation in National Standards Setting," March 30, 2002. Available at http://www.pollutionprobe.org/Reports/standardssetting.pdf.

13 Joan Russow, "Why I left the Green party: Once dedicated to principles above all else, the Greens have recently lost their way," *Ottawa Citizen*, December 6, 2005, A17 (Opinion).

14 Sierra Club of Canada, "A comparison of the official party platforms on the environment: 2004," June 2004. Available at http://www.sierraclub.ca/national/vote-canada/2004/scc-election-questionnaire.pdf.

15 The Greens led the pack in terms of total promised spending. For details about the other parties' promises, see J. Aubrey, "Conservatives rack up $75 billion in election spending promises," *Ottawa Citizen*, January 15, 2006, A3.

16 The Green Party's 2006 platform is available at http://main.greenparty.ca/platform_2006.html?&MMN_position=141:141.

17 Sierra Club of Canada, "Vote 2006: Analysis of Environmental Platforms of Federal Political Parties," January 2006. Available at http://www.sierraclub.ca/national/vote-canada/2006/scc-vote-2006.pdf.

18 Editorial, "Still in the wilderness. We conclude a series of editorials examining federal party platforms. Today, the Greens," *Ottawa Citizen*, January 13, 2006, A12.

19 J. Ibbitson, "Let's give the Greens some respect," *Globe and Mail*, December 1, 2005, A8.

20 Consortium spokesperson Jason MacDonald made his comments in C. Weeks, "The Greens would lower, raise GST," *Calgary Herald*, December 6, 2005, A6.

21 Green Party of Canada's online petition, available at http://www.greenparty.ca. (Accessed January 28, 2006).

22 J. Harris, "Let the Green Party into the debates," *National Post*, December 7, 2005, A20.

23 See Green Party of Canada Audited Financial Statements December 31, 2004. Available on the Elections Canada website at http://www.elections.ca/fin/rep/2004/green_2004.pdf. The largest loan ($439,754) came from Wayne Crookes, who also happened to be the party's 2004 campaign manager.

24 A large chunk of the 2006 election campaign loans ($400,000) again came from Wayne Crookes. Crookes suddenly resigned as campaign manager, just two weeks before the campaign began.

25 See J. Skikavich, "Vacation to keep Greens' candidate sidelined," *Whitehorse Star*, December 8, 2005, 2; A. McLean, "Green Party dumps candidate," *Edmonton Journal*, December 30, 2005, B4.

26 In 2004, approximately 10 percent of the party's candidates were parachuted into ridings. In 2006, the percentage dropped to 4.

27 As in any political party, candidates often go off-message. For example, in 2004, the Ottawa–West Nepean Green candidate told the *Ottawa Citizen* that he favoured abortion counselling, along with "certain restrictions on abortion." The party's official policy upholds a woman's right to choose. See S. Proudfoot, "Green candidate supports abortion counselling," *Ottawa Citizen*, June 12, 2004, B6.

28 George Read, National Campaign Manager, telephone interview with author, January 15, 2006.

29 David Chernushenko, Ottawa Centre candidate and Green Party deputy leader, telephone interview with author, February 22, 2006.

30 It was a change from 2004, when approximately $50,000 was sunk into Andrew Lewis's Saanich–Gulf Islands riding, for example. He finished only three thousand votes behind the third-place NDP, and combined Green-NDP votes were more than the first-place Conservative share. Nevertheless, the party decided he would not get special funding in 2006. As mentioned previously, his vote share dropped from 16.7 percent in 2004 to 9.9 percent.

31 Dermod Travis, Green Party Media Team Manager, telephone interview with author, January 14, 2006.

32 See http://www.jimharris.ca.

33 See, for example, S. Fairbairn, "Protest prompts Green Party to revisit stance on seal hunt," *The Chronicle-Herald*, April 17, 2004, A10; NTV's Weekly Headline News, "Green Party Wrangle," Newfoundland Broadcasting Co. Ltd., April 18, 2000. Available at http://72.14.207.104/search?q=cache:gu4Iny9GrcoJ:www.ntv.ca/news/viewEntries.php%3Fid%3D244+%22jason+crummey%22+and+%22green+party%22+and+%22seal+hunt%22&hl=en&gl=ca&ct=clnk&cd=10 (accessed February 10, 2006). Russow also had problems with the prospective candidate's support of the controversial Voisey's Bay project.

34 Jim Harris, Green Party leader, telephone interview by author, February 14, 2006.

35 Press Release, "Resignation of Mrs. Lori-Ann Martino from the Green Party of Canada," December 5, 2005. Available at http://openpolitics.ca/tiki-index.php?page=Lori-Ann%20Martino%20quits%20GPC,%202005-12-05&noredirect=y; and Lori-Ann Martino, telephone interview by author, February 21, 2006.

36 Media Release, "Green Party pledge to restore dignity to democracry," December 2, 2005. Available on the Green Party website at http://main.greenparty.ca/index.php?module=announce&ANN_id=82&ANN_user_op=view.

37 See, for example, Canadian Press, "Petroleum producers shrug off Greens' energy program," *Edmonton Journal*, December 22, 2005, A5; and T. Seskus, "Greens release energy policy: Petroleum producers say plan out of date," *Calgary Herald*, December 22, 2005, A4.

38 For details about taxes and subsidies for the resource sector, see, for example, "Improving the Income Taxation of the Resource Sector in Canada," Department of Finance Canada, March 2003. Available at http://www.fin.gc.ca/toce/2003/rsc_e.html.

39 L. MacKinnon, "The Green Machine," CBC, *The National*, December 13, 2005.

40 See, for example, D. Bueckert, "Watchdog in discussion with Greens over financing; Elections Canada responding to complaint over possible violations of election law," *Globe and Mail*, December 19, 2005; Canadian Press, "Violations investigated," *Leader-Post* (Regina), December 19, 2005; and I. Bailey, "Greens hope voters ignore legal troubles," *The Province*, December 20, 2005.

41 According to Harris during a telephone interview with the author on May 10, 2006, an amendment to his leadership expenses was subsequently submitted to Elections Canada.

42 Dermod Travis, Green Party media team manager, telephone interviews with author December 2005 and February 2006.

43 The new faces included former Progressive Conservatives David Scrymgeour and Tom Jarmyn (according to the party, the latter was brought in on an occasional contract basis to provide legal services). Dermod Travis, who describes himself as an unaffiliated political consultant, was hired to head the party's media team in the spring of 2004.

44 See, for example, the website OpenPolitics, available at http://openpolitics.ca/Green+Party+of+Canada, and M. Dobbin, "Green Party Blues. Can Jim Harris rescue the environment by mainstreaming the Greens?" *The Walrus*, July/August 2005, 41–7.

45 See Holloway resignation letter, available at http://openpolitics.ca/Kate+Holloway+resigns+GPC+Council,+Committees+and+nomination,+2005-06-08.

46 Jim Harris, Green Party leader, telephone interview by author, February 14, 2006.

47 Kate Holloway, former Green Party council member, telephone interviews by author, December 2005 and February 2006.

48 Steve Kisby, Green Party Membership Chair, telephone interview by author, February 7, 2006.

49 For full 1984 Green Party election results, see the Parliament of Canada website at http://www.parl.gc.ca/information/about/process/house/hfer/hfer.asp?Language= E&Search=Cres&canName=&canParty=119&ridProvince=0&ridName=&sub-mit1=Search.

50 Jon Burchell, *The Evolution of Green Politics: Development & Change within European Green Parties* (London: Earthscan Publications Limited, 2002), 1.

51 Trevor Hancock, former Green Party leader, telephone interview by author, February 14, 2006.

52 For more on factionalism within European Green parties, see, for example, E. Gene Frankland and Donald Schoonmaker, *Between Protest & Power: The Green Party in Germany* (Boulder, Colorado: Westview Press, Inc., 1992); Jon Burchell, *The Evolution of Green Politics: Development & Change within European Green Parties* (London: Earthscan Publications Limited, 2002); Eric H. Hines, "The European Parliament and the Europeanization of Green Parties," *Cultural Dynamics* 15, no. 3 (2003).

53 J. Burchell, "Evolving or Conforming? Assessing Organisational Reform Within European Green Parties," *West European Politics* 24, no. 3 (2001): 113–34.

54 Steve Kisby, Green Party Membership Chair, telephone interview by author, February 7, 2006.

55 In 1988, the Greens won 0.35 percent of the vote, in 1993, 0.23 percent. For full Green Party general election results, see the Parliament of Canada website at http://www.parl.gc.ca/information/about/process/house/hfer/hfer.asp?Language=E.

56 Wendy Priesnitz, former Green Party leader, telephone interview by author, February 8, 2006.

57 D. Crowe, "Alberta Greens," *Newsletter* 9, no. 1 (Winter 1996–97), 1. Available at http://davidcrowe.ca/Green/Newsletter/GreeNews1997-1.pdf (accessed February 8, 2006).

58 Russow, "Why I left the Green party."

59 Joan Russow, former Green Party leader, telephone interviews by author, December 2005.

60 Paul A. Taggart, *The New Populism and the New Politics: New Protest Parties in Sweden in a Comparative Perspective* (New York: St. Martin's Press, 1996), cited in Jon Burchell, *The Evolution of Green Politics: Development & Change within European Green Parties* (London: Earthscan Publications Limited, 2002).

61 M. Tempest, "A Tale of Two Parties: The German Greens Hit 25," *Speigel Online*, January 13, 2005. Available at http://www.spiegel.de/international/0, 1518,336637,00.html (accessed March 14, 2006).

62 Jim Harris, Green Party leader, telephone interview by author, February 14, 2006.

63 Claude Genest was the party's Quebec spokesperson during the 2006 campaign. He is a member of the shadow cabinet, responsible for the environmental economics portfolio.

64 Claude Genest, Green Party leadership candidate, telephone interview by author, February 26, 2006.

65 David Chernushenko, Green Party deputy leader, telephone interview by author, April 6, 2006.

66 Jim Harris, Green Party leader, telephone interview by author, May 10, 2006.

67 Under the Income Tax Act, registered charities "cannot be involved in partisan political activities." See Canada Revenue Agency website at http://www.cra-arc.gc.ca/tax/charities/policy/csp/csp-p02-e.html.

68 Elizabeth May, Executive Director, Sierra Club of Canada, telephone interview by author, March 22, 2006.

69 George Read, Green Party campaign manager, telephone interview by author, February 7, 2006.

CHAPTER SEVEN

Candidate Nomination in Canada's Political Parties
by William Cross

The defining characteristic of candidate nomination in Canadian political parties is the almost complete lack of public regulation. Political parties are left on their own to decide how they nominate their candidates. They can choose to elect a candidate through a vote of their local membership or not; they can allow their leader to unilaterally select candidates or not; and if they decide to permit contests, they determine all of the procedures including the timing, the venue, and the eligibility requirements both for voting and for standing as a candidate for nomination. Added to this is reluctance on the part of the parties to establish one set of rules governing all their nomination contests. Often these are left to provincial committees and can vary significantly from one region to another, while in other parties significant discretion over candidate selection is vested in the central campaign. When the latter is the case, the central campaign's involvement is typically uneven, leaving the electorally poor boroughs on their own while closely scrutinizing, sometimes orchestrating, the nomination process in constituencies that are electorally important to the party. The result is that there often is dramatic variance in the way candidates are nominated both within and between parties.

This very lack of consistent standards is one of the most commonly heard criticisms of the party candidate nomination process. More and more voices are being heard in support of public regulation of these contests. The argument in support of this position is essentially twofold. First, that candidate nominations are an integral part of the Canadian democratic process and thus should be subject to the same democratic standards of openness, fairness, and transparency that govern general elections. And second, that the political parties have not done an adequate job of organizing these contests in a manner consistent with these democratic norms. In this chapter, I begin with a discussion of why party candidate nominations are central to Canadian democratic practice, then consider the current state of these contests, and finally review the case for significant reform including increased public regulation.

WHY PARTY CANDIDATE SELECTION MATTERS

It has long been settled that candidate selection is one of the defining activities of political parties. In terms of legislative recruitment, distribution of power within parties, and defining the relationship between parties and their partisans, candidate nomination is a key event in all modern democracies.[1] Notwithstanding the fact that nominations are universally important, there are six features of Canada's electoral and party systems that raise the salience of candidate selection for voters:

1. the limited ability of voters to choose their preferred local representative in the general election;
2. the significant degree of regionalization of the party system resulting in regionally dominant parties and often reducing the general election to secondary importance;
3. the near monopoly of candidates nominated by the major parties on election to the House of Commons;
4. the tradition of brokerage-style parties accommodating many representational demands in their nomination processes;
5. the possible increase in free votes in the House of Commons; and
6. the opportunity party nomination contests offer for grassroots participation in the democratic process.

Each of these is discussed below.

The single member plurality electoral system (SMP) used in Canada limits the amount of choice voters have when casting their general election ballot. SMP allows voters to express only one opinion on the ballot, and this one preference influences both the selection of their local representative and the selection of the party to form the government. Unlike some other electoral systems, SMP does not allow voters to mark one preference for a local candidate and a separate one for their preferred party. The result is that most voters cast their ballot primarily based on their views of the national parties, their leaders, and their policy positions.

Research indicates that most often the identity and characteristics of the local candidates play a minor, secondary role in voters' decision-making.[2] This means that the only opportunity voters have to consider the type of person they would like to be their member of Parliament, and to influence this selection unencumbered with other considerations such as their views of the parties' leaders, is at the candidate nomination stage. Reflective of this is the frequency with which we hear anecdotes of voters "holding their nose" to vote for a local candidate they don't like because she represents their preferred party.

This can be contrasted with other electoral systems such as open list proportional systems. In these systems, general election voters are charged with selecting both individual representatives and their preferred party. What's important for our purposes is that, in these systems, voters have greater choice — casting separate ballots for their preferred party and their preferred candidates. In open list systems, voters choose representatives from a list of candidates presented by their favoured party. For example, a single district might have ten members to be elected. A party winning 40 percent of the vote is entitled to four of these ten seats. The party nominates ten candidates and voters choose which four are elected. By contrast, in the Canadian SMP system the party nominates a single candidate in each district and there is no intra-party, general election competition. The result is that the only chance voters have to influence the identity of a representative from their preferred party is during the candidate selection process.

The Canadian party system also influences the importance of party candidate selection in the choice of a parliamentary representative. In recent elections, the party system has been extremely regionalized, with individual parties dominant in parts of the country. For example, the Conservatives won every seat in the province of Alberta in the 2006 election. In twenty-five of the province's twenty-eight electoral districts, Conservative candidates defeated their closest opponent by more than thirty percentage points (and seventeen won by at least fifty percentage points). Even the Liberal Party, which suffered a significant decrease in its vote share, maintained regions where it was dominant. For example, in the strongly federalist Montreal area ridings of Mount Royal, Westmount–Ville-Marie, and Saint-Laurent–Cartierville, Liberal candidates won by an average of more than forty percentage points. In these areas of the country the general election is little more than a formality. The choice of a member of Parliament is made during the nomination contest of the regionally dominant party. Candidates are well aware of this; as one Conservative candidate in Alberta said, "For me the nomination is the election…. Once I'm nominated, the election is over."[3]

A third characteristic of the Canadian party system that highlights the importance of party candidate selection is the near monopoly the major parties have on the selection of members of Parliament. It is extremely rare for a candidate to be elected to Parliament in the first instance as an independent. In the 2006 election one of the 308 successful candidates was an independent (André Arthur in the Quebec City riding of Portneuf–Jacques-Cartier). Prior to this, the last candidate to be first elected to Parliament as an independent was Anthony Roman in the Toronto area riding of York North in 1984. The result is that essentially the only path to the House of Commons is through a party nomination contest. This can be contrasted with jurisdictions such as Ireland, where in each election a significant number of independent candidates are successful.[4] For example, in the Dáil elections of 2002, thirteen independent candidates were elected. This means that candidates have an alternate route and voters have the option of rejecting the offerings of the parties and selecting an independent candidate. Except in very rare circumstances, Canadian voters are essentially limited to choosing from among the candidates offered by the parties, making their selection process of greater consequence.

The Canadian tradition of big-tent brokerage parties also increases the importance of party candidate selection. The norm is for parties not to represent narrow, sectarian interests. This means that groups wanting to increase their representation in Parliament need to ensure their members are nominated by the parties in winnable constituencies. For example, Acadians in New Brunswick do not have their own political party (nor do francophones in Northern Ontario or anglophones in Quebec). Instead, if they wish to ensure that members of their community are elected to Parliament they need to ensure that they are nominated by the major parties. This can be contrasted with other countries such as Belgium, in which each of the major societal cleavages (largely based on language) is represented by its own party and there are no significant parties that transcend the divide. In this context French-speaking voters know that their interests will be represented in the general election by a party made up wholly from their community, as do German-speaking voters. In the Canadian case, voters from linguistic and identity groups without their own political parties need to focus on the party nomination process to ensure that an equitable number of candidates from their community are chosen. The same is true for groups such as women and visible minorities. There are no parties exclusive to these groups. Thus, in order to increase their numbers in the House of Commons they need to increase their representation among candidates nominated by the major parties.

There has recently been significant discussion relating to the role of the member of Parliament and a possible weakening of party discipline. Former prime minister Paul Martin raised the salience of this issue with his address on the so-called democratic deficit during his 2003 campaign to lead the Liberal Party. Martin promised to institute a three-line whip system that would allow for more frequent votes in the House in which backbench members (and, in rare instances, cabinet ministers) would not be required to follow a party line.[5] He did institute the three-line system upon becoming prime minister, but given his government's minority status the reform never was fully tested. The new Conservative government has also pledged to allow free votes. Their 2006 election platform includes both a pledge for a free vote on the issue of same-sex marriage and a general commitment to "make all votes in Parliament, except the budget and main estimates, 'free votes' for ordinary Members of Parliament."[6]

Should there be a significant increase in the occurrence of free votes, then party nomination contests take on a greater significance. In the current practice, voters need not be very concerned with the policy views of candidates for office as they are almost certain to reflect the views of their party should they be elected. However, if MPs become increasingly free to vote as they see fit in the House, then voters will have greater incentive to seek out and consider candidates' views in choosing their MP.[7] Given, as discussed above, that there is limited choice available to voters in a general election, the nomination contest takes on greater importance in this regard. For example, the Conservative Party supporter who strongly favours extending the definition of marriage to include same-sex partners will want to ensure that the party's nominee in her riding shares this view given the party's commitment to a free vote on the issue.

Party candidate selection potentially offers one of the few opportunities available to voters for meaningful participation in the country's democratic life. Very few voters will run for political office, attend a party's national convention, or travel to Ottawa to meet with members of Parliament. Because nominations typically take place at the constituency level, they offer the opportunity for widespread voter participation. Parties around the world are experiencing a crisis in terms of attracting supporters to active membership.[8] Canada is no exception and, in fact, compares unfavourably to most other Western democracies in terms of the proportion of voters who are active members of political parties.[9] Research indicates that voting in nomination campaigns is a key incentive to membership in Canada's political parties.[10] Given the findings of Young and Cross that voting in a nomination contest is one of the leading inducements to membership, open and accessible nomination contests are vital to the long-term health of parties as membership organizations.

Consistent with the criteria set out above, the evaluation of party candidate selection in this chapter primarily focuses on how open, fair, and transparent the process is for both voters and would-be candidates. In doing so, the following questions are highlighted: How much control do local voters have over the selection of their candidates? Are there significant barriers to participation for both voters and candidates in nomination contests? Are the contests organized in a fair and open fashion? Are they welcoming to candidates from underrepresented groups?

LOCAL PARTY MEMBERS AND CANDIDATE NOMINATION

Central Party Interference

It has long been argued that the norm in terms of party candidate nomination is for the local party members to have significant discretion in the choice of candidate. Some have observed that a defining characteristic of party organization in Canada is a trade-off between strong party discipline in the House of Commons and local discretion in the selection of candidates.[11] Put simply, the argument is that the local party members decide who to send to Ottawa, and once there the local representative is expected to follow orders from the central party elite. While the second part of this equation may still be true, the first is highly suspect. The 2006 election witnessed unprecedented central party involvement in the selection of local candidates. The reality is that in no instances are the local members able to select a candidate completely free from the interference of central party dictates, while in many cases the central party is able to select a candidate without local party members being able to influence the choice.

The single most important act influencing the character of candidate nominations in the 2006 election was the decision by party leaders Martin and Harper to ensure the renomination of all of their party's incumbent members of Parliament. The result was that in the 135 ridings won by the Liberals in the 2004 election, 121 of the incumbent MPs opted to run again and were renominated by their leader's fiat.[12] Similarly, of the 99 Conservatives elected in 2004, 89 opted to run again and were renominated by dictate of Mr. Harper. This means that in the vast majority of ridings in which the parties were most likely to elect an MP (those in which they had already proven electorally successful) local voters were given absolutely no say over who would be their local candidate. In the end, of the 124 Conservative candidates who were elected, 86 were incumbents who were renominated by the party leader, as were 96 of the 103 successful Liberals. At best, then, local party members were able to choose their candidate in less than one-third of the ridings the Conservative Party won compared with about one in fifteen for the Liberals.

This does not mean that there is no central party involvement in other nomination contests. Indeed, the central party leadership was actively involved in many other selections — particularly where it thought the party had a chance for electoral success. In the Liberal Party, the leader has routinely appointed non-incumbents as candidates in key ridings in recent elections. The practice began in 1993 with Jean Chrétien's appointment of fourteen new candidates and was repeated in his re-election campaigns in 1997 and 2000.[13] When Paul Martin became party leader he spoke against these appointments and suggested that he would break from this tradition. Prior to the 2004 election he said, "Essentially we are a democratic party, and a democratic party says you win your nomination."[14] Nonetheless, the party's central leadership unilaterally appointed a handful of Liberal candidates in the 2004 election and, in addition to reappointing all incumbents, appears to have arranged the nominations of preferred candidates in the 2006 election.

The party leaders' ability to control party nominations is enshrined in the Canada Elections Act. Beginning with the general election of 1972, party affiliation is listed next to the local candidate's name on the ballot paper. Elections Canada does not want to be in the position of sorting out who is and is not the official candidate of a party in each riding. Accordingly, it requires that local candidates have the signature of their party leader on their nomination papers in order for the party label to appear on the ballot. The ability to withhold this signature from a candidate who may be chosen by local party members and to bestow it on one with no indication of local party support essentially provides the party leader with absolute authority over candidate nominations.

Perhaps wary of criticism of too many centrally inspired candidate appointments, the parties sometimes orchestrate local events to ensure the nomination of their preferred candidate while not having to formally anoint him. An example of this from the 2006 election occurred in the riding of Etobicoke-Lakeshore, where the Liberal Party appears to have ensured the selection of Michael Ignatieff amidst significant local opposition. The local party president claims he learned late on a Friday that incumbent Liberal MP Jean Augustine was not running for re-election. At the same time he was informed the deadline for would-be nomination candidates to file their extensive nomination paperwork was 5:00 p.m. the next day. Not surprisingly, and despite the efforts of two local party members to become candidates, central party officials determined that only Ignatieff fulfilled the necessary candidacy requirements by the expedited deadline. According to a *Globe and Mail* editorial the nomination manoeuvring in this riding "smells to high heaven and makes a mockery of Prime Minister Paul Martin's claims to be a true believer in party democracy."[15]

Tensions often arise when there is a lack of communication between central party officials and both the local party association and would-be nomination candidates. Candidates often complain that the rules are changed or deadlines are imposed without their receiving adequate notice. Often they contend that these are deliberate efforts by the central party to favour other candidates. There are many examples from recent elections of would-be nomination candidates claiming that the deadline for filing nomination papers was expedited without their having adequate warning or that the deadline for signing up new members was moved forward without their having the opportunity to file the membership papers of their newly recruited supporters. The parties' nomination rules, which often set out such deadlines, usually allow for changes to be made by the central campaign committee for reasons such as electoral urgency, and thus there is no technical violation of the rules. Of course, even if there is, the only recourse a spurned candidate has is to appeal to the party itself for a remedy.

The central party has many tools at its disposal to influence a nomination contest short of unilaterally appointing a candidate. Generally, local associations require approval from party headquarters before they are able to hold their nomination contest. The central party often exercises control over things like the timing of the nomination. This permission can be withheld for a variety of strategic reasons, including, for example, a desire to bide time while the party tries to entice a particular high-profile individual to seek the nomination. In the 2006 campaign, this appeared to be the case in the Quebec riding of Vaudreuil-Soulanges, where former Liberal MP Nick Discepola was planning to seek the nomination and the local party's efforts to hold a contest were delayed by the central party. In the end, it became clear that the party was holding the riding in hopes that it could entice former astronaut Marc Garneau to be the candidate.[16]

As in the Ignatieff case, the central party's actions in support of Garneau reflect a desire to pave the way for so-called star candidates. Central party officials often find that this type of recruited candidate, who typically has not toiled in the party for long periods and does not have the extensive networks of grassroots community support necessary to be successful in a nomination contest, is reluctant to run without being assured of the nomination. In the cases of Ignatieff and Garneau this challenge was magnified by the presence of other candidates who had deeper connections with the local party and had been organizing for the nomination contest for some time. The party justifies these actions as a way of enticing quality individuals to electoral politics without requiring that they first spend months or years building local bases of support.

Would-be nomination candidates are required to have their candidacies approved by central party authorities. In the Liberal Party, and similarly in the other parties, nomination candidates are required to complete a lengthy "Nomination Contestant Personal Information Form." In addition to basic information such as name and date of birth, the candidate is asked to provide ten years of residential history, ten years of employment history, information on cultural and community organizations they have belonged to, information relating to matrimonial and custody proceedings, and details of any disciplinary action ever taken against them. They must also answer whether they have ever been suspended, expelled, or forced to withdraw from a post-secondary education institution; discharged, suspended, or asked to resign from any employment; involved in any employment-based lawsuits or charged with workplace harassment or fraud; disciplined by any professional association; denied entry into Canada or another country; subject to any outstanding tax liabilities; charged with plagiarism or cheating on school exams; charged with any crime, offence, or delinquency; declared bankruptcy; and whether they have any outstanding civil suit judgments or garnishments. They also must consent to a collection of information from "any person, government, educational institution, police force, military authority, investigative agency, retail credit agency, governing body or other organization...."[17]

The requirement that the central party give its approval to all nomination contestants is justified on the grounds of preventing extremist candidates or those whose nomination may embarrass the party (for example, someone facing ongoing court proceedings). Nonetheless, these practices provide the central party with another tool in influencing the nomination outcome. In attempting to ensure a desired outcome, party leaders can deny candidacy to all but their preferred candidate. Would-be candidates who are not permitted to run sometimes claim this is the motivation behind their denial. It is difficult to know how often this provision is utilized. Every election includes some high-profile cases of individuals being denied the ability to seek a nomination. For example, the Conservatives denied an application for candidacy from former Saskatchewan premier Grant Devine in 2004. The party provided no reason why Devine, wanting to run in the Saskatchewan riding of Souris–Moose Mountain, was denied candidacy, but it was apparently related to the scandals that had plagued his provincial administration. There are others, besides the few cases that reach the national media, whose applications for candidacy have been denied, but there is no way to be certain of the exact number.

The New Democratic Party, while generally allowing its local members more scope in the choice of a candidate, is unique in imposing a requirement that local associations conduct a meaningful search for female and minority candidates before they are allowed to hold a nomination meeting. This requirement is discussed further in a later section of this chapter considering how accessible nominations are to members of underrepresented groups.

Few Contested Nominations

One result of the central appointment of candidates in the vast majority of the ridings in which a party is likely to elect an MP is that there regularly are very few contested nominations. As one senior party operative explained to me, contests are not permitted in the most desirable constituencies (those the party currently holds), leaving a couple of dozen others where the party might be competitive and then a large number of ridings where the party has little or no chance of success. In these latter ridings, the local and central parties often work hard to ensure they have one credible candidate, never mind a contested nomination. Surveys of constituency associations in the past suggest that about one-third of local nominations are typically contested.[18]

Beginning with the 2004 election, Elections Canada requires local associations that hold a nomination meeting to file a report providing details within thirty days of the meeting. This analysis uses the data reported to Elections Canada by February 1, 2006. The major parties all claimed to have nominated a full slate of candidates by January 1, so all constituencies that held a nomination contest should have reported by this date. Nonetheless, the numbers vary dramatically by party: 206 Liberal associations filed reports by this date compared with 143 Conservatives, 112 New Democrats, and 73 Bloc. If a party does not hold an official nomination meeting it is not required to file a report, which may explain most of the missing data.

The available 2006 data support the finding that significantly less than half of all nominations are contested. Overall, about one-quarter of the constituency associations of the major parties report contested nominations for the 2006 election. There is, however, considerable variance among the parties. Slightly less than 10 percent of Liberal associations report holding a contested nomination, compared with 7 percent for the Bloc, 35 percent for the New Democrats, and 53 percent of Conservatives. However, these numbers have to be interpreted very carefully because of the different rates of reporting on nomination contests among the parties. Most of the associations not reporting are likely ones in which there was no formal nomination meeting and thus no contest, meaning the actual rate of contested nominations may be significantly lower than the data suggest (particularly for the NDP and Conservatives).

Data collected from the 2004 election provide a very different picture in terms of the number of contested nominations. Eagles, et al, report a significantly higher rate of contested nominations in this election.[19] However, they too rely on reports filed by constituency associations with Elections Canada and find that not all associations have reported (for example their sample includes about half of all NDP local associations). As they acknowledge, this likely means that the actual percentage of contested nominations is significantly lower than what they report. Nonetheless, the 2004 election in many ways provided a perfect storm in terms of the availability of nominations to be contested. First, none of the parties protected their incumbent MPs and many were challenged. This was the first time in several elections that Liberal incumbents were not protected, and there was likely some built-up ambition leading to challenges, along with remnants of the party's recent leadership struggles being played out on the ground with contests between Martin and Chrétien supporters. Second, a redrawing of electoral boundaries resulted in nomination contests between sitting MPs from the same party (for example, the high-profile Liberal cases of Sheila Copps and Tony Veleri in Hamilton East–Stoney Creek, and Carolyn Parrish and Steve Mahoney in Mississauga-Erindale). Third, the merger of the Canadian Alliance and Progressive Conservative parties almost immediately prior to the campaign resulted in local contests between representatives of the two former parties. In many ridings, the

Conservative Party's nomination contest became part of the continuing struggle for control of the new local organization between old Progressive Conservative and Canadian Alliance factions.

Barriers to Participation

While we cannot be certain of the exact numbers, it is clear that most nominations in the major parties in the 2006 election were claimed by only a single candidate. When there is a contested nomination, and the choice is left to the members, there are significant barriers to participation. Imagine a general election in which Elections Canada announced that as a cost-saving measure the following reforms will be implemented: a $10 poll tax, only one polling place per constituency, and the closure of the voters list seven to ninety days prior to the election (varying by province), with no on-site registration permitted. Surely, such rules would be met with outrage and would be successfully challenged as violating the Charter guarantee of the right to vote. Yet, these are the very rules that organize candidate nomination in our political parties.

All of the parties restrict voting in nomination contests to their dues-paying members. The cost of membership varies among the parties, and among provinces within some parties, but is typically in the range of $10. We know that many, if not most, nomination voters join the party for the sole purpose of participating in the choice of a candidate and partake in no other party activity.[20] Thus, the membership fee for these people is nothing more than the cost of eligibility to vote in the contest. Nomination candidates were widely believed to purchase bulk memberships for their supporters so that the poll tax would not be a disincentive. Opposed to such mass mobilizations, the parties have begun to insist that all new members pay their own fees, effectively meaning that anyone without the means of paying is disenfranchised.

All of the parties have cut-off dates by which members must belong in order to be eligible to vote in nomination contests. Again these vary widely both among parties and by province within some parties. The range seems to be from as many as ninety days to as few as seven days prior to the nomination contest. The purpose of the cut-off date is twofold. A minimal cut-off period is required so the party can ensure that members meet eligibility requirements (such as residency in the riding) and so all candidates can have access to a voters list. Those preferring a long cut-off date argue that it is illegitimate to allow voters who are not long-term members of the party to participate. They argue that the mobilization efforts in contested nominations that sometimes see thousands of new members joining are not in the party's best interest and are not fair to the long-term members who see their votes swamped at the nomination contest by newcomers who often have no established attachment or commitment to the party.

The effect of lengthy cut-off dates is compounded by the fact that many nominations occur well in advance of the election call. For example, the Conservative Party nominated almost all of its candidates by mid-May 2005 for the January 2006 election. In this case the early nominations partially reflected the possibility of the minority government falling at any moment. Nonetheless, research on elections following majority Parliaments shows that parties routinely nominate many of their candidates well before the official campaign begins.[21] This means that anyone wishing to vote in one of these nomination contests is required to belong to the party weeks before a nomination meeting and months before the election call. For the casual partisan of a political party who is not paying close attention months before an expected election call, the cut-off date may pass before they even know the nomination contest is occurring. And, unlike in general elections, there is no possibility of registering at the polls.

In fact there are no "polls" for nomination contests. In the 2006 general election, Elections Canada organized approximately twenty thousand voting locations across the country, an average of sixty-five per constituency. For nomination contests there is one polling station per constituency. This means that all interested voters have to travel to a single location in order to cast a ballot. This is an obvious impediment to participation, as in many ridings this can require travel of a hundred kilometres or more. Even in geographically compact urban ridings, this can require voters to travel to another part of their city to vote.

The number of voters participating in a nomination contest varies dramatically. Again, in terms of overall voter participation it is imperative to keep in mind that in most local parties there is no contest for voters to participate in. When there is a contest, the number of participants ranges from five thousand or more in the most hotly contested races to a few dozen in others. Two contests in the 2004 election provide examples of both extremes. In the Liberal nomination contest in Hamilton East–Stoney Creek there were 5,313 voters. This nomination was contested by two long-serving Liberal MPs, Sheila Copps and Tony Valeri, who were running against each other at least partially as a result of redistricting following the 2000 election. The total membership in the riding association was approximately eleven thousand, meaning that, even in this high-profile contest, only about half of those eligible to vote did so. Almost all of the members were recruited into the party by either the Valeri or the Copps campaign, as the number of memberships they reported selling to their supporters exceeded the total number of eligible voters. In the same election, forty-nine New Democrats gathered in the riding of Edmonton East, the only Alberta riding the party has ever won, to choose from among three candidates for their nomination. Most nomination contests lie somewhere in between in terms of the number of party members voting.

We do not have comprehensive information on the numbers attending nomination contests, as there is no requirement that the parties compile or report these data. In fact, in some contests, the local organizers will announce the winner but not the vote totals for individual candidates, making it even more difficult to know how many participated. A survey of local associations conducted after the 1993 election found that the mean attendance at contested nominations in the major parties was slightly less than six hundred.[22] The available evidence from more recent elections suggests that this is likely still a good estimate, though there is a tremendous range both within and among parties.

UNDERREPRESENTED GROUPS AND CANDIDATE NOMINATION

Voter Mobilization

One result of the rules governing participation in nomination contests is that the campaigns tend to be organized as recruitment and mobilization efforts. The first task of a nomination candidate is to identify his supporters and sign them up as party members. Most local party associations have a very small membership between elections. The result is that nomination contestants often seek to flood the local association with their supporters in advance of the membership cut-off date. This is a far more common practice in the Liberal and Conservative parties, where cut-off dates are typically twenty-one days or less before the contest, as opposed to the New Democratic Party, where they are as long as ninety days. The shorter cut-off period provides the candidates with more time to line up their supporters. The difference in practice is that contested NDP nomination meetings tend to have fewer voters and an electorate that is made up primarily of longer-term party members.

These recruitment campaigns often take place within ethnic communities. As far back as the 1962 election, Howard Scarrow observed large-scale recruitment in ethnic communities in the Ontario riding of Urban, where Scarrow estimates that three-quarters of the twelve hundred nomination voters were new Canadians.[23] The ethnic communities being mobilized change over time, but the dynamics remain the same. In the 2006 campaign, Liberal candidate Omar Alghabra, a former president of the Canadian Arab Federation, successfully sought the nomination in Mississauga-Erindale in part by mobilizing support in the Arab and Muslim communities; and Conservative David Xiao mobilized Chinese immigrants in support of his nomination bid in Edmonton Centre. In the 2004 campaign, Conservative Chuck Cadman was defeated in his bid for renomination in Surrey North by a candidate who mobilized significant support among Indo-Canadians. Recruiting support from ethnic communities is attractive to candidates needing to mobilize hundreds of supporters, as these are often hierarchical communities in which the endorsement of the leadership can result in a significant number of supporters.

Mobilization among new arrivals to Canada is often highly controversial. Unlike general election voters, nomination voters need not be citizens or eighteen years of age. Complaints are occasionally heard regarding large numbers of ethnic voters attending a nomination meeting, many of whom cannot speak either French or English, who appear to have limited understanding or interest in the contest other than voting for the candidate they've been instructed to support. While some argue that these lax rules provide a way into the democratic process for new arrivals, others contend that these participants are gaining nothing from the experience and are simply being used by candidates in need of supporters. There is evidence that virtually none of these ethnic voters who are mobilized into the parties for purposes of voting in a candidate nomination contest maintains a membership afterwards.[24]

Social conservatives, apparently mobilized largely around the same-sex marriage issue, were also active in recruiting voters in Conservative Party nomination contests in the 2006 campaign. An example of this is Darrel Reid, a former president of the group Focus on the Family Canada, who successfully sought the party's nomination in Richmond. An email message sent to members of a group called Defend Marriage (B.C.) urged them to take out membership in the party and support Reid's nomination bid.[25] Gloria Galloway identified "at least three riding associations in Nova Scotia, four in British Columbia and one in suburban Toronto [that] have nominated candidates with ties to groups like Focus on the Family, a Christian organization that opposes same-sex marriage."[26] Similar to mobilization in ethnic communities, these campaigns can cause dissension among the party's long-time members. In the Richmond case, the local party president quit in protest, "charging that the Tory party is 'getting dangerously close' to being overtaken by the religious right."[27]

Representativeness of the Candidate Pool

There are significant representational deficits in the Canadian Parliament. Both visible minorities and women are underrepresented. After the 2006 general election the number of women in the House of Commons dropped to sixty-four, representing less than 21 percent of all members. This is the fifth consecutive election in which the proportion of women elected has essentially stalled at just over one in five. Advocacy groups interested in increasing the number of female MPs have correctly identified the parties' candidate selection processes as a crucial barrier. Given the near monopoly the major parties have on the election of MPs, the key to electing more women to the House of Commons is for the parties to nominate more women in constituencies they have a chance of winning. The criticism of the parties is that they nominate too few women, and when they do nominate women they do so disproportionately in constituencies in which they have little chance of electoral success. Data from the 2006 election support both of these contentions.

As illustrated in Table 1, women were underrepresented in each of the parties' candidate pools in the 2006 elections. The numbers increased slightly from the 2004 election but remain far from the 50 percent level. There is a significant range among the parties, with just 12 percent of Conservative candidates being women, compared with 26 percent for the Liberals, 31 percent for the Bloc, and 35 percent for the New Democratic Party. Interestingly, Table 1 shows that women comprise a slightly higher percentage of MPs in the Bloc and NDP caucuses than they represent as a share of the candidate pool. This is not the case in the Liberal and Conservative parties, where the proportion of women in caucus is lower than the proportion in the candidate pool. This means that Liberal and Conservative female candidates are more likely to be nominated in ridings the party lost in 2006, while the Bloc and

NDP were slightly more likely to nominate women in ridings they won. This point is further illustrated in Table 2, which shows the number of female candidates nominated by each party by province for the 2006 election. The provinces in which the Liberal Party nominated the largest proportion of female candidates were Quebec and Alberta. Consistent with expectations at the outset of the campaign, the party won no seats in Alberta and suffered dramatic losses in Quebec — winning no new seats. Similarly, the Conservatives nominated one of their largest proportions of female candidates in Quebec, a province in which they anticipated few victories at the time the nominations were made.

Table 1
Female candidates by party
(1993–2006, as a percentage of all candidates)

	1993 nominated	1997 nominated	2000 nominated	2004 nominated/ elected	2006 nominated/ elected
Bloc	13	21	23	24/26	31/33
Liberal	22	28	22	24/25	26/20
NDP	38	36	31	31/26	35/41
PC/	23	19	13	-	-
Conservative	-	-	-	12/12	12/11
Reform/Alliance	11	10	10	-	-

Source: The 1993, 1997, and 2000 data come from William Cross, *Political Parties* (Vancouver: UBC Press, 2004) and the 2004 figures from Nikki Macdonald, "Women Beneath the Electoral Barrier," *Electoral Insight* (Ottawa: Elections Canada, January 2005).

When seeking the leadership of his party in 2003, Paul Martin appeared to agree with those who argue for the nomination of more women when he pledged, "We cannot go into this election campaign unless we have the largest number of women candidates in Liberal riding history.... We have to go out across this country and, in riding after riding, recruit young women who want to dedicate themselves to the public service."[28] Nonetheless, the party failed to make significant gains in either the 2004 or the 2006 campaign.

In prior elections, Jean Chrétien justified some of his candidate appointments on the basis of wanting to increase the number of women in the House of Commons. Similarly, in the 2006 election, in some ridings without a Liberal incumbent reoffering, the nomination appears to

Table 2
Female candidates by party and province, 2006

	Bloc	Conservatives	Liberals	NDP
Newfoundland (7)	-	1	1	4
P.E.I. (4)	-	0	0	2
Nova Scotia (11)	-	0	0	4
New Brunswick (10)	-	0	1	3
Quebec (75)	23	13	26	24
Ontario (106)	-	12	29	37
Manitoba (14)	-	3	3	3
Saskatchewan (14)	-	2	2	5
Alberta (28)	-	2	8	10
British Columbia (36)	-	4	7	15
Territories (3)	-	1	2	1
Total	23	38	79	108

have been reserved for a female candidate. An example of this is the riding of Ottawa West–Nepean, in which would-be candidate Jacques Shore dropped out of the nomination contest, telling his supporters that "the National Campaign Team advised him they want a woman to run."[29] A party official justified the pressure placed on Shore to drop out of the contest on the basis that it was consistent "with the Prime Minister's commitment to ensure the participation of more women in national politics."[30] While this may seem a laudable objective, and perhaps an acceptable justification for the curtailment of local democracy, the vast majority of cases in which the central party involves itself have nothing to do with gender and indeed guarantee the nomination of a disproportionate number of male candidates.

Like Martin, Harper has also expressed dissatisfaction with the number of women nominated by his party. Shortly after the 2006 election he told the media, "There really weren't the number of women candidates I'd like to see. I think there are things the party can do to assist the nomination of female candidates in the future."[31] It is not clear just what "things" Harper has in mind.

It is not by coincidence that the NDP both nominates more women than the other parties and nominates women disproportionately in constituencies that it has a chance of winning. The party has adopted a "Nomination and Affirmative Action Policy" that states that "New

Democrats are committed to the goals of gender-parity and diversity, and recognize that one of the ways to help move those goals forward is by ensuring that our candidate team is gender-balanced and reflects the diversity of the country." In support of these goals the party has set the following objectives: a minimum of 60 percent of ridings where the NDP has a reasonable chance of winning have women running as NDP candidates; a minimum of 15 percent of ridings where the NDP has a reasonable chance of winning have NDP candidates who reflect the diversity of Canada; and in ridings where incumbent New Democrats are not seeking re-election, special effort will be made to run affirmative action NDP candidates.

The NDP enforces these objectives through the following provision: "Ridings may only submit requests for nominations to a provincial or territorial committee charged with overseeing the federal process after the following steps have been taken: A) a Candidate Search Committee has been established reflecting the diversity of the riding; and, B) there are one or more candidates for nomination from affirmative action groups."[32] In order for a local association to hold a nomination meeting without a candidate from an underrepresented group, it must convince the central campaign that real efforts were made to recruit women and visible minorities to run. Previously, the party offered financial incentives to female nomination contestants. It has stopped this practice because of a belief that these contributions from the party to a nomination candidate are "no longer permitted under the Election Finances Act."[33]

One of the biggest factors working against an increase in the number of female candidates in the Liberal and Conservative parties is the guarantee of renomination for incumbents. These candidates are overwhelmingly male and they are running in constituencies that previous elections suggest are among the party's most competitive. The NDP's focus on ridings that they previously held and that they identify as winnable is crucial to a successful strategy of increasing the number of women in public office.

The 2006 data make it clear that when there are nomination contests, female candidates are likely to be among the contenders. Of the associations filing reports with Elections Canada by February 1, 2006, we find very few contested nominations, but, when there is one, women candidates are reasonably well represented. Table 3 illustrates the number of contested nominations by party and the number of these with a female candidate for the nomination.

The success rate for women contesting nominations varied significantly by party. In the NDP, seventeen of the twenty-six associations that

Table 3

Number of reported contested 2006 nominations by party
and the number of these with a female nomination candidate

	Bloc	Conservative	Liberal	NDP
Contested nominations	5	76	20	39
Number contested by a woman	1	23	10	26
Total nominations reporting	(73)	(143)	(206)	(112)

had a woman contesting the nomination chose a female candidate. In the Conservative Party a woman was successful in five of the twenty-three contests that had a female candidate, and the same was true in two of the ten Liberal contests. The sole contested Bloc nomination with a female candidate resulted in a woman being chosen. This suggests that for the Liberals and Conservatives the problem is that too few women are running for nominations, and they are not competing as well as men when they do.

There are twenty-three visible minority members of the House of Commons following the 2006 election, marking an increase of one from 2004. This represents 7.5 percent of all members, while this group comprises 14.9 percent of the Canadian population. Comprehensive data on the number of visible minority candidates in the 2006 election is not available at the time of writing. According to media reports, approximately 7 percent of the NDP's candidates were visible minorities, as were 12 percent of the Bloc Québécois' candidates. Liberal and Conservative officials report that they do not keep track of minority candidates.[34] In the 2004 election, as illustrated in Table 4, all of the parties nominated relatively few visible minority candidates. It is interesting that the Conservative Party led the way in nominating visible minority candidates while they trail far behind in the nomination of women.

Table 4

Visible minority candidates nominated by party in 2004
(number and percent of total candidates)

Bloc	5	(6.7)
Conservatives	33	(10.7)
Liberals	26	(8.4)
NDP	29	(9.4)

Source: Jerome H. Black and Bruce H. Hicks, "Visible Minority Candidates in the 2004 Feberal Election," *Canadian Parliamentary Review* (Summer 2006), pp. 15–20, 18.

REFORMING PARTY CANDIDATE NOMINATION

There have been many recent calls for reform of party candidate nomination processes. Groups advocating for greater numbers of women in politics, current and former parliamentarians, officials within the parties, academic and media observers, and leaders of public interest groups have all called for significant changes to the ways parties choose their candidates. A recent study of the nomination process by the Canadian Association of Former Parliamentarians concludes that "current practices are badly flawed and in need of substantive amendments in order to bring them into line with accepted democratic principles."[35] And Rudyard Griffiths, the executive director of the Dominion Institute, echoing a sentiment expressed by many observers, has argued, "It's time the parties got out of the business of running nominations and turned the process over to an independent body such as Elections Canada."[36]

As suggested at the outset, the governing norm of candidate selection has been that it is an internal party decision and accordingly it should be left to the parties to orchestrate the contests and set the rules governing them. This began to change in the 2004 election, when public regulation of the financing of nomination campaigns was put in place. This is a modest change, as the spending limit was set relatively high (at 20 percent of the general election limit or approximately $15,000) and evidence suggests that this affects spending in only the most exceptional races, as the vast majority of nomination candidates spend nowhere near this amount.[37] However, the general rule that the parties organize these contests as they see fit remains intact.

The legitimacy of this approach can be challenged on two grounds. The first is that candidate nomination is such an important part of Canadian democracy that it cannot be justifiably viewed as an internal matter of interest only to the parties. The second is that the parties either cannot or are not willing to effectively regulate these contests and ensure they are governed by generally acceptable democratic norms. The review of the current state of candidate nominations presented in this chapter supports both of these propositions.

The major parties themselves have begun to question the current norms of candidate selection. The Conservative Party platform for the 2006 election includes the following pledge: "A Conservative government will: Ensure that party nomination and leadership races are conducted in a fair, transparent and democratic manner," and "Prevent party leaders from appointing candidates without the democratic consent of local electoral district associations."[38] The wording of this platform plank suggests that the government may be considering more public regulation of these contests.

At their 2005 national convention, the Liberals considered several changes to their nomination rules proposed by the party's Ontario and Prince Edward Island wings. These included a prohibition on candidates being appointed by the leader, removing the right of the leader to prevent a party member from seeking a nomination, a uniform membership cut-off date of ninety days for eligibility to vote in a nomination contest, and a requirement that all members pay their own membership fees. The first three proposals were defeated at the convention while the fourth passed.

The most comprehensive proposal for reform of the candidate nomination process was made by the New Brunswick Commission on Legislative Democracy in 2005. The commission recognized that candidate nomination is an integral part of the province's democratic practice and reported, "The Commission heard from New Brunswickers that there should be a standard set of rules to ensure that these contests are conducted in a fair, open and transparent manner."[39] To accomplish this the commission made a series of recommendations, including that all nominated candidates be chosen by a vote of local party members, that nomination voters be subject to the same eligibility requirements regarding citizenship and age as are general election voters, that there be a standard membership cut-off date of seven days prior to the nomination contest, that the maximum membership fee a party can charge be set at $5, and that party leaders be required to certify that all local nominations are conducted in a fair and democratic manner.[40]

Some may argue that more open, democratically inspired nomination contests may lead to a decline in the number of women and minority candidates nominated. There is little to support this argument. While some party leaders justify their meddling in nominations as a way of increasing the number of female candidates, the reality is that most of this central party meddling is done on the behalf of male candidates (most often incumbents and "star" candidates). In addition, there is no systematic evidence that nomination voters will discriminate against women in democratically organized contests,[41] just as there is no evidence that voters discriminate against female candidates in general elections. The NDP example makes a strong case that the way for parties to increase their number of female candidates is through candidate recruitment and outreach in every constituency, and particularly in ridings where the party is competitive.[42] Women in the Liberal caucus were at the forefront in demanding regulation of the financing of nomination contests, and women MPs have been in the forefront of calls for greater democratization of the process to provide a more level playing ground among nomination candidates.

As observed at the outset, candidate nominations are key events in the life of every political party. As Schattschneider observed long ago, "the nominating process has become the crucial process of the party. He who can make the nominations is the owner of the party."[43] Similarly, Ranney contends that what is at stake in candidate nominations "is nothing less than control of the core of what the party stands for and does."[44] It is precisely because the stakes are so high that the parties will never be able to appropriately regulate candidate nominations themselves. When control over the party is at stake, competing interests will utilize whatever resources are available to them to ensure that they emerge successful. If candidate nomination simply had implications internal to party organization that would be acceptable. However, because these contests significantly influence which groups and interests are represented in Parliament they serve a much broader democratic purpose. It is this broader democratic purpose that demands that candidate nomination processes not be subsumed by internal fighting between party factions nor organized to serve the particular self-interest of a political party. The time has come for full public regulation of these important democratic contests in a manner consistent with the standards set for general elections.

NOTES

Valuable fact-finding and general detective work was provided by John Crysler. Thank you to the party operatives who provided insight on their nomination processes.

1   See for example, Richard S. Katz, "The Problem of Candidate Selection and Models of Party Democracy," *Party Politics* 7:3 (2001), 277–96; Michael Gallagher, "Introduction," in *Candidate Selection in Comparative Perspective: The Secret Garden of Politics*, ed. Michael Gallagher and Michael Marsh (London: Sage Publications, 1988); and Lars Bille, "Democratizing a Democratic Procedure: Myth of Reality?" *Party Politics* 7:3 (2001), 363–80.

2   See André Blais, E. Gidengil, A. Dobryzynska, and R. Nadeau, "Does the Local Candidate Matter? Candidate Effects in the Canadian Election of 2000," *Canadian Journal of Political Science* 36 (2003), 657–64.

3   David Xiao as quoted in "Three Scrappy Conservatives Fight for Edmonton-Centre Nomination," *Edmonton Journal*, May 5, 2005, B3.

4   Liam Weeks, "Explaining Voting for Independents Under STV Elections: the Irish Case," presented at the Annual Meetings of the American Political Science Association, Chicago (2004).

5   See Peter Aucoin and Lori Turnbull, "The Democratic Deficit: Paul Martin and Parliamentary Reform," *Canadian Public Administration* 46:4 (2003), 427–49.

6   *Stand up for Canada: Conservative Party of Canada Federal Election Platform* (2006), 44.

7   See William Cross, "Members of Parliament, Voters and Democracy in the Canadian House of Commons," *Parliamentary Perspectives* 3 (2000).

8   See Susan Scarrow, "Parties Without Members? Party Organization in a Changing Electoral Environment," in *Disaffected Democracies: What's Troubling the Trilateral Countries?* ed. Susan J. Pharr and Robert D. Putnam (Princeton, NJ: Princeton University Press, 2000), 129–56.

9   William Cross and Lisa Young, "The Contours of Political Party Membership in Canada," *Party Politics* 10:4 (2004), 427–44.

10   Lisa Young and William Cross, "Incentives to Membership in Canadian Political Parties," *Political Research Quarterly* 55:3 (2002), 547–69.

11   See, for example, R.K. Carty, "The Politics of Tecumseh Corners: Canadian Political Parties as Franchise Organizations," *Canadian Journal of Political Science* 35:4 (2002), 723–45 .

12   Belinda Stronach, elected as a Conservative in 2004, is included in the 121 Liberals renominated by Paul Martin for the 2006 election.

13   There appear to be three motivations for Chrétien's appointments: to pave the way for star candidates, to modestly increase the number of female candidates, and to prevent the nomination of "undesirable" candidates. See William Cross, "Grassroots Participation in Candidate Nominations," in *Citizen Politics: Research and Theory in Canadian Political Behaviour*, ed. Joanna Everitt and Brenda O'Neill (Toronto: Oxford University Press, 2002), 373–85.

14   "Arranging for Ignatieff," *Globe and Mail*, November 29, 2005, A20.

15   Ibid.

16   "Liberals Coy About Dumping Discepola for Astronaut Garneau," *Montreal Gazette*, November 23, 2005, A8. The party did nominate Garneau and he was defeated in the general election.

17   The candidate information form is included as an appendix to the "National Rules for the Selection of Candidates for the Liberal Party of Canada," as amended January 20, 2004.

18   R.K. Carty and Lynda Erickson, "Candidate Nomination in Canada's National Political Parties," in *Canadian Political Parties: Leaders, Candidates and Organization*, ed. Herman Bakvis (Toronto: Dundurn Press, 1991), 97–189, 120.

19   Munroe Eagles, Harold Jensen, Anthony Sayers and Lisa Young, "Financing Federal Nomination Contests in Canada — An Overview of the 2004 Experience," presented at the 2005 meetings of the Canadian Political Science Association, London, Ontario.

20   William Cross, *Political Parties* (Vancouver: UBC Press, 2004), Chapter 2.

21   Carty and Erickson, "Candidate Nomination," 97–189, 135.

22   William Cross, "Grassroots Participation in Candidate Nominations," in *Citizen Politics: Research and Theory in Canadian Political Behaviour*, ed. Joanna Everitt and Brenda O'Neill (Toronto: Oxford University Press, 2002), 373–85, 380.

23   Howard A. Scarrow, "Nomination and Local Party Organization in Canada: A Case Study," *Western Political Quarterly* 17 (1964), 55–62.

24   William Cross, *Political Parties* (Vancouver: UBC Press, 2004), 66.

25   Douglas Ward, "Religious Right Uses Its Clout," *Vancouver Sun*, July 30, 2005, C4.

26   Gloria Galloway, "Christian Activists Capturing Tory Races," *Globe and Mail*, May 27, 2005, A1.

27   Douglas Ward, "Religious Right Uses Its Clout," *Vancouver Sun*, July 30, 2005, C4.

28   Gloria Galloway, "Martin calls for 52 per cent Women MPs," *Globe and Mail*, November 14, 2003, A5.

29   Mohammed Adam, "Men Need Not Apply in Ottawa West — Nepean Liberal Race," *Ottawa Citizen*, June 28, 2005, B1.

30   Ibid.

31   Transcript of Stephen Harper's January 26, 2006, news conference reviewed at http://www.ctv.ca.

32   "Nomination and Affirmative Action Policy," in "NDP Prospective Candidate Information Package, Election 2005/06," section A, 4–6.

33   "NDP Prospective Candidate Information Package, Election 2005/06," section H, 18.

34   John Gray, "Once More, Few Women, Fewer Minorities," CBC.ca Reality Check Team, January 3, 2006.

35   "Analysis of the Canadian Association of Former Parliamentarians Survey: The Political Nomination Process in Canada," March 8, 2005 (Ottawa), 2.

36   Rudyard Griffiths, "Calling All Demagogues," *National Post*, January 10, 2006, A15.

37   Munroe Eagles, Harold Jensen, Anthony Sayers, and Lisa Young, "Financing Federal Nomination Contests in Canada — An Overview of the 2004 Experience," presented at the 2005 meetings of the Canadian Political Science Association, London, Ontario.

38   *Stand up for Canada*, 44.

39   *Final Report and Recommendations*, New Brunswick Commission on Legislative Democracy (2005), 80.

40   Ibid., 83.

41   See, for example, Carty and Erickson, "Candidate Nomination," 146–47.

42   This is consistent with the recommendation of the Royal Commission on Electoral Reform and Party Financing for the establishment of local candidate search committees mandated to encourage more women to seek party nominations.

43   E.E. Schattschneider, *Party Government* (New York: Rinehart, 1942), 101.

44   Austin Ranney, "Candidate Selection," in *Democracy at the Polls*, ed. David Butler, Howard Penniman and Austin Ranney (Washington, DC: American Enterprise Institute, 1981), 75–106, 103.

CHAPTER EIGHT

Electoral Legislation Since 1997:
Parliament Regains the Initiative
by Louis Massicotte

This chapter summarizes the development of Canada's electoral legislation since the 1997 election. It is intended as a follow-up to a chapter published in *The Canadian General Election of 1997*, in which I summarized and analyzed the changes brought about since the beginning of the decade.[1] The earlier chapter ended with the comment that the House of Commons was in danger of losing the initiative for the development of the body of laws that governs its own election, as rival actors were seizing the initiative. This view is no longer appropriate. Over the last nine years, Parliament has passed significant new legislation, and the government has been more successful than in the past when defending before the courts its policies in the field. Yet, the crisis of democratic governance that started in the late eighties is deepening. Younger generations keep disengaging from electoral politics at an alarming level, driving turnout from its usual 75 percent level to 61 percent in both the 2000 and 2004 elections. In 2006, turnout rose to 65 percent, not a bad score for a winter election, but still a relatively low one for an election leading to a change of government. (See Chapter Twelve.)

The chief developments of the period were the consolidation of the Elections Act in 2000, which put a cap on third-party election spending; the decennial redistribution of 2003; the political finance bill of 2003; the *Figueroa* case; and the emergence of a strong challenge to the existing plurality system.

A BRAND NEW ELECTIONS ACT, 2000

Since its latest overhaul in 1970, the Canada Elections Act had been amended piecemeal dozens of times, and there was a strong case for a wholesale consolidation to be carried out.[2] This was done in 2000 through

Bill C-2, "An Act respecting the election of members to the House of Commons, repealing other Acts relating to elections and making consequential amendments to other Acts."[3] Drawing on suggestions from the Lortie Commission, Chief Electoral Officer Kingsley's Statutory Reports,[4] the proceedings of the Standing Committee on Procedure and House Affairs, which culminated with its 35th Report (June 1998), plus various court decisions, the legislation was first introduced in October 1999. Instead of going next for second reading, it was referred under SO 73(1) to the Standing Committee on Procedure and House Affairs. The committee held twenty meetings and reported the Bill back to the House on December 3 with amendments. Further motions for amendment were dealt with on the floor of the House during three sitting days, and on February 22, 2000, the Bill, as amended, was concurred in with further amendments and read a second time. On February 28, the Liberals, with NDP support, rejected an Alliance motion objecting to numerous clauses, and the Bill was read a third time on division, with all four opposition parties voting against. An allocation of time motion had been passed earlier in order to speed up the process. The Senate later nodded in agreement and the Bill received Royal Assent on May 31, 2000. The legislation was not highly controversial, but more than fifty recorded divisions were held on its clauses, few showing unanimous agreement.

Like all documents of that nature, the Act encompassed scores of changes, some quite innocuous in scope. However, a few deserve comment.

Towards the Final Word on the Third-Party Spending Issue?

The most thorny issue Parliament had to deal with was third-party election spending; i.e., expenditures made by individuals and corporations or associations during election campaigns. This had been a problem since the introduction of spending ceilings for candidates and parties in 1974. As spending by political parties and candidates was strictly regulated, third-party spending could become a loophole that allowed moneyed interests to tilt the balance in favour of the parties and candidates they supported. The original provision that such expenditures had to be made "in good faith" led to ambiguous court decisions, and in 1983, the Trudeau government, with the support of both opposition parties, banned third-party spending altogether. This legislation was brought to court soon after and struck down as unconstitutional by the Alberta Court of Queen's Bench in

June 1984, on the eve of a general election.[5] This decision was not appealed by the government. As little advantage was taken of this new opportunity during the ensuing election, the issue vanished.

In the 1988 election, huge sums were spent by corporations to support the Free Trade Agreement with the United States, which was the chief issue of the campaign. However uncertain the impact of these advertising expenses actually was on the outcome of the election, many on the political left were quick to assume it had been decisive and accordingly pressed for another try at controlling third-party spending. The Lortie Royal Commission on Electoral Reform and Party Financing examined the issue with the dual concern of ensuring fair election campaigns and reinforcing the primacy of political parties at election times. This led Parliament in 1993 to deal with the issue with more liberal legislation that allowed for third-party spending subject to a ceiling of $1,000. In due course, the legislation was brought to court and again declared unconstitutional. This time, the government appealed the decision of the Alberta Court of Queen's Bench, but the latter was upheld three years later by the Alberta Court of Appeal.[6] The government chose not to appeal that decision.

Apprehended independent spending on a huge scale against the ruling party led the government to attempt a third time to regulate third-party spending, this time with more determination than before. Groups and persons were obliged to register with the Chief Electoral Officer if they had spent $500 on advertising to promote or oppose a party or a candidate. Such spending could not exceed $150,000 overall and $3,000 in each electoral district.[7] Collusion between various third parties in order to avoid spending limits was prohibited. Further, registered third parties had to disclose how much they had spent and where the money came from. To that extent, they were put more or less on the same footing as political parties and candidates, except they were not entitled to any reimbursement of their expenses, and the contributions they received were not eligible for any tax credit. The stated aim of this change was "to foster the level playing field that underlies the financial provisions of the Act. All Canadians have the right to know who is intervening in the political debate, and who is doing so through financial support."[8]

Less than three months after its enactment, this provision was brought to court by none other than former Reform Party MP Stephen Harper, then president of the National Citizens Coalition. The trial began on October 2, three weeks before the general election was called. The writs having been dropped, on October 23 Harper was granted by the Alberta Court of Queen's Bench an injunction that suspended third-party spending limits until the trial decision was rendered.[9] A protracted battle ensued involving three courts.[10] On November 10, following a ruling of the Supreme Court of Canada,[11] the Chief Electoral Officer reinstated the spending limits for the duration of the general election. However, it was announced that these limits would not be applied between October 22 and November 10 because of the earlier injunction. At the 2000 election, fifty third parties registered with Elections Canada and spent a total of $539,239.[12]

It was not until June 29, 2001, that the Alberta Court of Queen's Bench issued its decision on the essence of the trial. The impugned provision was struck down as unconstitutional.[13] This decision was upheld in December 2002 by the Alberta Court of Appeal.[14] This time, Ottawa decided to push the issue to the highest court of the land. Revealingly, the decision to appeal was announced at the same time as the government, shattered by accusations of unethical practices, was tabling its political finance bill (see below).

On May 18, 2004, the Supreme Court of Canada, in a split decision, reversed the rulings of both Alberta courts.[15] The spending limits were found not to be an encroachment either to the right to vote or to freedom of association. While agreeing that the limitations on third-party spending contravened freedom of expression, the majority held that this infringement was a reasonable limit under Section 1 of the Charter. This was in keeping with the rationale adopted by the Court in its ruling on the *Libman* case (1997). Even the dissenting judges wrote that "common sense dictates that promoting electoral fairness is a pressing and substantial objective in our liberal democracy, even in the absence of evidence that past elections have been unfair." While agreeing with the purpose of the legislation, they held that the limits were not proportional to this goal. The government's victory could hardly have been more complete. Both the *National Post* and the *Globe and Mail* lamented the decision.[16] Professor Alan Hutchison concluded, "The court shushes the rich."[17]

Thus ended the twenty-year-old judicial saga of third-party spending.[18] As in the *Carter* case on electoral boundaries, the Supreme Court had reached conclusions that were at variance with those of the U.S. Supreme Court.

A related issue was the time period during which political advertising could be made. Under the existing law, parties and candidates were prohibited from advertising at the beginning and at the end of the election campaign, while third parties could advertise at any time. Under the 2000 law, both sets of actors were prohibited from advertising on polling day.

Opinion Polls

Following the 1998 decision of the Supreme Court in the *Thomson Newspapers* case,[19] results of opinion polls could be published at any time throughout the election period. The new law prohibited the publication of polls on election day. A more innovative provision was a requirement that media reports on opinion polls specify who sponsored the survey, the pollster organization that conducted it, the date of the survey, and data on the sample, the rate of response, and the margin of error. Surveys not based on recognized statistical methods must be identified accordingly.[20]

Political Finance

The political financing provisions of the legislation were revisited. Parties were now required to file more comprehensive financial reports, including a statement of assets and liabilities and a statement on the sources of all contributions received as well as the funds transferred to candidates, riding associations, and trust funds for the election of a candidate. The threshold for disclosing the source of a contribution was raised from $100 to $200. Similarly, the threshold that entitles a donor to a tax credit of 75 percent was raised from $100 to $200. Numbered companies had to disclose the name of their chief manager.

In a subsequent (22nd) report, dated March 21, 2000, the House Committee on Procedure and House Affairs dealt with more general election law issues raised during its proceedings. The arguments raised by various witnesses on issues like proportional representation, the alternative vote, fixed election dates, women candidates, and the enhancement of participation by Aboriginals and other groups were mentioned, without the committee taking a stand.

Franchise Issues

Bill C-2 enfranchised returning officers for the first time. This meant that in the case of a tie between the two leading candidates in an electoral district after all votes had been counted, the returning officer would no longer be empowered to break the logjam by casting the decisive vote. Instead, a by-election would be held later for that purpose. Successive recommendations from the Chief Electoral Officer that the appointment of returning officers should no longer be left to the cabinet were ignored.

The legislation also provided that persons serving a prison sentence of two years or more would remain disenfranchised. However, in October 2002, the Supreme Court of Canada ended another twenty-year-old judicial debate by overturning a decision of the Federal Court of Canada (Appeal Division) and by ruling that all prisoners should be enfranchised.[21] This decision left only two Canadians deprived of the right to vote: the Chief Electoral Officer and the Assistant Chief Electoral Officer.

THE REDISTRIBUTION OF 2003

Compared with earlier experiences, the redistribution of 2003 went unusually smoothly. In March 2002, the Chief Electoral Officer disclosed what the representation of each province would be, based on the 2001 census figures. The size of the House rose to 308 seats, an increase of 7.[22] Ontario gained three seats, British Columbia and Alberta both got two more seats, while all other provinces had the same number as before, which meant for each a marginally smaller proportion of an expanded total. Table 1 provides the details of the computations.

The gap between the three faster-growing provinces and the others remains huge. The so-called senatorial floor rule now protects the four Atlantic provinces, resulting in an increase of nine seats from the preliminary allotment, while the grandfather clause adds a further eighteen seats (seven to Quebec, five to Saskatchewan, four to Manitoba, and one to both Newfoundland and Nova Scotia). As a consequence of these rules, ridings in Ontario, British Columbia, and Alberta have a population of 106,000 to 108,000, while the averages for provinces with a slower rate of growth range from 96,500 (Quebec) to 33,824 (P.E.I.). The faster-growing provinces, containing a total of 61.1 percent of the total population, have an aggregate 55.7 percent of the provincial seats. Strict representation based on population would have granted them sixteen more seats. While grumbling was heard in some quarters, there was no attempt to amend the redistribution rules adopted in 1985.

Once the representation of each province has been determined, electoral boundaries within each must be readjusted by a three-member boundary commission, even if the total number of districts has not been altered, in order to take into account population shifts and to ensure that Canadians remain fairly represented. Under the Electoral

Table 1
Representation formula — detailed calculations for 2001 census

	Senate Seat Allocation	Seats 33rd Parl	Population (2001 Census)	Divided by National Quotient: 107,220 (Rounded)	Rounded Result	Add'l Seats (Senate Clause)	Add'l Seats (Grandfather Clause)	Total Seats	Provincial Quotient (Rounded)
NL	6	7	512,930	4.784	5	1	1	7	73,276
PEI	4	4	135,294	1.262	1	3	0	4	33,824
NS	10	11	908,007	8.469	8	2	1	11	82,546
NB	10	10	729,498	6.804	7	3	0	10	72,950
QC	24	75	7,237,479	67.501	68	0	7	75	96,500
ON	24	95	11,410,046	106.417	106	0	0	106	107,642
MB	6	14	1,119,583	10.442	10	0	4	14	79,970
SK	6	14	978,933	9.130	9	0	5	14	69,924
AB	6	21	2,974,807	27.745	28	0	0	28	106,243
BC	6	28	3,907,738	36.446	36	0	0	36	108,548
Prov'l Total	102	279	29,914,315		278	9	18	305	90,080
NU	1		26,745					1	
NWT	1	2	37,360					1	
YT	1	1	28,674					1	
Nat'l Total	105	282	30,007,094					308	

Boundaries Readjustment Act, boundary commissions are expected to propose districts with populations that do not deviate by more than 25 percent of the provincial average, except in extraordinary circumstances. Actually, by 2001, forty-three of the districts created by the 1996 representation order (on the basis of 1991 population figures) exceeded this limit, with three deviating from the average by more than 50 percent, in addition to the two "extraordinary circumstances" districts. This only highlighted the need for change.

The composition of the ten provincial boundary commissions was announced on the same day and as usual included a few political scientists. For the first time since the thirties, the redistribution process went almost according to schedule, as there was no attempt by Parliament to interrupt the process in order to revisit the redistribution rules. The proposals of the boundary commissions were published during the summer of 2002, followed by public hearings thereon during the fall. More than 2,000 submissions or notices of intent to appear (including 151 from MPs) were received at this stage. The boundaries of no less than 241 of the proposed ridings were altered following public hearings.[23] All commissions had reported to the Speaker by the end of March 2003, and their reports were referred to the House of Commons Standing Committee on Procedure and House Affairs, which considered the objections filed by MPs. The boundaries of twenty-nine ridings were altered at this stage. The reports of the House Committee were transmitted to the boundary commissions, which had all made their final decisions by mid-August 2003. This allowed the new Redistribution Order to be proclaimed on August 25, just two months beyond the original schedule.

The existence of a statutory one-year delay between proclamation and enforcement might have postponed the coming into force of new boundaries if the next election had been called before August 25, 2004. However, by legislation Parliament moved to April 1, 2004, the earliest date for the new boundaries to be in force.[24] The next general election was called on May 23, 2004.

With the 2003 redistribution, the principle of equality of voting power was pushed further than ever. While commissions were allowed to deviate from the provincial average by as much as 25 percent, only 17 of the 305 provincial ridings actually deviated from the average by more than 15 percent.[25] Extraordinary circumstances were invoked to create two districts with smaller populations than allowed: Labrador (Newfoundland) and Kenora (Ontario). In the end, only 39 of the 301 districts delimited in 1996 survived the redistribution unaltered.[26]

The net impact of the boundary changes on party standings was modest. A transposition by Elections Canada of the 2000 election results in the new boundaries showed Liberals leading in 172 districts (+2), the Canadian Alliance in 70 (+4), and the Progressive Conservatives in 13 (+1), while the Bloc Québécois and the NDP showed no change, at 38 and 13 respectively. The increase for the Alliance stemmed from the addition of new seats in their strongholds of Alberta and British Columbia, while for the Liberals a slight decrease in two Atlantic provinces was more than compensated by an increase in Ontario.

The customary changes to the names of districts at the initiative of MPs were made in September 2003 through a single Bill (C-20), as had been done for the first time following the previous redistribution.[27] The names of thirty-eight ridings were altered. These changes were accepted by the Senate, though with some reluctance.[28] Most new names were longer than those they replaced, with the riding "West Vancouver–Sunshine Coast–Sea to Sky Country" competing strenuously with "Montmagny–L'Islet–Kamouraska–Rivière-du-Loup" and "Cumberland–Colchester –Musquodoboit Valley" for the distinction of having the longest name ever.

During the 2006 election campaign, Conservative Leader Stephen Harper noted the prejudice caused to rapidly growing provinces by existing redistribution rules and indicated his willingness to correct this problem "while ensuring that no province sees its number of MPs decline."[29] This might foreshadow a re-examination of the redistribution rules following the next census.

THE POLITICAL FINANCE BILL OF 2003

The basics of Canadian political finance legislation were established in 1974 by the Election Expenses Act. Actually, this landmark legislation dealt with more than its title suggested, as it regulated political contributions as well. Yet, it is fair to say that while the provisions dealing with election expenses, notably the issue of third-party spending, were extensively discussed and modified over the years, the contribution side of the regulatory regime survived pretty much unaltered for thirty years.

The approach underlying this regime was rather straightforward. The emphasis was on *disclosure*, viewed as *the* instrument for eliminating the worst excesses and for restoring public trust in the political system. Contributions from all kinds of sources were allowed, except from foreign companies (a proviso that was added in 1993). However, the amounts received had to be disclosed by parties and candidates in their financial returns, and the source had to be identified for donations exceeding $100 (a benchmark raised to $200 in 2000 in view of inflation). There was no limit on the size of donations. The rationale was that the public should know where the money came from, and that this would be enough to deter corruption, as contracts awarded in dubious circumstances could be traced to political donations. Big corporate money could flow to both the Liberals and the Tories, while big labour money could flow to the NDP. In order to encourage individuals to balance corporate and union money by contributing to parties, generous fiscal incentives were created.

Compared with the situation that had hitherto prevailed, with political party financing remaining shrouded in secrecy, this was a mighty improvement. Some provinces (like Ontario and New Brunswick) went further by capping the size of corporate donations, but it can fairly be said that the approach taken by Ottawa predominated in existing provincial legislation as well.

The main challenge to this approach came from Quebec. In 1977, under Premier René Lévesque, the province passed landmark legislation that banned corporate and labour union contributions and made individual electors the single source of donations to parties, subject to a yearly ceiling of $3,000. Acknowledging that *financement populaire* might not be enough to fill the void created by the ban on corporate donations, the law provided for a sum of $0.25 per elector (about $1 million) to be distributed by the state to parties, on the basis of the support they had received at the previous election. One cannot be surprised that this bold legislation was championed by a party that did not rely on corporate or union money for its own financing.[30]

For some time, the Quebec approach was viewed as an oddity on the federal scene, yet in Quebec it was acclaimed by most as a milestone that helped to eliminate corruption and to bolster the credibility of politicians. In the late eighties, adoption of this approach by Ottawa was championed by Tory MP François Gérin, who was close to the Parti Québécois (he joined the Bloc Québécois in 1990). Gérin's crusade was a failure within his own party, and both the Royal Commission headed by businessman Pierre Lortie and election law amendments passed thereafter ignored the Quebec approach. In part, it was dismissed as a sham in view of insistent rumours that the law was routinely evaded through corporate contributions disguised as individual donations.[31] This did not deter Manitoba from adopting the same approach in 2000.

What, then, led Jean Chrétien, a politician not known as a crusader for political reform, with many business connections despite his populist style, to challenge the existing consensus and to move in the opposite direction? Often it is a scandal that drives politicians to pass legislation designed both to curb corrupt practices and to restore trust in the system. During Chrétien's second and third terms, serious allegations (the so-called "Shawinigate," the Groupaction scandal) were raised against, though strongly denied by, the Liberal government. However, in August 2002, Chrétien was forced by a party revolt to announce he would retire by February 2004. This granted him an eighteen-month reprieve. The most plausible explanation for what followed is that the Prime Minister was troubled by the impact of these accusations on the public perception of his legacy and wanted to improve the way political financing was conducted. A supplementary consideration might have been that at this juncture in his career, he was aware that should the reform have harmful consequences for his party, it would be his successor who would have to live with them.

The substance of the legislation was hinted at in the Throne Speech of September 2002 and through leaks in December, and was disclosed on January 29 when Bill C-24, An Act to Amend the Canada Elections Act and the Income Tax Act (Political Financing), a bulky ninety-six-page document, was introduced in the House by Minister Don Boudria. It was the boldest attempt in this area in thirty years. The Bill banned corporate and labour union contributions, except those given to riding associations, nomination contestants, and candidates up to a maximum of $1,000. Only individual Canadians could contribute, and only up to $10,000 for each party (including its riding associations and candidates).

Anticipated shortages of funds resulting from these restrictions were to be compensated by the public purse. The tax credit for individual contributions was made more generous: the first $400 was entitled to a 75 percent tax credit, and the maximum amount of the tax credit was raised from $500 to $650.[32] More importantly, all parties that had secured 2 percent of the vote at the previous general election[33] were entitled to receive a quarterly allowance fund of $0.375 per vote received. Party riding associations had to be registered with the Chief Electoral Officer, thus eliminating the so-called black hole that many complained had allowed much money to escape the controls set by the law. The ceiling for party election expenses was raised from $0.62 to $0.70, and the portion thereof that was reimbursable was raised from 22.5 percent to 50 percent, while the threshold for candidates to be reimbursed for their election expenses was lowered from 15 percent to 10 percent of the vote. In addition, the definition of election expenses was broadened to include opinion polling.

The sweeping character of the reform was highlighted by the fact that the rules applying to contributions to and expenses by parties and candidates at elections were extended to leadership contestants and nomination contestants in ridings. The difficulty of determining a figure that would be appropriate for small as well as for big parties prevented the legislation from imposing a ceiling on total spending for leadership contestants.

The debate that surrounded Bill C-24 did not follow either the idealistic pattern of all parties agreeing in full harmony or the more familiar pattern of a government party imposing its will over some opposition parties.[34] Instead, at least outside the floor of the House, the battle mostly pitted Liberals against Liberals. Heated discussions took place within the government caucus before the Bill was tabled, and Prime Minister Chrétien threatened explicitly that he would call a snap election should the Bill be rejected. His rival Paul Martin openly deplored that the measure meant Canadian taxpayers would finance the Bloc Québécois, while the emergence of new parties would allegedly be hindered. Many of Martin's supporters within the Liberal caucus criticized the Bill sharply. Liberal Party President Stephen LeDrew openly restated the conventional wisdom by alleging that full disclosure was enough.[35]

Editorial comment on the Bill was mostly positive,[36] though some were unenthusiastic.[37] While Heritage Minister Sheila Copps fed the suspicions of many Canadians by stating that business contributions to the Liberal Party had been instrumental in slowing down the ratification of the Kyoto Protocol, perhaps the most revealing comment came from those who customarily provided the largest donations. Business executives as well as the Canadian Labour Congress let it be known that they saw no problem with the Bill.[38] The Bloc Québécois, then in deep trouble, was enthusiastic about the prospect of being rescued through federal public funds, while in Quebec the Bill was praised from all sides as an acknowledgement that the late René Lévesque had been right after all.[39]

As the views of dissenting Liberals found support only from the Canadian Alliance, while the Bloc Québécois, the NDP, and the Progressive Conservative Party supported the legislation, dissent within the Liberal caucus did not surface during the parliamentary consideration, with Paul Martin himself supporting the Bill at second reading.

So, in the end, the Prime Minister carried the day. How much it was his own decision is emphasized by the fact that Chrétien insisted on moving himself the second reading of a measure that was introduced by one of his ministers. The Bill was then supported by all parties but the Canadian Alliance.[40] The opposition from the latter did not stem from their reliance on corporate funding. Stephen Harper pointed out that 61 percent of the Alliance's funding in 2001 came from fifty thousand individuals, while of the Liberal Party's funding for the same year, only 19 percent came from five thousand individuals. His chief objection was summarized in an amendment to the motion for second reading, that "the Bill shifts the sources of contributions to political parties from the voluntary actions of people and organizations to a mandatory imposition on all Canadians, making political parties more dependent upon the state and less responsive to society" or, in cruder words, "the true nature of the Bill is simply the replacement by the government of its addiction to large business and union donations with an addiction to taxpayer funding."[41]

As it finally emerged from the parliamentary mills (after some eighteen meetings of the Committee on Procedure and House Affairs, plus the amendments passed at the report stage), the Bill was even more far-reaching than it had been upon its introduction. The ceiling on individual contributions was lowered from $10,000 to $5,000. An amendment introduced a spending limit for nomination contestants fixed at 20 percent of the limit allowed for a candidate's election expenses. Party and candidate expenses were to be reimbursed at a rate of 60 percent (only for the next election, in the case of parties). And the amount of the quarterly allowance for parties was raised to $0.4375, which on a yearly basis meant an increase from $1.50 to $1.75. The much-maligned party bagmen sitting in the Senate did not scuttle the Bill, which received Royal Assent on June 19, 2003, and came into force on January 1, 2004 (SC 2003, c. 19). A survey conducted during the 2004 election campaign found strong approval for five key provisions of the legislation, at least among those who had an opinion.[42]

The financial reports filed by the registered parties for the year 2004 offer an interesting insight on the extent to which parties are financed through voluntary individual contributions and through state subsidies. The Conservatives led with $10.9 million from 68,382 individuals, an average of $160 each. They were followed by the New Democrats, with $5.2 million from 30,097 individuals (an average of $173); the Liberals, with $4.7 million from 17,429 individuals (an average of $271); the Bloc Québécois, with $858,000 from 8,775 individuals (an average of $98); and the Greens, with $351,000 from 3,606 individuals (an average of $97). Contributions to the eight other registered parties totalled $308,378.

The total amount contributed by individuals to all political parties in 2004 was $22,378,265. This figure must be compared with the allocations paid to political parties for the same year, which totalled $23,196,130, and with the reimbursements of election expenses o parties ($30.5 million) and to candidates ($24.8 million) following the 2004 general election. Keeping in mind that individual donations are compensated by generous tax credits, the extent to which political parties are henceforth funded by the state is obvious.

TOWARDS A PROPORTIONAL REPRESENTATION SYSTEM?

The expectation that the regionally lopsided outcomes of the 1997 election would spark a new debate on the pros and cons of a proportional representation (PR) system was not immediately fulfilled. Following the 2000 election, there was renewed interest in the issue, but with a different perspective. Hitherto most grievances expressed against the plurality rule were based on its potentially harmful effect on national unity. The rationale, first expressed by political scientist Alan Cairns in 1968, was that plurality artificially restricted national parties in a few regions, thereby hampering their ability to take a national view of issues and exacerbating regional cleavages.[43] This time, plurality tends to be indicted on more classical grounds, as an impediment to the emergence and survival of smaller parties. An important development is the rise of interest groups dedicated to PR. Fair Vote Canada, the most important of these groups, takes the view that any parliamentary majority based on a mere plurality of the popular vote is a "phoney majority." The elections of 2004 and 2006 gave more salience to the issue, as the Green Party secured 4 percent of the vote in both cases. Political scientists have shown keen interest in the issue and have generally been supportive of PR.[44]

In the provinces, serious attempts to reform the electoral system have been made, many of them still ongoing at the time of writing, but none having been successful so far.[45] The most innovative approach has been the creation in British Columbia in 2003 of a non-partisan forum called the Citizens' Assembly, composed of 160 individuals selected by lot from among the general electorate. It included two people from each provincial riding (on the basis of gender parity), plus two representatives from the Aboriginal population. The assembly convened in 2004.

Members were lectured on the mechanics and implications of electoral systems by experts. This was followed by hearings of the public throughout the province and by a deliberation that unexpectedly led not only to the near-unanimous rejection of the plurality rule but also to the selection of the Irish single transferable vote system (STV) as the alternative.[46] Politicians agreed to be excluded completely from the process and to the direct submission of the system selected by the Citizeens' Assembly to the people through a referendum, with the proviso that they would feel bound by the outcome only if the formula secured the approval of 60 percent of the valid votes and a majority in 60 percent of the ridings.

The referendum was held on May 18, 2005, simultaneously with the general election. With politicians abstaining from taking sides, STV won the support of 57 percent of the vote and came ahead in seventy-seven districts out of seventy-nine. The Legislative Assembly decided that another referendum would be held later, simultaneously with the next general election, but on the basis of a more specific proposal including the proposed boundaries for multimember electoral districts. In 2006, Ontario set up a Citizens' Assembly on the same lines, but without setting in advance a threshold for victory.

In Quebec, the issue of proportional representation, which had been debated in the early and late seventies as well as in the early eighties, had remained in limbo since, despite a brave promise in the Parti Québécois' program in 1994 that such a reform would be made as soon as possible. But after winning the 1998 election with a smaller number of votes than the Liberals, the PQ decided to shelve its promise until after Quebec had become sovereign country. Interest was revived unexpectedly in 2001, when a committee of the National Assembly was empowered to study the issue, and when *États généraux* were set up with Claude Béland as chairman to deal with scores of political reform issues like referendums, the introduction of a U.S.–style presidential system, the drafting of a distinct constitution for Quebec, and electoral system reform. Though the *États généraux* held in February 2003 opted massively for a mixed electoral system, the steering committee chaired by Béland chose to recommend the introduction of a list PR system based on regions. The Charest government opted instead for a type of mixed member proportional (MMP) system, which was formulated in a draft bill released in December 2004.[47] A special committee of the National Assembly, enlarged with eight citizens selected by lot from among more than two thousand applicants, heard expert witnesses and toured the province in early 2006. The introduction of any PR system is strenuously opposed by the Parti Québécois, which won the 1998 election with a smaller proportion of the vote province-wide than the Liberal Party.

In New Brunswick and Prince Edward Island, commissions were set up to explore electoral reform. New Brunswick's Commission on Legislative Democracy, a royal commission in all but the name, had broad terms of reference including not only the electoral system but electoral boundaries, referendums, and parliamentary reform. Its report, released in January 2005, recommended the adoption of an MMP system broadly patterned on the formula introduced in New Zealand during the previous decade, but with list MLAs elected within four regions rather than province-wide.[48] No immediate action, except the preparation of new electoral boundaries for *single*-member districts, has followed. In Prince Edward Island, a one-person commission composed of a retired judge also adopted the MMP approach.[49] However, the proposal met with the hostility of both main parties and, at a referendum held on November 2005, it was overwhelmingly rejected by the electorate.[50]

Ottawa's response to the call for PR has been lukewarm. The Law Commission of Canada commissioned research on the issue and heard citizens before issuing in 2004 a detailed report recommending the introduction of a MMP system.[51] In a House of Commons of 304, there would be 197 elected by plurality in single-member constituencies and 107 elected through party lists in a compensatory way. Voters would vote for a constituency MP and, as they wished, support either the closed list of a party or a single candidate on a party list. List seats would be allocated within each province except in Ontario and Quebec, which would be divided into three and two regions respectively. Candidates would be allowed to run both in a constituency and on a party list. No threshold would prevent the election of members from small parties, but only parties with candidates in one-third of the constituencies would be eligible for list seats.[52]

However, as the debates held in the House over the issue in February 2001 and September 2003 suggested, most MPs are decidedly hostile to the very notion of PR.[53] The merger in December 2003 of the Canadian Alliance and Progressive Conservative parties to create the new Conservative Party of Canada weakened the case for alternative formulas on this side of the political spectrum, leaving the NDP, the Greens, and PR activists as the sole defenders of the idea. During both the 2004 and 2006 campaigns, NDP Leader Jack Layton repeatedly advocated PR.

The NDP took advantage of its pivotal position in the minority Parliament elected in June 2004 to extract from the ruling Liberals, with the support of all other parties, an amendment to the Address empowering the Standing Committee on Procedure and House Affairs "to recommend a process that engages citizens and parliamentarians in an examination of our electoral system with a review of all options."[54] The committee heard expert witnesses on the issue and travelled to various countries in order to get acquainted with the STV and MMP systems.

In its 43rd Report, tabled June 16, 2005, the committee rejected the citizens' assembly approach, as it excluded MPs from the decision-making process on electoral system reform. Rather, it advocated a complex approach involving both a special committee of the House and a "citizens' task force" working in parallel and later comparing their respective conclusions, with MPs having the last word. The task force, whose composition and working methods remained unspecified, would report on the values and principles that Canadians would like to integrate in their democratic and electoral system. The special committee would be empowered to hold hearings throughout Canada. Both bodies were expected to meet in November to discuss their respective findings. The task force would thereafter report its findings to the special committee, which would submit its recommendations to the House by the end of February 2006. In separate reports, both the Conservatives and the Bloc Québécois highlighted how slim the consensus among parties was. The former supported a citizens' assembly on the B.C. model, while the latter expressed concerns about the creation of a citizens' task force. No action followed, as the attention of the public was already monopolized by the political crisis stemming from the sponsorship scandal, which later led to the downfall of the Martin government and its defeat at the January 2006 election.

The new Conservative government elected in 2006 is committed to deal with the issue. The Speech from the Throne of April 4, 2006, stated, "Building on the work begun in the last Parliament, this Government will seek to involve parliamentarians and citizens in examining the challenges facing Canada's electoral system and democratic institutions."[55]

THE *FIGUEROA* CASE AND ITS AFTERMATH

In a perceptive comment on the political finance bill, columnist Hugh Windsor argued that Chrétien's political finance bill included some of the first steps towards proportional representation.[56] A few provisions of Bill C-24 can indeed be interpreted as fostering a more diverse political picture. This is the case not only for the provision that state subsidies, now the chief source of political funds, will be apportioned on the basis of the popular vote cast for parties having secured 2 percent of the vote, rather than on the percentage of seats won,[57] but also for the lowering to 10 percent of the threshold allowing candidates to be reimbursed for their expenses. Another important judicial decision might well be identified in the future as a harbinger of change.

Since 1970, the Canada Elections Act has included provisions for the registration of political parties. Registration entitles parties to privileges like issuing receipts for the contributions they receive, being allotted broadcasting time, and having their candidates identified as such on the ballot papers. The Act made life more difficult for emerging parties, as it required that for a new party's registration to come into force, and to be maintained, fifty candidates had to be sponsored. New parties that could not reach this benchmark were not registered. Registered parties who failed to field fifty candidates lost their status as registered parties. In 1993, this misfortune happened to a few small parties, including the Communist Party of Canada, which was obliged to liquidate its assets, to pay all its debts, and to transmit the balance to the Chief Electoral Officer.

The leader of the party, Miguel Figueroa, challenged this benchmark as an encroachment on the right to run for office under Section 3 of the Charter. A lower Ontario court agreed with this view in 1999 and ordered the threshold to be lowered to two candidates.[58] This ruling was reversed by the Ontario Court of Appeal the next year, though the judge acknowledged that non-registered parties should be allowed to have their names on the ballot paper.[59]

The issue reached the Supreme Court of Canada. In an important decision released in June 2003, the Court fully agreed with Figueroa and invalidated the fifty-candidate threshold.[60] Indeed, the ruling read in some parts as a plea for small political parties.

> The capacity of a political party to provide individual citizens with an opportunity to express an opinion on governmental policy and the proper functioning of public institutions is not dependent upon its capacity to participate in the governance of the country subsequent to an election.... The members and supporters of political parties that nominate candidates in fewer than 50 electoral districts do play a meaningful role in the electoral process. They are both a vehicle for the participation of individual citizens in the open debate

occasioned by the electoral process and an outlet for
the expression of support for political platforms that
are different from those adopted by political parties
with a broad base of support.[61]

The Court agreed to postpone the coming into force of this ruling
for a year in order to grant Parliament the opportunity to adjust the legislation accordingly. The government introduced a measure to that
effect. Despite the preference of some members for a higher figure, Bill
C-3 reduced the threshold from fifty candidates to one. Parties applying
for registration were required to submit signed declarations of support
from at least 250 members and to have no fewer than four party officers.
The most thorny issues were the addition in the Canada Elections Act of
a definition of a political party as "an organization one of whose fundamental purposes is to participate in public affairs by endorsing one or
more of its members as candidates and supporting their election" and
the resulting obligation for the Chief Electoral Officer to make value
judgments, before granting the application, as to whether the appli-
cant's "fundamental purpose" was to participate in public affairs, by
looking at documents like the party's constitution, internal rules, and
political manifesto. Despite the understandable misgivings expressed by
Chief Electoral Officer Jean-Pierre Kingsley and some witnesses, the legislation was passed with the understanding that it was imperative, on
the eve of a general election, to fill the legal vacuum created by the
Supreme Court, and that the issue would be re-examined later.[62]

PERSPECTIVES FOR THE FUTURE

The 2006 election resulted in the formation of a new government that
immediately showed that electoral reform would be one of its priorities.
As noted above, the Speech from the Throne announced that the public would be consulted on the electoral system. More specific reforms
were included in the massive Federal Accountability Bill (C-2) tabled on
April 11, 2006.

After a quarter of century, the recommendations of the Chief
Electoral Officer to end the appointment by the cabinet of returning
officers in constituencies were accepted. The Bill would wipe the slate
clean by declaring vacant the offices of incumbent ROs. Returning officers will be appointed in the future by the Chief Electoral Officer on

the basis of merit for a renewable term of ten years, and may be removed by the same.

The ceiling for individual contributions to registered parties, independent candidates, and leadership contestants will be reduced from $5,000 to $1,000. A new annual limit of $1,000 will be created on contributions to registered associations, nomination contestants, and candidates of a registered party. Contributions by corporations, trade unions, and associations will be banned totally. The period within which a prosecution for an electoral offence may be instituted will be extended to ten years from the commission of the offence. Registered parties and candidates will be prohibited from transferring money to candidates directly from a trust fund.

Finally, in May 2006, Prime Minister Harper announced that his government would introduce legislation providing for federal elections to be held at fixed dates every four years, a move that was hailed by all opposition parties but the Liberals.

CONCLUSION

The most important developments in Canadian election law since 1997 occurred undoubtedly in the area of political finance. Third-party spending, which potentially could have made a mockery of the spending limits introduced in 1974, has been curbed. Instead of relying on large donations from corporations and labour unions, parties now depend chiefly on public subsidies and individual contributions. Corporate contributions are limited in size and may go only to candidates. The contrast between this regime and the way campaigns are financed in the United States was repeatedly and favourably mentioned.

As noted above, political finance laws aim at restoring the public trust in the political system and those who operate it following a huge scandal. The irony is that the passing of Bill C-24 came *before* the disclosure of corrupt practices (the sponsorships) of unsuspected scope that brought the mighty Liberal administration to an end and, for a time, seemed to have the potential to lead to the dislocation of the country. Public outrage was immense in the wake of the revelations by Jean Brault and others during the Gomery Commission's hearings, and trust in politicians reached historic lows. This episode has driven home an important point: Canadians are no longer in a mood to forgive corruption at the top, a point that will hopefully be remembered by the political class in the future.

By uncovering the shady practices that had marred the financing of the Liberal Party in Quebec under the previous rules, the Gomery inquiry may have ultimately proved that the rationale for Bill C-24 was sound. It is revealing that the Gomery report did not see fit to make recommendations dealing with the way political parties were financed. In this field, at least, the ruling Liberals had pre-empted the strike. The new government, far from questioning the internal logic of the legislation, intends to go further in the same direction.

NOTES

1   Louis Massicotte, "Electoral Reform in the Charter Era," in *The Canadian General Election of 1997*, ed. Alan Frizzell and Jon H. Pammett (Toronto: Dundurn Press, 1997), 167–91.

2   Earlier consolidations of the Elections Act (apart from the periodic comprehensive revisions of all federal statutes) were made in 1874, 1900, 1906, 1920, 1934, 1938, 1960, and 1970.

3   The short title is the *Canada Elections Act* (S.C. 2000, c. 9).

4   Canada, Chief Electoral Officer, *Canada's Electoral System. Strengthening the Foundation. Annex to the Report of the Chief Electoral Officer of Canada on the 35th Election*, Ottawa, 1996; *Report of the Chief Electoral Officer of Canada on the 36th General Election*, Ottawa, August 1997.

5   *National Citizens Coalition* v. *Canada (AG)* (1984), 11 D.L.R. (4th) 481.

6   *Canada (AG)* v. *Somerville* (1996), 136 D.L.R. (4th) 205.

7   These figures are subject to inflation adjustments. At the November 2000 election, the actual limits were $152,550 and $3,051 respectively. By the January 2006 election, they had risen to $172,050 and $3,441.

8   *Report of the Chief Electoral Officer of Canada on the 37th General Election held on November 27, 2000*, p. 68.

9   *Harper* v. *Canada (AG)*, [2000] A.J. No. 1226.

10   The federal government appealed from the injunction to the Alberta Court of Appeal, but lost: *Canada (AG)* v. *Harper*, [2000] A.J. No. 1240. An appeal was launched to the Supreme Court of Canada, which suspended the application of the injunction decision until it could hear the injunction application, which meant that spending limits were reinstated.

11   *Canada (AG)* v. *Harper*, [2000] 2 S.C.R. 764.

12   The figures for the 2004 election were sixty-three registered third parties spending a total of $717,979. In 2006, seventy-seven third parties registered. Figures kindly provided to the author by Alain Pelletier, Elections Canada, April 2006.

13   *Harper* v. *Canada (AG)*, [2001] 9 W.W.R. 650.

14   *Harper* v. *Canada (AG)*, [2002] 223 D.L.R. (4th) 275.

15   *Harper* v. *Canada (AG)*, 2004 CSC 33.

16   "A body blow to free speech," *National Post*; "The court seals off a Charter freedom," *The Globe and Mail*; both May 19, 2004.

17   Alan C. Hutchinson, comment published in the *Globe and Mail*, May 19, 2004.

18 This might prove only a temporary conclusion, as the person who lost the case became prime minister of Canada in 2006, if at the helm of a minority government,

19 *Thomson Newspapers Co.* v. *Canada (AG)*, [1998] 1 S.C.R. 877.

20 Ss. 326(1) of the Act.

21 *Sauvé* v. *Canada (Chief Electoral Officer)*, [2002] 3 S.C.R. 519.

22 Had the previous "amalgam" redistribution formula remained, the total size of the House would have reached 373 under the 2001 census figures. See Russell Williams, "Comparing Federal Electoral Redistributions: Straining Canada's System of Representation," paper presented at the CPSA Annual General Meeting, Quebec City, May 2001.

23 Figures kindly provided to the author by Herschell Sax, Elections Canada, April 2006.

24 Bill C-5, assented to March 11, 2004 (S.C. 2004, c. 1).

25 Canada, Chief Electoral Officer, *Enhancing the Values of Redistribution. Recommendations from the Chief Electoral Officer of Canada following the Representation Order of 2003*. Ottawa, May 2005, p. 22.

26 These figures include the three districts of the Territories, which were not subject to alteration.

27 S.C. 2004, c. 19. Two other changes were passed in February 2005, one being actually a return to the earlier name.

28 In its 8th Report, dated May 6, 2004, the Standing Committee of the Senate on Legal and Constitutional Affairs, while reporting the Bill without amendment, restated its earlier objections to the custom of altering the names of electoral districts through legislation, noting that such changes entailed costs of about $500,000. Senators approvingly quoted a remark found in the 16th Report of the House Committee of Procedure and House Affairs (April 2004) that "it seems pointless to us for House business to be needlessly taken up with name changes from the commissions."

29 Canadian Press, "Green Party, NDP support move toward PR system," *The Guardian* (Charlottetown), January 9, 2006, p. A8.

"31 This view has slowly become conventional wisdom and has been confirmed by some of the revelations arising from the Gomery hearings in April 2005.

32 The full formula reads as follows: the tax credit is equal to 75 percent of the first $400 of a donation, plus 50 percent of the next $350, plus one-third of the portion exceeding $750, up to a total tax credit of $650. This meant that beyond $1,275 the donation does not bring any tax credit beyond the maximum.

33 Parties scoring less than 2 percent nationwide were nevertheless entitled if they had secured an aggregate 5 percent of the vote in the districts where they had fielded candidates.

34 On this issue, see Louis Massicotte, "La réforme du mode de scrutin: L'unanimité des partis est-elle indispensable?" *Éthique publique* 7, no. 1 (2005): 38–47.

35 Stephen LeDrew, letter to *The Globe and Mail*, April 28, 2003.

36 See "To tame the excesses of political donations," *The Globe and Mail*, January 30, 2003; André Pratte, "Il était temps," *La Presse*, January 24, 2003, p. A10.

37 "This is not real reform," *The Gazette*, January 30, 2003; Anthony Westell, "You call this an electoral reform bill?" *Globe and Mail*, February 3, 2003.

38 Brian Laghi and Janet McFarland, "New rules to bend traditional party ties," *Globe and Mail*, January 30, 2003.

39 Michel Vastel, "Chrétien et Lévesque : même vertu!" *Le Soleil*, January 30, 2003; Vincent Marissal, "René Lévesque et Jean Chrétien, même combat," *La Presse*, January 30, 2003, p. A6; Raymond Giroux, "Chrétien s'inspire de René Lévesque ... et va plus loin," *Le Soleil*, January 30, 2003.

40 However, a motion for time allocation was passed against the wishes of all opposition parties in order to shorten the report stage and third reading.

41 House of Commons, *Debates*, February 11, 2003.

42 For example, the ban on corporate and labour union contributions was approved nine to one, with 34 percent having no opinion. My thanks to André Blais and to the Canadian Election Study Team, who conducted the survey and provided the relevant figures.

43 Louis Massicotte, "Changing the Canadian Electoral System," *Choices* (The Institute of Research on Public Policy) 7, no. 1 (2001).

44 Larry Gordon and Doris Anderson, "Political scientists from 34 Canadian universities call for national referendum on electoral reform," January 2002. A total of 103 political scientists signed the petition sponsored by Fair Vote Canada.

45 Ken Carty, "Regional Responses to Electoral Reform," *Canadian Parliamentary Review* 29, no. 1 (2006): 22–6; Peter Aucoin, Louis Massicotte, and David E. Smith, "Round table on the process to be used for electoral reform," *Canadian Parliamentary Review* 28, no. 2 (2005): 23–5.

46 British Columbia Citizens' Assembly on Electoral Reform, *Making Every Vote Count. The Case for Electoral Reform in British Columbia, Final Report* (Vancouver, December 2004), is a short brochure outlining the assembly's work and conclusions. It was distributed to all homes in the province. More details can be found in the *Technical Report* issued by the same body, December 2004, 264.

47 This author contributed to the preparation of the government's model. See Louis Massicotte, *In Search of a compensatory mixed electoral system for Quebec. Working Document*, Quebec, December 2004. The actual model actually put forward by the government differed slightly from the formula recommended in this document.

48 New Brunswick, Commission on Legislative Democracy, *Final report and Recommendations*, January 2005.

49 Prince Edward Island Electoral Reform Commission, *Report*, December 2003; *Final Report*, October 2005. See also John A. Cousins, "Electoral Reform for Prince Edward Island," *Canadian Parliamentary Review* 25, no. 4 (2002): 26–36.

50 See Jeannie Lea, "The Prince Edward Island Plebiscite on Electoral Reform," *Canadian Parliamentary Review* 29, no. 1 (2006): 4–8. Premier Binns decided that the threshold for victory would be 60 percent support for the formula, and stated that he would feel bound by the outcome of the referendum only if turnout was high. Actually, the referendum was held in late November. Ostensibly for budgetary reasons, the number of polling stations was reduced by 90 percent, with an average of more than one thousand electors in each, which made it more difficult for the voters to reach them. No list of electors was used, which obliged would-be voters to answer five questions before casting their vote. About one-third of the electorate showed up at the polls, and the "NO" side carried the day with 64 percent of the vote.

51 Law Commission of Canada, *Voting Counts: Electoral Reform for Canada*, Ottawa, 2004, 209 pages.

52 For an application of this formula to the 2004 election, see Ian Gray and James Gray, "Proportional representation — The Scottish Model applied to the 2004 Canadian election," *Canadian Parliamentary Review* 27, no. 3 (2004): 19–22.

53 House of Commons, *Debates*, February 20, 2001, and September 30, 2003. The NDP motion that sparked the second debate called for a referendum to determine whether Canadians wished to replace the current electoral system with a system of proportional representation and, if so, the appointment of a commission to consult Canadians on the details of the model. It was rejected by the Liberals with the

support of the Progressive Conservatives, and was supported by the NDP and the Canadian Alliance.

54 *Journals of the House of Commons*, October 18, 2004.

55 This came as a surprise, for at its first policy convention in 2005 the new Conservative Party had deleted from the party platform the idea of creating a citizens' assembly to adopt proportional representation, as well as the recall of elected members. See Ross Marowits, "Conservatives heading to political centre," Canadian Press, March 19, 2005.

56 Hugh Windsor, "Proportional representation inches forward," *Globe and Mail*, January 31, 2003, A4.

57 At the time of writing (April 2006), the 2 percent threshold was undergoing a Charter challenge before the Ontario Superior Court of Justice, *Canadian Action Party* et al. v. *Canada (AG)*.

58 *Figueroa* v. *Canada (AG)* [1999], 43 O.R. (3rd) 728 (Ontario Court, General Division).

59 *Canada (AG)* v. *Figueroa* [2000], 50 O.R. (3rd) 161 (Ontario Court of Appeal).

60 *Figueroa* v . *Canada (AG)*, [2003] 1 S.C.R. 912.

61 Para. 44 and 45 of the *Figueroa* decision.

62 S.C. 2004, c. 24. See H. McIvor, "The Charter of Rights and Party Politics. The Impact of the Supreme Court Ruling in *Figueroa* v. *Canada (Attorney General)*," Institute of Research on Public Policy, *Choices* 10, no. 4 (2004), 26.

CHAPTER NINE

The Media and the Campaign
by Christopher Waddell and Christopher Dornan

Political parties invariably resent the coverage they receive from the media. They feel as though they are forced to fight election campaigns on two fronts, the first against their political opponents and the second against a press corps reflexively opposed to their ambitions for office. Now that the 2006 federal election is history, who has grounds to complain about how the media coverage played out?

Not the Conservative Party. For the most part, the press corps was impressed by the discipline of the Conservatives' campaign, so much so that three weeks into the contest many commentators wondered aloud why the superior Conservative effort had yet to gain traction with voters. Then the NDP released a letter it had received from the RCMP confirming a criminal investigation had been launched into leaks from the federal Department of Finance that may have been used for improper financial gain. The Conservatives had not been hammering the Liberals on the integrity issue — they judged that with the memory of the sponsorship scandal still fresh the Liberals' record on integrity would speak for itself — but the story could not help but play in their favour. That week, the first surges in Conservative support registered in the polls and the party went on to form the government.

The Conservative victory came neither because of the media coverage nor despite it. The Conservatives have no call to object to how the media covered their campaign.

The same is true of the Liberals. As infuriated as Liberal Party operatives may have been with the campaign coverage they received, it hardly mattered in the party's fortunes. Liberals complained that their party and its leader could not catch a break from the media. But the media did not make the Liberals' campaign hapless. They merely reported on its difficulties. There were simply too many missteps, and the Conservatives outmanoeuvred the Liberals at every turn. The seeds of the Martin defeat were sown long before the media started reporting an upturn in Conservative support right after the Christmas break. Media coverage was not a determining factor in how the Liberals fared.

The New Democrats were not happy with their media coverage either. They believed they were given short shrift in national media coverage, relegated to a sub-plot recognized only in passing. The NDP may well have been eclipsed in news coverage by the contest between the failing Liberals and the ascendant Conservatives, but the party remained a constant presence in the wings. If nothing else, the NDP put the prospect of strategic voting squarely on the agenda by appealing to skittish Liberal voters to "lend us your vote." And in the end, the New Democrats gained seats. Who is to say whether their media coverage helped them do so or blunted their chances of winning even more?

The Green Party, similarly, complained about being dismissed by the mainstream media. It was not accorded the same attention as the more established parties. Nonetheless, the media themselves made an issue of their own attention to the Greens. The party's exclusion from the leaders' debates, for example, triggered an automatic protest and an equally automatic news story about whether the Greens should be included. This provided an occasion for the media to point out how well the Greens had done in the previous election and that the Greens themselves were not without their internal party divisions. The Green Party, like the NDP, might protest its lack of prominence in the election news agenda, but its failure to win any seats was not a consequence of its treatment at the hands of the media.

Nor were the fortunes of the Bloc Québécois determined by the party's coverage. The Bloc won the lion's share of seats in Quebec. And yet the party was the author of its own misfortune. Overly confident too early in the contest — where could the threat to its candidates come from, given the implosion of Liberal support? — the BQ speculated about winning more than 50 percent of the Quebec vote in a federal election. Speculating on results is always a dangerous business for a political party, as it leaves it open to ridicule if the prediction doesn't come true.

It was an aspiration frustrated in part by the surprise victories of Conservative candidates in Quebec. At Christmas, no one expected the Conservatives to take a single seat in the province. And yet they took ten, and it was not the doing of the news media.

As a consequence, the only actors with cause to regret the media coverage of the 2006 election may be the news media themselves. At the time, they thought they were behaving responsibly in how they covered the campaign. In the aftermath, they may have their doubts.

The proper role of the news media in an election campaign is a delicate balancing act. On the one hand, they are obliged to provide a public platform whereby the political parties can put their respective policies before the electorate. It is not their place to hijack the contest by imposing their own agenda. At their best, they dutifully document the various parties' platforms and pronouncements, they cultivate interest in the course of the election on the part of the public, and they moderate the debate with a view to informing the electorate as comprehensively as possible.

But this does not mean the news media should limit themselves to mere stenography. They may be the main conduits through which the politicians appeal to voters, but they should not be inert. Imperfectly, perhaps, the media are still the public's representatives during an election contest. It is within their mandate to pose questions to the politicians on the public's behalf — to raise issues of public interest and electoral consequence no matter that these might be discomfiting to the parties, each of which has a script to which it would prefer to hew and issues it would rather not address.

The Conservative strategy of releasing a policy announcement a day in the opening weeks of the election was not simply a device to methodically unveil the party's platform. It was a mechanism to seize control of the news agenda, to dominate the day-to-day coverage, and it was therefore a media management technique. Compelled by their own responsibilities to document each announcement as it came, the media as a result had few openings or opportunities to raise issues that were not on the Conservatives' playlist. The range of issues on which the party's social conservatism had in the past made many voters uneasy simply never arose with any prominence. Abortion, same-sex marriage, federal funding for the arts and culture, the future of the CBC, and so on — these were by and large absent concerns.

The Conservatives were aided in this regard by an incident on the first day of the campaign in which a reporter asked Stephen Harper "Do you love Canada?" Charitably, one might view the question as an awkward attempt to ask what version of Canada the Conservative leader imagined for the future, but it was seen at the time as the sort of ambush antagonism that gives journalism a bad name, implying as it did that Harper's policies amounted to an attack on all that the country holds dear. Even people who had no intention of voting for the Conservatives rolled their eyes in exasperation with the press. That put paid to any further impertinence on the part of the media, who henceforth merely reacted to campaign events rather than seize the lead in the electoral dance.

Ironically, then, what impressed the reporters covering the Conservative campaign — in particular the party's tight message discipline — was the very thing that neutralized the media, that made them bit players in the Conservatives' ultimately successful script for victory. In the main, the news media were even-handed and responsible in how they documented the course of the campaign. At the same time, they largely and inadvertently surrendered their role as autonomous agents.

The consequences of that became clear once the Conservatives assumed power. The new government's conduct toward the national press corps was an extension of its campaign strategy: the media were to be corralled, controlled, circumvented, and sidelined, just as the party's own members were to be strictly circumscribed in their dealings with the press. Some media access to ministers was restricted. The Prime Minister's handlers would determine who in the press corps could pose questions to the leader and under what conditions. Cabinet meetings would be held in secret. The press might not even be informed of visits by foreign heads of state.

All the elements of this approach have been tried by previous governments upon taking office to impose their own stamp on media relations, to avoid contradictions, and to keep everyone focused on the messages those in the Prime Minister's Office want delivered to Canadians. It sometimes works for a brief period of time but doesn't survive the ups and downs of a parliamentary session, the Commons question period, and the fact that government communications are too diverse to be controlled by any central organization. This attempt to keep the media subordinate is unlikely to work either. Politics is a turbulent business and managing the media is a mug's game. But for the Conservatives, at least, one of the lessons of the 2006 election was that the media *can* be played to electoral advantage.

Media complaints about this treatment left Canadians cold, as three months after the election opinion polls showed support for the new government at higher levels than the Conservatives received on election day. Nonetheless image is a crucial element of politics. While doing no immediate damage to Harper, if media relations becomes the first of many examples of centralization it could cumulatively threaten the credibility of the message Harper delivered during the campaign that he would run a different, less centrally controlled government than the Liberals.

The lack of public sympathy for media complaints may also reflect the degree to which some media predictions about the election were simply wrong. It had been a quarter of a century since Canadians last voted for a federal government in the middle of winter after a campaign that stretched over the Christmas–New Year's holiday. It had been almost as long since a campaign lasted fifty-six days. For the media as much as for the politicians, these were the initial challenges in the 2005–06 election campaign. No one could predict whether readers, listeners, and viewers would be interested in election news for that length of time or how much the weather might disrupt the campaign and the media's ability to cover it. There were fears that the weather and an uninterested electorate would conspire to keep voters at home, dropping turnout another step closer to only 50 percent of Canadians voting.

In the late November days leading up to the minority Liberal government's defeat in the House of Commons, the media predicted with seeming certainty that this would be the nastiest election campaign in Canadian history, full of personal attacks, and that the public would be very angry at having their holidays disrupted by electioneering. Politicians would pay the price. As it turned out, both predictions were wrong. Canadians were interested in the campaign from the start and even took heed of a key event that took place over the Christmas holidays that likely shaped the outcome: the NDP announcing that the RCMP would launch a criminal investigation into a possible leak from the office of Finance Minister Ralph Goodale of a government decision not to tax income trusts. Rather than being nasty, the 2005–06 election campaign was more about policy and less about personality than any campaign since the free trade election of 1988.

NEWS ORGANIZATIONS AND THEIR AUDIENCES

Throughout the campaign, Carleton University's School of Journalism and Communication and Decima Research Inc. conducted a series of Internet-based surveys, asking a sample of Canadians to complete a weekly emailed election questionnaire. In late November before the parliamentary defeat of the Liberals, Decima asked approximately twelve thousand members of the online eVox panel, which it uses for a range of email-based surveys, if they were planning to vote and wanted to be part of the election survey. The poll would track weekly changes in voters' attitudes over the course of the campaign about election issues, advertising, news coverage, and the performance of the media. Approximately nine thousand people agreed to participate. Between forty-five hundred and seven thousand responded to each weekly survey within seventy-two hours of receiving it.

The initial survey, between November 26 and December 1, established basic data about where Canadians get political news and what news organizations they would rely on during the campaign. Respondents could indicate as many different newspapers, networks, and channels as they wished. It was no surprise that television networks scored well, as that is how the majority of Canadians get their news. An almost equal number of people selected CTV and CBC television. Only the option of "your daily local newspaper" registered with more respondents, but this meant different papers according to where in Canada respondents lived. The importance of television as the dominant medium for campaign coverage is even more obvious when the responses naming CBC or CTV are combined with those mentioning cable news channels, CBC Newsworld, and CTV Newsnet.

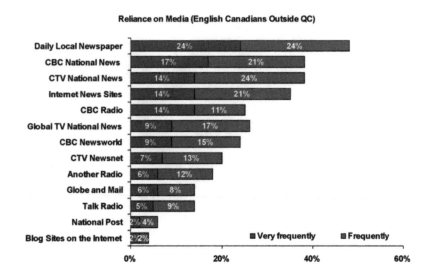

Among francophones (largely but not exclusively in Quebec), television is even more important than in the rest of Canada as the primary election information source. One-third more people named one of the television networks than selected "your daily local newspaper."

Reliance on Media (Francophone Quebecers)

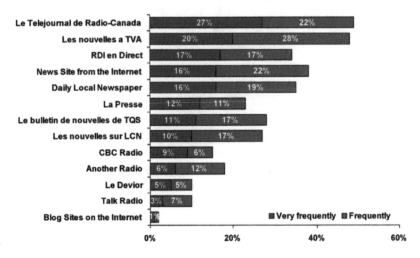

More than one in three English Canadians (38 percent) outside Quebec said they would rely, but not exclusively, on CBC's main television newscast, *The National*, frequently or very frequently during the campaign. Albertans were the least likely to name *The National* (at 32 percent) and Atlantic Canadians the most (45 percent). Liberal (46 percent) and NDP voters (42 percent) were more likely than Conservative voters (33 percent) to say they would rely on *The National*. Along the same lines, 53 percent of those who say they are on the centre-left of the political spectrum were more likely to rely in part on *The National*. Its audience is slightly older and has higher incomes than the national average.

Similar numbers (38 percent) said they would rely on *CTV National News*. Slightly fewer British Columbia and Alberta residents than Central Canadians planned to rely on CTV, and CTV had a marginally larger audience in Ontario than CBC among survey respondents. Roughly equal percentages of Liberal and Conservative voters planned to rely on CTV, but fewer NDP voters were interested in CTV coverage. More people who described themselves in the centre and on the centre-right of the spectrum and more middle-income individuals planned to watch CTV than CBC.

The survey also found a significant share of the 26 percent who preferred *Global National* lived in B.C. and Alberta. Its newscast attracts a greater percentage of Conservative voters than supporters of either of the other parties. More Global viewers are female than male and they see themselves as more on the right and in the centre of the political spectrum.

The *Globe and Mail* was the leading newspaper, with 11 percent saying they would rely on it frequently or very frequently. The *Globe*'s audience for election coverage, more male than female and with higher incomes, spanned the political spectrum, but had slightly more readers who say they are left of centre than who say they are on the right. Almost half (46 percent) of those who named the *Globe* had at the campaign's start already decided how they would vote, with 47 percent choosing the Liberals, 25 percent Conservatives, and 13 percent NDP.

About half as many people (6 percent) planned to rely on the *National Post*. Its readers in the Carleton-Decima survey were more likely to be upper income and politically right of centre. More than half (55 percent) had already decided how they would vote, with 49 percent backing the Conservatives, 31 percent Liberals, and 13 percent NDP.

Almost one-quarter (22 percent) of those in the survey said they would rely in part on CBC Radio for campaign coverage. More of that group was male, upscale, and left of centre, and found in Atlantic Canada, Ontario, and B.C. The 13 percent of respondents who planned to rely on talk radio was predominantly male, older, and Conservative, and was composed of more decided than undecided voters.

The gap between television and newspapers was not as pronounced when people identified the single news organization they would rely on the most during the campaign.

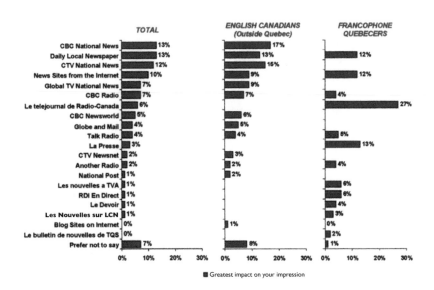

CBC's *The National* and local dailies were tied at the top of the list with 13 percent each. *CTV National News* was cited as the single most relied upon news organization by 12 percent. CBC's program led CTV among men, Liberal and NDP voters, and in all regions except Ontario. CTV led very narrowly among women, in Ontario, and more clearly among Conservative voters. Internet news sites were next most frequently picked, selected by 10 percent. The *Global National* newscast and CBC Radio were each cited by 7 percent. In this survey, Global's audience is largest in B.C. and Alberta, and somewhat right of centre. Quebec residents were most likely to cite Radio-Canada's *Téléjournal* (23 percent), followed by local dailies at 15 percent, Internet news sites at 13 percent, and *La Presse* at 12 percent.

The choice of Internet news sites as the most important source for election coverage is remarkably high in this survey, almost equalling television. While there is no question that more and more people are getting their news from the Internet, the strong results for Internet news sites reflect the degree of Internet interest and sophistication among those responding to the survey.

COVERING THE CAMPAIGN

The length of the campaign was one factor influencing media coverage. Equally important for newspapers was the state of the long-running circulation war among the major dailies. The battle was at its height during the 2000 election, the *National Post*'s first federal campaign. Challenging the *Globe* for national newspaper supremacy, the *Post* matched its established rival almost story for story.

By the 2004 campaign the war was almost over, with the *Globe* proclaiming victory. The *Post* had been bought by CanWest and the new owners had cut staff and costs sharply to curtail losses. In 2004, the *Post* made no effort to match the range of the *Globe*'s coverage. That was still largely true in the 2005–06 campaign, even though the *Post* was in better shape than two years earlier. Its losses had stabilized and the paper was even hiring reporters, but it did not return to a head-to-head fight with the *Globe*. It was more selective in what it covered and how it went about doing so. It did not match the number of features the *Globe* printed, the national scope of the *Globe*'s coverage, or the regular daily opinion polling that was a cornerstone of the *Globe*'s approach to this campaign.

The 2005–06 campaign lasted half as long again as the one in 2004. Predictably, the country's major newspapers all published many more stories this time around than in the thirty-six-day campaign in May–June 2004. The campaign also occurred during what is traditionally the slowest time of the year for news — December and January — which meant less competition from other news for space in papers or time on television.

The examination of newspaper coverage in this chapter builds on the studies done for *The Canadian General Election of 2000* (Dornan and Pyman) and *The Canadian Election of 2004* (Waddell). It is based on a database containing all campaign stories published in the *Globe and Mail* and the *Toronto Star* as they appeared in the Factiva electronic database from November 28, 2005, the day before the government fell, up to and including the published results of the election on January 24, 2006. The database also includes all election stories from the *National Post* in the FP Infomart electronic database between the same dates.

The *Globe* and *Post* both publish Monday to Saturday and the *Star* is a seven-days-a-week operation, but the *Globe* ran many more election stories than its competitors, just as in 2004.

Table 1
Election stories

	Globe	*Post*	*Star*
2000	764	710	522
2004	518	391	389
2006	978	796	779

Along with more stories came a shift in the type of stories carried by the three papers. For years, newspapers have struggled to respond to television as the primary source of news for Canadians. How can papers present fresh information in the morning, when their readers may have seen the same story on television the night before? That became an even larger problem with the rise of all-news cable channels in Canada that present news twenty-four hours a day. The all-news landscape changed in the summer of 2005, when the Canadian Radio-television and Telecommunications Commission eased licence restrictions on CTV Newsnet. Whereas it had been restricted to providing only headline news, the new relaxed rules allowed it to compete directly with CBC Newsworld, which it did vigorously in this campaign. That not only put pressure on its TV competitor but also put more pressure on newspapers. Newspapers have responded to the immediacy of all-news television by shifting campaign coverage away from hard news. They have placed greater emphasis and prominence on columns and columnists that mix opinion and analysis, playing off the news and taking their readers beyond television's more immediate and terse hard news coverage. Newspaper editors and owners are betting that readers have already seen the facts on TV and are seeking context, depth, and analysis.

It has been easy for newspapers to make this shift, as the past several federal election campaigns have largely centred on personality rather than policy. Campaign strategy, advertising, media relations, and party war rooms that produce charges and counter-charges every campaign day — that kind of drama captivates reporters and columnists and makes for more colourful copy than policy differences between the competing parties.

This time, though, neither the media nor the other parties anticipated that from the outset the Conservatives would adopt a strategy that saw leader Stephen Harper announce a new policy every day and continue to do so well into January. His approach forced the media to cover this campaign differently. Newspaper and television reporters fight a daily battle for space and time for their stories with the pressure from editing desks always for shorter and tighter reports. When the campaign trail story became a new policy announcement every day, reporters had to devote time and space to details and background of the policy and its possible impact. They also needed to include a quotation or two from Harper and some specific policy reaction from other parties or interest groups. That frequently left no time or room for personality, strategy, or the mindless back and forth between leaders' tours that may have fascinated the media in the past but left the public cold.

Some of the announcements were unexpected, such as a commitment to cut the Goods and Services Tax (GST) by one percentage point, or a plan to provide tax relief for parents with children playing sports. The details of the Conservatives' proposal to provide $100 a month towards child care payments for all children under the age of six were likewise news. The Conservatives also made life easy for reporters on their leader's tour. Each announcement was simple and straightforward, with two or three central points that were easy to understand and readily explained to radio and television audiences and newspaper readers. The party restricted itself to a single announcement per day, and so that is what the media covered. By contrast, in the two weeks before the election the Liberals had flooded the country with spending announcements. That left them with nothing new to talk about once the campaign began. When the party began its policy announcements in January, they often came in flurries of two or three, which reduced their impact as reporters had trouble figuring out which was most important to highlight and found it equally tough to squeeze them all into their stories.

In response to the policy-driven Conservative campaign, newspapers adjusted their coverage balance to increase news and reduce columns and opinion. All three papers did so and devoted an almost identical share of coverage to news stories — one of many similarities in how they covered the campaign. The shift towards more news coverage also reflected the fact that newspapers have an advantage over television in a policy-driven campaign. Television cannot adequately present the details of policy announcements in a two-minute news report. It can just touch on the highlights. So anyone interested in the substance of policies had to read the papers or turn to Internet sources. The newspapers capitalized on the natural advantage of the print medium to flesh out and examine in detail the policies that surfaced in the campaign.

Table 2
News stories (as a percentage of total number of stories)

	Globe	Post	Star
2000	45	60	53
2004	47	40	55
2006	57	61	60

This change was least apparent in the *Toronto Star* because it had retained a stronger focus on news in past campaigns than the other two papers. News coverage jumped in the *Globe and Mail* but the most dramatic change was at the *National Post*. Job cuts there prior to 2004 meant fewer reporters, so the paper's columnists had been responsible for most of the coverage of that campaign. That also injected more opinion into the news pages of the paper, opinion that often reflected conservative viewpoints. By contrast, in the 2005–06 campaign, the *Post* followed the trend, devoting more space to news while columnists took a back seat. Of the three papers, the *Globe* remained the most heavily committed to columns and columnists.

Table 3

Columns (as a percentage of total number of stories)

	Globe	Post	Star
2000	32	21	28
2004	28	30	33
2006	25	22	20

All three papers printed more editorials about the campaign than they had in 2004. However, because all the papers had also increased the overall quantity of news, the proportion of coverage devoted to editorials actually decreased.

Table 4

Editorials (as a percentage of total number of stories)

	Globe	Post	Star
2000	5	7	9
2004	6	8	6
2006	5	5	5

None of the papers gave much space to the opinions of those not on their staff. Such a policy-intensive campaign would have been perfect for showcasing as wide a cross-section of views as possible on the policies proposed by the parties from such groups as business, social policy activists, the environmental movement, and foreign policy and defence advocates. As in 2004, the *Globe* gave the smallest share of its overall coverage to op-ed pieces, even though it publishes the most influential opinion page in the country.

Table 5

Op-ed stories (as a percentage of total number of stories)

	Globe	Post	Star
2000	7	8	1
2004	4	9	2
2006	4	6	6

Feature stories also played a less prominent role than they did in 2004 at both the *Globe* and the *Post*. Only the *Star* increased the share of coverage devoted to features from its 2004 levels.

Table 6
Features (as a percentage of total number of stories)

	Globe	*Post*	*Star*
2000	6	6	8
2004	15	13	4
2006	9	6	10

The most striking aspect of newspaper coverage is the degree to which all three papers made the same decisions about how to apportion their coverage between news, features, editorials, and columns. At a time when newspapers are losing readers to television and the Internet, none of the three was willing to take a chance in this campaign and do something dramatically different from its rivals. The lack of distinctiveness is obvious when comparing how the three papers allocated their coverage during this campaign.

Table 7
Types of coverage (as a percentage of total coverage)

	Globe	*Post*	*Star*
News	57.4	60.8	60.2
Editorial	4.7	5.4	4.6
Column	25.5	21.7	20.0
Op-ed	3.8	5.8	5.6
Feature	8.7	6.3	9.5

That uniformity even extended to the percentage of coverage devoted to each of the parties. All three papers paid greater attention to the Liberals than the Conservatives, even though in the second half of the campaign it was increasingly clear the Conservatives were going to form the next government. There were two minor anomalies: the Bloc received less coverage in the *Toronto Star*, as it wasn't running candidates where most *Star* readers lived, while the NDP did relatively better in the *Star*, in part reflecting the strength of the party in Toronto-area constituencies.

Table 8
Party coverage (as a percentage of total coverage devoted to parties)

	Globe	Post	Star
Liberal	42.8	43.8	44.6
Conservative	38.7	35.0	36.3
NDP	11.2	13.7	14.8
Bloc	5.5	5.4	2.9
Green	1.8	2.1	1.3

There were differences, though, in how the papers used their front pages. The *Globe* leaned towards the Liberals in the number of front-page stories it ran while the *Star* had slightly more Conservative stories than Liberal ones on its front page. There were an equal number of stories for each party on the *Post*'s front page. A good percentage of those stories at all three papers were negative rather than positive but at least the two parties appeared regularly on all three front pages. That's not true for the NDP, which complained with considerable justification that the media devoted much less time and space to its leader and its policies than to the other two parties.

Throughout the entire campaign, only two front-page headlines in the *Globe* mentioned the NDP. One on December 3 reported the decision of Canadian Auto Workers union president Buzz Hargrove to support Paul Martin and the Liberals instead of the New Democrats. The other, on December 12, stated "Liberals snatch NDP votes in Ontario; New Democrats' support level drops to single digits as Grits reach their highest mark since May." The NDP was furious about the headline, saying the story was flat out wrong. It took the *Globe* three days to admit the error. Even then it only ran a small and obtuse correction on page two that stated, "Figures for party support in Ontario were incorrect in a story published Monday. Poll respondents were asked which party had the most momentum going into the Jan. 23 federal election as well as which party they would support. Those momentum numbers were wrongly cited as each party's level of support." The correction then noted the correct level of support for each party but did not state explicitly that there was no change in NDP support over the days in question. Angry with that delay in correcting the record, the NDP turned down an invitation to meet with the *Globe*'s editorial board in what became a campaign-long feud.

The New Democrats believed the *National Post*, the paper ideologically most distant from the NDP, actually gave it the most balanced coverage of the three papers. Front-page headlines support the NDP's view. The stories were not always favourable but at least the NDP appeared on the *Post*'s front page.

The *Globe*'s attention to the Bloc Québécois, even though very few of its readers could vote for the party, reflected both the paper's traditionally higher circulation in Quebec than either the *Post* or the *Star* and the fact that early in the campaign it appeared the Bloc might win the support of more than 50 percent of voters in Quebec, something no sovereigntist party had ever done.

Table 9
Front-page stories (as a percentage of total election front-page stories)

	Globe	*Post*	*Star*
Liberal	46.0	29.8	29.0
Conservative	36.8	29.8	33.9
NDP	0.0	5.3	1.6
Bloc	2.3	1.8	1.6
Green	0.0	1.8	0.0

The editorial pages of the three papers were more balanced in their treatment of the three national parties. The *Globe* paid more attention to the Conservatives than it did to the Liberals; and whereas in 2004 it had endorsed the Liberals, this time it called on its readers to support the Conservatives on the grounds that it was time for a change. Both the *National Post* and the *Toronto Star* stuck with their 2004 picks. The *Post* again backed the Conservatives while the *Star* as always called for another Liberal government.

Table 10
Editorials (as a percentage of total editorials during the campaign)

	Globe	*Post*	*Star*
Liberal	30.4	34.9	22.2
Conservative	37.0	27.9	19.4
NDP	4.3	7.0	8.3
Bloc	2.2	0.0	0.0
Green Party	0.0	0.0	0.0

There were some differences in the issues each paper chose to high-light and some things each chose to forego. For instance "reality checks" — a feature of past campaigns in which party statements and policies are tested against the facts of an issue — virtually disappeared from the three papers, although they remained a staple of television coverage.

The Globe and Mail

The *Globe* anchored its campaign coverage with a separate theme page each day of the week, usually on page five. On Monday it was campaign issues, Tuesday youth and media, Wednesday behind-the-scenes activi-ties, Thursday belonged to candidates, Friday to strategy, and Saturday was the week in review. It was a smart innovation and effective as a daily focus for coverage. A diary of interesting election snippets or a cam-paign notebook usually filled out the page.

With many predicting a close result, the *Globe* also reported weekly on the views of individual undecided voters across the country, some-thing it had not done in 2004. The other main focus for the *Globe* and the other papers was candidates. In an era of complaints about cam-paign coverage being too preoccupied with party leaders, the *Globe* devoted about 10 percent of its coverage to individual candidates and interesting races. As in 2004 the anchor for this was columnist Roy MacGregor, who travelled from coast to coast, profiling candidates and bringing a human dimension to elections and politics.

The largest chunk of the *Globe*'s news coverage was directed at party and campaign strategy. The other papers did the same thing. Each devoted almost one-fifth of their news coverage to strategy issues. Ethics received more attention in the *Globe* than in either the *Post* or *Star*, as did federal-provincial relations and Quebec sovereignty. That was con-sistent with the *Globe* paying more attention to the Bloc Québécois than either the *Post* or the *Star*.

In the months after the 2004 election the *Globe* launched a separate British Columbia section only in papers distributed in that province. Reporters from the paper's Vancouver bureau filed forty-seven stories during the 2005–06 campaign that appeared only in that section, beyond the British Columbia stories that ran across the country in the paper's national edition. As a result, West Coast *Globe* readers received much more local coverage of issues such as the Chinese head tax and B.C. candidates and races than they had in the 2004 campaign.

The National Post

Almost 15 percent of the *Post*'s coverage centred on the leaders, compared to 11 percent at the *Star* and 10 percent at the *Globe*. Supplementing that, the *Post* injected some humour and coverage of off-beat issues with columns that almost daily asked the leaders questions that were often frivilous. An equally large chunk of the *Post*'s coverage was devoted to candidates, anchored by the paper's Ottawa columnist John Ivison, who played a similar role to Roy MacGregor's at the *Globe*, travelling the country, profiling candidates and close races. Consistent with the paper's conservative leanings, the *Post* had more than double the percentage of news stories on taxes, especially the Conservative pledge to cut the GST, than did the *Globe*. It also had a larger percentage of stories on federal budget issues than the *Globe*, but the *Globe* devoted a greater share of its space to Canada–U.S. matters than did the *Post*. None of the papers paid much attention to any other foreign policy issues, matching the way the parties ignored foreign policy during the campaign. The *Post* had a smaller share of social policy stories than either the *Globe* or the *Star*, while all three papers almost completely ignored the same-sex marriage issue.

The Toronto Star

The *Star* is always true to its Toronto roots, championing urban and social issues, and that was no different this time. The paper paid more attention than the others to candidates, although it concentrated almost exclusively on those running in the Greater Toronto Area. Of the three papers, the *Star* had the smallest percentage of stories on ethics issues and devoted only about two-thirds as much coverage as the *Post* did on the leaders. Campaign strategy was also slightly less prevalent in *Star* stories than in the other papers. More *Star* stories than *Globe* or *Post* stories dealt with youth and youth voting issues. The *Star* also paid more attention to voting rules and how to vote than the others. Not surprisingly, urban issues were a *Star* preoccupation, particularly crime, gun control, and handguns.

The core of the *Star*'s analytical coverage came from highly experienced columnists James Travers, Chantal Hebert, Graham Fraser, and Thomas Walkom, all of whom have been covering elections for at least twenty years. That experience showed in the sophistication of their analysis and commentary. The paper frequently used its Ottawa bureau chief Susan Delacourt as analyst and explainer of campaign developments under the tag line "Campaign Decoder." It was an effective variant of the now abandoned reality check concept.

TELEVISION

Just as the parties during an election campaign are locked into a contest with one another for voters' support, so too are news organizations locked into a contest with one another for readers, viewers, and listeners. It is in their interests, therefore, to engage the public in the election, particularly since covering elections in this vast country is an expensive proposition.

Noteworthy during this election were the campaign coverage innovations on the part of the networks to kindle viewer interest in the contest. In addition to the standard reportage from the campaign trail, the panels of commentators, the in-studio arguments between party operatives, and the town hall–style meetings with party leaders, all the networks resorted to unconventional features aimed at capturing eyeballs. CTV, for example, deployed six-year-old Daniel Cook — star of his own television program aimed at the primary school set — as a campaign correspondent. The leader in campaign coverage theatrics, however, was CBC's *The National*, which introduced a range of features designed to make the election fun. These included:

- a segment in which candidates pitched their parties to undecided voters via "speed-dating" (also done by CTV);
- a regular "Taxi Chat" segment in which candidates got behind the wheel of a cab while a camera recorded their encounters with the members of the public they picked up as fares;
- the use of comedians — the Toronto comic Sean Cullen and a Winnipeg group called the Content Factory — to inject levity into the coverage;
- a regular segment called "Campaign Confidential" in which an anonymous former campaign insider (eventually revealed to be strategist Rick Anderson) offered his commentary on the contest as it unfolded;
- a regular "Road Trips" segment in which reporter Mark Kelly accompanied members of the electorate as they visited distant parts of the country: a voter from Montreal, for example, encountering the political culture of Alberta; and

- a feature in which the parties were given the opportunity and the airtime to produce their own news accounts of the campaign events of that day.

No doubt some viewers found these innovations frivolous, but in the main it was gratifying to see a little creativity being applied to the coverage. Elections are serious affairs, but that does not mean that the media should comport themselves at all times in deadly earnest.

POLITICAL COVERAGE — THE BROADER CONTEXT

Polls, Polls, Polls

Despite regular criticisms by academics and even some journalists that the media rely too much on public opinion poll results to shape how they cover campaigns, polls continued to play a central role. This was true for all media, even though the CBC proclaimed as it did in 2004 that it did not commission polls itself or report directly on other poll results. In truth that meant the CBC wouldn't report on polls unless they were interesting. When polls suggested public opinion was starting to shift towards the Conservatives just after the new year, the CBC reported and pursued that story just as aggressively as all the other news organizations.

There was a polling innovation in 2004, the daily tracking poll conducted by SES Research for the Canadian Public Affairs Channel (CPAC). The network and SES did it again just as successfully in this campaign. Each day at 2:00 p.m., CPAC placed the results of the previous day's polling of four hundred Canadians on its website and reporters logged on to get the latest update. It was the main topic of reporter conversation on the campaign trail once each day's numbers were released. Who was up and down on a daily basis framed how the media viewed and reported each party's campaign. CPAC's daily tracking poll merged the results of the previous three days' polling, dropping the oldest day as each new day was added. The media's faith in the accuracy of this poll was no doubt bolstered by the fact that the final SES results in 2004 were closest among all pollsters to the actual election results.

The *Globe and Mail* adopted a similar approach for this campaign, abandoning weekly polls for a daily tracking poll published in the paper. It was conducted by the Strategic Counsel, with former Progressive Conservative pollster and Strategic Counsel executive Allan Gregg as the spokesperson and analyst. With the Liberals leading and Conservatives showing no sign of movement before Christmas despite their daily policy announcements, the tracking poll wasn't featured prominently in the *Globe*'s coverage but it was there every day at the top of the rotating feature page. The tracking poll results moved into the spotlight in early January when they began to detect Conservative momentum, as the party moved past the Liberals both nationally and in Quebec. That was a major surprise, as Bloc Québécois voters were moving to the Conservatives, dashing the Bloc's dream of finally winning the support of 50 percent of Quebecers for a sovereigntist party in an election. In the final ten days, poll results not only drove *Globe* coverage, they were featured in front-page headlines and created controversy.

On January 16 the *Globe* announced in a front-page headline, "Tories enter home stretch just shy of majority, poll finds." The story stated that the Conservatives had the support of 40 percent of Canadians and had opened a thirteen-point lead over the Liberals. Two days later and just five days before voting, the paper reported the gap had widened to seventeen points — 41 percent to 24 percent. No other polling firm gave the Conservatives that much support or such a substantial lead over the Liberals. Even though differing methodologies used by individual companies makes it risky to compare results of polls done by separate firms, the *Globe*'s numbers seemed out of whack. Even corporate cousin CTV played down these results in its national nightly newscast, apparently fearing it was a rogue poll, the one in twenty that does not fall within the usual polling margin of error.

Then, as tracking poll results showed the Conservatives falling back to levels of support that other polling firms believed they had never exceeded, *Globe* coverage proclaimed the Liberals were narrowing the gap opened by the Conservatives. On January 20, the top of the paper's front page bluntly stated "Harper's lead takes a hit," noting that the gap was now 37 to 28 percent — much closer to the results other pollsters had shown all along. It was also a margin other polling companies believed had been relatively constant during the campaign's final week. The way the *Globe* treated the poll left a crucial question unanswered. Were the Liberals repeating the last weekend comeback that gave them a minority government in 2004, or did the *Globe* proclaim Harper's lead had taken a hit simply to avoid admitting its earlier headlines and polling results were wrong? Some viewed it even more cynically as either an attempt to scare people into voting Liberal to avoid a Conservative majority government or the result of having a Conservative pollster doing the polling. Neither was a credible complaint. The apparent surge in Conservative support seems more likely to have been an error in methodology under the pressure of conducting a large number of telephone interviews every night.

The last week's shenanigans highlighted how much the *Globe* built its coverage around poll results. Approximately 18 percent of the paper's front-page stories during the campaign dealt with polls or polling. That was significantly more than on the front pages of either the *National Post*, which used the *Globe*'s former polling partner Ipsos-Reid, or the *Toronto Star*, which used Ekos Research. Each devoted only about 11 percent of its front-page stories to polls and polling results. (See Chapter Ten.)

The *Star* followed the traditional once every week or ten days approach to polling through the first half of the campaign. But in the campaign's last two weeks, it matched the *Globe*'s daily tracking polls with its own. Ekos Research made up to five hundred calls a night, turning that night's numbers around for the next morning's paper. Every day reporters compared the *Globe* and *Star* results with those from SES/CPAC. The fluctuations in daily results revealed some of the methodological difficulties in turning around large tracking polls every night for morning newspapers. There is no time to call back people in the original sample selected at random who don't answer the phone, so others are added to make up the total, and that can skew the results. First edition deadlines and the three-hour time difference to British Columbia also meant the West Coast was probably underrepresented in most nights' results. Results also bounced up and down a great deal from night to night, making it hard to identify anomalies.

There had been concern about possible polling errors earlier in the campaign. On January 10, the *National Post* reported that Ekos, the *Star*, and *La Presse* had delayed publishing the results of a weekend poll that showed a surprising double-digit jump in support for the Conservatives because they were concerned about its accuracy. They added seven hundred calls to the original five hundred that had turned up a remarkable spike in Conservative support. The extra calls confirmed the initial sample's findings. The tide was turning towards the Conservatives and quickly.

While polls track changes in party support, it is much more difficult to figure out what impact poll results during a campaign may have on voting intentions. Voters know the polls exist, as 91 percent of those in the Decima-Carleton survey said they had noticed media coverage of opinion poll results. Almost half (49 percent) of the 4,972 people who returned email questionnaires between January 13 and 15 thought there was about the right amount of poll coverage in the media, while 41 percent said there was too much. Those who describe themselves on the left were more likely to think poll coverage was excessive than those on the right. Many of those surveyed were also quick to discount any impact of poll coverage. Slightly more than half, 53 percent, of the survey's respondents said reading or hearing about poll results in the news has no impact on which party they will support.

However, opinion polls may contribute to some strategic voting. With the Conservatives leading in polls and an Ontario sample that was evenly split between Liberal and Conservative supporters, 19 percent of undecided voters said the poll results made them more likely to vote Liberal while only 11 percent said they were more likely to vote Conservative based on polls reported in the media.

Playing the Seat Projection Game

In the 2004 campaign, the major news organizations took their poll results and used them to project how many seats each party would win on election day. They were wrong: the results failed to match the predictions. The seat projection models in 2004 were based on the assumption that Progressive Conservative and Canadian Alliance voters from 2000 would all vote for the new Conservative Party in 2004. Having been burned once, the media were not keen to risk such predictions again.

Ironically the seat projection models would have worked much better in this election, as the same parties were running in 2006 as ran in 2004. But voter turnout was the potential spoiler this time around. The last winter election highlights the potential problem. In May 1979, 76 percent of Canadians voted, giving Joe Clark and the Conservatives a minority government. In the election the following February that returned a Liberal majority under Pierre Trudeau, winter weather meant that turnout fell to 69 percent. If the 2004 summer and 2006 winter election followed that pattern, turnout would drop to about 54 percent from the 61 percent of voters who went to the polls in 2004. The possibility of a seven percentage point drop in turnout when less than five percentage points separated first and second in more than fifty seats in 2004 made seat projections in this campaign an extremely risky business. News organizations did not want to be embarrassed two elections in a row. That was a smart call. As it developed, voter turnout would have undermined any seat projections but not the way many had anticipated. Turnout on January 23 was 65 percent, four percentage points higher than in 2004, and no model could have predicted which party those extra voters would support.

Matching its aggressive use of opinion poll results, the *Globe and Mail* was more adventurous on seat projections than its competitors. A two-line headline across the width of the front page on January 13 proclaimed "Pollster's seat projection puts Harper on the cusp of a majority." Almost all of the thirteen inches of the story on the front page highlighted the inexact nature of the seat projection game. It then continued without missing a beat in deciding that "with speculation focused on whether the Conservatives could form a majority government, the *Globe and Mail* has opted to publish the numbers based on the Strategic Counsel's polls." It was a questionable decision followed the next week by the prominent coverage given first to the poll that found the huge lead for the Conservatives and then to the Liberals apparently reducing that advantage. The final ten days of an election campaign is not the time to splash a story across a front page that could most charitably be described as only interesting if true.

Old Habits Die Slowly

Two other disturbing trends in recent political coverage also played a role in this campaign — the use of anonymous quotes and selective advance "leaks" of pending policy announcements, with the latter coming back to haunt the Liberals.

The reliance by political reporters on anonymous quotes has reached epidemic proportions in newspapers, and these dubious quotes appeared regularly in all three papers during the campaign. The use of unnamed sources and anonymous quotes has been blamed for a steady decline in media credibility in the United States, forcing leading news organizations such as the *New York Times*, the *Washington Post*, and the *Los Angeles Times* to introduce policies that limit the use of quotes from unnamed people. In Canada the media appear not to be concerned about the degree to which they encourage negative or derogatory attacks on politicians and others by protecting the identity of those who make unsubstantiated allegations.

In this campaign, the *Globe and Mail* ran a front-page story on January 10 by the paper's senior political reporter, Jane Taber, and reporter Bill Curry that was critical of the Liberal campaign. The story included direct and indirect quotes attributed variously to three different unnamed candidates, a veteran Liberal, a Martinite, some Liberal staffers, another Liberal staff member, some Ontario candidates, and a senior Liberal. Heritage Minister Liza Frulla, defending the campaign, appeared in paragraph twenty as the first named person in the story. While that was the most flagrant abuse, all three papers regularly included quotes from unnamed people in their stories. Readers had no idea who these people were, what axes they had to grind, or even whether they were fictions designed to allow reporters to inject their own comments into their stories. All the parties were victims of these media smears.

The Liberals also discovered they could no longer count on the media management strategy they had perfected during years in government. The Liberals took advantage of competition between news organizations to be first with news by providing advance information about upcoming policy announcements to selected television and newspaper reporters, allowing them to claim they had received "leaks" of government plans. Of course the leaks were carefully designed to highlight whatever aspects of any planned announcement the government wanted to emphasize. The media were too frequently willing accomplices in advancing the government's agenda.

The Liberals found themselves on the defensive early in this campaign, as they were unprepared for the daily Conservative policy announcements. They mistakenly believed that Canadians would start paying attention only after the holidays but realized they had to respond after more than a week of Conservatives grabbing the headlines. So they tried out one of their old media management tricks. On December 8 the newspapers all contained stories with selected details of a handgun ban Paul Martin would announce the next day in Toronto in response to a series of murders in the city. The "leak" worked just as it had when the Liberals were in government, giving the proposed ban two days of publicity. First came the pre-announcement story with officially approved highlights of what was going to be announced without any reaction, and then the second day's stories featured the actual announcement and reaction.

Things did not turn out as well when the party returned to the same media management strategy in early January. Resuming the campaign after New Year's, the Liberal campaign told reporters that Martin would deliver a major lunchtime speech in Winnipeg on January 3 to highlight Liberal values, co-ordinated with new television advertisements. It was all designed to kick off what Liberals believed was the real campaign. The speech was well received and initially reported, but later that day the campaign team heard rumours the Conservatives would announce the following morning a promise to repeal the $975 fee charged to immigrants. The Liberals responded by leaking that night their own hastily conceived plan to do the same thing. The Liberal immigration story made the front pages the next morning, reducing the coverage of the Conservative announcement that day but also obliterating coverage of Martin's speech and undermining the advertising strategy. They had been too smart by half and scooped themselves. It was not a good start to part two of the campaign.

Two days later Canadian Press ran what seemed to be a real leak, stating the Liberals would reveal the next day a plan to offer first- and final-year undergraduate university students free tuition. The story caught the Liberal communications team off guard, and they would only tell reporters on the Martin plane that the story was not entirely correct. That refusal to confirm the story and provide advance details of the next day's announcement led to heated confrontations with reporters on the tour. A bizarre series of stories followed in which reporters and columnists speculated on the possibility that a mole inside the Liberal campaign was leaking campaign announcements to the media and, improbably, to the Conservatives. No reporter ever presented any evidence to substantiate this assertion, but that did not stop media across the country speculating about the prospect for several days.

This all came as opinion polls picked up growing support for the Conservatives and that, combined with the troubles of the Liberal campaign, began to dominate media coverage. The campaign team had not helped its cause by delaying policy announcements until the second half of the campaign and then releasing them in clusters, rather than following the Conservatives' lead, perfected in December, of simple single daily announcements. The Liberal announcements were complicated and hard to distinguish from the flurry of spending announcements made in the two weeks before the campaign began. Reporters did not know what was new and what had been announced before so they decided to ignore much of it. Besides, with polls showing the Liberal support falling and Conservative support growing, particularly in Quebec, it was easier to ask questions about campaign strategy and fortunes. That was the way the last few campaigns had been covered by the media. Reporters and columnists were back on the ground many found more familiar, talking tactics, strategy, and personality — and demanding that politicians react to statements by another leader or anyone else for that matter. This kind of reporting required less research than trying to understand and explain complex policy proposals.

A perfect example was the day of the Liberal tuition announcement. Filing for *CTV National News* that night, Ottawa bureau chief Robert Fife, who had been in the midst of the leak fight on the plane the day before, ignored the details of the announcement completely in his story. Instead he focused on verbal stumbling in Martin's presentation, the small number of people in the room watching the Liberal leader speak, and criticism of the state of the Liberal campaign. The CBC television story that evening provided some of the details of the tuition policy, but in the days that followed CTV coverage of the Liberals, viewed through the same lens of the daily poll results it shared with the *Globe and Mail*, continued to ignore the substance of whatever Martin was saying on the campaign trail. Night after night CTV coverage of the Liberals focused on strategy and tactics, delivering a harshly negative impression of the state of the party's campaign and the effectiveness of its leader while ignoring its platform proposals. It was a theme other news organizations picked up in the campaign's final ten days. By then, much of the media had concluded that Martin was likely to lose the election, and whatever he was saying at this point was of minimal importance.

The Public Knows Best

Public reaction to the televised leaders' debates is an excellent demonstration of the gap that exists between how reporters view elections and what interests the public. In this campaign there were two sets of debates — the first pair in mid-December in Vancouver and the second in Montreal two weeks before voting day. The debate format in 2004 had quickly devolved into a two-hour, four-person, non-stop shouting match, interrupted by the occasional question. It was widely criticized. Those "debates" looked particularly bad when compared with the civilized and informative series of debates between George W. Bush and John Kerry in the U.S. presidential campaign in the fall of 2004. The television network organizers of the 2005–06 Canadian debates responded by introducing a much more rigid format. Each leader would answer specific questions directed to him, and then the others leaders could briefly comment, within the limits of a strict time schedule. While each leader was speaking, the others had to remain silent. There would be no verbal free-for-alls.

Most reporters and commentators instantly concluded as soon as the first two-hour session ended that the new format was a loser. They pushed the leaders in the post-debate scrums to agree that the event was boring. The leaders disagreed. In the process reporters revealed the degree to which they were out of touch with the opinions of Canadians. The Carleton-Decima survey discovered after the first set of debates on December 15–16 that almost half (45 percent) of those surveyed thought the new format was an improvement over the format of the 2004 debates while only 23 percent thought it was worse. That wasn't true in Quebec, where only one-quarter of those surveyed liked the new approach while 42 percent found it worse. Nationally, support for the new format was consistent across the ideological spectrum of voters while slightly more women than men preferred it.

Additional questions in the survey about which network Canadians chose to watch the debates backed up earlier findings about the ideological differences between each network's viewers. CBC debate viewers were more likely to be on the left of centre while a greater share of CTV and Global viewers leaned to the right. CTV and Global also had more female than male viewers. CBC had a larger male than female audience.

Ideological differences in audiences also emerged when decided voters for each party were asked which single news organization they relied on the most to help them reach conclusions about the debates. Liberals and New Democrats turned more to CBC television and radio for debate analysis while Conservative voters were more likely to rely on CTV, local talk radio, and the Internet. Among newspapers, Liberals and New Democrats more often selected the *Globe and Mail* while Conservatives looked to the *National Post.* In Quebec, Radio-Canada/RDI was selected by 30 percent of Bloc Québécois voters and TVA/LCN was chosen by 28 percent of those who would vote for the Bloc.

Table 11
Main media source for debate conclusions
(percentage of each party's decided voters)

	Liberal	Conservative	NDP	BQ
CBC TV/Newsworld	25	15	26	1
CTV/Newsnet	18	23	13	-
Global	7	7	8	-
Globe and Mail	4	2	3	-
National Post	1	3	-	-
CBC Radio	3	2	8	-
Local talk radio	0	6	2	-
Internet	4	7	2	-

The survey also found almost one-third of those responding did not consult the media at all in reaching their conclusions about the debate. Instead they relied on their own perceptions from watching the event.

Table 12
Most influential factor in shaping debate conclusions (percentage)

The debates themselves	31
Newspapers the day after	11
Immediate post-debate TV analysis	8
TV newscasts that night	8
All-news channels	4
Internet news sites	4
Internet blogs	1

Backing the Blackout

In 2006, election rules once again prevented news organizations from broadcasting or publishing any results until polls closed in the region of the country where the broadcast would be seen or heard. Internet news sites were prohibited from reporting results from anywhere in the country until the last polls closed in British Columbia at 10:00 p.m. EST, and satellite TV signals originating in Canada faced the same restrictions. Following the 2000 election, Paul Bryan, who ran a B.C.–based website, was charged by police with violating the Elections Act when he posted Eastern Canadian election results on his site before the polls had closed in B.C. He was acquitted prior to the 2004 election and that temporarily killed the blackout. An appeal court reversed the original acquittal, bringing the blackout back for 2006. That decision was appealed to the Supreme Court of Canada and a group of news organizations went to the Supreme Court asking for a quick hearing of the case prior to election day that might end the blackout. The Court, however, refused to juggle its hearing schedule to accommodate the media.

Almost one-third of those in a Decima-Carleton email survey in late December supported an end to the media blackout. In British Columbia almost half of those surveyed supported it. Across the country one-quarter of the 6,380 people questioned said they would take steps through websites, blogs, emails, and text and instant messaging systems to circumvent the blackout and get results before their polls closed. Those potential lawbreakers included 35 percent of B.C. respondents and 40 percent of those surveyed in the Vancouver area. One-third of those on the right but only one-quarter of those on the left said they would try to get around the blackout. That suggests the blackout is a bigger issue for small-*c* conservatives than small-*l* liberals.

Siding with the Winner

The Carleton-Decima survey also asked Canadians both early and later in the campaign whether they thought the coverage provided by various news organizations showed bias and which party they thought most journalists covering the campaign wanted to form the next government.

The questions were asked between December 7 and 9, before the first set of debates and with the Liberals holding a steady lead in published public opinion poll results. While a majority said either they could detect no leanings or they were unsure, 29 percent believed the *National Post* leaned towards the Conservative party, while 26 percent believed CBC television leaned towards the Liberals and 22 percent believed CBC radio had the same tendencies. Only 4 percent thought CBC television leaned towards the Conservatives and 3 percent had that same view of CBC Radio.

In Quebec a similar majority were unsure or could not detect any leanings towards a specific party, but 29 percent believed Radio-Canada and *La Presse* both favoured the Liberals, while 26 percent thought TVA leaned towards the Bloc Québécois.

At the same time in early December, 40 percent of those surveyed believed that most journalists covering the campaign wanted the Liberals to form the next government, while only 15 percent believed most journalists wanted a Conservative victory. As the table indicates, those who describe themselves on the right of the political spectrum and Conservative voters were the most convinced that journalists were Liberal supporters.

The survey also asked whether respondents thought media coverage of each of the leaders had been too positive, too negative, or struck about the right balance. Opinion was most divided about Conservative Leader Stephen Harper and Liberal Leader Paul Martin.

The survey posed the same questions again between January 13 and 15. At this point in the campaign, the opinion polls showed a solid Conservative lead and the media were already speculating on the possibility of a Harper majority government. Opinion about media bias among the same group of people quizzed in December matched the change in opinion poll results. Now 40 percent said that most journalists wanted the Conservatives to win while only 19 percent thought most journalists wanted a Liberal victory. Those on the left were most likely to say most journalists wanted the Conservatives to win.

Perceptions about how the media treated the two main party leaders had also sharply changed. Now twice as many people (40 percent versus 19 percent in December) believed that media coverage of Paul Martin was overly negative. That view was strongest in British Columbia (47 percent) and weakest in Alberta (32 percent). Almost half as many (11 percent in mid-January versus 19 percent in December) now believed media coverage of the Liberal leader was overly positive. Views had also flipped on Stephen Harper. Almost twice as many as in December (27 percent versus 16 percent) now considered coverage of him as overly positive, but there was only a slight drop in the number who now viewed coverage of the Conservative leader as overly negative. On both occasions more than three-quarters (77 percent) of those surveyed believed coverage of New Democratic Party Leader Jack Layton struck about the right balance.

CONCLUSION

If audience satisfaction is the main determinant of success then the media did well in the 2006 election. In the campaign's second week, almost three-quarters of those responding to the Carleton-Decima survey said the media had done a good or excellent job covering the campaign. Those who planned to vote for the Conservatives were least likely to endorse the quality of media coverage, but 70 percent of even this group said coverage was good or excellent. Overall opinion had not changed among the entire group when they were asked the same questions as the campaign entered its final week. This time 75 percent viewed campaign coverage as good or excellent. However, the views of Conservatives had changed. With the party looking like a winner, 80 percent of Conservative supporters viewed the media's performance as good or excellent. It was a perfect example of the degree to which the media's performance in election campaigns is judged through partisan eyes.

There is a good explanation of public satisfaction with campaign coverage in 2005–06. The Liberal defeat in Parliament ended a minority government in which the antics of all the parties and the media coverage of those antics alienated many Canadians. Non-stop allegations of

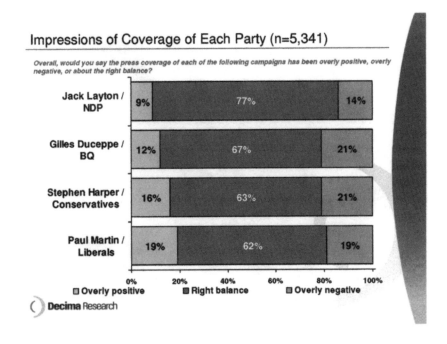

Impressions of Coverage of Each Party (n=5,341)

Overall, would you say the press coverage of each of the following campaigns has been overly positive, overly negative, or about the right balance?

Party	Overly positive	Right balance	Overly negative
Jack Layton / NDP	9%	77%	14%
Gilles Duceppe / BQ	12%	67%	21%
Stephen Harper / Conservatives	16%	63%	21%
Paul Martin / Liberals	19%	62%	19%

☐ Overly positive ■ Right balance ☐ Overly negative

◯ Decima Research

sleaze and scandal, name-calling, political manoeuvring, and backstabbing reduced parliamentary proceedings to the level of schoolyard bickering. That's what the media covered day after day. For many Canadians that's what political reporting and politics had become. It left them cold and they stopped listening, watching, and reading. Had the 2006 election been a nasty, aggressive slanging match it is unlikely that the campaign coverage would have received such positive reviews.

Instead the political players dropped the single-minded devotion to scandal they had demonstrated in Parliament over the previous eighteen months and talked policy day after day. This caught the Liberals completely off guard and forced the media to cover issues and policies. That change from concentrating on theatrics to focusing on substance captured the attention of Canadians in December. It also caught the Liberals and even the media by surprise. The predicted antagonism over a Christmastime election never materialized and the public turned out to be wide awake, not dozing off, during the campaign's first four weeks.

It was only in the campaign's final ten days that the pre-election media focus on personality and charges and counter-charges returned when the Conservatives ended their policy announcements. They had concluded, correctly, that they had said enough to get elected if they made no big mistakes in the final few days.

Even though the public was generally very satisfied with the 2005–06 election campaign coverage, there remain issues for the media to ponder. The use and misuse of public opinion data remains the largest concern. News organizations are continually searching for new gimmicks to promote the distinctiveness of their campaign coverage in a very competitive market where the Internet increasingly is crowding newspapers, radio, and television. That led directly to the seat projection debacle in 2004 and the controversies surrounding the accuracy of daily tracking polls in 2006. Both of these undermined rather than enhanced the media's credibility with the public. The parties shape their campaigns around their own polling, so the media needs to be polling as well to understand campaign decisions. However, poll results should be just one element of a news organization's campaign coverage strategy. Instead they have become the prism through which all campaign events are reported and analyzed, threatening public confidence in campaign coverage because polls are sometimes wrong.

Then there is the matter of sameness of coverage. The future of newspapers is being called into question by television and the Internet, which with their ability to deliver news instantly can steal readers. That should be a reason for each paper to be distinctive, to take different angles on stories, and to find different approaches designed to give the paper a clear identity that will build a loyal readership. Instead, the overwhelming impression of campaign coverage in the *Globe and Mail*, the *National Post*, and the *Toronto Star* is uniformity. All three papers covered the same issues the same way, leaving the impression that they are collectively interchangeable rather than individually essential. That's not a good strategy for survival.

This was also the first campaign in several in which newspapers increased their news coverage and reduced the amount of attention given to columns and opinion. Substance and issues, not superficiality and impressions, dominated newspaper, radio, and television reporting of the 2006 election and Canadians liked that. This was also the first election since 1988 — also an issues-based campaign about free trade with the United States — in which voter turnout did not drop. It rose by four percentage points over the turnout in 2004 to 64.9 percent of eligible voters. That is enough to argue that an election campaign where the media devoted more time and space to issues rather than personalities and concentrated on news rather than opinion may be the long-sought antidote to growing apathy about politics and public policy. It is an intriguing theory for the media and the parties to test when Canadians next go to the polls.

CHAPTER TEN

Public Opinion and the 2006 Election
by Michael Marzolini

Public opinion is civilization's most powerful currency. It starts and ends wars, changes governments, determines people's behaviour, creates and maintains the market for all products and services, and impacts on every decision made by both the public and private sector. The art and science of measuring public opinion is rarely of more interest to Canadians than during a federal election campaign. Most major media organizations employ a pollster to explore the attitudes and opinions of the voters and determine their likely behaviour at the ballot box. Political parties also retain a "pollster of record" whose job is to strategically "manage" public opinion between and during elections, using communications, positioning, and imaging techniques to maximize public support for their party and leader, while minimizing that of their opposition. The measuring, interpretation, and reporting of public opinion, whether by media pollsters or party pollsters, are a public trust. This trust also extends to the media organizations that publish public opinion results, though this often creates tension between choosing an interesting headline versus reporting what a poll actually says.

The following chapter explores the ebb and flow of public opinion during the 2006 federal election, while noting how the public trust of accurate public opinion interpretation at times yielded ground to media sensationalism. It also examines the performance and accuracy of the individual media organizations, political parties, and the polling firms they retained.

In the 2006 federal campaign some media relied too heavily on polls and used them to manufacture news stories, even when the news was not worth reporting. The best example of this occurred early in the campaign, when public opinion was stagnant, voters were paying very little attention, and the overall horse-race poll numbers showed no change. "Liberals surge in Ontario" was the front-page headline of one daily, based on a statistically insignificant shift within a regional sub-sample of its national survey. The next day, when that regional shift stabilized by the same statistically insignificant amount, the unapologetic headline was "Tories receive bump in Ontario."

Granted, headlines like these prove better value for media organizations than publishing "Nothing happened again today" at the top of a poll-tracking graph containing only parallel lines. Newspapers engage pollsters to help sell newspapers. The public is fascinated by what they and their fellow citizens are thinking, and print and broadcast media organizations use their pollsters to find headlines and, when sensational headlines are not available, to manufacture filler content. Often this filler content, covering concerns over issues, attitudes toward various party policies, and impressions of various attributes of the party leaders, gives the public an insight into strategy and tactics of the various campaigns. Voters are able to gain an understanding of why a particular topic was introduced into a campaign speech, or why a certain advertisement is running, or why a party is pouring resources and leader time into one province and not another.

Not so insightful, but of greater interest to media and the public, are the horse-race voter-preference numbers. These simply reveal the comparative levels of support for each party, ideally providing a context, when viewed with the policy and leadership data, to determine whether various party strategies and tactics are working. Unfortunately, many media organizations often publish only the horse-race data, leaving the question "why is support shifting from one party to another?" open to individual interpretation and the mercy of journalists who have little understanding of public opinion methodology.

Canada's media and their pollsters started their work for the 2006 campaign under a shadow of distrust from the previous election. In 2004, the media had been preoccupied with the "voodoo science" of electoral seat projections, an unscientific extrapolation of the nationwide polls intended to determine how voters of each individual riding would cast their ballots. These projections can often be quite accurate, if the survey sample is large enough, and if the seat projection model is based only on regional poll changes, and not national changes, which do not necessarily affect support in all ridings. These projections adjust historical election results upwards and downwards based on new polling data.

The problem in 2004 was that there were no historical election results for the new Conservative Party of Canada. The CPC was formed by a merger of the Canadian Reform Conservative Alliance (which delivered all of its support to the new party) and the Progressive Conservative Party of Canada (which saw large portions of its vote transfer to the Liberal Party). The seat projection models did not take this into account and hence severely over-emphasized the strength of the CPC, predicting a CPC minority rather than the actual Liberal minority.

Despite the misleading seat projections, the last public opinion results of the 2004 election were actually very accurate, showing a significant Conservative lead at the time, but were all conducted too early to predict the outcome. The final polls were taken between five and eight days ahead of the vote. This timing is not usually problematic — the electorate has usually reached a consensus by the campaign's final week — but this time many voters were still undecided until late in the campaign.

Yet a competent analysis of the media polls would have revealed the fluidity of the electorate. All of the final polls showed the Liberals rebounding and the Conservatives falling. Moreover, the foundation of support for the Conservatives was seen to be crumbling. Fewer people wanted to see them form a government than said they would vote for them. This suggests that the Conservatives were further trending downward and would likely fall further. These clues, and others, were contained in all of the opinion polls that were released but were obscured by the news media's preoccupation with horse-race numbers and smothered by their concentration on seat projections. Canada's pollsters received a black eye, deserved in part for their reluctance, and that of their clients, to continue polling through to election day.

The 2006 election would be different. Pollsters regrouped and designed new methodologies. All would be prepared to poll right up to the weekend before the vote, and some would go further than that — polling on election eve, and even during the day when people were heading off to cast their ballots. Some, like SES, which would prove the most reliable of the media pollsters in 2006, doubled their sample size. None would stoop to provide seat projections. Most would delve deeper into public opinion than the horse-race numbers and try to anticipate changes in support by examining attitudes toward the leaders, the issues, and the policy planks of the parties, as well as campaign momentum and other diagnostics.

The media also regrouped. Some changed their pollsters, echoing the words of Robert Hurst, president of CTV News: "We were left out to hang by our pollsters last time." CTV and the *Globe and Mail* would choose the Strategic Counsel, led by Allan Gregg, who as former chief pollster to the Progressive Conservative Party had provided public opinion strategy for Brian Mulroney, Joe Clark, and Kim Campbell and was widely respected.

The *National Post* and the Global Television Network would replace their traditional pollster, COMPAS, with Ipsos-Reid, the country's largest, and arguably most recognized, public opinion polling organization. CPAC, the Cable Public Affairs Channel, would continue to retain SES, a small polling firm, led by a former PC pollster for Joe Clark, that had built a solid reputation through its provision of daily tracking in 2004.

The *Toronto Star* and *La Presse* would continue to use Ekos Research, an Ottawa-based consultancy specializing in the public sector, while a number of news services would use Léger Marketing, a Quebec-based firm in the process of growing into a national company. Canadian Press would retain Decima Research, an established firm founded in the eighties by Allan Gregg, while Reuters and Rogers Media would both use POLLARA, a strategic polling firm that had served as chief pollsters to the Liberal Party during the Chrétien years and before that had polled for, among others, CTV, *Toronto Star*, and Sun Media newspapers.

The CBC continued its practice of not conducting its own polls but relying internally on Environics Research, which would produce very in-depth surveys for the guidance of CBC's senior news staff, but aside from some pre-writ and post-writ polling, none was ever broadcast.

Few of these pollsters are paid. Most polling firms subsidize their clients, spending far more money collecting data than could be reimbursed by their sponsors. Most work for name-recognition and profile, trusting that this will assist their firm's marketing efforts. Others poll out of pride and reputation, wanting to demonstrate their accuracy and analysis and hoping to be the firm with the most accurate poll of the election. There are very few opportunities other than elections and referendums in which pollsters can prove the accuracy of their craft.

In 2006, most of these pollsters would prove themselves uncannily accurate and worthy of the public trust. Some would make glaring errors, allowing methodological issues to produce misleading results mid-campaign. Others would allow their work to be tainted by bad analysis by reporters and on a few occasions by bad analysis by the pollsters themselves.

Unlike the media pollsters, the two major parties' pollsters are usually given a budget of between $750,000 and $1.2 million. While a media pollster may ask six questions in a survey, a party pollster will ask more than a hundred, with a much larger sample. Focus groups testing messages and discussing leader image, policies, advertising, and strategy are conducted nightly. Surveys into key ridings, as well as nightly tracking, often interviewing as many as a thousand people a night, are continuous throughout the campaign. Party pollsters try to "shift the needle," determining which hot buttons and levers will solidify their party's core vote and which will serve to poach support from the other parties. They are usually the first and last word in election tactics and strategy on each campaign team.

The Liberal pollster was David Herle of The Gandalf Group, formerly Earnscliffe Research, a long-time loyalist of Paul Martin. A lawyer by training, his first attempt at polling a national campaign in 2004 was confused and unfocused, not yielding the necessary ballot question as to why voters should choose the Liberals. Indeed, the Liberals campaigned not on their strengths, like their economic performance, but more on their weaknesses, such as cleaning up government patronage. This resulted in a muddled campaign that caused them to lose the majority status they had enjoyed for eleven years and almost caused them to lose the election itself. Only a last-minute voter backlash against Conservative campaign errors and fear over Stephen Harper having a right-wing "hidden agenda" allowed the Liberals to salvage a minority government.

Also polling for the Liberal Party of Canada, oddly, was long-time Tory pollster and campaign manager John Laschinger. Though never a federal Liberal, he had been an advisor to once-Conservative MP Belinda Stronach, and he continued to provide her with advice and polling when she sat as a Liberal. He would be used by the Liberals to poll soft Conservative voters in the suburbs outside of Toronto, searching for ways to bring them into the Liberal fold. However, the Liberals regarded his $70,000 contract only as a way of preventing Laschinger from working for the Tories — they would not use his data to any material effect.

The Conservatives' 2004 campaign had also been lacking in cohesive strategy from their polling. The "hidden agenda" fears at the end of that campaign should have been countered; Stephen Harper's lack of decisiveness on the abortion issue was an Achilles heel that their pollster should have insisted be dealt with. In the last week Harper spoke continually of forming a majority government, scaring voters who might have trusted him with a minority but certainly not with a majority. This disastrous strategy, which prompted an electoral run on the bank, was aimed at attracting Quebec supporters — the feeling being that Quebecers would jump on the Conservative bandwagon if they appeared likely to form a government. It was a clear miscalculation, and one that could have been rectified by competent polling analysis of how these issues should have played out.

Having learned from past mistakes, the Conservative Party had a very professional team effort heading into the 2006 election. Dimitri Pantazopoulos would again collect the polling data. David Crapper, who had distinguished himself in several previous Progressive Conservative campaigns, would advise on public opinion analysis. This would feed up to Patrick Muttart, a straight-talker with a superb grasp of how to design and execute political strategy.

The team analyzed the demographics of the party's core voters, the soft Conservatives and soft Liberals who would be their key targets, and quite unusually but brilliantly simplified the process by giving each demographic an ordinary person's name. Creative directors of the Conservative advertising firms, for example, could then design an ad designed to appeal to "Peter" or "Margaret" rather than having to deal with a dozen confusing demographics that could result in a mediocre message. This simplification approach was an innovation that removed much of the mystery to the art of electoral targeting and made it more useable to organizers on the ground. The Conservative campaign could "narrowcast" rather than "broadcast." It could maximize its appeal to receptive voters, while ignoring those voters who were not attainable. This proved to be effective.

Neither the NDP nor Bloc Québécois had any sophisticated opinion polling programs in 2004 or 2006. Their surveys were regional or riding-specific only and were not subjected to a high level of strategic development. Perhaps as a result, neither campaign distinguished itself in either election.

THE PUBLIC OPINION ENVIRONMENT

Shortly after the loss of its majority status in 2004, the Liberal government announced through their spokesman John Duffy that they would "govern on the numbers." This phrase was correctly interpreted by the media as meaning they would govern by focus group and opinion poll. Policies that the public believes to be important would be acted upon. Other issues, perhaps even more vital to the nation but not visible on the radar screen of public opinion, would be ignored.

This was the Liberals' first mistake of the 2006 election. Public opinion should never dictate public policy. The public's views should always be taken into account, but the philosophy of parliamentary democracy involves electing representatives of the people to intensively study the issues, develop policies that will address their needs, and make informed and deliberative choices. If they are leading, rather than following, public opinion, they must be prepared to explain their choices to the electorate, because in order to get re-elected, they must receive the endorsement of the public. The pollster can assist with this, providing the messages and contexts that will be most effective at explaining government decisions and attaining public buy-in. "Governing on the numbers" is essentially mob rule. This basically means dismissing the parliamentarians while relying on pollsters to run the government.

This was the growing view of the Martin Liberal government from its inception to its replacement. Rather than choose four or five things it would do, and do well, it reached too far, trying to apply itself to too many issues. Every issue was a priority as the party tried to be all things to all people. It dispersed its energy and resources to the point where its accomplishments were overshadowed by its failures.

In 2003 the public had very high expectations of the much-anticipated Martin government, but these expectations were not met by his performance. Some frustration resulted, and Martin's impression rating fell significantly in 2004. The advertising sponsorship scandal, a fixture in the news for more than a year by that time, reached new proportions with a new, more detailed report from the auditor general. Rather than deal with these unlawful acts in the tried and true manner — leaving it to the RCMP to find and punish the perpetrators — and get on with governing, Martin's pollsters tried a bizarre new strategy. They considered the scandal a fortunate opportunity to portray Martin as different from the previous Liberal prime minister and thereby ditch all the baggage collected through ten years of Liberal government. By cleaning up the mess, they thought, Martin would be seen as the agent of change that Canadians desired.

The Prime Minister crossed the nation, talking up the sponsorship scandal and making it the focus of national attention. He promised to deal with it, but rather than rely only on law enforcement agencies he appointed a Commission of Inquiry to ensure maximum exposure. It was a miscalculation, damaging the Liberal brand and divorcing Martin from the accomplishments of the government in which he had served effectively as minister of finance. Furthermore, it destroyed the lead that the Liberals had enjoyed over their nearest competitor for the past ten years. The drop in support was most damaging in Quebec, and the fallout from the Gomery inquiry would also dangerously raise public support for independence in that province.

For close to two years, both before and after the 2004 election, the Liberal government was paralyzed, not by the public's reaction to the ongoing inquiry but by its own lack of creative policy. The throne speeches and budgets of the Liberal government were lacklustre, mediocre affairs that contained little that would motivate voters or stimulate their interest. Federal-provincial agreements to provide more money for health care were met with cynicism — the public had seen that ritual many times yet never perceived any progress in fixing the health care system. A child care agreement with the provinces was new, but government child care, a fixture of Liberal platforms for more than twenty years, has never attracted much public appetite. It was a priority for some but not for a majority of Canadians.

The lack of policies and vision that the Liberals demonstrated during their 2004 election campaign was a damaging overlay to the next seventeen months of office. All voter concerns continued to be priorities. The government slavishly followed a host of badly interpreted opinion polls, aimed at all times at the squeaky wheels of society, not at the public as a whole. The Liberals struck an accord with the NDP: in exchange for the latter propping up the government, the Liberals promised to spend more than $5 billion on "priorities" that had not been important when they wrote the 2005 budget. Canadians considered this cynical and unethical. Liberal voter support remained steady, as the public didn't think the Conservatives would be an improvement, but Martin's impression rating fell and the foundations of Liberal support were in tatters.

In the summer of 2005, it was only Stephen Harper who kept Liberal support out of the gutter. Harper was seen as unelectable. His preoccupation with opposing the same-sex marriage issue was translated as "intolerance" by most Canadians, even opponents of same-sex marriage. Many suspected he would show the same intolerant attitude toward women and abortion and visible minorities. His repertoire seemed to consist of nothing but outrage over the sponsorship scandal and outrage over same-sex marriage. People saw him only as an opposition leader, not as a prime minister. This negativity, combined with Harper's lack of personal warmth, repelled much potential electoral support. The electorate considered him not yet ready for prime time. Disaffected Progressive Conservatives launched a "dump-Harper" campaign, prompting much concern in Liberal ranks over the prospect of losing what they considered their best asset.

The Liberals eased up on Harper, refusing to go for the jugular or to define him in their own terms. He had to be preserved to deliver the

Liberals their majority. This erroneous and dangerous strategy, giving Harper a free ride on vulnerable issues like same-sex marriage, allowed him to repair the damage and build a fresh and very positive image. He was allowed to make his appeal to the electorate during the entire first half of the campaign without substantive criticism from the Liberal Party. This opportunity enabled Harper to gradually transform into the leader the public wanted him to be. By the time the Liberals reacted, in the first week of 2006, Harper had far more credibility than Martin, and it was impossible to re-label him as being cold, intolerant, and mean-spirited.

The week before the November non-confidence vote in the House of Commons, which many expected would presage an election, saw the harvest of the "governing on the numbers" strategy. Scores of Liberal spending announcements were suddenly unleashed on the public, often on an hourly basis and up to thirty a day, promising huge sums of money for every conceivable "priority" listed in the opinion polls. Forest industry money in British Columbia, theme parks in P.E.I., conference centres in Nova Scotia, immigrant integration in Ontario, police training, art gallery renovations, modernization of the immigration system, new aircraft for the military, and infrastructure spending in almost every province were among the hundreds of promises made. Altogether, by some estimates, over $24 billion would be promised in new spending, more than one-seventh of the entire federal budget. As a senior Liberal cabinet minister said to an advisor, "I hope they defeat us soon. The country can't afford us."

The result of these scattered announcements was the creation of more public frustration and cynicism. The voters already suspected, from the expensive accord with the NDP, that the Liberals were willing to do anything to remain in office. Now they were sure of it. After a seventeen-month drought of ideas, policy, or government activity, they now had more than they could absorb. The spending appeared desperate, jumbled, and out of control. Realization set in that these announcements were only promises, and many people were confused as to whether they would still be valid after the election. This rain of promises discontented the voters, but while it worsened their impression of Martin once more, the public was still unhappily resigned to voting Liberal. There seemed to be no alternative — at the start of the campaign Stephen Harper appeared to lack policies, ideas, or vision. His platform was still limited to pointing out Liberal breaches of public trust. The media described him as more a public prosecutor than a potential prime minister. Horse-race polls showed him trailing the Liberals by between 5 and 10 percent.

THE 2006 ELECTION CAMPAIGN

The first poll of the 2006 election campaign, released by POLLARA–Reuters News on November 28, 2005, at the exact hour in which the government was defeated in Parliament, showed the Liberals at 36 percent, versus the Conservatives with 31 percent. This five-point gap still indicated that the Liberals would retain their minority government. Anything less than a twelve-point margin over the second-place party yields only a minority government.

Day one of the election campaign started with a risky strategy for Stephen Harper that raised the eyebrows of armchair political strategists across the country. It appeared to be business as usual, with the routine attack on Liberal corruption and a strong emphasis on Conservative opposition to same-sex marriage. Pundits reacted negatively. Many said that he was throwing the election away again, just as he had in 2004. Former PC prime minister Kim Campbell publicly predicted that Harper would lose the election. Liberal war room staffers were elated. Others, such as *Globe and Mail* columnist Jane Taber, who put Harper in her "Who's Hot?" listing of her campaign notebook, realized what few suspected, that this was actually a very workable strategy.

Putting the controversial same-sex marriage issue front and centre removed it as a "hidden agenda" item, essentially flushing it from the campaign and making it a non-issue. The Conservatives had now dealt with it — they didn't need to raise the subject again. The Liberals did not pursue it. They were more concerned about peaking too early and figured Harper was now dead in the water.

Indeed, the Liberals anticipated that Harper would run a very negative campaign focusing on the sponsorship scandal. Shortly before the election, Prime Minister Martin had announced that his campaign would be about values — Liberal versus Conservative. In other words, it would be a replay of the 2004 campaign, demonizing Stephen Harper for being a scary, right-wing zealot with a hidden agenda. The expectation was that Harper would spend all of his time demonizing Martin for the sponsorship scandal. The public expected a negative campaign. And the first day of the election fed this expectation.

If Harper had indeed run a negative campaign, he would have lost very badly, and the Liberals might have attained a majority. Any good poll analysis showed that while the Liberals did not get high marks for competence, they were still viewed as far more competent than the Conservatives and much less risky than the alternative. Canadians are by nature risk-averse. That is why they deserted the Conservatives in the last week of 2004. If Harper were to show any electoral strength at all during the course of the campaign, he was expected to lose it once more during the last week.

Two phases of the campaign were expected, divided by the new year. The first phase was expected to be a "phoney war," with parties keeping their gunpowder dry and holding back on policy, promises, resources, and advertising. The public, after all, were busy preparing for the holidays. They would not be paying a lot of attention, and it would be best to save energy for after the new year. The Liberals expected to make the breakthrough to their majority in 2006, and they, along with the media, assumed that the Conservatives would hold off as well.

In truth, there was little movement in the polls going into December. The consensus among the media pollsters was that the Liberals had a lead of between 5 and 8 percent. Strategic Counsel and SES both unveiled daily tracking polls that effectively made most of the other polls irrelevant. Past elections had seen only two or three polls released per week; now the poll intensity was three to five per day. Moreover, daily tracking polls could essentially conduct a couple of hundred new interviews each night, drop the oldest interviews from a few days before, and report brand new results. This was far more economical, and almost as accurate, than one-time surveys conducted all at once — reported and then discarded.

Media "poll clutter" dissuaded most of the remaining pollsters from conducting their customarily high number of polls. The normally prolific Ipsos-Reid would release only six polls in the first phase of the campaign, Decima four, POLLARA and Léger three each, and Ekos only one. However, daily trackers SES and Strategic Counsel would release twenty-six and twenty poll reports respectively, dominating most of the poll-driven media coverage.

Though the public was paying little attention, it would not benefit Harper to conserve his energies during the first phase of the election campaign. He was trailing in the polls, many of the media and the public had written him off as an effective leader, and there was an expectation that the Liberals would likely glide to a disappointing minority, or manage in January to get the lift necessary to form a majority government. With such low expectations, and with the Liberals "keeping their powder dry," there was great opportunity to make an impact. And any impact whatsoever could hardly fail to exceed expectations and give Harper and the Conservatives a boost.

Within this environment, and after what had been termed a disastrous first day, Harper confounded his opposition with a new and unexpected strategy. On only the second day of the campaign he announced one of his key and most effective policies — the reduction of the GST from 7 percent to 5 percent. Reducing this hated tax was good politics, though perhaps not good economics. POLLARA referred to this policy as a "magic bullet" in a *Globe and Mail* commentary on December 2. It was easy to understand, visible, and unlike most other campaign promises would actually make a difference to the average Canadian.

The Liberals, unhappy but trapped into defending an unpopular tax, went into action, mobilizing economists to criticize the GST reduction. Income tax cuts, they said, were a far more effective way of putting money back into people's pockets. In this they may well have been right. However, polling on the last three federal tax cuts had shown that most people had trouble understanding the impact of those "major" cuts on their household budget. Once they did understand, they were disappointed to find they were only minor and often trivial. They had been unimpressed by the Liberal tax cuts announced pre-writ, most of which were back-ended five years into the future. Income tax cuts also suffer from a lack of accountability. As a focus group respondent asked when discussing the two most recent tax measures announced by the federal and Ontario Liberals, "How come when they cut our taxes, I save $48, but when they raise them, it costs me $900?" The GST reduction, however, could actually be seen. Savings could be easily computed. And it fit the mood of Conservative target voters, people who were frustrated by elites freely spending huge sums of money and who perceived very little benefit trickling down to them.

Strategic Counsel confirmed the efficacy of the GST reduction in their polling, reporting in the *Globe and Mail* that 67 percent of Canadians liked the tax cut, but that "only" 28 percent said it would influence how they vote. "It's not the silver bullet," claimed Allan Gregg, in a bizarre interpretation of his own findings. Party pollsters search endlessly for any policy that will influence more than 5 percent of the electorate to support their political party. They rarely find a policy impacting on as much as 10 percent of the electorate, much less 28 percent. The Liberals' 1993 Red Book, for example, largely regarded as the greatest asset of that campaign, attracted some 15 percent of voters to the Liberals. Mike Harris's much-valued Common Sense Revolution platform moved 9 percent to the Ontario PC Party. These percentages sound quite low to the general public but of course constitute massive voter swings during a campaign. With only a 5 percent gap between the Liberals and the Conservatives, Harper's GST reduction's impact on 28 percent of all voters, and even higher among soft Liberal and NDP supporters, was actually the most effective political policy advanced in many decades.

The GST policy was not left alone on the table for long. The following day Harper announced a new and popular policy on health care wait times. He finished off his first week promising tougher penalties for drug crimes and clearly dominated the first week of election coverage. He would do the same in the second week, continuing to win the news cycle with daily policy announcements such as tax credits for sports enrolment for children and a grant for child care.

The Liberals reacted lethargically, explaining that voters were not yet tuned into the election, and the Tories were clearly going nowhere, as witnessed by a flurry of media polls showing that the Liberals had actually made some small gains in the first weeks and the Conservatives had lost ground.

These polls were many, and while the numbers varied, the trend of a slightly widening gap at the expense of the Conservatives was accurate. SES, Ipsos, and POLLARA all showed that the Liberals had increased their support by 3 percent by the end of the first week, while the Conservatives had dropped between 1 and 3 percent. Only Strategic Counsel had party support basically unchanged from the start of the campaign. The consensus appeared to be that there was very minor movement, but that the public was not yet heavily tuned in. The media, however, like the Liberals, swooped on these early poll results and assigned them great importance.

What was the importance of these early campaign shifts? There was none. The pollsters were largely wasting their time, conducting some 80 percent of their interviews with people who were not paying attention to the campaign. This is normal in the first two weeks of a campaign. Political parties often unveil their best policies and speech lines early, allocate massive resources, and then are frustrated at seeing no traction, positive or negative, in the daily opinion tracking. For the first two weeks of an election campaign only 20 percent of the population pays a lot of attention. This group consists of elites, media, Internet bloggers, political junkies, and people working in the public affairs arena. The average Canadian is uninterested, not ready to shop for a political party until usually the third week of the campaign. However, in 2006 the campaign was eight weeks long, rather than five, and the Christmas holidays bisected the timeline. It would take longer than two weeks for people to connect to this election. Indeed, the starting flag for public engagement into the campaign would be January 2, 2006, when the holidays were over.

What the pollsters should have done, and which indeed the Strategic Counsel actually did, two weeks into the election, was ask the simple question "How much attention are you paying to this election campaign?" But while the *Globe* pollsters may have collected the information, they did not analyze it properly. They failed to take the 19 percent of respondents they found to be "paying a lot of attention," tabulate their results separately to compare against the rest of the population, and see where the momentum was shifting. Without this vital clue, the *Globe* pollsters concluded that a Liberal victory was largely a done deal for Martin, because "almost everybody in the country is paying attention to this campaign." They came to this astounding conclusion by adding the 19 percent of "alert voters" to the 60 percent of respondents who claimed to be "paying some attention." "Paying some attention" is a mediocre response that should correctly be interpreted as meaning "I know that there is an election, but I haven't been following it."

In response to such analysis, POLLARA provided an interview to the *Globe and Mail*, headlined "The Intersection Point" on December 17, in which POLLARA stated with complete confidence that Stephen Harper's Conservative Party would overtake the Liberal Party during the first week of January. Though this analysis shocked many reporters and commentators, while others considered the prediction risky, all of Canada's media pollsters could have come to the same conclusion if they had analyzed the views of those "alert voters" who were "paying a lot of attention" to the campaign. Among this group, Harper had traction.

The "alert voters" comprised only about one in five voters until the final three weeks of the campaign, when the number would soar to four in five. Those paying early attention appreciated the Conservatives' new emphasis on policy rather than negativity and personal attacks. They found these policies attractive and responsible, and they began to view Stephen Harper in a much more positive way than they had in the past. They started to consider voting for him. They were the only ones at the time who were doing so. The rest of the population, the 80 percent paying little attention, were providing pollsters with opinions based on their views of him from the past and never updated. Once that update took place on January 2, POLLARA concluded, traction would occur, the polling numbers would intersect, and the Conservatives would be on the brink of forming a government.

What could not be determined was whether there would be a second intersection point. Would there be a voter backlash against Stephen Harper in 2006 as had happened in 2004? It would depend on whether Harper could not just gain support but gain both credibility and trust in even greater proportions, enough to surpass Paul Martin. If he could, Harper would be inoculated against the expected Liberal counterattack.

For Canada's pollsters, the real election campaign would start on January 2. For Stephen Harper, his job would be half completed by that time. His work in the first two weeks of December had laid the foundation for an early January surge. At the same time, Paul Martin's strategy had laid a very poor foundation for his party's future. The media polls would pick this up and reflect it accurately beginning in the first week of January.

The Liberal strategy is traditionally more difficult to design than those of its opponents. As a national party, the Liberals have to fight multi-front battles, while their opponents just pour resources into one province or a few regions where they have the basis of support. In 2006 the Liberals decided upon a "holding action" against the Conservatives in terms of policy, first matching income tax reductions against GST reductions. Then they pitted an enhancement of their state-operated day care plan against Harper's policy of simply sending parents money to spend as they choose. Neither Liberal policy fared well in the comparison, especially after the pratfalls of two of Martin's key advisors who insisted that Harper's day care scheme was bad because irresponsible parents may spend the money on "beer and popcorn." Like the infamous 2003 press release from Conservative Ontario Premier Ernie Eves describing his Liberal opponent Dalton McGuinty as "an evil reptilian kitten eater from outer space," the "beer and popcorn" remark was a seminal moment of the campaign. It broke through the issue clutter and impacted on those Canadians who never read a newspaper or watch television news. The entire electorate, not just the alert voters, took notice. It did not change their vote; they merely added it to the rest of the data they would later consult to make their voting decision.

Martin's campaign advisors were equally clumsy at setting traps for Harper's Conservatives. Martin's announcement of a "Canada Handgun Ban" was deliberately leaked ahead of time to try to provoke a response from the more reactionary Conservative MPs who were known to oppose such a policy. Gun control would have been a fine wedge issue for the Liberals to take on the Conservatives — polling data suggests the Liberals would have won handily — but the lure had less cunning than a Wile E. Coyote Roadrunner trap, and nobody took the bait.

The major battlefront for the Liberals in the first phase of the campaign was not against the Conservatives, though it should have been. Rather, Martin upped the ante against the Bloc Québécois, suggesting that the election in Quebec was in fact a referendum on Quebec's desire to stay in Canada or to leave it. The Bloc, with more than 50 percent of support in the province, were ecstatic. They just had to deliver their existing support to the ballot box and their cause would advance further than they could have dreamed.

The gamble would have been a better one if Martin's own leadership ratings in Quebec had been positive. However, the fallout from the sponsorship scandal had ravaged Liberal support, and those who were still Liberal loyalists were uncomfortable with their party. They would have preferred a different federalist option, but neither the Conservatives nor the New Democrats were perceived to have any chance of winning seats in the province.

A good portion of the Liberals' challenge centred on their political approach to Quebec. Martin, according to *Maclean's* columnist Paul Wells, had a tin ear for matters in that province. He consistently misjudged the mood of the Quebec people — passing every speech, policy, or discussion through the filter of the national unity debate. He, like the Chrétien government since the 1995 referendum, had fallen into the trap of letting the Liberals' opponents, in this case the separatist opposition, set the agenda. Liberal communications seemed designed only to react to separatist concerns rather than to address the people of Quebec directly. Voters considered this patronizing. The overlay of the sponsorship scandal multiplied the resentment. Ordinary people wished to debate real issues, such as crime and quality of life, without these concerns being compromised by jurisdictions, political ego, and a surplus of "tact" that suggested Quebec was not just a distinct society but also a "problem case." There was an appetite for a straight-talking approach to Quebec issues, without continuous reference to national unity. By trying to make the federal election a referendum on sovereignty, Martin had ignored public opinion and crafted an electoral quagmire for the Liberals.

Paul Martin also faced a challenge from his dealings with the New Democratic Party. Traditionally, the Liberal Party had always been positioned as the spectrum spanner — centrist, where most voters reside, but with a beachhead on both the left and right of the political spectrum. The Liberals, along with most of the public, could be socially progressive while economically conservative — a balanced approach that suited the Liberals as long as they maintained the credibility to do so. The credibility came from the team. The government of Jean Chrétien had two left-leaning cabinet ministers, Lloyd Axworthy and Sheila Copps, who could foray to the left, while economically conservative Finance Minister Paul Martin and Industry Minister John Manley could anchor the right.

However, Paul Martin's government no longer had any champions of the left. Copps had been expelled in an ugly party feud and Axworthy had retired, while other left-leaning MPs, like former CIDA minister Maria Minna, were not invited into the Martin fold. An accord had been signed with the NDP, and many socially progressive initiatives from the Chrétien period, such as same-sex marriage and marijuana decriminalization, were still on the agenda, but they lacked visible left-leaning champions. Martin tried to fill this void himself. Again he would try to be all things to all people — personally making forays into the left rather than maintaining the solid centre while delegating his ministers to be his "stalking horses." The result was that he lost credibility, further confused people as to where he stood politically, and left the political centre vulnerable to his opponent. This would not have been problematic if Harper had marginalized himself on the right, but Harper was taking aim at the centre himself, traditional Liberal ground where most of the votes are.

All of this activity still appeared to be having very little effect on public opinion. December poll results, hampered by Christmas shopping and seasonal parties, showed very little decisive movement. The "alert voters" were starting to embrace Harper, but this wasn't apparent from any of the polls in the media. The public, even after a televised December leaders' debate that attracted only half the expected audience, was still not tuned in.

Despite the apathy, there was no shortage of election coverage in the media. The *Globe and Mail*, with its new Strategic Counsel tracking poll, wrote story after story on public opinion, devoting whole sections to how the public was reacting to the campaign. No facet of the *Globe*'s campaign coverage was without some polling orientation. It started off as good analysis. They had well-produced, easy-to-read tracking graphs on their website and promised "an unprecedented degree of insight every day" from their polling. With the *Globe*'s resources, commitment, and highly reputable pollsters, it held the promise of having the best media polling package seen to date. All it needed was a horse race to make it work, though in December the horses were still in the paddock.

The problems started on the second day of the campaign, when the horse-race poll numbers did not deviate from those of the first day. The third day ran into the twentieth day, and there was still absolutely no change outside of the poll's margin of error. The SES-CPAC tracking for the same period was slightly more volatile but also had a wider margin of error. The truth was that public opinion was not moving much during this period. A consensus of all the polls would indicate that there was some very minor pro-Liberal shifting in the first two weeks, and some tightening after that, but it was not worth any headlines.

The *Globe and Mail*, however, had a very strong appetite for headlines. After the first few days they had exhausted the topic of "what is the public thinking today?" and their stories were in danger of getting repetitive. They had a choice — shift their coverage away from polling and poll-driven stories or milk what they had for sensationalist headlines, going beyond responsible polling analysis to make news where none existed. The first such front-page headline, "Liberals Surging in Ontario," hit the newsstands December 5. The story reported a 2 percent Liberal gain, well within the poll's 4.1 percent margin of error. It was meaningless. Liberals were quoted in the paper commenting on this "surge" and saying it portended great things to come as they quested for their majority. Strategists commented on how Paul Martin's low profile and defining messages on national unity were no doubt working to great advantage. The following day, the *Globe*–Strategic Counsel poll numbers stabilized. The trivial change had reversed itself, again within the margin of error. The *Globe* ran the headline "Tories receive 'bump' in Ontario" together with the usual commentary and insight into poll numbers that in truth meant absolutely nothing.

A week later the *Globe* would again strain the public trust of accurately reporting people's opinions with a third front-page headline, "Liberals Snatching NDP Votes in Ontario" (December 12). The NDP had seemingly fallen overnight, from 17 percent to just 9 percent. "The strategy of driving those NDP supporters closer to the bosom of the Liberal Party seems to be working," commented pollster Allan Gregg. Credit was given to Buzz Hargrove, the union leader who had urged New Democratic supporters to vote Liberal in ridings the NDP couldn't win. CTV ran the same story. Other news organizations picked it up. The NDP appeared to be crippled. If the poll had been true, it would have been the most devastating blow ever to impact a Canadian political party overnight.

Nobody from the mainstream media questioned this poll. Nobody from the polling industry tried to determine why it didn't match their own data, nor did they contradict it. It was left to a couple of Internet bloggers to actually pore through the poll report and discover the error. The journalists had quoted numbers off the wrong page of their report!

NDP support had not fallen; somebody had just mixed up "voter intent" with "campaign momentum." The NDP was still at 17 percent, though its Ontario candidates were panicked and the party risked damage by the media and the public's perception that they were in free fall. The error was widely reported over the Internet on December 12, but the *Globe* offered no correction on December 13, by which time the error was a major topic amongst both the mainstream media and the blogging community. Finally, a terse correction, but no apology, was printed on December 14.

Meanwhile, the rest of the media were not altogether innocent of exaggerating the importance of poll-driven stories. Canadian Press, for example, reported that most Canadians were not impressed with the minimalist Conservative election ads, and that these ads would not cause people to flock to Stephen Harper. Was this relevant? Not really — most election ads are not designed to appeal to the general public or even to be popular. They are targeted toward specific demographics — often maybe only a few percent of the population — and an ad's effectiveness cannot be accurately judged just by asking people if it changed their vote or not. The purpose of these ads was to help redefine Stephen Harper's image. Most polling firms have sophisticated ad-testing systems that they use to develop and test creative concepts and executions. None can be applied in a quick general public political poll.

Other polls attempted to measure the impact of Paul Martin's verbal attack on the United States government over the Kyoto accord and softwood lumber disputes. After the U.S. ambassador objected to this tough talk, Martin escalated the war of words, consistently attacking the U.S. at every opportunity. Some early polls showed that while it wasn't yet impacting heavily on voter support, his standing up to the Americans was popular.

Many of these polls were conducted too soon. It is always popular for a national leader to take a decisive, firm position against another country. Brian Tobin, as fisheries minister during the Spanish-Canadian fishing dispute in the early nineties, saw his popularity soar to record levels. This surge usually disappears almost as quickly, once the electorate has a chance to reflect on the action. As Paul Martin's self-portrayal as the Canadian underdog confronting the U.S. bully continued, it began to be perceived as opportunistic and anti-American, a stance that was inconsistent with Martin's traditional pro-American positioning. Though popular in the short-term, it would reinforce his growing image as being desperate for votes, willing to do and say anything to stay in office.

The year ended with an announcement of the RCMP's decision to investigate insider trading as a result of a Liberal pre-election announcement on income trusts. These proceedings would later be blamed by many in the media, and in the Liberal Party, for causing the sea change in public opinion that was shortly to follow. The evidence is to the contrary. The income trust scandal was certainly not irrelevant to the 2006 election, but the die was already cast. It merely served as a lightening rod that typified and collected together all the existing perceptions of Liberal scandals and entitlements of the previous few years. However, these perceptions were already in the mindset of the "alert voters," the 20 percent of Canadians who were "paying a lot of attention" to the campaign. Those voters had been shifting to Harper steadily since the second week of the campaign. During the holidays some of their attention transferred to their family and friends. SES, the only pollster surveying through the holidays, began to show a buildup of Conservative momentum and support well before the income trust scandal broke. Few people actually understood the income trust scandal. To most of them, it was just a title for all the other abuses, real and perceived, that typified the Martin Liberal government. It was a convenient excuse voters could offer to Liberal candidates at the door.

The phoney war ended on January 2, 2006. People returned to work and school, and life settled back into routine. First on the agenda for Canadians was dealing with the intrusive election campaign — which they had managed to keep at a distance during the holidays. The first day back, Liberal support fell by a couple of points in all of the SES, Ekos, and Strategic Counsel polls. The trend would be confirmed a few days later by the Ipsos-Reid and Decima polls. The perceptions and attitudes of the "alert voters" predictably impacted on the newly awakened voters. Conservative policies like the GST reduction and child care allowance began to find appeal and traction with voters who had not paid them much attention during the first round. Harper's first act of 2006, quite astutely, was to review his top five priority policies, thereby ensuring that the newly connected voters could catch up.

By the end of the first week in January, all of Canada's media polling firms had the Conservatives ahead of the Liberals by an average of 4 or 5 percent. The Liberals' response to their drop in support was slow but would swiftly escalate to negative. There was as yet no Liberal policy platform released. The voters knew what Harper stood for, but Martin was still an enigma. Martin's campaign was unfocussed and muddled. It was not that he hadn't tried to define himself to the voters but that he done so in too many different ways. His government had been seen as a place-holder, stricken into inactivity by the sponsorship scandal and Martin's lack of agenda. Canadians had the option of awarding him a majority government, hoping that he would do better, or looking around for another party to endorse.

For many years, the Reform/Alliance/Conservative opposition had appeared to be risky and right-wing, almost an extremist alternative. The Liberals had always successfully portrayed them this way. However, the Conservatives had now redefined themselves as competent, compassionate, innovative, and politically centrist. The Liberals had passively allowed this. As one pollster said at the time, "Two months ago the Liberals had Stephen Harper lying in a coffin with a stake through his heart, with the word 'unelectable' tattooed on his forehead, and then they just walked away and let him get up."

The image of Paul Martin as a ditherer, a rootless, rudderless, and indecisive man, took hold. Reporters and columnists had formed this impression of him more than a year before the election, but the public did not accept it at the time. They had wanted to give him a chance. When he in a sense abdicated the campaign, awarding Stephen Harper a clear month to lay the foundations, unfettered, for a public perception of the Conservatives as an alternative risk-averse government with a popular centrist-agenda that Canadians could live with, Martin invited comparisons that would prove his undoing. Harper was really no different than a Liberal. He had less baggage and fewer scandals, was more decisive, and had an actual agenda.

On January 2, as Harper rattled off the five priorities of a Conservative government — reducing the GST, instituting an accountability act, getting tougher on crime, sending cheques to parents to go towards child care costs, and cutting patient wait times in the health care system — Martin was touring a bagel factory for a photo opportunity. Martin's time in early January, like that of the entire month of December, was not well spent. The Conservatives were climbing each and every day in the opinion polls, while the Liberals were falling.

Martin's campaign attempted a strategy based on telling Canadians the "fundamental" differences between the Conservatives and the Liberals. He did so emotionally and eloquently. However, the public, and in particular those alert voters who had followed the campaign from the start, did not think the differences were all that great, did not believe the Liberals had much credibility on any of those issues, and thought that the Conservative approach was actually preferable.

The greatest difference between the two parties was on child care policy. The Liberals' institutionalized child care program, run by government, was backed by a majority of hard-core Liberals and New Democrats. The Conservative option, to give cheques to parents to fund their own child care, whether in the home or in existing child care facilities, was preferred by a very large number of Conservatives and many soft Liberals. The greatest electoral boost was to the Tories. Soft Liberals were more likely to back Harper than hard-core New Democrats were to support Martin. However, since child care had never ranked as a very important issue during Canadian election campaigns, as John Turner had discovered when he proposed a similar program in 1984, the policy was useful only in showing contrast between the parties, not as a vote-producer.

Any contrast campaign, where the goal is to show the differences between party approaches, quickly lends itself to negativity about the opponent. The Liberals are traditionally good with this type of strategy and the negative advertising and hard-hitting messaging that go with it. However, the Liberals' 2006 advertising team, like their strategy and polling team, was relatively inexperienced and untried. None had ever led a successful national election. Their internecine wars, cliquishness, and dysfunctional nature had purged all the professionals from the team. Martin was left with a corporal's guard of hard-core loyalists, despised by many in the Liberal Party, who had failed him in 2004 and were on track to do so again in 2006.

The most bizarre Liberal strategy was to passively count on a slingshot effect. David Herle, the chief Liberal pollster, anticipated that a drop in Liberal support would motivate a "stop Harper" movement. In 2004, when Harper had boasted of possibly winning a majority, the electorate had indeed reacted. They were willing to trust him with a minority, but the prospect of a majority had reopened fears about Harper's hidden agenda. A majority Conservative government, people reasoned in 2004, would outlaw abortion and treat minorities with intolerance. Many soft Conservatives shifted their support back to the Liberals, allowing the Liberals to salvage a fragile minority.

In 2006 there was an expectation that if the Conservatives looked really strong, and enough voters panicked about it, then the resulting backlash would swing the numbers all the way to a Liberal majority. If the Conservatives were ahead, the national media would scrutinize the frontrunner more intensely and fuel the panic. The Liberals would try to stampede this panic by using a mixture of tough talk from Martin — on the dangers and even the possible breakup of the country that could result from a Conservative government — and very tough negative advertisements.

A good analysis of the media polling in the public domain, much less the more in-depth party polling, would have likely dissuaded the Liberals from following this bizarre strategy. The Conservatives had laid a good foundation. They were not scary. A national Conservative convention had removed abortion from the party platform. Harper was reaching out to new Canadians and spending a lot of time in Quebec talking issues and policy. Most importantly in that province, he talked about Quebec's place "on the ice and not on the bench" within Canadian federalism, without paying undue and unwelcome attention to national unity concerns. He was an unthreatening alternative. The slingshot effect was a long-shot concept.

The Conservatives nevertheless effectively inoculated themselves from negative Liberal advertising with an ad of their own. Anticipating Liberal strategy, which was expected to be a rerun of their scare tactics of the 2004 campaign, the Tory ad stated that the Liberals were desperate and would soon run very negative ads. This warning removed much of the wind from the sails of the Liberal attack ads that followed. When the ads ran, it would in fact make the Liberals appear desperate and undermine their credibility.

It is possible that many of the Liberal ads could have worked. It is likely that one in fact did have some positive effect on Liberal fortunes. A quote from Stephen Harper in his own words, claiming that Atlantic Canadians were basically lazy and lacking entrepreneurship, was aired across the Atlantic. SES reported a significant decline in Conservative support throughout the region. Harper had apologized for that remark in December, but it needed to be restated for the 80 percent of Atlantic residents not paying attention to his apology at the time. He did not do so, and the Liberals regained a few points in the regional polls.

Most of the ads, however, did not fare so well. Most of them did not use Harper's own words but only deliberately misleading and twisted interpretations of his words. All had the tag line "we're not making this up" to explain the gravity of "Harper's statements." Many voters could see that what Harper said and what the Liberals claimed he meant were not the same thing. The ads violated the basic principle of such attack ads — that a candidate's own words must be used if it is to be believed. Most of the ads stretched the truth too far. The greatest stretch was the infamous "Soldiers in our Cities" ad, in which an announcer gravely told Canadians "Stephen Harper actually announced he wants to increase military presence in our cities. Canadian cities. Soldiers with guns. In our cities. In Canada. We did not make this up."

This ad, which was authorized for production but not for distribution, and was mistakenly distributed to the media, was so over-the-top that it blew away much of the Liberal campaign's credibility. Paul Martin was seen as increasingly desperate — his spin doctors on pundit panels looked increasingly beleaguered and haggard — and the Liberal advertising campaign became a target of ridicule and jokes on television and the Internet.

Liberal support continued to decline — down six points in the first twelve days of January, according to both SES and Strategic Counsel. The Conservatives were up 6 percent, putting them 9 percent ahead in the SES poll (Conservative minority territory) and 12 percent ahead in the Strategic Counsel poll (a possible Conservative majority). The New Democrats were stagnant, despite Liberal efforts to provoke strategic voting that would swing New Democrat votes to the Liberals to defeat the Tories. And the Bloc Québécois had actually lost support, from more than 50 percent down to about 45 percent. And surprisingly, it was beginning to look like the Conservatives could win seats in that province, though the lack of poll segmentation between Montreal and the rest of the province did not allow much seat-by-seat speculation.

Regional analysis became a major poll issue during the 2006 campaign. The Conservatives were ahead in Ontario, but the stark difference between Tory support in the rural areas versus the major urban centers did not appear in the media polls. The samples were not robust enough to get a good read on Montreal, Toronto, or Vancouver. Strategic Counsel had conducted some spot polling in those cities earlier, but like SES provided no tracking numbers. The other one-off pollsters did not present a very detailed picture either. Yet the numbers were reversed between the big cities and rural Canada. The Liberals still had a big lead in Toronto while trailing badly across the rest of Ontario. They also enjoyed strong support in Vancouver and Montreal. The public was not aware of this.

By the last week of the campaign, uncertainty about the strength of the Conservative lead fed a minor variation of the Liberal's much-vaunted slingshot effect. The media's and public's ignorance of the urban-rural vote split increased public apprehension in some regions that the Conservatives were headed toward a majority government. The voters once again edged slowly back to the Liberals, but by only a few points, moving back into Conservative minority territory.

This "correction" was exacerbated by several Tory errors in the last week of the campaign. First were Harper's comments trying to ease public fears of a Conservative majority, which he correctly deduced from his polling was dangerous ground. He pointed out that Canada still had Liberal-appointed judges that would limit the power of a Conservative government. This did not have the calming effect it was supposed to. Paul Martin latched onto his words, charging Harper once more with having a secret hidden agenda that would be thwarted by the courts until such time as Harper could appoint his own judges. The abortion issue was once more a force in public opinion.

Second, Harper lost control of his agenda during that last week. Critical days in which he could have been promoting his five-point priority program were lost as he defended himself on Liberal ground. Some of this was necessary, but opportunities for positive news coverage were wasted as he spent his time, three of the last seven days, attacking his detractors — Martin, Layton, and labour leader Buzz Hargrove. To maintain his media momentum, Harper should have remained positive and delegated his negative and defensive messaging to his campaign chairman.

And third, and worst of all for the Conservatives, was their inexplicably negative last-minute advertising. Formerly it had been disciplined and positive and very much in tune with public opinion. New negative ads aimed at the Liberals were unnecessary and gratuitous, taking the entire Conservative campaign off-message and diluting the effect of the positive policy platform. Many of Harper's previous ads had been contrast, but all had an upbeat message. Harper had been surging because he put forward solid popular policies, reinforced by his advertising, and the public reacted positively. The Liberal attacks he was trying to counter were bruising but not damaging — his old ads would have weathered the storm. He had no reason to go negative.

A fourth wild card was present among the fumbles that dogged the Tories in the last week of the election. This one was not their fault, however. It was a pollster's. The most cautious and conservative of the pollsters during the campaign was the *Globe and Mail*'s Strategic Counsel. Despite some sensationalist and misleading headlines that could be blamed on reporters, some debatable analysis, and one major error in understating the NDP vote by almost half, their polling numbers were very stable. No unexplained shifts had taken place, and unlike some of the other media polls their sample size was large enough that the vote intent numbers moved up and down by only a point or two each day. It was a well-presented tracking poll that befitted the *Globe and Mail* and arguably was the most relied upon public opinion survey of the campaign.

On January 17, however, six days before the vote, the *Globe*'s polling went awry. The Conservatives, according to Strategic Counsel, had vaulted into an 18 percent lead over the Liberals. SES disagreed, reporting the Conservatives at only 5 percent ahead, and Ekos showed an 8 percent lead. But it was the *Globe and Mail* that had the greatest media penetration. Its polls dominated all others, and anybody concerned that the Tories were heading to a huge guaranteed majority had good reason to think so.

Was this poll correct? According to Allan Gregg, "What happens sometimes, if you have a single night where the numbers appear abnormally high or low (yes, one out of twenty times this should happen), their effect is muted by the inclusion of the results of the other two nights (i.e. the total of three that we report). When you dump the abnormally high or low results from your three day total however, the numbers will 'jump'."

Gregg is right that such a problem can occur. Adding a new night of tracking and dropping an old can create some variation, a couple of points' worth, but not enough to explain the huge variation within this poll. Terence Corcoran, writing for the rival *National Post*, called it "way off course and flat wrong." Other pollsters would come up with different methodological theories to explain these numbers. Gregg himself, after the election, would say that Strategic Counsel did not take into account the effects of incumbency and hence underestimated the Liberals. However, this incumbency theory does not hold water. Pollsters ask voters what they will do at the ballot box, and the aggregated results take into account both popular and unpopular incumbents as well as local candidates.

Rather, this poll was wrong because of an unwitting mistake in the questionnaire. A question placed in front of the vote-preference question skewed the results, exaggerating the Conservative vote and reducing the Liberal vote. The first question in the Strategic Counsel survey reads, ""Do you support a change in government?" If a respondent answers, "Yes," indicating they believe the Liberals should be defeated, it then becomes difficult to follow with "I'm voting Liberal" when asked for vote choice. Many voters did believe that Canada needed a change in government, yet they could not bring themselves to vote Tory, and there was no other alternative for them but to vote Liberal. But they have just told an interviewer that they support a change of government. In order not to appear stupid or inconsistent, they answer that they will vote for the Conservatives. This does not affect all respondents, but if it affects even one-tenth of them, then the problem in this poll is explained.

Proof is found during the testing of this phenomenon by POLLARA during the 2003 Ontario provincial election. It was observed that in surveys where the "change of government" question was placed in front of the vote question, the results were very different from when the question was asked cleanly. A split-sample poll was conducted: five hundred people were asked the question one way and five hundred the other, all on the same day. A 12 percent difference between the polls was found, outside the margin of error. As with the Strategic Counsel poll, the electoral advantage went to the challenger, not the incumbent, in the poll where the inter-item bias was suspected.

There was no untoward intention or incompetence in the Strategic Counsel poll for the *Globe and Mail*. It was only inexperience on the part of the questionnaire design team and on the part of the survey analysts. However, no *mea culpa* was published, and the following nights of *Globe* tracking, which dropped the inter-item bias question, predictably produced a rapid free fall in Conservative vote that was reflected nowhere else. Such a perception, at its worst, is potentially damaging to the electoral process.

When a political party experiences a run on the bank, a major decline in a short period of time, there exists the potential for a bandwagon effect among other voters. In this case, the Conservatives "lost" 5 percent of their support in two days, while the Liberals "gained" 4 percent. Of course there was absolutely no such movement — the starting point was a badly skewed poll, which the *Globe* and pollsters did not disavow. Though the argument is made that polls do influence election campaigns, the *Globe and Mail* poll could have done a major disservice to the Conservative Party.

Polls do usually have an influence on election campaigns. There is nothing wrong or problematic with this. Media coverage, election signs, comments from friends and family, brochures, and endorsements all can influence the vote. If a householder notices that all the election signs on his street are for a different candidate than the one he supports, he likely will not change his mind, but he might take a long look at the other candidate to see if he is missing anything. Similarly, a poll reader may wonder why one party she hadn't considered is surging in popularity. She may then give it a second look, treating the poll results as an endorsement of that party by other Canadians.

There is no evidence that the *Globe* poll had this effect. That may well argue that the influence of media polls on the electoral system is exaggerated or that many Canadians did not take the *Globe* poll seriously in the last week. The plethora of last-minute campaign polls also likely diluted the impact of the swift and artificial decline reported by the *Globe*. SES, which called the election results the most accurately of the pollsters, showed only a half-point Tory drop when Strategic Counsel was showing a 5 percent decline. Ipsos showed no decline at all. That is not to say that the sharp poll decline had no effect — if it had not been reported, could the Conservatives have done better?

Whether the poll hampered their support or not, the Conservative Party's three self-inflicted wounds of the final seven days — being off-message, being sidetracked, and running negative ads — certainly did. Was it for the better? According to most of the polls, which showed the largest number of Canadians desiring a Conservative minority, rather than a Liberal minority or a Conservative majority, it certainly was. The electorate was successful at getting what it wanted.

The Conservatives ended the election with 36.3 percent, the Liberals 30.2 percent, the New Democrats 17.5 percent, the Bloc 10.5 percent, and the Greens 4.5 percent. Paul Martin resigned as Liberal leader, ensuring at least a year of being able to govern as if it had a majority for the Conservatives, though for them to claim this in public would severely damage their popularity. A very strategic minority resulted, in which the Conservatives could not be defeated in the House of Commons without the participation of the leaderless Liberals and at least one other party.

The Liberals will have a chance to regroup, shake off the baggage collected over the last thirteen years of governing, cleanse itself of the sponsorship scandal, develop new policies, select a new leader, and renew itself. They will need to review their appeal to rural and Western Canada and develop an approach based on something greater than the potential for Conservative mistakes in these regions. The Conservatives will have their long-awaited chance at making a difference, but tempered by their failure to win any seats in Toronto or to make much impact on urban women, new Canadians, and visible minorities.

So how did the pollsters fare on election day? Their results were, collectively and individually, very accurate indeed. Each pollster who surveyed until the end, or close to the finish, ended up with results accurate to plus or minus 3 percent of the actual vote totals.

	CPC	LPC	NDP	BQ	GPC
Election Results	36.3%	30.2%	17.5%	10.5%	4.5%
SES/CPAC	36.4%	30.1%	17.4%	10.6%	5.6%
Léger/Independent	38%	29%	17%	11%	4%
Strategic Counsel/					
Globe and Mail	37%	27%	19%	11%	6%
Ekos/*Toronto Star*/*La Presse*	37%	27%	20%	12%	5%
Ipsos-Reid/*National Post*	38%	27%	19%	12%	5%
Decima/Canadian Press	37%	27%	18%	11%	7%

The final polls of Strategic Counsel, Ekos, Ipsos-Reid, and Decima erred only in underestimating Liberal support by 3 percent, an allowable difference within the margin of error of their polls. However, the first three of these four firms claimed a smaller margin of error for their polls than was actually the case, 1 percent for Ipsos Reid and 2 percent for both Strategic Counsel and Ekos. It is a common mistake in media polling when the pollster quotes margin of error based on sample size and not on the actual valid responses for each party, which is more statistically correct. Media polls, however, like many media stories, are often simplified for the reader.

The most accurate pollsters on the final day of the campaign were SES Research, just 1.1 percent too high for the Green Party, followed by Léger Marketing, just 2 percent too high for the Conservatives.

Could they have done a better job? They could not have been much more accurate. Six polling organizations, all with results within 3 percent of the election totals, are creditable in any election campaign. Sample sizes were robust; there were none of the small nationwide samples that had provided erratic jumps and dives during past campaigns. Pollsters remained in the field until the end of the campaign, and some even polled through the holiday season.

There were some issues with frequency of reporting, the daily tracking pollsters SES and Strategic Counsel having significant more media and public attention than the one-off pollsters such as Ipsos-Reid, Léger, Decima, and Ekos. Altogether, Canada's seven major opinion research firms released 123 voter-intent polls. The two daily tracking firms produced 83 of these.

Urban polling is one area for improvement that all media pollsters should work on for the next election. While the daily tracking provided results for the four major regions of Canada, it never gave any reflection of the key battlegrounds of Toronto, Montreal, and Vancouver. These areas voted so differently from their surrounding provinces that to combine them with the larger regions dilutes the value of the poll results. Next election, the Conservatives will be seeking to hold their support in rural and Western Canada while making inroads into the three urban battlegrounds. The Liberals will be attempting to defend their support in the cities, while attracting support in rural and Western Canada. The NDP is a greater factor in urban areas than rural and will have to be taken into account in the battle for the three cities.

It will not be enough for pollsters just to segment urban and rural vote intent, as has sometimes been done in the past. Not all large cities are as Liberal as Toronto, Vancouver, and Montreal. Edmonton and Calgary, for example, voted heavily Conservative in 2006, and their inclusion into "urban" would just cause confusion. Rather, it will be critical for good election analysis to survey a large sample in each of the three major cities. This means additional cost for the polling firms and, since they are already subsidizing a great deal of the media's polling cost, should also require a greater contribution from their clients.

Altogether, in terms of accuracy, Canada's pollsters acquitted themselves very well in 2006. All of the firms were accurate to at least a 3 percent margin of error and they won back their reputation, tainted in 2004, by the expedient of polling longer and closer to election day. The analysis was not always stellar. Some of the media, particularly the *Globe and Mail*, sometimes preferred sensationalized headlines rather than responsible analysis, and this requires some review on their part. There were also some issues with interpretation and methodological errors. But any rogue polls were corrected by election day, and the public trust was by and large maintained collectively by Canada's pollsters, who reflected public opinion to the best of their abilities and technology. As such, the public was well served.

CHAPTER ELEVEN

After Fifty-Six Days ... the Verdict
by André Turcotte

Most analyses of elections focus on what decides elections. However, it is also important to examine what elections decide. On January 23, 2006, the Canadian electorate was asked to go to the polls, again, to make decisions about what to do with the Martin government and the minority Parliament it had elected less than two years prior, as well as with the potential alternatives to the Liberals. As democratic theorists suggest,[1] through a series of individual vote choices, Canadians rendered a collective judgment. Above the noise of electoral rhetoric, the voices of voters combined to produce results matching the sum of their individual intentions and apprehensions. Through the sum of their individual vote decisions, Canadian voters elected a plurality of Conservatives (124) to Parliament and, in so doing, returned to power a political party they had decimated a little more than a decade ago.

By electing 103 Liberals, voters put an end to thirteen years of Liberal rule but decided that despite scandals and misconduct, Canada's "natural governing party" should remain a competitive force in Ottawa. As a result, Canadians will continue to be governed by a minority Parliament. The NDP, with its twenty-nine seats, has its strongest parliamentary representation since 1988, and the Bloc Québécois can continue to strongly represent Quebec's interests in Ottawa, albeit with a reduced contingent (fifty-one seats). However, while none of the alternatives to the Liberals were compelling to enough Canadians to deserve a clearer mandate, the final vote tally meant the end to the political career of Paul Martin.

This chapter looks at the factors that led to the voters' judgment, their decisions and indecision. To do so, key events of the campaign will be examined. The chapter will also put the results of the 2006 election in perspective by looking at the impact of issues, the flow of the vote, the impact of leaders and parties, as well as the campaign itself, on vote choice. Comparisons with previous elections, especially with the 2004 election, will be made in order to isolate what was unique about the voters' judgment in 2006 but also what were the signs of continuity in their decision. The analysis is based on the results of a poll conducted by POLLARA on January 25 and 26, 2006.[2] General conclusions will be drawn about the outcome and the meaning of the people's verdict.

A LONG WINTER ELECTION CAMPAIGN

After seventeen months of near misses, machinations and empty threats, the Conservative Party, the NDP, and the Bloc finally united to defeat the Liberal government in a non-confidence vote in the House of Commons. By a vote of 171 to 133, the opposition parties decided to make history on that particular November 28, 2005. It was the first time in more than forty years that a government was defeated on a non-confidence motion, and Canadians would be treated to a Christmas election campaign for the first time since 1979. Moreover, it was to be the second January vote in Canadian history; the last time was in 1874. The vote also set the stage for a fifty-six-day campaign, the longest campaign in twenty-one years. Despite the histrionics, the campaign quickly settled into common themes and expected jostling.

Liberal Leader Paul Martin opened his campaign by addressing the perennial issues of Canadian election campaigns: his strong record on the economy; his accomplishments in dealing with social issues, notably health care and day care; and a warning against another sovereignty referendum in Quebec. For his part, Stephen Harper chose to focus on the need for change, Liberal corruption, tax cuts, and fighting crime. NDP Leader Jack Layton unveiled a campaign that encouraged voters to think locally about what a New Democrat MP could do for them. He also emphasized ethics, the need to fight against private health care, and the need to protect the environment. The central and almost exclusive theme of the Bloc Québécois campaign was a call to Quebecers to punish the Liberal Party for the sponsorship scandal and, in so doing, reaffirm their national pride by telling Ottawa that Quebec's continued presence within Confederation was not for sale.

On the third day of the campaign, the focus was put on the economy with Stephen Harper's proposal to reduce the GST from 7 percent to 5 percent within four years. The Liberals countered by stating that their focus was on income tax reduction that could bring targeted benefits to those who need it most, namely the poor and the middle class. Jack

Layton criticized Harper's proposal and stated that his priority was not to reduce taxes but to use Ottawa's financial capacity to address important issues such as protecting the environment, reducing high tuition fees, and creating jobs. Canadians were thus presented with different options on tax reduction while awaiting even clearer distinctions on issues that mattered most to them, especially the one that had dominated the previous three elections — health care.

The three main parties decided to blur their position when it came to health care. They all pledged to do more to fix the system and committed themselves to strengthen the public health system. Harper's commitment focused on demanding that provinces provide timely access to key medical treatments by the end of next year or pay to send patients to other jurisdictions. It was unclear how the Conservative leader was going to enforce his commitment, if at all, since he ruled out providing more cash to cut waiting lists. Harper did not address his intentions with regards to private sector involvement, refusing to rule out private delivery of publicly funded care, and saying he would not close private clinics already in existence. In a line reminiscent of the ill-fated Canadian Alliance Leader Stockwell Day, Harper asserted that "there will be no private parallel system."[3] The Liberals also promised to allow patients to travel to other jurisdictions when health care is not available within an acceptable time in their own province, with the difference that funds would be made available to cover the costs. Jack Layton responded by attacking Harper's position; he held up a health card and a credit card, saying that only his party will ensure that a health card is all that is needed for health care in Canada. With the Liberals, New Democrats, and Conservatives jockeying over health care, Bloc Leader Gilles Duceppe was musing about the need to have a Quebec team in international hockey competition.

One would expect that the mix of issues chosen by the parties reflected, in part, what was on the mind of Canadians. After all, one of the consistent determinants of electoral success in Canadian federal elections has been the winning party's ability to position itself favourably on what was seen as the most important issue facing the government at the time.[4] The 2006 federal election was different in this regard. When asked about the most important issue in the election, slightly more than one-third of Canadians could not identify one. The inability of the electorate to identify an important campaign issue was significantly higher in 2006 than in the previous election (19 percent). It was also higher than in 2000 and 1997 when it reached 29 percent and was already a cause for concern.[5]

Moreover, it stands in sharp contrast with elections in the eighties when very few people were unable to identify an important issue.[6] The consequences of this situation will likely impact the ability of the Conservative Party to implement any kind of policy agenda. Clearly, the Harper Conservatives have been given an "absent mandate" — as the concept was introduced in the literature on Canadian voting behaviour in the eighties and early nineties[7] — and they will be facing an electorate ready to remind the new prime minister of how fickle their support is and how quickly the amalgam of voters that got them elected can unravel.

Table 1
Most important campaign issues, 1993–2006

ISSUE	2006	2004	2000	1997	1993
Health care	12%	32%	31%	8%	3%
Unemployment, jobs	1	1	2	24	44
Economy	3	3	3	4	8
Deficit, debt	3	4	6	10	18
Taxes	4	3	7	3	-
National unity, Quebec, regionalism	2	1	3	13	4
Resources, environment	2	2	2	1	-
Social issues	9	1	4	2	1
Government, trust, parties' accountability, leaders	14	18	8	3	7
Sponsorship scandal	6	4	-	-	-
Time for change	2	-	-	-	-
Crime, safety, guns	4	-	-	-	-
Other	4	12	5	3	4
None, don't know	34	19	29	29	10

Source: 1993 Insight Canada Research Post-election survey; 1997-2006 POLLARA Post-election surveys. Percentages sum to 100 percent in each column.

This situation also points to the possibility that the Canadian party system is in the process of reverting to the brokerage model that was disrupted by the successful emergence of the Reform Party and the Bloc Québécois in 1993. For most of Canada's electoral history, the main political parties have followed a non-ideological approach to winning elections. They focused on building short-term coalitions and brokering diverse interests and issues with the sole purpose of ensuring parliamentary majorities. This pattern of brokerage politics had been disrupted from time to time, most recently in 1993. It can be argued that the early success of Preston Manning and the Reform Party was based on a different approach to politics in which the party made specific attempts to distinguish itself from the others, notably on deficit reduction, democratic reform, and national unity. Looking at Table 1, one can see that only 10 percent of voters failed to identify an important campaign issue in 1993. In both the 1993 and 1997 elections, Manning could rely on a set of voters who clearly aligned their issue priorities with Reform's.[8] But, ultimately, Manning Reformers were unable to dislodge the governing Chrétien Liberals and the experiment was electorally unsuccessful.

Looking at the issue mix in 2006, parties would have been hard pressed to anchor their campaign around a key theme. Unlike in 2000 and 2004, when health care unequivocally surfaced as an important issue that benefited the Liberals, only 12 percent of Canadians continued to identify this as their most important issue. That explains the decision of the main parties to avoid the health care issue during most of the 2006 campaign. Similarly, while economic issues dominated the agenda for most of the seventies, eighties, and early nineties, they remained marginal for the third consecutive election. The sponsorship scandal was mentioned by only 6 percent of voters, and even if we combine this issue with the more general theme of "government trust and accountability," only 20 percent of Canadian voters perceived the issue that dominated the campaign discourse as their most important one. The picture that emerged from the lack of issue priorities and from the dynamic of the first few days of the campaign was one in which three of the four main parties — the Bloc being the exception — were trying to shed some of the political baggage they had accumulated over the last few years and take care of the unfinished business from the 2004 election. In doing so, they moved closer to restoring some of the enduring features of Canadian electoral politics.

The period between 1993 and 2006 was reminiscent of the one preceding the Diefenbaker landslide in 1958. The Mackenzie King–Louis St. Laurent era was one of Liberal dominance over a weak opposition. Throughout that period, the Conservatives spent more time fighting amongst each other than attacking the Liberals and saw their base of support drift away to the Progressives, the CCF, and Social Credit. Similarly, the Chrétien Liberals benefited from a divided opposition with the Bloc Québécois and the Reform Party (and subsequently the

Canadian Alliance), preventing the Progressive Conservatives from rebuilding along the pillars of the archetypal PC winning formula, namely a cobbling up of a coalition of Western conservatives and decentralists alongside nationalistic Quebecers. A first step towards remedying this situation occurred on May 31, 2003, when the newly elected PC Leader Peter Mackay entered into discussions with Stephen Harper to merge with the Canadian Alliance.[9] The two party leaders had won their respective leadership races on their commitment to preserve and strengthen their own parties but within a few weeks simply turned around and reneged on their words. Peter Mackay broke his own commitment to David Orchard and the PC membership while Harper reneged on the *raison d'être* of the Reform/Canadian Alliance populist ideals. But history tends to look favourably at results, and Mackay and Harper will be remembered as those who managed to reach a deal where others had failed. Consequently, for the first time since 1993, the Liberals faced a united conservative force in 2004. The experiment was partly successful.

In the 2004 election, Conservatives could once again depend on a single group of potential supporters, but forming the government remained elusive. Despite the Alliance-PC merger, the Conservatives' performance was only marginally better than the Alliance's in 2000 in terms of popular vote. The new party lost the support of a significant segment of former PC voters and relied on discontented Liberals. It also depended on a stagnant group of Reform/Alliance voters and seemed unable to grow beyond that core. The Harper Conservatives were marginal in Quebec, and despite a scandal-plagued Liberal government, Harper was unable to unify, let alone increase, the conservative vote in Ontario. Regardless of their ninety-nine seats, Conservatives needed to address the fact that, with only 29.6 percent of Canadians supporting them, they were the most unpopular unified conservative party in more than fifty years.[10] A look at the flow of the vote between 2004 and 2006 indicates that the Conservatives did address those weaknesses.

THE FLOW OF THE VOTE

The Conservative minority victory can be explained by four factors. First, the Conservatives were, by far, the most effective at retaining their previous vote and in so doing were able to build on a solid core of supporters. As Table 2 indicates, 83 percent of 2004 Conservative voters continued to support their party in 2006. In contrast, 67 percent of 2004 Bloc voters, 57 percent of 2004 NDP voters, and 53 percent of 2004 Liberal voters demonstrated the same commitment to their respective party. Second, the Harper Conservatives were able to attract one in five Liberal defectors. This is higher than their performance in 2004, when they managed to attract only 13 percent of those voters and lagged behind the NDP as the choice for disaffected Liberals.[11] Third, the most improbable Conservative gains were made to the detriment of the Bloc Québécois. Unlike in the 1997 (9 percent), 2000 (9 percent), and 2004 (3 percent), elections when only a marginal number of disenchanted Bloc voters turned to the right-of-centre alternative,[12] 19 percent of Bloc defectors supported the Conservatives in 2006. This translated into ten Conservative seats in Quebec and made the difference between a potentially contested electoral outcome and a Harper minority government.

The success of the Conservatives was also the result of the partial failures of their opponents to meet their own strategic objectives. For the Liberals, the goal in 2006 was to reverse, or at least stop, the erosion of support suffered in 2004. In that election, they were able to retain only 59 percent of their 2000 supporters. This was lower than the retention rates of 64 percent in 2000[13] and 63 percent in 1997[14] when they won two majorities.

THE PATTERNS OF VOTING

Table 2
Vote stability and change, 2004–2006

| | | 2004 Behaviour | | | | | |
		Non-Voters	Liberals	PC	NDP	BQ	Others
2006 Behaviour	Liberals	17%	53%	4%	13%	1%	8%
	Cons.	7	20	83	10	19	25
	NDP	3	12	5	57	2	29
	BQ	2	1	-	1	67	4
	Others	3	5	2	9	6	33
	Did Not Vote	69	9	6	10	5	1
	N=	239	336	191	78	69	24

Source: POLLARA Post-Election Survey. Percentages sum to 100 percent in each column.

Unfortunately for Martin, the repeated attacks, scandals, and accusations took their toll; barely half (53 percent) of 2004 Liberal voters continued to express their loyalty to the party in 2006. The final outcome could have been worse for the Liberals had it not been for their ability to attract 13 percent of 2004 NDP voters. Moreover, despite the overall erosion in Liberal support, Liberal incumbents were apparently able to rely on a solid core of supporters in their ridings, since ninety-nine of them were returned to Ottawa, the largest group of veterans amongst the four main parties.

Back in 2004, it was the New Democrats that were most responsible for denying the Liberals their fourth consecutive majority, when 14 percent of 2000 Liberal voters switched to the NDP. The Liberals hit back in 2006. In the closing days of the campaign, Martin was appealing directly to NDP voters to stop the Harper Conservatives.[15] As stated above, the Liberal strategy worked to some extent, with the NDP losing 13 percent of its 2004 support to the Liberals, compared to 10 percent to the Conservatives. Moreover, the erosion of Liberal support to the NDP was slightly less damaging in 2006 (loss of 12 percent). However, the Liberals needed much more than that to stay in power.

As in every election since their breakthrough performance in 1993, the Bloc Québécois fought for relevance in 2006. There will always be some incongruity with a separatist party in the House of Commons, and no one knows this better than Bloc Leader Gilles Duceppe. Ever since he ran as a separatist candidate in a federal by-election in Laurier–Ste-Marie on August 13, 1990, Gilles Duceppe has been written off. Even after winning that by-election to become the first openly sovereigntist Quebec MP to be elected to the House of Commons, few believed he or the Bloc Québécois would have a lasting impact on Canadian politics. When Duceppe replaced Lucien Bouchard and suffered a setback by winning only forty-four seats in the 1997 election, many believed the days of the Bloc were numbered. Then it was the Martin juggernaut that was supposed to bury the Bloc and re-establish the federal Liberals as the voice of Quebec. But Duceppe had other plans.

In 2004, Duceppe succeeded in keeping the sovereignty issue alive despite the defeat of the Parti Québécois in the 2003 provincial election. He ran a smart campaign focused on Quebecers' resentment over the then emerging sponsorship scandal and capitalized on the fact that the Liberals simply gave up on winning Quebec. He was rewarded with a strong victory. With 48.8 percent of the Quebec popular vote in 2004, Duceppe almost matched the Bloc's best showing in 1993 when they garnered 49.3 percent of the vote under Lucien Bouchard's leadership. The Bloc also succeeded in preventing the Conservatives from rebuilding the Mulroney coalition and, in the process, denied them any chance of forming government.[16]

After the election, the revelations from the Gomery inquiry about the role of Quebec federal Liberals in the sponsorship scandal only strengthened the Bloc's position in Quebec, and expectations ran high in 2006 (see Chapter Five). In the opening days of the campaign, the Quebec media were convinced that the only remaining question about the Bloc's performance was whether or not it would do better than its 1993 showing when it elected fifty-four MPs.[17] *La Presse* released a CROP poll in late November giving the Bloc a thirty-point lead (53 percent to 23 percent) over the second-place Liberals, with the Conservatives coming in fourth — behind the NDP — with the support of only 9 percent of decided voters.[18] But the electorate never appreciates being taken for granted. Moreover, Harper's fluency in French meant that for the first time in years, Quebecers would hear a decentralist message from someone other than the Bloc. As a result, not only did the Bloc fail to match its 1993 performance, it actually elected a slightly smaller contingent of MPs. For their part, the Conservatives did much better than anticipated in Quebec, almost matching the Liberals in terms of seats. The remainder of the present analysis will offer potential explanations for the performance of the four main parties, starting with a look at the key factors affecting vote choice.

FACTORS IN THE VOTE DECISION

For the last ten federal elections, Canadians have been asked to identify the most important factors in influencing their vote choice. The question format first asks whether party leaders, local candidates "here in this constituency," or parties as a whole were most important in deciding whom to support in the election. Then, a follow-up question queries whether the choice of leader or candidate was motivated by issues or by the personal qualities of the individuals, or in the case of the parties whether it was the party's general approach or specific issues that was most important. Table 3 summarizes the findings for the 2006 election as well as for each election since 1974. The table indicates in a set of parentheses the proportion of the leader, candidate, and party vote that was motivated by "issues" rather than personal qualities or the general approach of parties.

For the sixth consecutive election, at least 50 percent of Canadians identified "parties" as the most important factor influencing their vote choice. The resilience of this factor is significant and partly explains the resurgence of the Conservatives. Once they managed to move beyond the permutations from the right of the spectrum — from Progressive Conservative Party and Reform to the Alliance and the Democratic Representative Caucus and finally the Conservative Party — and were able to present a stable political vehicle to the electorate, Canadians were ready to give them a second look. In 2006, slightly more than one in two Canadians (53 percent) cited parties as the most important influence on their vote choice, matching 2004 findings but down from 58 percent in 2000. Local candidates (24 percent) were more important than party leaders (23 percent) for only the third time since 1974.

Table 3
Most important factors in voting, 1974–2006
(Percent citing issue basis in parentheses)

Election	Party leaders	Local candidates	Party as a whole
2006	23% (54)	24 (46)	53 (49)
2004	25% (60)	22 (49)	53 (51)
2000	22% (60)	21 (58)	58 (46)
1997	20% (71)	22 (59)	58 (57)
1993	22% (62)	21 (52)	57 (54)
1988	20% (71)	27 (57)	53 (57)
1984	30% (56)	21 (46)	49 (37)
1980	36% (53)	20 (40)	44 (43)
1979	37% (54)	23 (43)	40 (45)
1974	33% (58)	27 (48)	40 (43)

Sources: 1974–84 Canadian National Election Studies; 1988 re-interview of 1984 CNES; 1993 Insight Canada Research post-election survey; 1997–2006 POLLARA Post-Election Surveys.

The decline of leaders as the key factor in determining vote choice is, to some extent, surprising. After all, the four main parties prominently showcased their leaders throughout the 2006 campaign, but our findings indicate that their strategy failed to resonate with voters. Moreover, there has been a decline in the importance of the issue stance of leaders, parties, and candidates in 2006; these findings go against historical trends but are further evidence that this last election was not dominated by issues. In specific terms, since 1974, the issue stance of party leaders has been most important when the election was fought by well-known political leaders, notably in 1988 when Mulroney, Turner, and Broadbent fought over free trade and in 1997 when Chrétien, Manning, and Charest tried to give shape to the aftermath of the 1993 collapse of the PC Party. In contrast, the arrival of new leaders shifted the focus towards image over substance, such as in 1979 when Joe Clark ran in his first election as PC leader; in 1984 with the appearance of Mulroney, Turner, and Broadbent; and to some degree in 2000 with Stockwell Day. This pattern was not repeated in 2006. Despite the presence of four well-known party leaders, there was a decline in the importance of their respective issue stances. The next section further examines the impact of leadership on the dynamics of the campaign and on the final outcome.

THE CAMPAIGN, THE LEADERS, AND THE FINAL OUTCOME

Since the 2006 election campaign was the longest in two decades, it is important to look at the interactions between campaign dynamics, the leaders, and the vote. First, the campaign itself continues to play an increasing role in shaping vote choice. In specific terms, less than half (49 percent) of voters had already made up their minds by the time the election was called, down only marginally from 2004 (-1 percent) but down 11 percentage points since 2000. About one-quarter (24 percent) of voters made up their mind during the campaign, presumably to find out more about the issues, leaders, and parties. This is unchanged from 2004 but significantly higher than in 2000 (18 percent) and 1997 (16 percent). Some 26 percent of the electorate (+1 percent) waited until the final days to decide which party to support.

Turning our attention to the impact of campaign dynamics on vote choice, it would appear that, once again, the Conservatives had trouble keeping their momentum in the final days of the campaign. The same scenario occurred in 2004. As we recall, the Liberal campaign unravelled in early June when Paul Martin's top political adviser, David Herle, was quoted — on the front page of the *Globe and Mail* — as saying that the Liberals were "in a spiral."[19] This led Harper to commit his most important mistake of the campaign. He began to talk about the possibility of winning a majority government and to talk confidently about his chances of forming the government.[20] Voters who were then likely to be voting against the Liberals — as a way to punish them for the sponsorship scandal and their arrogance in power despite their misgivings towards the Conservatives — returned to the Liberal fold to prevent a Conservative victory. Incredibly, Harper committed the same mistake in 2006 when he tried to reassure voters against the prospect of a Conservative majority, suggesting that the Liberal-dominated Senate and the Supreme Court could act as checks on the new government, inviting concern that this new Harper government may need to be kept in check. But unlike 2004, the Liberals were unable to attract the bulk of those worried voters, who instead turned to the NDP and other parties in significant numbers.

Table 4
2006 vote by time of vote decision

	Before Election Called (40% - -2%)*	When Called (9% - +1%)	During Campaign (26% - +1%)	Final Days (24% - n/c)
Liberals	32%	36%	28%	25%
Conservatives	44	48	37	33
NDP	12	10	17	24
Bloc	10	3	10	6
Other	2	3	8	12
N=	314	54	164	24

* change from 2004 election

Another way to look at the impact of the campaign on vote choice is to examine the composition of party support and the timing of the vote decision. As Table 5 shows, a majority of Conservative (57 percent), Liberal (55 percent), and Bloc (54 percent) voters had made up their minds by the time the election was called. But in the final days of the campaign, it appears that those who remained undecided were unable to bring themselves to support either of the two main national parties (as well as the Bloc in Quebec). As a result, 79 percent of those who voted for other parties in 2006 — most notably the Green Party — decided to do so during the campaign, especially in the closing days. Similarly, 65 percent of NDP voters also came to their decision during the campaign. This reinforces my earlier assertion that a significant number of Canadians concluded that, even after a fifty-six-day campaign, a minority Parliament remained a good option since none of the alternatives to the Liberals were compelling enough to deserve a clearer mandate.

Table 5
Vote choice and the timing of decision

	Liberals	Conservatives	New Democrats	Bloc	Other
Before election is called	45%	47%	30%	51%	17%
When called	10	10	5	3	4
During campaign	23	22	26	27	31
Final days	22	21	39	19	48
N=	218	297	119	63	48

THE DEBATES

One of the important events of recent campaigns has been the leaders' debates. It is a time when party leaders can talk directly to a relatively large number of voters and are given the opportunity to present key elements of their platform in the hope that it will resonate with voters. It is also an opportunity to try to discredit their opponents. This is not to suggest that debates always have a direct and significant impact on the final outcome. In 2004, the influence of the leaders' debates was more about reinforcing voter intentions than conversion. Of the 18 percent of Canadians who thought Martin won the debates, 77 percent voted Liberal. That was almost identical to Chrétien's showing in 2000 when 75 percent of those who picked him as winner voted for the Liberals.[21] Similarly, 76 percent of those who chose Stephen Harper as debate winner in 2004 supported the Conservatives, while in 2000, 74 percent of voters who chose Day voted for the Alliance.[22]

Because of the length of the campaign and because of the hiatus during the Christmas celebrations, four debates were held during the 2005–06 campaign. The first two — one French and one English — were held in December and two more were held in January. A similar proportion of voters (41 percent) mentioned they had watched part or all of the first or second set of debates. Of those who watched the debates, 73 percent tuned in for both the December and January debates, while 8 percent watched only the debates in December and 19 percent watched only the final debates in January.

Stephen Harper was perceived as the clear winner in both December (30 percent) and January (38 percent) and improved significantly from 2004, when only 22 percent preferred his performance over the others'.

Once more, the leadership debates were more about reinforcing voter intentions than converting voters — especially by the time the January debates were aired. Looking at the data reported in Table 6A, among the 30 percent who picked Harper as winner, 70 percent voted Conservative, while 69 percent of those who those who preferred Martin's performance ended up voting for the Liberals. The same pattern repeats itself when we look at data from the January debates. As Table 6B shows, of the 38 percent of Canadians who thought Harper won the last debates, 70 percent voted for the Conservatives. In the same vein, 73 percent of those who chose Martin as winner voted for the Liberals.

One important difference between the first and the second set of debates is that Harper emerged as a clearer winner in January. Moreover, when results from Quebec are analyzed separately, Harper's debating skills may have had an impact on the surprising Conservative performance in that province and on the erosion of Bloc support. Of the Quebecers who watched the December debates, a plurality (13 percent) thought Duceppe was the clear winner, slightly ahead of Harper (12 percent). In January, Harper emerged with a slight lead, with 17 percent of Quebecers who watched the debates choosing him as the winner, ahead of Duceppe at 11 percent. While the difference between the two leaders was marginal, the results suggest that the Harper Conservatives were picking up some momentum in the province of Quebec, and for the first time since 1988, a Conservative message was resonating with enough Quebec voters to turn support into seats.

Table 6A
2006 vote by perceived debate winner — December debates

	Martin (16%)	Harper (30%)	Layton (16%)	Duceppe (13%)
Liberals	69%	10%	23%	26%
Conservatives	13	70	26	28
New Democrats	10	6	46	9
Bloc	1	8	2	32
Other	7	6	3	5
N =	62	113	71	47

Table 6B
2006 vote by perceived debate winner — January debates

	Martin (16%)	Harper (38%)	Layton (13%)	Duceppe (11%)
Liberals	77%	9%	35%	17%
Conservatives	16	76	15	10
New Democrats	6	9	44	19
Bloc	-	3	2	51
Other	1	3	4	3
N =	82	54	101	109

An analysis of the 2006 campaign would not be complete without a look at leaders' images. Unlike the previous election when we had three new party leaders, Martin, Harper, Layton, and Duceppe were back in 2006 for repeat performances, and party strategies were strikingly similar to those adopted in the previous election. Once again, Liberal strategists perceived Martin to be their main asset, and the Liberal campaign was built around the personal appeal of the leader. A lot was made of the fact that Martin had been exonerated of any wrongdoing in the sponsorship scandal by Justice Gomery, and the Liberals hoped that this would be sufficient to regain the support of those Liberals who had deserted the party in the previous election. Similarly, both the Conservatives and the New Democrats organized their campaign around their leaders and tried to address perceived shortcomings from the previous election. In 2004, Stephen Harper had been seen as aloof, elitist, and devoid of a sense of humour, and effort was made throughout the campaign to present a more personal side of him. Jack Layton was no longer a newcomer on the federal scene, and his relatively good showing in 2004 held the promise of better things to come, despite his problems in being taken seriously by the media.[23] To make an important electoral breakthrough, Layton had to improve his image in seat-rich Ontario and Quebec, where his impression ratings were the lowest in 2004. Bloc Leader Gilles Duceppe was popular in his home province, but his party, ever since Lucien Bouchard's departure, had tended to downplay its leadership in favour of its mission to preserve and protect the interests of Quebec in Ottawa. Accordingly, the Bloc campaign message focused on asserting its *raison d'être* with constant attacks on Liberal corruption, with Duceppe being only the messenger. Accordingly, for fifty-six days Canadians were given ample opportunity to evaluate the leaders.

As it has done since the 2000 election, the POLLARA study asked Canadians to rate their impression of each party leader on a scale of 1 to 10, where 1 is "not at all impressed" and 10 is "very impressed." Overall, Harper received the highest ratings at 5.5, ahead of Layton (5.1), Martin (4.4), and Duceppe (4.1). In comparative terms, Harper's ratings are significantly higher than they were in 2004 (4.6) and he is significantly better perceived than his predecessor was in 2000 (4.6). Layton's impression ratings are also better than in 2004 (5.1) and better than Alexa McDonough's before him (4.6), while Duceppe, with his 4.1 ratings, has been in a steady decline since 2000.

Table 7
Leaders' evaluations

	2006	2004	2000
Chrétien	-	-	4.8
Martin	4.4	5.1	-
Day	-	-	4.6
Harper	5.5	4.6	-
McDonough	-	-	4.6
Layton	5.1	4.6	-
Duceppe	4.1	4.5	4.6

Source: 2000–2006 POLLARA Post-Election Surveys.

But the real story is the decline in Paul Martin's image. Ever since he entered public life, Martin had led a charmed and seemingly effortless political career, receiving glowing performance reviews as finance minister and favourable media coverage. His 1995 budget was hailed a milestone budget — a budget that re-established Canada's credibility with the international financial community[24] — and when he officially became Canada's twenty-first prime minister on December 12, 2003, pundits and political observers were agreeing on the inevitability of a fourth consecutive Liberal majority.[25] But as some of his predecessors, notably John Turner and Kim Campbell, had realized, the media was much more aggressive with Martin as prime minister than in his previous subordinate posts. He proved unable to adjust, and his image was tarnished by his handling of the sponsorship scandal and his inability to meet the high expectations he had created. Within three years, Martin had gone from unassailable to unpalatable. A look at leaders' evaluations from a regional perspective shows the extent of the damage to Martin's image.

As Table 8 demonstrates, Paul Martin's image deteriorated in every region of the country. His decline was negligible in British Columbia (-0.3) and in Ontario (-0.4) but devastating everywhere else. Martin's ratings dropped from 5.8 to 4.7 (-1.1) in Atlantic Canada, from 4.9 to 3.9 (-1.0) in the Prairies, and from 4.6 to 3.7 (-0.9) in Quebec. More telling is the reality that Martin trailed the others in impression ratings in every region of the country, even where the Liberals were able to minimize electoral losses. Clearly, all those Liberal candidates and incumbents who once looked to Martin as their main electoral asset managed to win their seats in 2006 despite him.

The regional picture was more positive for the other two national leaders. While the NDP may not have managed the electoral breakthrough it was hoping for in 2006, Layton met his strategic objective by improving his image in Quebec and Ontario. His overall impression improved significantly in Quebec (+0.9), Ontario (+0.9), and Atlantic Canada (+1.3). More importantly, Layton comes out of the 2006 election as the best regarded leader in Ontario. His objective will be to translate this popularity into seats in the next federal election.

We do not have any evidence showing that the Canadian electorate has warmed up to Stephen Harper's personality, but his impression ratings have definitely improved across the country. Harper made the most significant improvements in Quebec (+1.5) and Ontario (+1.3), but his ratings also went up in B.C. (+0.7), the Prairies (+0.6), and Atlantic Canada (+0.6). Unlike Layton, Harper was able to translate an improved image into more seats.

Table 8
Evaluation of leaders by region

	B.C.		Prairies		Ontario		Quebec		Atlantic	
	2006	2004	2006	2004	2006	2004	2006	2004	2006	2004
Martin	4.5	4.8	3.9	4.9	4.9	5.3	3.7	4.6	4.7	5.8
Harper	5.2	4.5	6.0	5.4	5.3	4.6	5.6	4.1	4.9	4.3
Layton	5.0	5.0	4.9	4.8	5.4	4.7	5.0	4.1	5.6	4.3
Duceppe							5.3	6.1		

Source: 2004-2006 POLLARA Post-Election Surveys.

While Martin was the clear loser in the 2006 election, the results should also give Gilles Duceppe reasons to be concerned. His impression ratings have deteriorated significantly in Quebec, dropping from 6.1 to 5.3 in the nineteen months between the last two elections. Duceppe should also be concerned by the fact that he rates slightly lower than Harper (5.6) and barely ahead of Layton (5.0) in his home province. The Bloc's decision to run a negative campaign focused almost exclusively on Liberal corruption may have eroded the positive image of its leader. The decision may have also opened the door to Harper's Conservatives to add to the coalition of Western conservatives the decentralists and nationalistic Quebecers they need to form a majority government.

CONCLUSION

With the return to power of the Conservatives, albeit in a minority position, the Canadian political landscape appears to be struggling to return to the pre-1993 party system. This development should not be dismissed nor its significance minimized. Many had argued that the Liberals seemed poised to maintain their dominance of Canadian electoral politics for an extended period of time.[26] However, such analyses dismissed the inherent volatility of the Canadian electorate. Despite the devastation of 1993, the Conservatives only had to move beyond the permutations from the right of the spectrum — from PC and Reform to the Alliance and the DRC and finally the Conservative Party — and present a stable political vehicle to the electorate. Once this was achieved, Canadian voters were ready to give the party a second look. The results of the present analysis indicate that the electorate liked some of what they saw — enough to make Stephen Harper Canada's twenty-second prime minister.

Analysts should be prudent and not jump to conclusions about the consequences of the Liberal defeat. After all, the Liberals have been punished by the electorate in the past. The Liberal hold on power from 1993 to 2006 was the longest since the King–St. Laurent era. As was the case in 1957, 1979, and 1984, Canadian voters decided that the Liberal Party had been in power for too long and its growing arrogance needed to be kept in check. They turned to the Conservatives as the vehicle to deliver that message. The 2006 election will prove to be either a similar episode or the beginning of something different. The outcome rests on a set of specific factors.

First, parties need to address the growing gap between what the electorate wants and what they decide to offer to voters during the campaign. Voters have consistently mentioned that parties, and not leaders, are the most important factor in influencing their vote decision. In 2006, parties and local candidates were more important than leaders in influencing vote choice. In this context, leader-centred campaigns may not be the best way to win elections, and the voters' reluctance to elect a majority government may be the consequence of their lack of familiarity with what the main parties purport to represent.

Second, our analysis suggests that each party should be facing the future with a combination of hope and apprehension. The NDP managed to leave the political cellar it had occupied since 1993 and can once again claim its cherished role of "conscience of Canada." But more could be in store for the NDP. Layton's emerging popularity in Ontario creates an opening for the NDP, and the next election will decide whether Layton's favourable image can be translated into seats. For its part, the Bloc is once again at a crossroads. The sponsorship scandal offered a golden opportunity for the party to increase its stranglehold on the province and promote the cause of sovereignty. The party made a strategic mistake in concentrating its campaign efforts almost exclusively on Liberal corruption instead of offering a compelling vision for change. In doing so, it has tarnished the image of its popular leader and will have to worry about Harper's growing popularity.

Obviously, the most important unanswered question deals with interpreting the Conservative victory. Unequivocally, the gamble taken by Stephen Harper and Peter Mackay in merging the PC and Alliance paid off. The Conservatives are in power, a feat that seemed unreachable less than five years ago. Stephen Harper managed to improve his appeal to Canadian voters between 2004 and 2006, especially where it counted the most — in Quebec and Ontario. The nature of the Conservative gains in Quebec is particularly interesting since they show signs of the re-emergence of traditional Conservative vote patterns. The Conservatives took eight of their ten seats from Bloc incumbents. Some of the seats, such as Lotbinière–Chutes de la Chaudière, Jonquière-Alma, and Lévis-Bellechasse, have a conservative tradition going back to the days of the Union Nationale. They represent a solid base from which to rebuild. However, in 2006 the Conservatives were facing the most scandal-plagued Liberal Party in decades and still managed to form only a minority government. We saw that in the final days of the campaign, those who remained undecided were unable to bring themselves to support the Conservatives and drifted to the NDP and other parties. The Liberal Party will have a new leader in the next election and the sources of disapproval of the Liberal record will have dissipated. The manner in which Harper deals with this new reality will dictate whether he will be able to repeat Diefenbaker's feat of turning the 1957 minority victory into a landslide victory a year later or if his government — like the 1979 Clark government — will be remembered as a footnote in history.

NOTES

1   See for instance, C.B. Macpherson, *The Life and Times of Liberal Democracy* (Oxford: Oxford University Press, 1977); Morris Fiorina, *Retrospective Voting in American National Elections* (New Haven: Yale University Press, 1981); and David Held, *Models of Democracy* (Palo Alto: Stanford University Press, 1977).

2   A total of twelve hundred telephone interviews were conducted for this study. The author would like to thank Mr. Michael Marzolini, Chairman of POLLARA, for his generous contribution.

3   Gloria Galloway, "Harper vows to rush wait-time solution," *Globe and Mail*, December 3, 2005, A4.

4   See André Turcotte, "Canadians Speak Out," in *The Canadian General Election of 2004*, ed. Jon H. Pammett and Christopher Dornan (Toronto: Dundurn Press, 2004), 324–7. For a more general discussion see Harold D. Clarke et al., *Absent Mandate*, 3rd edition (Toronto: Gage Educational Publishing Company, 1996).

5   See discussions of issues in Jon H. Pammett, "The People's Verdict," in *The Canadian General Election of 2000*, ed. Jon H. Pammett and Christopher Dornan (Toronto: Dundurn Press, 2001); and Jon H. Pammett, "The Voters Decide" in *The Canadian General Election of 1997*, ed. Alan Frizzell and Jon H. Pammett (Toronto: Dundurn Press, 1997).

6   See Jon H. Pammett, "The 1988 Vote" in *The Canadian General Election of 1988*, ed. Alan Frizzell, Jon H. Pammett, and Anthony Westell (Ottawa: Carleton University Press, 1989).

7   For a full discussion see Clarke et al., *Absent Mandate*, 174–5.

8   See Nevitte, Neil, et al., *Unsteady State: The 1997 Canadian Federal Election* (Toronto: Oxford University Press, 2000), especially chapter 8.

9   As reported by Curtis Gillespie, "After Eleven Years of Smug Liberal Rule, Is Stephen Harper Going to Be any Better?" *Toro*, Summer 2004, 85.

10 For the full analysis, see Turcotte, "Canadians Speak Out."

11 Ibid., 319.

12 For 1997, see Jon H. Pammett, " The Voters Decide"; for 2000, see Pammett, " The People's Verdict"; and for 2004, see Turcotte, "Canadians Speak Out."

13 Pammett, "The People's Verdict."

14 Pammett, "The Voters Decide," 228.

15 Allan Woods and Mark Kennedy, "Liberals question game plan," *The Gazette*, January 18, 2006, A1.

16 Turcotte, "Canadians Speak Out," 317–8.

17 Vincent Marisal, "Le premier minister Stephen Harper?" *La Presse,* November 29, 2005, A2.

18 "Le Canada en Elections," *La Presse*, November 29, 2005, A1.

19 Jane Taber, "The Liberals are in a spiral, top Martin adviser says," *Globe and Mail*, June 10, 2004, A1.

20 Jane Taber, "Confident Harper talks majority," *Globe and Mail*, June 11, 2004, A1.

21 Pammett, "The People's Verdict," 308.

22 Ibid.

23 John Ibbitson, "Passionate and ruthless, Martin looks like he's fighting to survive," *Globe and Mail*, June 16, 2004, A1.

24 This point was made in Edward Greenspon and Anthony Wilson-Smith, *Double Vision: The Inside Story of the Liberals in Power* (Toronto: Doubleday Canada Limited, 1996); Susan Delacourt, *Juggernaut: Paul Martin's Campaign for Chrétien's Crown* (Toronto: McClelland & Stewart Ltd., 2003); and John Gray, *Paul Martin: The Power of Ambition* (Toronto: Key Porter Books, 2003).

25 Drew Fagan, "How Martin came back from brink," *Globe and Mail,* June 29, 2004, A1.

26 André Blais, Elisabeth Gidengil, Richard Nadeau, and Neil Nevitte, *Anatomy of a Liberal Victory: Making Sense of the Vote in the 2000 Canadian Election* (Peterborough: Broadview Press, Ltd., 2002).

CHAPTER TWELVE

Voter Turnout in 2006:
More Than Just the Weather
by Lawrence LeDuc and Jon H. Pammett

A winter election would mean lower turnout. That seemingly simple proposition led many to expect that the federal election of January 2006 would be a low-turnout affair, possibly even eclipsing the historic low turnout of the 2004 election. We also know that voting turnout in Canada has been in a more or less continuous downtrend over the past two decades, for reasons that we have explored in some detail elsewhere and will discuss further in this chapter.[1] However, rather than thinking of the 2006 case as a winter election, we might also frame it as an election that resulted from the parliamentary defeat of a government, as one involving a major political scandal, or as one that in the end resulted in a change of government. These factors are all related in a way to the timing of the election, but they each have the potential to contribute either positively or negatively to turnout in different ways. The fact that the election brought about a change of government speaks to the competitiveness of this election, a factor that we will address more directly in this chapter.

Greater efforts by the electoral authorities and others to improve turnout, in part a response to the turnout declines of previous elections, may have had some positive effects. The sponsorship scandal and its aftermath may have motivated some voters to vent their anger at the governing party, or it may have augmented many citizens' negative feelings about politics and politicians — a condition that has in fact contributed to the broader turnout decline of recent years.[2] In the end, turnout in the 2006 election rose to 64.9 percent of the electorate as estimated by Elections Canada, a notable increase over the 60.5 percent nadir of the 2004 election (Figure 1). But, given the strength and persistence of the turnout decline that has taken place in Canada and many other democratic nations in recent years, it is unlikely that the modest reversal of 2006 signals the beginning of a new trend of rising turnout. Rather, the explanation for the modest increase in turnout in 2006 more likely lies in the particular context of this election and in the various short-term factors associated with it that may have offset some of the longer-term forces that have persistently been driving turnout in elections down. Because of the complexity of circumstances under which the 2006 election took place, there are a number of different hypotheses that might be advanced regarding turnout in the unusual election of 2006. We will explore these patterns further in the subsequent sections of this chapter.

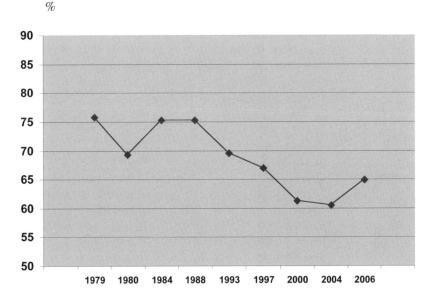

Figure 1
Turnout in federal elections, 1979–2006

SEASONALITY

The argument that there is a seasonality to turnout in elections is difficult to test, given the relatively small number of cases available and the plethora of other factors that can affect turnout. Further, the reasons that we might expect a winter election to produce lower turnout are rather unclear. Is it because severe winter weather might deter voters from going to the polls? If so, the proposition might in reality prove to be literally as variable as the weather, both in different regions of the country and from one case to another. Snowbirds might have decamped to warmer climes and thus be unavailable for, or inattentive to, an election taking place during a Canadian winter. But more readily available postal

Table 1
Turnout in federal elections, 1874–2006

Election Date	Turnout
January 22, 1874	69.6
September 17, 1878	69.1
June 20, 1882	70.3
February 22, 1887	70.1
March 5, 1891	64.4
June 23, 1896	62.9
November 7, 1900	77.4
November 3, 1904	71.6
October 26, 1908	70.3
September 21, 1911	70.2
December 17, 1917	75.0
December 6, 1921	67.7
October 29, 1925	66.4
September 14, 1926	67.7
July 28, 1930	73.5
October 14, 1935	74.2
March 26, 1940	69.9
June 11, 1945	75.3
June 27, 1949	73.8
August 10, 1953	67.5
June 10, 1957	74.1
March 31, 1958	79.4
June 18, 1962	79.0
April 8, 1963	79.2
November 8, 1965	74.8
June 25, 1968	75.7
October 30, 1972	76.7
July 8, 1974	71.0
May 22, 1979	75.7
February 18, 1980	69.3
September 4, 1984	75.3
November 21, 1988	75.3
October 25, 1993	69.6
June 2, 1997	67.0
November 27, 2000	61.2
June 28, 2004	60.5
January 23, 2006	64.9

voting, advance polls, or even a rising U.S. dollar could mitigate this factor. Or is it because in an election in which the campaign spans part of the traditional holiday season, voters' attentions are likely to be directed elsewhere? One can as readily think of some seasonal factors that might pull in the opposite direction. In an election taking place during the school year, university students might be attentive to politics and better able to vote. Parents of school-age children might likewise be more readily available for an unexpected trip to the polls, at least in comparison with periods of the year when school is not in session.

Table 2
Turnout in federal elections by month and season, 1874–2006

	N	Turnout		N	Turnout
June	9	71.0	Spring	9	74.4
October	5	71.4	Summer	10	69.7
November	5	72.0	Autumn	13	71.6
September	4	70.6	Winter	5	67.6
March	3	71.2			
January	2	67.2	All seasons	37	71.2
February	2	69.7			
July	2	72.3			
December	2	71.4			
April	1	79.2			
May	1	75.7			
August	1	67.5			

Clearly, seasonal factors play a role from time to time in determining when an election takes place. Historically, June has been by far the preferred month for federal elections in Canada, but autumn has been the more popular season (Tables 1 and 2). The seasonal classifications shown in Table 2 are of course somewhat arbitrary and may not in themselves reflect some of the seasonal factors that we typically think about when considering the timing of elections. Four of the nine June elections (1896, 1949, 1968, and 2004) occurred in the last week of June (after the vernal equinox) and would thus be considered summer elections when a strictly seasonal method of classification is employed, as in Table 2. But these could well be different in their potential turnout effects than a summer election taking place in August (only 1953), a much more traditional family holiday period. Likewise, an autumn election occurring in December is likely to be viewed very differently than one occurring in October or November, the more popular autumn months (Table 2). For our purposes, we could just as easily classify the two elections that have taken place in December (1917, 1921) as winter elections, because of the probability of colder weather and the possible intrusion on a traditional holiday period. Likewise, two of the three elections that occurred in March (1940, 1958) are probably very similar in possible seasonal effects to the only one that took place in April (1963), since all three of these cases fall within a few days of each other. But the one that took place in the first week of March (1891) could readily be grouped with the two February elections (1887, 1980), given the more likely similarity of winter weather patterns throughout the country.

A government that calls a snap election during the traditional holiday or vacation seasons might expect to be criticized for such a decision. But an election brought about by the defeat of the government in Parliament is not subject to these types of calculations. It occurs when it will, and any potential turnout effects become merely a small part of the larger election context. A "Christmas election," as much of the press insisted on calling it at the beginning of the 2005–06 campaign, is nevertheless an unusual event in Canada. Only once before in Canadian history has there been an election in January — in 1874 when Alexander Mackenzie, who had become prime minister in November 1873 because of parliamentary defections resulting from the Pacific scandal, opted for an immediate election.

In all, there have been only five winter elections, including that of 2006, in all of Canadian history, and they have indeed produced somewhat lower than average turnouts (Table 2). But the cases themselves are too few and varied to permit much in the way of generalization. Even if the two December elections were added to the "winter" group as shown in Table 2, the patterns would be inconsistent, since one of the two December elections — the wartime election of 1917 — had a robust turnout of 75.0 percent, while the other (1921) was significantly lower at 67.7 percent. Comparing sequential elections occurring in different months tells us little more. The 1874 election — the only other one occurring in January — yielded a turnout of 69.6 percent, little different than the election following it in 1878 (69.1 percent), which took place in September.[3] The election of March 5, 1891, yielded a low turnout (64.4 percent), but the one following in June 1896 produced an even lower one (62.9 percent). The preceding election of February 1887 yielded a better turnout (70.1 percent), but little different than the one before that (70.3 percent) in June 1882.

These elections, of course, took place long ago, making them dubious reference points for a twenty-first-century winter election in Canada. However, much of our expectation for turnout in the 2006 election was shaped by the only modern-day winter election — that of February 1980. When the Clark government was defeated in Parliament on December 13, 1979, the chain of events created a context strikingly similar to that of the 2006 election. And indeed, in the election that took place on February 18, 1980, turnout registered 69.3 percent — a substantial decline from that of the May 1979 election (75.7 percent) and also considerably lower than the one following in September 1984 (75.3 percent).

Given the similarity of circumstances, there was thus some reason to expect that the timing of the 2006 election might lead to lower turnout. But there were some important differences to consider as well. Given the steady decline in turnout of the three preceding elections, turnout in federal elections was already at historic lows. And the combination of vigorous voter awareness campaigns and administrative changes designed to make the process of voting easier could conceivably mitigate any effects that the weather or other seasonal factors might have. In the end, unseasonably pleasant winter weather throughout much of the country on election day, with temperatures of -3 in Halifax, -5 in Montreal, +3 in Toronto, -2 in Winnipeg, +3 in Saskatoon, +10 in Calgary, and +8 in Vancouver, may well have moderated any of the potentially more adverse seasonal effects. While weather patterns in Canada are never uniform, election day was simply a nice day throughout much of the country.[4]

THE TURNOUT DECLINE: A CONTINUING TREND?

From the postwar period onward, the normal expectation was that about three-quarters of registered electors would exercise their right to vote. The only exceptions to that pattern after 1945 were the February 1980 election, as discussed earlier, and the 1953 election — the only federal election ever to have occurred in August. It seemed difficult to raise turnout much above the 75 percent level, but there also seemed to be no reason to expect it to be significantly lower unless an election took place at a particularly unusual time of the year. The interest level of the elections in 1984 and 1988 was uncharacteristically high, judging by the dramatic nature of the campaign and the results. Both the Mulroney sweep and the free trade election were unusual circumstances in the broader history of Canadian elections, owing to the upsurge of support for the Progressive Conservatives in the 1984 instance and the continual heated discussion of the proposed Free Trade Agreement throughout the 1988 campaign. Yet turnout in both of those elections registered only what had seemingly become the more or less standard level of 75 percent of eligible voters participating.

Research for the Royal Commission on Electoral Reform and Party Financing, published in 1991, recommended ways to increase turnout by improving access to the voting process through such measures as more readily available advance voting opportunities, mail ballots, weekend voting, and other changes.[5] A number of these proposals were indeed adopted, but the expected improvements in voter turnout did not appear. Instead, turnout in elections after 1988 began to decline.

Starting with the 1993 federal election, voting participation began a steady downward slide, decreasing by a full 15 percentage points by 2004. The decline was gradual, with stops at 70 percent in 1993, 67 percent in 1997, 61 percent in 2000, and 60.5 percent in 2004. Turnout in provincial elections similarly declined over much of the same period, suggesting that the forces that were driving turnout down did not derive from federal politics alone.[6] Research found that the rise in non-voting was very strongly associated with age, as many young newly eligible citizens did not avail themselves of opportunities to go to the ballot box.[7] Over time, the normal process of generational replacement began to be reflected in lower voting turnout patterns. These underlying demographic factors pushing turnout down were to some extent offset in the 2004 election by increased competition between the parties, particularly in Ontario — the one province where turnout rose appreciably in 2004 over 2000. But turnout was higher in 2006 in *all* of the provinces than it had been in the previous election, thereby suggesting a more general rise in public interest in the 2006 contest.

Table 3
Turnout by province, 2000–06

	2006	2004	2000
Newfoundland	56.8	49.2	57.1
Prince Edward Island	73.7	70.7	72.7
Nova Scotia	63.6	61.7	62.1
New Brunswick	69.1	62.1	67.7
Quebec	63.3	58.9	64.1
Ontario	67.3	61.7	58.0
Manitoba	62.7	56.5	62.3
Saskatchewan	65.7	59.1	62.3
Alberta	62.4	59.4	60.2
British Columbia	64.3	63.6	63.0
TOTAL CANADA	64.9	60.5	61.2

An examination of voting turnout for the last three federal elections in the provinces reveals some interesting patterns (Table 3). In many provinces, the 2006 turnout is very similar to that of 2000, making 2004 appear to be the outlier. Newfoundland, for example, had turnout around 57 percent in both 2006 and 2000, with an intervening dip to 49 percent in 2004. The pattern in New Brunswick, Quebec, and Manitoba is similar. The other Western provinces, as well as Nova Scotia and Prince Edward Island, show more modest rises in 2006, to levels slightly above *both* 2004 and 2000.

The main exception to these patterns in 2006 occurred in Ontario. In that province, voting participation rose by a more substantial amount, reaching 67.3 percent and displaying a more consistent pattern of *increasing* turnout since the 2000 election. This figure is well above that for any province other than Prince Edward Island, where turnout has traditionally been exceptionally high in comparison with other provinces. In our analysis of turnout in the 2004 election, we argued that the changed competitive situation of the political parties had particularly acted to increase turnout in Ontario.[8] Our hypothesis, therefore, is that the continuing rise in competitiveness in 2006 is likewise part of the explanation for the additional turnout increase in Ontario.

A post-election survey conducted by POLLARA that included a question on "reasons for not voting" can help to provide further evidence

Table 4
Reasons given for not voting in 2000 or 2006 federal elections

	2000	2006
Lack of Interest		
Not interested; didn't care; apathy	23.2	29.3
Vote meaningless; wouldn't count; results a foregone conclusion	7.8	4.7
Forgot; unaware	2.2	4.7
Too complicated; confusing	0.4	2.0
	33.6	**40.7**
Negativity		
No appealing candidates/parties/issues	12.6	4.7
Lack of faith/confidence in candidates/parties/leaders; regional discontent	11.4	10.7
Lack of information about candidates/parties/issues	3.3	3.3
	27.3	**18.7**
Personal/Administrative		
Too busy with work/school/family	13.7	19.3
Away from riding/province/country	10.3	1.3
Registration or moving related problems	6.7	7.3
Illness; health issues	2.9	8.0
Didn't know where or when; polling station problems; no transportation	3.3	4.0
Religious reasons	1.5	1.3
	38.4	**41.2**
N =	1,036	150

Notes: 2000 data from Elections Canada survey; 2006 from POLLARA post-election survey. Data are weighted. First response only from 2000. Category of "other; unclassifiable; none" reasons removed.

regarding Canadians' perceptions of the efficacy of their vote in the present Canadian setting. The reasons given by individuals in the 2006 election who were eligible to vote but decided not to do so are shown in Table 4. This question was open-ended so that no potential reasons were given

to prompt non-voters for their response. These are placed in the same categories of reasons established by the authors in a study of non-voting in
the 2000 election, thereby facilitating comparison across time.[9] A major
feature of the earlier study was its sample design, whereby a much larger
than usual group of respondents was interviewed who reported not having voted in the election. Thus, we can have a higher degree of confidence
in the distribution of reasons given in the first column of Table 4.

Non-voters give reasons for their behaviour that broadly fall into
three categories. The first is lack of interest in politics in general and/or
the election in particular. Included in this category is a view that their vote
would be meaningless, in the sense that the outcome was not in doubt or
that the parties were all the same. A second set of reasons taps public negativity toward the political process in any of its many manifestations.
Those turning away from elections out of distaste or disgust are likely to
say that politicians are not to be trusted or have not addressed the important problems facing the country. Finally, there is a set of reasons that
relate to the respondents' personal circumstances. This includes illness,
absence, or relocation of residence. It also includes difficulties with the
registration process; a number of people, particularly young people, do
not receive a voter information card because they are not on the permanent List of Electors. None of these items represents an actual barrier to
voting, should the individual be interested in taking the time to overcome
the perceived difficulty. However, if voting is a marginal political act for
people, such hindrances do act as inhibitions to voting. Finally, there are
those who report that they are too busy to vote, because they have conflicting activities involving their work, school, or family lives.

For the reported non-voters in the POLLARA 2006 survey (used
extensively in Chapter Eleven to analyze the voting behaviour in 2006),
the results are broadly similar to those for 2000. About 40 percent of
those reporting they did not vote in 2006 gave reasons relating to their
lack of interest in the election. Slightly less than 20 percent cited negativity, and another 40 percent or so gave personal or administrative reasons for their lack of voting participation. Once again in 2006, the category of personal or administrative reasons was dominated by those saying they were too busy to vote. Although the numbers are small, and
caution should be used in their interpretation, the relationship of age
with those citing the "too busy" reason is interesting. Of non-voters
aged eighteen to twenty-four, 32 percent said they were too busy to vote.
For the twenty-five to thirty-four group, 25 percent gave that reason,
and this number declined to 21 percent for the thirty-five to forty-four

age group, to 14 percent for the forty-five to fifty-four group, and to virtually nothing for older voters.

This propensity for young citizens to cite being too occupied with other things to take the time to vote is, in a way, a statement that non-voting need not be a permanent state of affairs for them. If they had more time next time, they might be saying, they would consider participating. The difficulty with this position, of course, is that habits of voting or not voting become ingrained over time. The sense of civic duty, which produces the feeling that it is important to vote regardless of the context, is not developed. Rationalizations of a lack of public action of all sorts, including voting, become easier to invoke. A syndrome of non-participation is in danger of developing among many Canadian youth.

TURNOUT AND COMPETITION

Research in Canada and elsewhere supports the hypothesis that voting turnout is positively related to the degree of competition between the sides contesting an election.[10] This research establishes that the context of the election, represented by the short-term images of political parties, leaders, and candidates, and the discourse around issues provide a competitive balance that energizes the electorate to a greater or lesser degree. The competitive balance may have a number of different dimensions. It can be perceived by potential Canadian voters at the level of the individual constituency, with local candidates vying for their attention. In the local arena, incumbency may play a part in determining the degree of competition — a popular (or unpopular) local member seeking re-election may provide a quite different competitive context for the voter than that indicated by national polling numbers.

The closeness of the result of the previous election, in this case the election of 2004, will also provide a background to the present contest. Perceptions of the degree of competition can also be directed to the national race, where frequently published opinion polls (see Chapter Ten) gauge the fortunes of the major parties and their leaders. And these perceptions may also be directed toward the regional or provincial level. The "battle of Quebec" or "battle of Ontario" is often reported separately from the analysis of the fortunes of the national parties. Even though the national contest in 2006 was quite competitive, and the outcome uncertain, potential voters in Alberta may not have perceived it that way, given expectations that the Conservatives would easily sweep that province.

Measuring competition in these several dimensions is therefore a complicated analytical task. Not only are there many arenas of competition, but the perceptions of voters are also involved. If the competitive context changes significantly from one election to the next, voters may or may not be aware of that change, depending on their degree of attentiveness to politics more generally. We know from a previous analysis that the degree to which observers feel their vote would make a difference in their constituency interacts with an objective measure of the margin of victory to make a major difference in constituency turnout. In the 2000 study, ridings where the margin of votes between the winner and the runner-up was narrow and where people subjectively felt that their votes would make a lot of difference in the outcome saw an 82.5 percent rate of turnout; in the opposite situation, where the winning margin was very large and people felt their votes would make no difference in the outcome, only 40 percent voted.[11]

Table 5 presents the relationships for the last two elections between constituency turnout and the objective competitiveness in those constituencies, as measured by the margin of victory of the winner, that is, the number of votes between the first- and second-place finishers. While there are certainly other potential measures of competition that take more factors into account (for example, the distance between the first three finishers could be used), this straightforward measure illustrates the connection between this factor and turnout well enough for our current purposes. For Canada as a whole, using all 308 constituencies, the correlation for 2006 was -.276, up from -.191 in 2004. The negative nature of this relationship tells us that the smaller the margin of victory, the higher the percentage of voters. Therefore, we have a moderately strong, statistically significant, relationship between competition in the ridings and the number of people who go out to vote in them.

We would not expect to find large changes in the competitive circumstances at the riding level between two elections occurring within nineteen months of each other. This will especially be true when a large number of incumbents are seeking re-election, as was the case in 2006. Indeed, the simple correlation between the majority obtained by the winning candidate in 2006 and that in 2004 is quite high (.78), as is also the correlation between turnout at the riding level in the two elections (.86). We would not therefore expect to see a large change in turnout at the constituency level unless the competitive situation at that level changes significantly from one election to the next.

The pattern of relationships between competition and turnout is presented in Table 5 for all of the provinces, including the Northern territories. There is considerable variation in these locations, as might be expected since in some places there are quite small numbers of cases. In the Territories, Newfoundland, and New Brunswick, there is actually a *positive* relationship between the margin of victory and turnout, indicating that in these locations the ridings where the victorious candidates won by more votes tended to have higher turnout. But these findings are based on three, seven, and ten ridings, respectively. In Prince Edward Island's four ridings, there was a strong relationship between turnout and margin of victory in 2004, but none in 2006. Saskatchewan and Alberta display little evidence that variation in competition at the riding level has much effect on turnout.

Table 5
Turnout by margin of victory, 2004 and 2006 federal elections

[Pearson r]

	2004	2006
TOTAL CANADA	-.191**	-.276**
Newfoundland	-.506	.166
Prince Edward Island	-.745	-.006
Nova Scotia	-.020	-.101
New Brunswick	.182	.200
Quebec	.005	-.174
Ontario	-.356**	-.313**
Manitoba	.158	-.388
Saskatchewan	-.055	-.051
Alberta	-.031	-.039
British Columbia	-.276	-.364*
Territories	-.112	.892

** significant at < .01
* significant at < .05

In several parts of the country, however, there was an important relationship in 2006 between competition and turnout. In particular, British Columbia, Ontario, Manitoba, and Quebec give indications from Table 5 that there was a stronger connection between these two variables than was found in other places. All of these areas appeared to be more competitive in 2006 than 2004. All four of these provinces featured three-way races in many constituencies. In the case of British Columbia, Ontario, and Manitoba, the Conservatives, Liberals, and New Democrats were close contenders in a large number of ridings. In Quebec, the story of the election was the emergence of the Conservative Party, which won a total of ten seats, some coming from the Liberals and some from the Bloc Québécois. This competitive situation appears to have sparked considerable interest on the part of voters and encouraged them to participate on the grounds that their votes would be more likely to count in determining the outcome.

The constituencies divide about evenly between those where the level of competitiveness (as measured by margin of victory for the winning candidate) increased in 2006 (150) and those where it declined (158). There is little difference in the overall level of competitiveness at the constituency level between the elections. The average margin of victory for the winning candidate in 2006 (20.7 percent) is little different than that found in 2004 (20.5 percent). In those few constituencies where large changes in the level of competitiveness occurred, there were often special circumstances relating to incumbency. For example, the constituency in which the largest decrease in competitiveness occurred was Edmonton-Beaumont, which had been narrowly won (by 0.33 percent) by David Kilgour, running as a Liberal in 2004. Kilgour later left the Liberal caucus to sit as an independent and voted in favour of the non-confidence motion that brought down the government on November 28. He did not seek re-election in 2006, and the riding was won by a Conservative by an overwhelming majority (37.5 percent). At the opposite end of the competitiveness index, the riding of Labrador had been won by Liberal Lawrence O'Brien in 2004 by a very large margin (46.5 percent). But O'Brien died during the minority Parliament, and the riding suddenly became competitive. It was retained by the Liberals in 2006, but by a much narrower margin (10.8 percent). In all but one of the 150 constituencies where competitiveness increased in 2004, turnout rose or was virtually unchanged. In a few instances, it went up quite substantially. The increase in turnout in O'Brien's former riding, for example, was 13.4 percent. The average increase for all of the more competitive ridings, however, was a more modest 4.8 percent.

In constituencies where competitiveness decreased, the pattern was somewhat more mixed. Turnout in those constituencies rose by an average of 3.6 percent — about in line with the increased turnout in the election as a whole. The turnout increase in Kilgour's former riding was 2.6 percent — below the average for the entire country. But although the turnout increases that might be attributable to changes in party competition at the constituency level were modest (Pearson r = .15), the pattern found is in the hypothesized (positive) direction, and it is statistically significant. We can therefore argue that the greater competitiveness of the 2006 election, both nationally and at the local level, accounts for *some* of the improvement in voter turnout found in the 2006 election. We do not know, of course, the extent to which these changes in the local competitive situation were well perceived by the voters before the election took place. But it could be argued that a perception of changed competitive circumstances would certainly be more likely in those instances where an incumbent was not seeking re-election, or where a party that had not previously been competitive in a particular riding was running a more active and visible campaign.

Many of the constituencies that saw substantial changes in local competitiveness in 2006 were in Quebec, and this was often attributable to the presence of a more competitive Conservative candidate. In Roberval, for example, the Bloc incumbent retained the seat in 2006, but by a much narrower margin (8.0 percent) than in 2004 (36.2 percent). In the constituencies of Charlesbourg and Beauport, Bloc incumbents who had won by comfortable margins in 2004 were narrowly defeated in 2006 by Conservative candidates. In Beauce, on the other hand, a Liberal incumbent who had retained the riding by a narrow margin in 2004 was overwhelmed by a Conservative in 2006, with the Bloc candidate running a distant second. A number of competitive changes were also found in some rural Ontario ridings where Conservative candidates who had been elected for the first time in 2004, often in fairly tight contests with a Liberal incumbent, were re-elected in 2006 by a much wider margin, rendering those constituencies substantially *less* competitive in 2006. At the same time, some suburban Ontario ridings became *more* competitive, as a Liberal incumbent who had won by a large margin in 2004 retained the riding by a much narrower margin in 2006. Constituencies such as Mississauga South or Oakville fall into this group.

Table 6

Predictors of turnout in constituencies, 2006

[multiple regression]

	MODEL 1		MODEL 2	
	B (SE)	BETA	B (SE)	BETA
Margin of Victory 2006	-.086 (.032)**	-.261	-.062 (.016)**	-.188
Margin of Victory 2004	-.015 (.030)	-.047	.020 (.016)	.061
Incumbent wins	-.493 (.837)	-.036	-.955 (.427)*	-.070
Conservative wins	1.641 (.654)**	.154	.302 (.337)	.028
Turnout in 2004			.773 (.026)**	.835
R square =	.109		.769	

** significant at <.01
 * significant at <.05

Using the aggregate data, we can estimate through multiple regression analysis how much of the variance in turnout at the constituency level can be explained by factors related specifically to competition. Table 6 presents two regression models. We have entered here two measures of competition, the first measuring the margin of victory in 2006 (as used in Table 5 to correlate with turnout), and the second measuring the same factor in the previous election (2004). The theory behind using this measure as well as the 2006 one is that voters might be considering the competitive situation as a result of the previous election and extrapolating that situation to the current context. The margin of victory in 2006 would of course be known only after the election had taken place, but it is not an unreasonable assumption that many people would be aware of how close a race would likely be on the basis of commentary and occasional surveys during the campaign.

Two additional factors are added to the models in Table 6. Since the main story of the 2006 election involves the increased support for the Conservatives and the likelihood that they would form a government, we entered a variable that identifies those ridings across the country that the Conservatives won. The reasoning here was that these areas might engender more interest since their outcomes could be particularly relevant to the formation of a new government, with attendant possibilities of Cabinet representation or at least possible benefit for the area. Finally, a variable is added measuring whether the incumbent won the election in the riding. The reasoning here was that incumbent victories would indicate seats that were more likely to be safe, making votes count less.

Model 1 displayed in Table 6 shows that these four factors together explain 11 percent of the variance in turnout in the constituencies in 2006. Only two of the four factors are statistically significant, however. The most important predictor is the 2006 margin of victory, with the negative sign indicating that the narrower the victory the higher the turnout. The presence of a Conservative winner was also associated with increased turnout. The other two factors are not important predictors of turnout, though their effects are in the predicted direction.

Model 2 in Table 6 adds the factor of the 2004 turnout as a predictor of 2006 turnout. As can be seen, this has a dramatic effect on the result, raising the predictive power to the point where 77 percent of the variance in turnout can be explained by the five factors acting together. Constituencies can be seen as having consistent histories, or cultures, which are a cumulation of a variety of factors acting in the local context. These could be related to the patterns of representation engaged in by members of Parliament over the years, to long-term patterns of competition, to demographic concentration of groups more or less likely to participate, or a number of other factors. While this measure of the turnout history is very important in explaining why an individual riding would have a certain level of turnout in 2006, it is not the only factor. The 2006 margin of victory explains additional variance over and above this previous turnout measure. Thus, we see that the competitive situation, particularly where it changed, was instrumental to the rise in turnout in 2006 in many parts of Canada, as well as in a number of specific constituencies.

REVERSING THE TURNOUT DECLINE

As we have argued earlier in this chapter, the decline in voting turnout that has taken place in Canada and in other countries is part of a longer-term trend that is not likely to be reversed in a single election. The demographic factors that are driving this trend are powerful, and they are not easily offset by the types of shorter-term elements that may be associated with a particular set of electoral circumstances. Yet, we also know that the trend *was* at least partly or temporarily reversed in the 2006 election, as turnout rose from the historic low point of 60.5 percent recorded in the 2004 election to 64.9 percent in 2006. The increase in turnout in the most recent election is more than a trivial one, and it represents a hopeful sign that turnout need not necessarily keep going down further with every election. It is true that, by historical standards, turnout in Canadian elections is still well below the levels that were routinely recorded during the seventies and eighties. But any sign that the turnout decline may be reversing should be welcomed by those who are concerned that declining turnout represents part of a growing democratic deficit in Canada and other Western democracies.

Figure 2
Turnout in six countries (last five elections)

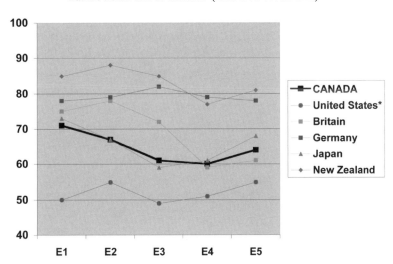

* Percentage of voting age population voting in presidential elections in United States.
  All others are percentage of registered voters in parliamentary elections.

In fact, it is entirely possible that the modest increase in turnout recorded in the 2006 federal election in Canada represents more than merely a blip in a trend that has generally been viewed with considerable pessimism. Recent elections that have taken place in several other countries have likewise seen either a modest reversal or a flattening of the longer-term pattern of turnout decline. In Britain, where a steep decline to a historic low of 59.4 percent occurred in 2001, turnout recovered slightly to 61.5 percent in the 2005 election (Figure 2). A more substantial increase in turnout also took place in the most recent U.S. presidential election, likewise following a period of sustained (if more uneven) decline.[12] Elections in the past year in Japan and New Zealand also saw increases in voting turnout, in both instances following upon a longer period of decline. Among the six countries compared in Figure 2, only Germany shows the turnout decline continuing into its most recent (2005) election. But in the German case, the turnout decline has been slight, and at 77.7 percent in the most recent election, the participation rate was considerably higher than Canada's. Among the countries compared in Figure 2, only New Zealand (80.9 percent) is higher, although it too has experienced a decline from the levels of a decade earlier.

As in Canada, we cannot tell whether the modest reversal in a pattern of declining turnout that has taken place is specific to a particular election or if the increase in turnout can be sustained over a longer period of time. In several of the countries compared in Figure 2, arguments similar to those that we have examined here appear plausible. The last U.S. presidential election was highly competitive and also saw extensive voter mobilization efforts by the political parties, local electoral authorities, and other interested groups. In Britain, the Electoral Commission has conducted extensive publicity campaigns directed at involving young people in particular in the electoral process.[13] Similar efforts by the electoral authorities, political parties, NGOs, media, and other interested groups may well be having an effect that is capable of being sustained beyond one election. Civic education programs, where these have been pursued, may gradually begin to engage young voters.[14] Mock elections, conducted in many high schools, were much in evidence during the recent federal election, and a number of Elections Canada's efforts to increase voting turnout were particularly directed at young people. As political scientist Mark Franklin has argued, getting newly eligible voters to participate in one election might be the key to developing the habit of voting over the life cycle. If these efforts are indeed successful over time, one might expect to see at least a slowing of the turnout decline followed by a modest reversal. The effects would be gradual, but they would be sustained.

To the extent that some of the reversal of the turnout decline is attributable to the emergence of a more competitive politics, the prognosis is more uncertain. The fact that one election is more competitive, or the outcome more uncertain, does not in itself mean that the next one will be. However, in Canada, the defeat of the Liberals and the emergence of a conservative party capable of winning an election suggest that the federal political arena will be more competitive for some years ahead. Thus, to the extent that this election result will send a strong signal to potential voters that elections matter, the increase in turnout that occurred in 2006 could well carry forward into the future.

However, the argument that the 2006 election was more competitive than the three preceding elections does not apply at the constituency level. As noted earlier, there has been little change from one election to the next in the degree of competition between candidates at the riding level, and the average margin of victory for winning candidates in 2006 was little different than in the previous election. In our parliamentary democracy, it is the degree of competitiveness at the constituency level that matters most, because it is only at that level that a person's vote can make a difference. Unlike U.S. presidential elections, in which voters can split a ticket, Canadian voters have only a single vote to cast and that vote must be cast for a candidate running in a local constituency.

The 2006 election campaign brought many appeals for strategic voting by parties and party leaders, and in some instances these may have had some effect on voting choice.[15] But strategic voting, however justified, is inherently frustrating for the voter. For it to be effective, voters must not only estimate the competitive situation at the constituency level with some accuracy but also be willing to cast a vote for a candidate or party who is not their true preference in order to (hypothetically) prevent someone else from being elected. When political scientist André Blais asks the question "Why is there not more strategic voting in Canadian plurality rule elections?" the answer might well be straightforward from the voter's perspective.[16] It can sometimes be much simpler, and more satisfying, to decide not to vote at all when there is no one to vote *for*.

While some have proposed measures such as simpler voting procedures, Sunday voting, postal ballots, or programs of civic education as potential solutions to the turnout decline, others have focused on the electoral system itself. In our 2000 survey of non-voters conducted for Elections Canada, we found that Canadians generally were receptive to the idea of electoral reform, although this does not necessarily mean that they would vote for such a change in a referendum if the choice were presented to them directly.[17] It is more than coincidental, however, that, in the comparison of turnout trends shown in Figure 2, the two countries that have consistently shown the highest turnout (and the smallest declines) are those with proportional voting systems.[18] In systems structured along these lines, voters do not face the unhappy choice of voting for candidates that they do not want in order to make their vote count. In Canada, the turnout decline, together with the frustration felt by voters in making their votes effective in an often uncompetitive political system, has given considerable impetus to the electoral reform movement in recent years. While turnout may have gone up in 2006, there is nothing in the outcome of this election that is likely to reduce these pressures in the near future, even if the aggregate result was more uncertain and the election outcome more exciting.

The so-called Emerson affair, occurring shortly after the 2006 federal election, illustrates graphically some of the many anomalies that can occur under our first-past-the-post electoral system and the ways in which these might over time impact negatively on turnout. When David Emerson changed political parties to join the Conservative cabinet only a few days after having been re-elected as a Liberal candidate in Vancouver Kingsway, many voters in that constituency understandably felt betrayed. Some of those may have been strategic voters who supported Emerson specifically to *prevent* the election of a Conservative. Others were undoubtedly sincere voters seeking to support the re-election of the Liberal government. In both cases, the votes of more than twenty thousand citizens in that riding were effectively miscounted, at least in partisan or strategic terms. The Vancouver Kingsway case, whatever its longer-term significance, could strengthen the case for electoral reform in Canada, or alternatively it may contribute further to the trend towards non-voting.

CONCLUSION

The reversal of the turnout decline in 2006 is good news for those who have been concerned about the health of Canadian electoral democracy, but it is at best a small step in a more positive direction. It is possible that the emergence of a more competitive political system, both nationally and at the level of the constituency where it most affects the voter, may help to sustain the modest trend towards higher turnout in the 2006 election. It is also quite possible that some of the measures that have been directed at reversing the turnout decline in recent years are beginning to have some effects. However, the forces that have contributed to the decline over the past decade are powerful ones, and they will not easily be reversed over the longer term. Some of these are demographic, and like most powerful demographic trends, they play themselves out over a considerable period of time. Others are systemic, embedded in the nature of our electoral institutions, which have become increasingly dysfunctional for citizens seeking to have their voices heard and their votes counted. The winter election of 2006 did not bring the lower turnout that many observers of past trends might have expected. But neither did it resolve the many problems that have contributed to the turnout decline in recent years. For students of politics, the future will provide an empirical test of many of the arguments advanced here. Both in Canada and elsewhere, the turnout decline, its causes and consequences, and its possible reversal, will remain a subject of the highest importance.

NOTES

1   Jon H. Pammett and Lawrence LeDuc, *Explaining the Turnout Decline in Canadian Federal Elections: A New Survey of Non-voters* (Ottawa: Elections Canada, 2003).

2   Jon H. Pammett and Lawrence LeDuc, "Four Vicious Circles of Turnout: Competitiveness, Regionalization, Culture and Participation in Canada," paper presented to the European Consortium of Political Research Joint Sessions Workshops, Uppsala, Sweden, April 14–18, 2004.

3   The first two elections — those of 1867 and 1872 — are excluded from consideration here because voting took place over a period of several months.

4   *Globe and Mail*, January 24, 2006, A8.

5   See the articles in Herman Bakvis, ed., *Voter Turnout in Canada* (Toronto: Dundurn Press, 1991).

6   Pammett and LeDuc, "Four Vicious Circles."

7   Pammett and LeDuc, *Explaining the Turnout Decline*. See also André Blais, Elisabeth Gidengil, Richard Nadeau, and Neil Nevitte, *Anatomy of a Liberal Victory: Making Sense of the Vote in the 2000 Canadian Election* (Toronto: Broadview, 2002), Chapter 3; Jon H. Pammett and Lawrence LeDuc, "Behind the Turnout Decline," in *The Canadian General Election of 2004*, ed. Jon H. Pammett and Christopher Dornan (Toronto: Dundurn Press, 2004).

8   Pammett and LeDuc, "Behind the Turnout Decline," 349–50.

9   Pammett and LeDuc, *Explaining the Turnout Decline*, 17.

10 Some Canadian evidence is presented in Pammett and LeDuc, "Four Vicious Circles." For multinational evidence, see Mark Franklin, *Voter Turnout and the Dynamics of Electoral Competition in Established Democracies Since 1945* (Cambridge: Cambridge University Press, 2004).

11 Pammett and LeDuc, "Behind the Turnout Decline," 352.

12 There are different methods of reporting turnout in the United States, which has no national voters list. Here, we use the simplest method, which bases turnout on the total of "voting age" population as registered by the census. Other methods that attempt to correct this calculation by removing certain groups of people not eligible to vote will often show a higher percentage turnout figure. On turnout in the 2004 U.S. presidential election, see Paul Abramson, John Aldrich, and David Rohde, *Change and Continuity in the 2004 Elections* (Washington: CQ Press, 2006), Chapter 4.

13 U.K. Electoral Commission, *The Youth Democracy Report*, 2004. See also International Institute for Democracy and Electoral Assistance, *Youth Voter Participation: Involving Today's Young in Tomorrow's Democracy*, 1999.

14 On this topic, see Orit Ichilov, ed., *Political Socialization, Education and Democracy* (NY: Teachers' College Press, 1990). See also Henry Milner, *Civic Literacy: How Informed Citizens Make Democracy Work* (Hanover, NH: University Press of New England, 2002).

15 On the issue of strategic voting more generally, see Blais et al, *Anatomy of a Liberal Victory*, Chapter 13.

16 André Blais, "Why Is There Not More Strategic Voting in Canadian Plurality Rule Elections?" *Political Studies* 50 (2002): 445–55.

17 About 71 percent of the entire sample (including both voters and non-voters) indicated that they would be supportive of a change to proportional representation. Pammett and LeDuc, *Explaining the Turnout Decline*, 47–9.

18 Both Germany and New Zealand use a mixed member proportional system, in which some members are elected from constituencies and others proportionally from party lists. For a discussion of these issues as they might apply in Canada, as well as other comparisons, see Henry Milner, ed., *Making Every Vote Count* (Toronto: Broadview, 1999). On the relationship between voting turnout and electoral system type, see Andre Blais and Agnieszka Dobryzynska, "Turnout in Electoral Democracies," *European Journal of Political Research* 33 (1998): 239–61.

KEY TO APPENDICES

BQ	Bloc Québécois
CA	Canadian Action Party
CHP	Christian Heritage Party
Comm	Communist Party
Cons	Conservative Party
GP	Green Party
IND	Independent
Liberal	Liberal Party
Libert	Libertarian Party
MP	Marijuana Party
ML	Marxist-Leninist Party
NDP	New Democratic Party
No Affiliation	
PCP	Progressive Canadian Party

APPENDIX A: Results of the 39th Federal Election by Percentage of Votes and Number of Seats Each Party Received

	Canada		AB		BC		MB		NB		NL		NT		NS		NU		ON		PE		QC		SK		YT	
	# seats	% votes	# seats	% votes	# seats	% votes	# seats	% votes	# seats	% votes	# seats	% votes	# seats	% votes	# seats	% votes	# seats	% votes	# seats	% votes	# seats	% votes	# seats	% votes	# seats	% votes	# seats	% votes
BQ	51	10.5																					51	42.1				
CA	0	0	0	0.1	0	0.1	0	0	0	0	0	0							0	0			0	0				
CHP	0	0.2	0	0.2	0	0.2	0	0.6	0	0					0	0.3			0	0.3	0	0.1	0	0	0	0.2	0	0.9
Comm	0	0	0	0	0	0	0	0.1											0	0			0	0	0	0		
Cons	124	36.3	28	65	17	37.3	8	42.8	3	35.8	3	42.7	0	19.8	3	29.7	0	29.6	40	35.1	0	33.4	10	24.6	12	48.9	0	23.7
GP	0	4.5	0	6.6	0	5.3	0	3.9	0	2.4	0	0.9	0	2.3	0	2.6	0	5.9	0	4.7	0	3.9	0	4	0	3.2	0	4
IND	1	0.5	0	1	1	0.6	0	1.1	0	0.7	0	0	0	0.9	0	0.3	0	0	0	0.2	0	0.3	1	0.9	0	0.2		
Liberal	103	30.24	0	15.3	9	27.6	3	26	6	39.2	4	42.8	0	34.9	6	37.2	1	39.1	54	39.9	4	52.5	13	20.7	2	22.4	1	48.5
Libert	0	0			0	0.1													0	0			0	0.1				
MP	0	0.1	0	0	0	0.1	0	0	0	0					0	0.1	0	7.8	0	0.1	0	0.3	0	0.1			0	2.4
ML	0	0.1	0	0	0	0.1									0	0.1			0	0.1			0	0.1				
NDP	29	17.5	0	11.7	10	28.6	3	25.4	1	21.9	0	13.6	1	42.1	2	29.8	0	17.6	12	19.4	0	9.6	0	7.5	0	24	0	23.9
No Affiliation	0	0	0	0	0	1													0	0					0	0.1		
PCP	0	0.1	0	0											0	0.3			0	0.2				0.1				
	308		28		37		14		10		7		1		11		1		106		4		75		14		1	

APPENDIX B

Percentage of Votes Received by Constituency

NEWFOUNDLAND

AVALON
CONS	51.6
LIB	38.6
NDP	9.1
GP	0.8

BONAVISTA–GANDER–GRAND FALLS–WINDSOR
LIB	52.0
CONS	40.3
NDP	7.0
GP	0.7

HUMBER–ST. BARBE–BAIE VERTE
LIB	52.9
CONS	31.2
NDP	14.9
GP	1.0

LABRADOR
LIB	50.5
CONS	39.7
NDP	9.1
GP	0.7

RANDOM–BURIN–ST. GEORGE'S
LIB	45.5
CONS	40.8
NDP	12.3
GP	1.4

ST. JOHN'S EAST
CONS	46.6
LIB	34.9
NDP	17.5
GP	1.0

ST. JOHN'S SOUTH–MOUNT PEARL
CONS	44.7
LIB	33.0
NDP	21.7
GP	0.6

PRINCE EDWARD ISLAND

CARDIGAN
LIB	56.2
CONS	33.7
NDP	7.5
GP	2.6

CHARLOTTETOWN
LIB	50.2
CONS	34.1
NDP	11.1
GP	3.1
MP	1.0
CHP	0.5

EGMONT
LIB	53.2
CONS	31.0
NDP	9.5
GP	5.2
IND	1.1

MALPEQUE

LIB	50.5
CONS	34.6
NDP	10.2
GP	4.7

NOVA SCOTIA

CAPE BRETON–CANSO

LIB	53.2
CONS	24.2
NDP	20.1
GP	2.5

CENTRAL NOVA

CONS	40.7
NDP	32.9
LIB	24.6
GP	1.6
ML	0.3

DARTMOUTH–COLE HARBOUR

LIB	42.3
NDP	32.5
CONS	22.8
GP	2.2
ML	0.1

HALIFAX

NDP	46.9
LIB	30.9
CONS	18.0
GP	3.9
ML	0.3

HALIFAX WEST

LIB	49.4
NDP	24.4
CONS	23.0
GP	3.2

KINGS–HANTS

LIB	45.6
CONS	32.2
NDP	19.0
GP	2.2
MP	1.0

CUMBERLAND–COLCHESTER–MUSQUODOBOIT VALLEY

CONS	52.0
LIB	23.9
NDP	20.7
GP	2.1
IND	1.2

SACKVILLE–EASTERN SHORE

NDP	52.9
LIB	23.0
CONS	21.9
GP	2.2

SOUTH SHORE–ST. MARGARET'S

CONS	36.8
NDP	28.5
LIB	28.4
CHP	3.4
GP	2.9

SYDNEY–VICTORIA

LIB	49.9
NDP	28.5
CONS	18.3
GP	3.3

WEST NOVA

LIB	39.2
CONS	38.1
NDP	18.8
GP	2.3
IND	1.5

NEW BRUNSWICK

ACADIE–BATHURST

NDP	49.9
LIB	30.7
CONS	16.9
GP	1.4
IND	0.7
IND	0.4

BEAUSÉJOUR

LIB	47.5
CONS	32.2
NDP	16.7
GP	2.8
IND	0.8

FREDERICTON

LIB	41.8
CONS	34.7
NDP	21.2
GP	1.9
IND	0.4

FUNDY ROYAL

CONS	48.3
LIB	27.3
NDP	21.1
GP	3.3

MADAWASKA–RESTIGOUCHE

LIB	38.0
CONS	35.6
NDP	23.0
GP	3.4

MIRAMICHI

LIB	42.3
CONS	34.1
NDP	16.9
IND	5.0
GP	1.8

MONCTON–RIVERVIEW–DIEPPE

LIB	47.7
CONS	30.1
NDP	18.9
GP	2.9
CA	0.3

NEW BRUNSWICK SOUTHWEST

CONS	54.8
LIB	26.8
NDP	15.6
GP	2.8

SAINT JOHN

LIB	42.9
CONS	39.3
NDP	15.6
GP	2.1

TOBIQUE–MACTAQUAC

CONS	43.8
LIB	42.9
NDP	11.5
GP	1.9

QUEBEC

ABITIBI–TÉMISCAMINGUE

BQ	52.3
CONS	22.6
LIB	13.8
NDP	8.5
GP	2.7

AHUNTSIC

BQ	38.9
LIB	37.2
CONS	12.3
NDP	7.9
GP	3.7

ALFRED-PELLAN

BQ	43.0
LIB	27.6
CONS	18.9
NDP	7.1
GP	3.4

ARGENTEUIL–PAPINEAU–MIRABEL

BQ	52.1
CONS	23.3
LIB	13.4
NDP	6.5
GP	4.6

BEAUCE

CONS	67.0
BQ	20.0
LIB	7.9
NDP	2.6
GP	2.5

BEAUHARNOIS–SALABERRY

BQ	47.5
CONS	26.5
LIB	15.0
NDP	7.6
GP	3.4

BEAUPORT–LIMOILOU

CONS	39.5
BQ	37.9
LIB	10.0
NDP	8.0
GP	4.1
ML	0.5

BERTHIER–MASKINONGÉ

BQ	48.5
CONS	31.4
LIB	10.4
NDP	6.1
GP	3.6

BOURASSA

LIB	43.4
BQ	32.0
CONS	15.8
NDP	5.2
GP	3.2
ML	0.4

BROME–MISSISQUOI

BQ	38.3
LIB	28.0
CONS	20.4
NDP	5.9
PCP	4.0
GP	3.5

BROSSARD–LA PRAIRIE

BQ	37.2
LIB	35.0
CONS	16.9
NDP	7.5
GP	3.3
ML	0.2

CHAMBLY–BORDUAS

BQ	54.7
CONS	20.6
LIB	11.3
NDP	8.4
GP	5.1

CHARLESBOURG–HAUTE-SAINT-CHARLES

CONS	41.0
BQ	38.3
LIB	8.8
NDP	6.2
IND	3.2
GP	2.5

MONTMORENCY–CHARLEVOIX–HAUTE-CÔTE-NORD

BQ	49.1
CONS	32.3
LIB	8.8
NDP	6.4
GP	3.4

CHÂTEAUGUAY–SAINT-CONSTANT

BQ	51.4
CONS	20.4
LIB	18.7
NDP	5.2
GP	4.3

CHICOUTIMI–LE FJORD

BQ	38.5
LIB	29.2
CONS	24.7
NDP	5.1
GP	2.5

COMPTON–STANSTEAD

BQ	42.8
CONS	24.3
LIB	22.3
NDP	6.2
GP	4.4

DRUMMOND

BQ	49.7
CONS	22.3
LIB	16.4
NDP	6.3
GP	5.3

GASPÉSIE–ÎLES-DE-LA-MADELEINE

BQ	42.7
CONS	32.2
LIB	19.3
NDP	3.0
GP	2.9

GATINEAU

BQ	39.2
LIB	31.3
CONS	16.8
NDP	10.0
GP	2.7

HOCHELAGA

BQ	55.6
LIB	17.2
CONS	12.2
NDP	8.9
GP	4.9
MP	0.7
ML	0.5

HONORÉ-MERCIER

LIB	38.2
BQ	34.8
CONS	17.4
NDP	6.2
GP	2.9
ML	0.4

HULL–AYLMER

LIB	32.7
BQ	29.3
CONS	17.3
NDP	15.5
GP	5.0
ML	0.2

JEANNE-LE BER

BQ	40.2
LIB	34.1
CONS	11.8
NDP	9.2
GP	4.7

JOLIETTE

BQ	54.1
CONS	26.8
LIB	9.9
NDP	5.2
GP	3.9

JONQUIÈRE–ALMA

CONS	52.1
BQ	39.3
NDP	3.9
LIB	3.0
GP	1.8

LAC-SAINT-LOUIS

LIB	48.2
CONS	26.7
NDP	10.7
BQ	7.7
GP	6.8

LA POINTE-DE-L'ÎLE

BQ	60.5
CONS	15.2
LIB	14.1
NDP	7.0
GP	3.2

LASALLE–ÉMARD

LIB	48.4
BQ	28.7
CONS	12.8
NDP	6.0
GP	3.2
IND	0.6
ML	0.3

LAURENTIDES–LABELLE

BQ	53.8
CONS	20.3
LIB	14.5
NDP	6.5
GP	4.9

LAURIER–SAINTE-MARIE

BQ	54.7
NDP	16.7
LIB	12.5
GP	8.3
CONS	6.4
MP	0.7
IND	0.3
ML	0.3
COMM	0.2

LAVAL

BQ	44.3
LIB	25.6
CONS	18.6
NDP	8.1
GP	3.4

LAVAL–LES ÎLES

LIB	39.3
BQ	33.1
CONS	17.1
NDP	7.2
GP	2.9
ML	0.4

LÉVIS–BELLECHASSE

CONS	46.4
BQ	29.0
LIB	8.2
IND	7.6
NDP	4.6
GP	4.1

LONGUEUIL–PIERRE-BOUCHER

BQ	55.2
CONS	18.8
LIB	12.6
NDP	8.6
GP	4.0
MP	0.8

LOTBINIÈRE–CHUTES-DE-LA-CHAUDIÈRE

CONS	54.3
BQ	29.6
NDP	6.8
LIB	5.4
GP	3.8

LOUIS-HÉBERT

CONS	34.5
BQ	34.1
LIB	15.0
NDP	9.1
GP	4.3
IND	1.9
IND	1.0
CHP	0.2

LOUIS-SAINT-LAURENT

CONS	57.7
BQ	24.2
LIB	6.4
NDP	5.7
IND	3.0
GP	3.0

MANICOUAGAN

BQ	51.1
CONS	19.0
LIB	14.3
NDP	12.8
GP	2.3
IND	0.5

MARC-AURÈLE-FORTIN

BQ	51.0
CONS	20.5
LIB	15.5
NDP	8.0
GP	5.0

HAUTE-GASPÉSIE–LA MITIS–MATANE–MATAPÉDIA

BQ	46.0
CONS	29.7
LIB	13.1
NDP	6.2
GP	2.7
IND	2.3

MÉGANTIC–L'ÉRABLE

CONS	49.8
BQ	32.6
LIB	10.4
NDP	3.9
GP	3.2

MONTCALM

BQ	62.3
CONS	19.3
LIB	8.3
NDP	6.7
GP	3.5

MOUNT ROYAL

LIB	65.6
CONS	17.9
NDP	6.7
BQ	5.7
GP	3.8
ML	0.3

NOTRE-DAME-DE-GRÂCE–LACHINE

LIB	43.8
BQ	20.3
CONS	17.4
NDP	11.8
GP	6.0
LIBERT	0.3
ML	0.3

ABITIBI–BAIE-JAMES–NUNAVIK–EEYOU

BQ	46.6
LIB	22.4
CONS	20.9
NDP	6.1
GP	4.0

OUTREMONT

LIB	35.2
BQ	29.0
NDP	17.2
CONS	12.7
GP	4.8
IND	0.2
PCP	0.2
ML	0.2
IND	0.2
IND	0.1
IND	0.1

PAPINEAU

BQ	40.7
LIB	38.5
CONS	8.3
NDP	7.7
GP	3.6
ML	0.7
CA	0.4

PIERREFONDS–DOLLARD

LIB	51.1
CONS	23.1
BQ	12.4
NDP	7.7
GP	5.5
ML	0.2

PONTIAC

CONS	33.7
BQ	28.7
LIB	24.2
NDP	10.0
GP	3.2
ML	0.2

PORTNEUF–JACQUES-CARTIER

IND	39.8
BQ	25.9
CONS	22.7
LIB	4.9
NDP	3.9
GP	2.8

QUÉBEC

BQ	41.5
CONS	29.8
LIB	11.4
NDP	9.2
GP	4.7
IND	1.6
PCP	1.0
LIBERT	0.6

REPENTIGNY

BQ	62.4
CONS	18.1
LIB	8.7
NDP	7.7
GP	3.1

BAS-RICHELIEU–NICOLET–BÉCANCOUR

BQ	55.9
CONS	23.4
LIB	13.0
NDP	4.5
GP	3.2

RICHMOND–ARTHABASKA

BQ	47.9
CONS	32.2
LIB	10.4
NDP	4.9
GP	4.6

RIMOUSKI-NEIGETTE–TÉMISCOUATA–LES BASQUES

BQ	46.4
CONS	22.2
LIB	19.3
NDP	9.8
GP	2.3

RIVIÈRE-DES-MILLE-ÎLES

BQ	53.9
CONS	20.9
LIB	12.8
NDP	7.0
GP	5.4

MONTMAGNY–L'ISLET–KAMOURASKA–RIVIÈRE-DU-LOUP

BQ	52.4
CONS	25.1
LIB	14.1
NDP	4.6
GP	3.8

RIVIÈRE-DU-NORD

BQ	59.1
CONS	20.8
LIB	9.3
NDP	7.2
GP	3.7

ROBERVAL–LAC-SAINT-JEAN

BQ	45.2
CONS	37.2
LIB	7.7
NDP	5.5
GP	4.3

ROSEMONT–LA PETITE-PATRIE

BQ	56.0
LIB	15.8
NDP	11.5
CONS	9.3
GP	6.6
MP	0.8

SAINT-BRUNO–SAINT-HUBERT

BQ	50.3
CONS	19.8
LIB	16.4
NDP	8.3
GP	4.5
IND	0.7

SAINT-HYACINTHE–BAGOT

BQ	56.0
CONS	24.8
LIB	9.8
NDP	5.5
GP	3.9

SAINT-JEAN

BQ	54.0
CONS	22.1
LIB	12.4
NDP	7.0
GP	4.6

SAINT-LAMBERT

BQ	45.3
LIB	23.3
CONS	19.7
NDP	7.4
GP	3.9
ML	0.4

SAINT-LAURENT–CARTIERVILLE

LIB	59.8
BQ	14.6
CONS	13.2
NDP	7.7
GP	4.3
ML	0.4

SAINT-LÉONARD–SAINT-MICHEL

LIB	57.2
BQ	18.7
CONS	14.4
NDP	6.8
GP	2.3
ML	0.5

SAINT-MAURICE–CHAMPLAIN

BQ	44.3
CONS	33.0
LIB	11.6
NDP	7.6
GP	3.5

SHEFFORD

BQ	43.1
CONS	24.8
LIB	23.4
NDP	4.7
GP	4.0

SHERBROOKE

BQ	52.2
CONS	20.7
LIB	13.2
NDP	8.9
GP	4.3
IND	0.6

TERREBONNE–BLAINVILLE

BQ	59.2
CONS	20.0
LIB	9.0
NDP	7.5
GP	4.3

TROIS-RIVIÈRES

BQ	45.9
CONS	31.7
LIB	10.8
NDP	7.8
GP	3.1
MP	0.8

VAUDREUIL-SOULANGES

BQ	43.1
LIB	28.4
CONS	19.0
NDP	5.5
GP	3.9

VERCHÈRES–LES PATRIOTES

BQ	57.4
CONS	21.8
LIB	8.7
NDP	8.2
GP	3.9

WESTMOUNT–VILLE-MARIE

LIB	45.7
CONS	17.6
NDP	15.4
BQ	12.6
GP	8.3
ML	0.2
COMM	0.2

ONTARIO

AJAX–PICKERING

LIB	49.4
CONS	32.7
NDP	12.8
GP	4.2
CHP	0.8

ALGOMA–MANITOULIN–KAPUSKASING

LIB	38.2
NDP	34.5
CONS	23.3
GP	2.7
FPNP	0.9
IND	0.4

ANCASTER–DUNDAS–
FLAMBOROUGH–WESTDALE
CONS	39.1
LIB	34.5
NDP	21.3
GP	4.4
IND	0.5
ML	0.2

BARRIE
CONS	41.9
LIB	39.2
NDP	12.2
GP	6.8

BEACHES–EAST YORK
LIB	40.4
NDP	35.0
CONS	18.0
GP	6.1
PCP	0.4
ML	0.2

BRAMALEA–GORE–MALTON
LIB	50.7
CONS	32.7
NDP	12.7
GP	3.4
ML	0.5

BRAMPTON–SPRINGDALE
LIB	47.3
CONS	30.8
NDP	17.7
GP	3.9
COMM	0.2

BRAMPTON WEST
LIB	49.1
CONS	35.7
NDP	11.1
GP	4.1

BRANT
LIB	36.9
CONS	36.0
NDP	21.3
GP	4.6
CHP	0.9
IND	0.4

BURLINGTON
CONS	43.1
LIB	39.1
NDP	12.4
GP	5.3

CAMBRIDGE
CONS	43.8
LIB	33.6
NDP	16.9
GP	5.2
CA	0.4

CARLETON–MISSISSIPPI MILLS
CONS	56.2
LIB	23.6
NDP	12.5
GP	6.5
MP	0.6
PCP	0.6

CHATHAM-KENT–ESSEX
CONS	42.8
LIB	31.3
NDP	22.4
GP	3.6

DURHAM
CONS	47.0
LIB	30.0
NDP	17.3
GP	4.6
CHP	1.1

DAVENPORT
LIB	51.9
NDP	32.6
CONS	10.8
GP	3.7
COMM	0.4
CA	0.3
ML	0.3

DON VALLEY EAST
LIB	54.0
CONS	29.2
NDP	12.9
GP	3.9

DON VALLEY WEST

LIB	53.4
CONS	33.3
NDP	9.1
GP	3.5
LIBERT	0.4
CA	0.3

DUFFERIN–CALEDON

CONS	47.9
LIB	30.0
NDP	12.1
GP	10.0

EGLINTON–LAWRENCE

LIB	52.9
CONS	30.3
NDP	11.5
GP	5.1
NO AFFILIATION	0.2

ELGIN–MIDDLESEX–LONDON

CONS	45.6
LIB	26.3
NDP	19.2
GP	5.6
CHP	2.0
PCP	1.0
CA	0.2

ESSEX

CONS	40.4
LIB	34.1
NDP	22.7
GP	2.6
ML	0.2

ETOBICOKE CENTRE

LIB	52.4
CONS	33.2
NDP	9.6
GP	3.8
PCP	0.7
ML	0.2

ETOBICOKE–LAKESHORE

LIB	43.6
CONS	35.2
NDP	15.6
GP	5.1
COMM	0.3
ML	0.2

ETOBICOKE NORTH

LIB	61.6
CONS	22.3
NDP	10.6
GP	2.6
PCP	1.5
IND	0.8
ML	0.6

GLENGARRY–PRESCOTT–RUSSELL

CONS	41.6
LIB	41.2
NDP	12.7
GP	4.5

BRUCE–GREY–OWEN SOUND

CONS	48.2
LIB	27.6
GP	12.9
NDP	11.3

GUELPH

LIB	38.4
CONS	29.8
NDP	22.0
GP	8.7
CHP	0.9
COMM	0.2
ML	0.1

HALDIMAND–NORFOLK

CONS	48.3
LIB	34.3
NDP	12.8
GP	3.5
CHP	1.0

HALIBURTON–KAWARTHA LAKES–BROCK

CONS	49.0
LIB	28.8
NDP	17.2
GP	5.0

HALTON

CONS	44.2
LIB	41.4
NDP	8.8
GP	5.6

HAMILTON CENTRE

NDP	51.3
LIB	23.5
CONS	20.3
GP	4.2
CA	0.7

HAMILTON EAST–STONEY CREEK

NDP	36.0
LIB	35.2
CONS	25.3
GP	2.9
COMM	0.6

HAMILTON MOUNTAIN

NDP	37.4
LIB	31.9
CONS	27.1
GP	2.6
CHP	0.8
ML	0.2

HURON–BRUCE

LIB	39.8
CONS	38.0
NDP	16.3
GP	3.4
CHP	1.9
IND	0.5

KENORA

LIB	36.5
CONS	31.0
NDP	29.9
GP	2.5

KINGSTON AND THE ISLANDS

LIB	45.9
CONS	26.1
NDP	19.2
GP	8.0
IND	0.5
CA	0.4

KITCHENER CENTRE

LIB	43.3
CONS	32.1
NDP	18.4
GP	5.6
COMM	0.5

KITCHENER–CONESTOGA

CONS	41.2
LIB	38.5
NDP	14.9
GP	5.4

KITCHENER–WATERLOO

LIB	46.9
CONS	28.3
NDP	17.9
GP	6.5
IND	0.3
ML	0.2

LANARK–FRONTENAC–LENNOX AND ADDINGTON

CONS	51.1
LIB	24.7
NDP	16.2
GP	5.2
PCP	1.2
MP	0.8
CA	0.7

LEEDS–GRENVILLE

CONS	54.6
LIB	24.3
NDP	15.3
GP	5.8

LONDON–FANSHAWE

NDP	34.5
LIB	32.6
CONS	29.0
GP	3.9

LONDON NORTH CENTRE

LIB	40.1
CONS	29.9
NDP	23.7
GP	5.5
PCP	0.5
ML	0.3

LONDON WEST

LIB	37.7
CONS	35.5
NDP	21.4
GP	4.8
PCP	0.5
ML	0.1

MARKHAM–UNIONVILLE

LIB	61.9
CONS	26.7
NDP	8.0
GP	2.2
PCP	0.6
IND	0.6

LAMBTON–KENT–MIDDLESEX

CONS	46.4
LIB	31.0
NDP	17.2
GP	4.0
CHP	1.5

MISSISSAUGA–BRAMPTON SOUTH

LIB	53.9
CONS	30.8
NDP	10.9
GP	3.8
ML	0.6

MISSISSAUGA EAST–COOKSVILLE

LIB	51.7
CONS	31.4
NDP	11.4
GP	3.1
IND	1.1
CHP	1.0
ML	0.4

MISSISSAUGA–ERINDALE

LIB	44.8
CONS	39.3
NDP	11.1
GP	4.4
IND	0.5

MISSISSAUGA SOUTH

LIB	44.2
CONS	40.1
NDP	10.8
GP	4.6
CA	0.2
ML	0.1

MISSISSAUGA–STREETSVILLE

LIB	45.9
CONS	34.8
NDP	13.3
GP	4.5
PCP	1.4

NEPEAN–CARLETON

CONS	55.0
LIB	28.0
NDP	11.5
GP	5.5

NEWMARKET–AURORA

LIB	46.2
CONS	38.0
NDP	9.6
GP	4.8
PCP	1.2
CA	0.1

NIAGARA FALLS

CONS	40.4
LIB	34.5
NDP	21.0
GP	4.1

NIAGARA WEST–GLANBROOK

CONS	47.4
LIB	30.7
NDP	16.0
GP	4.0
CHP	2.0

NICKEL BELT

LIB	43.3
NDP	38.7
CONS	12.6
PCP	2.3
GP	2.1
MP	0.9
ML	0.1

NIPISSING–TIMISKAMING

LIB	44.7
CONS	34.5
NDP	17.3
GP	3.5

NORTHUMBERLAND–QUINTE WEST

CONS	41.2
LIB	36.0
NDP	18.1
GP	4.7

OAK RIDGES–MARKHAM

LIB	47.1
CONS	38.5
NDP	9.9
GP	4.6

OAKVILLE

LIB	43.4
CONS	42.1
NDP	9.7
GP	4.8
CONS	38.6
NDP	33.5
LIB	24.0
GP	3.8
ML	0.2

OTTAWA CENTRE

NDP	36.9
LIB	29.2
CONS	22.7
GP	10.2
MP	0.6
IND	0.2
COMM	0.2
ML	0.1

OTTAWA–ORLÉANS

CONS	41.1
LIB	39.1
NDP	15.1
GP	3.8
IND	0.9

OTTAWA SOUTH

LIB	44.2
CONS	37.4
NDP	13.2
GP	4.7
PCP	0.4

OTTAWA–VANIER

LIB	42.3
CONS	28.7
NDP	21.8
GP	6.6
PCP	0.4
ML	0.2

OTTAWA WEST–NEPEAN

CONS	43.1
LIB	34.1
NDP	16.2
GP	4.9
IND	1.5
CA	0.2

OXFORD

CONS	46.5
LIB	28.1
NDP	17.4
GP	3.1
CHP	2.9
MP	1.6
LIBERT	0.4

PARKDALE–HIGH PARK

NDP	40.4
LIB	35.9
CONS	17.1
GP	5.5
MP	0.6
ML	0.2
NO AFFILIATION	0.2

PARRY SOUND–MUSKOKA

CONS	40.1
LIB	40.0
NDP	11.9
GP	8.0

PERTH–WELLINGTON

CONS	46.1
LIB	25.8
NDP	18.6
GP	6.5
CHP	2.9

PETERBOROUGH

CONS	35.9
LIB	32.4
NDP	25.7
GP	5.1
MP	0.7
IND	0.3

PICKERING–SCARBOROUGH EAST

LIB	52.7
CONS	31.7
NDP	11.6
GP	3.6
IND	0.3
CA	0.1

PRINCE EDWARD–HASTINGS

CONS	48.7
LIB	31.6
NDP	14.8
GP	4.2
IND	0.7

RENFREW–NIPISSING–PEMBROKE

CONS	57.7
LIB	24.2
NDP	12.5
GP	3.1
IND	2.5

RICHMOND HILL

LIB	53.6
CONS	31.9
NDP	10.0
GP	4.6

ST. CATHARINES

CONS	37.5
LIB	37.0
NDP	20.5
GP	4.0
CHP	0.8
ML	0.2

ST. PAUL'S

LIB	50.3
CONS	25.8
NDP	19.2
GP	4.8

SARNIA–LAMBTON

CONS	41.0
LIB	33.1
NDP	20.0
GP	3.2
CHP	2.1
IND	0.6

SAULT STE. MARIE

NDP	38.9
LIB	34.2
CONS	24.0
GP	2.3
FPNP	0.5
ML	0.1

SCARBOROUGH–AGINCOURT

LIB	62.6
CONS	23.8
NDP	11.1
GP	2.5

SCARBOROUGH CENTRE

LIB	55.4
CONS	27.3
NDP	14.0
GP	3.3

SCARBOROUGH–GUILDWOOD

LIB	53.3
CONS	28.7
NDP	14.2
GP	3.0
IND	0.4
CA	0.2
IND	0.2

SCARBOROUGH–ROUGE RIVER

LIB	65.6
CONS	20.4
NDP	10.8
GP	1.6
IND	1.0
LIBERT	0.5

SCARBOROUGH SOUTHWEST

LIB	47.8
CONS	24.0
NDP	23.1
GP	4.4
IND	0.4
COMM	0.3

SIMCOE–GREY

CONS	49.8
LIB	30.9
NDP	11.2
GP	5.6
CHP	2.6

SIMCOE NORTH

CONS	40.4
LIB	38.4
NDP	14.1
GP	6.0
CHP	1.1

STORMONT–DUNDAS–SOUTH GLENGARRY

CONS	54.7
LIB	27.2
NDP	13.5
GP	3.3
CHP	1.3

SUDBURY

LIB	41.6
NDP	32.0
CONS	21.7
GP	2.7
PCP	1.6
ML	0.2
COMM	0.1
IND	0.1

THORNHILL

LIB	53.1
CONS	33.7
NDP	7.8
GP	3.4
PCP	1.9

THUNDER BAY–RAINY RIVER

LIB	35.1
NDP	33.4
CONS	27.2
GP	3.1
MP	1.1

THUNDER BAY–SUPERIOR NORTH

LIB	36.0
NDP	35.0
CONS	22.0
GP	5.7
MP	1.2

TIMMINS–JAMES BAY

NDP	50.6
LIB	34.3
CONS	13.6
GP	1.5

TORONTO CENTRE

LIB	52.2
NDP	23.7
CONS	18.2
GP	5.2
COMM	0.2
NO AFFILIATION	0.2
AACEV PARTY OF CANADA	0.1
ML	0.1

TORONTO–DANFORTH

NDP	48.4
LIB	34.2
CONS	9.9
GP	7.1
ML	0.3

TRINITY–SPADINA

NDP	46.0
LIB	40.1
CONS	9.0
GP	3.8
PCP	0.6
ML	0.2
CA	0.1

VAUGHAN

LIB	59.7
CONS	26.0
NDP	8.3
GP	4.9
LIBERT	1.1

WELLAND

LIB	35.5
NDP	30.7
CONS	29.2
GP	3.4
CHP	0.9
ML	0.2

WELLINGTON–HALTON HILLS

CONS	50.7
LIB	29.2
NDP	12.3
GP	6.1
CHP	1.1
IND	0.6

WHITBY–OSHAWA

CONS	43.9
LIB	38.8
NDP	13.0
GP	3.6
LIBERT	0.4
CA	0.3

WILLOWDALE

LIB	55.2
CONS	29.3
NDP	11.4
GP	4.1

WINDSOR–TECUMSEH

NDP	44.6
LIB	26.4
CONS	25.3
GP	3.2
ML	0.4

WINDSOR WEST

NDP	49.5
LIB	25.4
CONS	20.1
GP	3.0
PCP	1.3
IND	0.5
ML	0.2

YORK CENTRE

LIB	52.7
CONS	30.1
NDP	13.6
GP	3.7

YORK–SIMCOE

CONS	47.9
LIB	30.7
NDP	13.3
GP	6.9
CHP	1.1

YORK SOUTH–WESTON

LIB	57.1
NDP	21.3
CONS	17.4
GP	3.8
IND	0.5

YORK WEST

LIB	63.8
CONS	18.6
NDP	14.1
GP	3.0
IND	0.6

MANITOBA

BRANDON–SOURIS

CONS	54.4
NDP	20.2
LIB	18.0
GP	4.6
IND	1.6
CHP	0.8
COMM	0.3

CHARLESWOOD–ST. JAMES–ASSINIBOIA

CONS	47.0
LIB	36.4
NDP	12.8
GP	3.8

CHURCHILL

LIB	40.7
NDP	28.4
IND	17.2
CONS	11.6
GP	1.6
IND	0.6

DAUPHIN–SWAN RIVER–MARQUETTE

CONS	59.1
NDP	18.3
LIB	18.2
GP	3.7
CHP	0.8

ELMWOOD–TRANSCONA

NDP	50.8
CONS	32.1
LIB	12.3
GP	3.6
CHP	1.1

KILDONAN–ST. PAUL

CONS	43.1
LIB	33.5
NDP	20.2
GP	2.7
IND	0.5

PORTAGE–LISGAR

CONS	69.8
LIB	11.4
NDP	11.0
GP	5.1
CHP	2.7

PROVENCHER

CONS	65.7
LIB	15.8
NDP	13.7
GP	4.8

SAINT BONIFACE

LIB	38.6
CONS	35.0
NDP	21.9
GP	3.9
CHP	0.7

SELKIRK–INTERLAKE

CONS	49.0
NDP	37.0
LIB	10.0
GP	2.9
IND	0.6
CHP	0.5

WINNIPEG CENTRE

NDP	48.4
LIB	24.3
CONS	19.5
GP	7.1
COMM	0.7

WINNIPEG NORTH

NDP	57.2
LIB	21.1
CONS	17.6
GP	2.9
CHP	0.8
COMM	0.5

WINNIPEG SOUTH

CONS	41.4
LIB	41.2
NDP	13.7
GP	3.1
CHP	0.6

WINNIPEG SOUTH CENTRE

LIB	39.2
CONS	31.5
NDP	21.8
GP	4.5
PCP	2.2
IND	0.6
CA	0.2

SASKATCHEWAN

BATTLEFORDS–LLOYDMINSTER

CONS	54.0
NDP	15.8
NO AFFILIATION	14.4
LIB	12.8
GP	2.1
CHP	1.0

BLACKSTRAP

CONS	48.0
NDP	30.6
LIB	16.9
GP	3.3
IND	1.0
COMM	0.2

DESNETHÉ–MISSINIPPI–CHURCHILL RIVER

LIB	41.4
CONS	41.1
NDP	15.4
GP	2.2

CYPRESS HILLS–GRASSLANDS

CONS	66.5
NDP	16.8
LIB	12.9
GP	3.8

PALLISER

CONS	43.0
NDP	33.0
LIB	20.2
GP	3.4
CA	0.3

PRINCE ALBERT

CONS	54.4
NDP	23.8
LIB	19.4
GP	2.3

REGINA–LUMSDEN–LAKE CENTRE

CONS	42.1
NDP	28.1
LIB	26.6
GP	3.1

REGINA–QU'APPELLE

CONS	41.2
NDP	32.4
LIB	23.1
GP	3.3

SASKATOON–HUMBOLDT

CONS	49.1
NDP	29.5
LIB	16.9
GP	3.7
IND	0.9

SASKATOON–ROSETOWN–BIGGAR

CONS	45.5
NDP	39.0
LIB	12.1
GP	2.5
CHP	0.9

SASKATOON–WANUSKEWIN

CONS	49.4
LIB	24.1
NDP	22.1
GP	3.6
CHP	0.9

SOURIS–MOOSE MOUNTAIN

CONS	62.8
LIB	18.5
NDP	14.0
GP	4.7

WASCANA

LIB	51.8
CONS	30.0
NDP	14.7
GP	3.5

YORKTON–MELVILLE
CONS	63.5
NDP	18.9
LIB	14.0
GP	2.8
IND	0.9

ALBERTA

FORT MCMURRAY–ATHABASCA
CONS	64.7
LIB	14.8
NDP	14.6
GP	4.9
FPNP	1.1

CALGARY EAST
CONS	67.1
LIB	13.6
NDP	10.9
GP	7.4
COMM	0.6
CA	0.5

CALGARY CENTRE-NORTH
CONS	56.0
NDP	16.8
LIB	13.7
GP	11.8
IND	0.7
FPNP	0.4
ML	0.3
CA	0.3

CALGARY NORTHEAST
CONS	64.9
LIB	22.1
NDP	7.8
GP	4.4
IND	0.9

CALGARY–NOSE HILL
CONS	68.5
LIB	17.1
NDP	7.9
GP	6.5

CALGARY CENTRE
CONS	55.4
LIB	19.2
NDP	13.3
GP	11.7
CA	0.5

CALGARY SOUTHEAST
CONS	75.2
LIB	10.3
NDP	7.7
GP	6.8
CONS	72.4
LIB	11.4
NDP	8.1
GP	7.7
CHP	0.5

CALGARY WEST
CONS	58.7
LIB	22.1
GP	10.3
NDP	8.3
CA	0.4
ML	0.2

CROWFOOT
CONS	82.6
NDP	7.4
LIB	5.6
GP	4.5

EDMONTON–MILL WOODS–BEAUMONT
CONS	58.6
LIB	21.1
NDP	14.6
GP	4.5
IND	1.0
COMM	0.2

EDMONTON CENTRE
CONS	44.9
LIB	38.6
NDP	10.8
GP	5.3
IND	0.4
ML	0.2

EDMONTON EAST

CONS	50.1
LIB	26.2
NDP	18.5
GP	5.2

EDMONTON–LEDUC

CONS	60.5
LIB	19.5
NDP	13.8
GP	6.2

EDMONTON–ST. ALBERT

CONS	59.7
LIB	20.3
NDP	14.0
GP	6.0

EDMONTON–SHERWOOD PARK

CONS	64.0
LIB	14.4
NDP	14.3
GP	7.4

EDMONTON–SPRUCE GROVE

CONS	66.8
LIB	16.8
NDP	10.5
GP	5.9

EDMONTON–STRATHCONA

CONS	41.7
NDP	32.5
LIB	17.8
GP	5.9
PCP	1.1
MP	0.7
ML	0.2

LETHBRIDGE

CONS	67.3
NDP	13.7
LIB	11.2
GP	3.5
CHP	2.8
IND	1.4

MACLEOD

CONS	75.5
LIB	9.2
NDP	6.5
GP	6.2
IND	2.1
CA	0.5

MEDICINE HAT

CONS	79.7
LIB	8.4
NDP	8.0
GP	3.9

PEACE RIVER

CONS	57.0
IND	20.3
NDP	11.1
LIB	9.4
GP	2.3

RED DEER

CONS	75.7
NDP	9.9
LIB	9.2
GP	5.2

VEGREVILLE–WAINWRIGHT

CONS	74.2
NDP	9.2
LIB	7.6
GP	7.5
WBP	0.8
CHP	0.7

WESTLOCK–ST. PAUL

CONS	68.2
LIB	15.0
NDP	10.0
GP	4.9
IND	1.0
IND	0.9

WETASKIWIN

CONS	75.2
NDP	9.3
LIB	9.2
GP	6.3

WILD ROSE

CONS	72.2
GP	10.8
LIB	9.7
NDP	7.3

YELLOWHEAD

CONS	71.2
NDP	10.9
LIB	9.4
GP	6.6
CHP	1.8

BRITISH COLUMBIA

ABBOTSFORD

CONS	63.3
NDP	17.0
LIB	12.7
GP	5.8
MP	0.7
CA	0.4
ML	0.2

BURNABY–DOUGLAS

NDP	35.6
LIB	33.0
CONS	27.7
GP	3.5
COMM	0.3

BURNABY–NEW WESTMINSTER

NDP	38.8
LIB	29.9
CONS	27.6
GP	3.7

CARIBOO–PRINCE GEORGE

CONS	44.9
LIB	24.1
NDP	23.2
GP	5.5
CHP	1.2
CA	0.6
ML	0.2
FPNP	0.2

CHILLIWACK–FRASER CANYON

CONS	56.0
NDP	20.9
LIB	16.9
GP	4.0
CHP	2.0
ML	0.2

DELTA–RICHMOND EAST

CONS	48.4
LIB	31.9
NDP	14.7
GP	5.0

PITT MEADOWS–MAPLE RIDGE–MISSION

CONS	40.2
NDP	35.0
LIB	20.3
GP	3.3
MP	0.6
IND	0.5
ML	0.2

ESQUIMALT–JUAN DE FUCA

LIB	34.9
NDP	31.3
CONS	27.5
GP	5.7
WBP	0.5
CA	0.1

FLEETWOOD–PORT KELLS

CONS	33.5
LIB	31.6
NDP	25.2
IND	7.4
GP	2.4

KAMLOOPS–THOMPSON–CARIBOO

CONS	39.3
NDP	30.8
LIB	25.2
GP	4.7

KELOWNA–LAKE COUNTRY

CONS	49.2
LIB	25.8
NDP	16.6
GP	8.0
CA	0.4

KOOTENAY–COLUMBIA

CONS	54.4
NDP	25.9
LIB	13.3
GP	6.1
CA	0.3

LANGLEY

CONS	52.6
LIB	23.1
NDP	18.4
GP	5.6
CA	0.4

NANAIMO–ALBERNI

CONS	41.4
NDP	32.2
LIB	19.1
GP	5.4
IND	1.5
CHP	0.2
CA	0.2
ML	0.1

NANAIMO–COWICHAN

NDP	46.8
CONS	32.1
LIB	15.3
GP	5.1
CA	0.5
ML	0.2

NEWTON–NORTH DELTA

LIB	34.2
NDP	32.0
CONS	30.6
GP	1.9
IND	0.7
COMM	0.3
IND	0.2

NEW WESTMINSTER–COQUITLAM

NDP	38.3
CONS	32.5
LIB	23.5
GP	3.0
IND	2.3
IND	0.2
ML	0.1

OKANAGAN–SHUSWAP

CONS	44.9
NDP	26.7
LIB	22.6
GP	4.1
NO AFFILIATION	0.8
IND	0.7
CA	0.3

NORTH VANCOUVER

LIB	42.3
CONS	36.8
NDP	13.2
GP	7.5
ML	0.2

OKANAGAN–COQUIHALLA

CONS	50.2
LIB	23.0
NDP	19.2
GP	7.6

PORT MOODY–WESTWOOD–PORT COQUITLAM

CONS	41.1
LIB	27.1
NDP	23.1
IND	4.8
GP	3.3
LIBERT	0.6

PRINCE GEORGE–PEACE RIVER

CONS	59.9
NDP	17.0
LIB	15.7
GP	6.4
IND	0.9

RICHMOND

LIB	42.8
CONS	38.7
NDP	14.0
GP	4.5

SAANICH–GULF ISLANDS

CONS	37.2
NDP	26.5
LIB	26.1
GP	9.9
WBP	0.3

SKEENA–BULKLEY VALLEY

NDP	48.3
CONS	33.0
LIB	12.7
CHP	3.2
GP	2.8

BRITISH COLUMBIA SOUTHERN INTERIOR

NDP	49.0
LIB	20.2
CONS	19.3
GP	11.3
ML	0.3

SOUTH SURREY–WHITE ROCK–CLOVERDALE

CONS	46.7
LIB	30.7
NDP	16.9
GP	5.3
PCP	0.5

SURREY NORTH

NDP	45.7
CONS	27.6
LIB	19.6
GP	2.7
IND	1.4
IND	1.2
CHP	1.2
PCP	0.6

VANCOUVER CENTRE

LIB	43.8
NDP	28.7
CONS	20.5
GP	5.8
LIBERT	0.5
MP	0.5
CHP	0.2

VANCOUVER EAST

NDP	56.6
LIB	23.4
CONS	13.3
GP	6.0
CA	0.7

VANCOUVER ISLAND NORTH

NDP	41.7
CONS	40.6
LIB	12.8
GP	4.8

VANCOUVER KINGSWAY

LIB	43.5
NDP	33.5
CONS	18.8
GP	2.8
LIBERT	0.6
COMM	0.4
CA	0.3
ML	0.1

VANCOUVER QUADRA

LIB	49.1
CONS	28.9
NDP	16.1
GP	5.1
IND	0.5
MP	0.3
ML	0.1

VANCOUVER SOUTH

LIB	48.0
CONS	27.1
NDP	21.1
GP	3.3
ML	0.5

VICTORIA

NDP	38.5
LIB	27.5
CONS	24.6
GP	8.1
MP	0.5
IND	0.5
WBP	0.3

WEST VANCOUVER–SUNSHINE COAST–SEA TO SKY COUNTRY

LIB	37.5
CONS	36.0
NDP	20.1
GP	6.2
ML	0.2

TERRITORIES

YUKON

LIB	48.5
NDP	23.9
CONS	23.7
GP	4.0

WESTERN ARCTIC

NDP	42.2
LIB	35.0
CONS	19.8
GP	2.1
IND	0.9

NUNAVUT

LIB	40.0
CONS	29.1
NDP	17.2
MP	7.9
GP	5.9

CONTRIBUTORS

ÉRIC BÉLANGER is an Assistant Professor in the Department of Political Science at McGill University. His research interests include political parties, public opinion, voting behaviour, as well as Canadian and Quebec politics. He has written or co-written articles published in *Comparative Political Studies*, *Electoral Studies*, the *European Journal of Political Research*, *Acta Politica*, *Publius*, *French Politics*, the *British Journal of Politics and International Relations*, the *International Journal of Public Opinion Research*, and the *Canadian Journal of Political Science*.

STEPHEN CLARKSON, who teaches political economy at the University of Toronto, has written the chapter on the Liberal Party of Canada for every federal election book since the 1974 campaign, when the series began. In October 2005, the University of British Columbia Press published his revision and compilation of these studies as *The Big Red Machine: How the Liberal Party Dominates Canadian Politics* — a subtitle that condemned his book to a three-month shelf life.

WILLIAM CROSS is a member of the Department of Political Science at Carleton University. He is a student of Canadian and comparative political parties. His recent work focuses on questions of intra-party democracy in a comparative perspective. He has published in many academic journals and is author of *Political Parties* (UBC Press, 2004) and co-author of *Rebuilding Canadian Party Politics* (UBC Press, 2000).

CHRISTOPHER DORNAN is an Associate Professor in the School of Journalism and Communication at Carleton University, and the co-editor with Jon H. Pammett of two previous volumes in this series. Along with

Christopher Waddell, he wrote the Mediawatch column for the *Globe and Mail* during the 2006 federal election. In the fall of 2006, he will be an Erasmus Mundus fellow at the Danish School of Journalism in Aarhus and City University in London.

FARON ELLIS is Director of the Citizen Society Research Lab at Lethbridge College. He is author of *The Limits of Participation: Members and Leaders in Canada's Reform Party* and various other publications on Canadian politics and political parties. This is his fifth contribution to the Canadian Election series.

SUSAN HARADA is an Assistant Professor in the School of Journalism and Communication at Carleton University. Prior to joining Carleton, she worked for more than two decades as a journalist, for the most part with the CBC. Her experience includes eight years as a National Parliamentary Correspondent based out of the CBC's Ottawa Bureau, where she contributed to the coverage of, among other things, three federal election campaigns and numerous national leadership conventions and first ministers' conferences between 1993 and 2001. She also spent seven years as a documentary journalist for the CBC's flagship current affairs show *The Journal*, producing national and international documentaries on a wide variety of issues.

LAWRENCE LEDUC is Professor of Political Science at the University of Toronto. His publications include *Comparing Democracies 2: New Challenges in the Study of Elections and Voting* (with Richard G. Niemi and Pippa Norris) and *The Politics of Direct Democracy: Referendums in Global Perspective*.

MICHAEL MARZOLINI is Chairman and CEO of POLLARA Strategic Public Opinion & Market Research, the largest Canadian-owned public opinion firm. For twelve years he served as chief pollster and strategist to the prime minister of Canada, and was the architect of the electoral strategies for the Liberal Party of Canada's three back-to-back election victories between 1993 and 2000. Over the past twenty years, he has provided data-driven electoral strategies to some 410 political candidates across North America and Europe, 86 percent of whom were elected to office. He has also served as media pollster to CTV News, the *Toronto Star*, Southam Newspapers, Canwest-Global News, Sun Media, and *Maclean's*.

LOUIS MASSICOTTE is Associate Professor of Political Science at the Université de Montréal. He co-authored *Establishing the Rules of the Game: Election Laws in Democracies*. He was technical advisor to the Quebec government for the preparation of a mixed electoral system model. For 2006–07, he will be Visiting Professor in Democracy and Elections at the American University, Washington, D.C.

RICHARD NADEAU is Professor of Political Science at the Université de Montréal. His fields of specialization include voting behaviour, public opinion, and political communication. He has published extensively on these topics in major journals including the *American Political Science Review*, *The American Journal of Political Science*, *Journal of Politics*, *The Canadian Journal of Political Science*, *Public Opinion Quarterly*, *Electoral Studies*, *The British Journal of Political Science*, *Poltical Behavior*, *The European Journal of Political Research*, and *The International Journal of Public Opinion Research*.

JON H. PAMMETT is Professor of Political Science and Associate Dean of the Faculty of Public Affairs at Carleton University. He is co-author of *Political Choice in Canada* and *Absent Mandate*, as well as several earlier volumes in this election studies series. He has worked in the fields of voting behaviour, declines in voter participation, political education, and socialization.

ANDRÉ TURCOTTE is Assistant Professor in Mass Communication at Carleton University's School of Journalism and Communication. He holds a PhD in Political Behaviour from the University of Toronto. At Carleton, he lectures and conducts research in advanced quantitative communication, political communication theory, and persuasion. Over the years, Dr. Turcotte has provided strategic research advice to many leading private sector firms as well as several government organizations.

CHRISTOPHER WADDELL is an Associate Professor, holder of the Carty Chair in Business and Financial Journalism, and Associate Director of the School of Journalism and Communication at Carleton University. From 1993 to 2001 he was Parliamentary Bureau Chief for CBC Television News and responsible for campaign and election night coverage for the 1997 and 2000 federal elections. Prior to joining the CBC he worked at the *Globe and Mail* as a reporter in the *Report on Business*, a reporter and then bureau chief in the paper's Ottawa bureau through the 1988 federal election, and then became first the *Globe's* associate editor and then its national editor.

ALAN WHITEHORN is Professor of Political Science at the Royal Military College of Canada, cross-appointed in the Department of Political Studies at Queen's University, and an Associate of the Institute for Humanities at Simon Fraser University. He is the author of *Canadian Socialism: Essays on the CCF-NDP*, co-author with Keith Archer of *Political Activists: The NDP in Convention,* and *Canadian Trade Unions and the New Democratic Party.* He is co-editor with Hugh G. Thorburn of *Party Politics in Canada,* 8th edition. He has contributed chapters to this election studies series since 1988.

PETER WOOLSTENCROFT teaches Canadian politics in the Department of Political Science, University of Waterloo. He has published essays on party politics, the politics of education, political geography, the federal and Ontario Progressive Conservative parties, leadership conventions, international electoral cooperation, and has contributed, singly or jointly, to this series of election studies since 1993.

DATE D'